STAGE LIGHTING

STAGE LIGHTING:
Practice and Design

W. Oren Parker
Carnegie-Mellon University

R. Craig Wolf

Holt, Rinehart and Winston, Inc.

| New York | Chicago | San Francisco | Philadelphia |
| Montreal | Toronto | London | Sydney | Tokyo |

Copyright © 1987 by Holt, Rinehart and Winston, Inc.

All rights reserved. No part of this publication may be reproduced or transmitted in any form or by any means, electronic or mechanical, including photocopy, recording or any information storage and retrieval system, without permission in writing from the publisher.

Requests for permission to make copies of any part of the work should be mailed to: Permissions, Holt, Rinehart and Winston, Inc., 111 Fifth Avenue, New York, New York 10003.

Printed in the United States of America
7 8 9 032 9 8 7 6 5 4 3 2

ISBN 0-03-032938-0

Library of Congress Cataloging-in-Publication Data

Parker, W. Oren (Wilford Oren)
  Stage lighting.

  "A version of the more comprehensive textbook by the same authors, Scene design and stage lighting, limited to the chapters on stage lighting"—Pref.
  Bibliography: p.
  Includes index.
  1. Stage lighting. I. Wolf, R. Craig. II. Parker, W. Oren (Wilford Oren). Scene design and stage lighting. III. Title.
PN2091.E4P37   1987   792'.025   86-18429

Holt Rinehart and Winston, Inc.
The Dryden Press
Saunders College Publishing

To Gilbert Hemsley, Jr.

Preface

Stage Lighting: Practice and Design is a version of the more comprehensive textbook by the same authors, *Scene Design and Stage Lighting* limited to the chapters on stage lighting. Its publication reflects the increasing interest in the study of stage lighting as a related yet independent area within the broader field of design in the theatre. Although this book is conceived as a *basic* text for beginning designers, it is aimed toward a professional level of practice and design.

The most visible change from *Scene Design and Stage Lighting* is in the chapter on color. Color plates have been added to better illustrate the origin of color, mixing techniques, and the phenomenon of color vision. The interaction of colors and color modification are also discussed as they relate to lighting design and the use of color filters. Some equipment up-date as well as a new section on "care and handling" has been added to Chapter Five, and the final section on special effects has been expanded.

Chapters have been arranged to guide the reader through the traditional progression of electricity, sources, optics, instrumentation, control, color, and, finally, practice. However, it may be desirable to proceed to Chapter Eight (Stage Lighting Practice) after reading the introductory chapter and then return to the established sequence (Chapter Eight was written with this possibility in mind). In this way, the reader gains fuller appreciation of how the nuts-and-bolts mechanics relate to practice and design. However, experience has shown that such a progression tends to increase learning time a bit.

We wish to express appreciation to William Nelson and Michael Garl for photographs from the Carnegie-Mellon University Department of Drama and for the use of the department's Lighting Laboratory.

The authors wish to gratefully acknowledge the inspiration of lighting designer Tharon Musser and the help of Gilbert Hemsley, Jr., Pat Simmons, John Ezell, Susan Dandridge, Lee Watson, David Segal, Nancy Jo Smith, and Teschie Parker. Without their assistance and support this book would not be of the quality that it is.

W.O.P.
R.C.W.

Contents

PREFACE

1 · INTRODUCTION TO STAGE-LIGHTING DESIGN

Stage Lighting   3
Stage Lighting and Theatrical Form   4
Qualities of Light   8
Stage Lighting and the Fundamentals of Design   10
The Functions of Stage Lighting   14
Development of a Lighting Designer   18

2 · STAGE LIGHTING AND ELECTRICITY

Atomic Theory   19
Conductors and Insulators   21
Sources of Electric Current   23
Electric Units of Measurement   25
Direct and Alternating Current   27
Electric Services   28
Series and Parallel Circuits   30
Stage Connectors   31
Switches   34
Circuit Protection   35
Testing Equipment   36
Electrical Safety   37

3 · LIGHT SOURCES

Incandescent Lamp   39
R and Par Lamps   42
Tungsten-Halogen Lamps   44
Lamp Life   45
Identifying and Purchasing Lamps   47
Color Temperature   48
Low-Voltage Lamps   48
Arc Lights   49

Gaseous Discharge Lamps   51
Safety and Light Sources   52

4 · REFLECTION AND REFRACTION

Reflection of Light   54
Reflectors   55
Refraction of Light   58

5 · DISTRIBUTION CONTROL

Spotlights   63
Beam Projector   72
Par Can   74
Floodlights   74
Striplight   75
Follow Spots   76
Automated Fixtures   78
Care and Handling   79

6 · INTENSITY CONTROL

Archaic Forms of Dimming   84
Autotransformer Dimmers   85
Elements of Electronic Control   88
Types of Electronic Control   93
The Operator and Remote Control   101

7 · COLOR AND LIGHT

Color and Light   104
Color Mixing   105
Color Vision   108
Color Perception   109
Designing With Color   111
Color Media   117

8 · STAGE LIGHTING PRACTICE

Lighting the Actor   120
Lighting the Background   132
Design Decisions   134
The Light Plot   137
Realizing the Plot   146
The Lighting Lab   148
Lighting for the Commercial Theatre   149

Broadway Practices   150
Planning the Lighting   152
Regional Theatres   158

9 · LIGHTING FOR THE PROSCENIUM THEATRE

The Realistic Interior   161
Realistic Exteriors   170
Wing-and-Border Settings   174
Other Types of Proscenium Staging   180

10 · LIGHTING FOR OTHER PRODUCTION FORMS

Arena Production   182
Thrust Stage Production   189
The Flexible Stage   195
Lighting Dance   196

11 · SCENIC PROJECTION, PRACTICALS, AND SPECIAL EFFECTS

Light as Scenery   202
Projected Scenery   203
Practicals   223
Special Effects   228
Effect Properties   233

GLOSSARY

ADDITIONAL READING

INDEX

STAGE LIGHTING

1

Introduction to Stage-Lighting Design

The design of lighting often begins with the scene designer's sketch which presents a suggestion of the light that will illuminate the scene. It may appear to be coming from such natural sources as the sun, the moon, or a fire, or from artificial sources as table lamps or ceiling fixtures. In contrast, the sources may be frankly arbitrary and depend on the position and color of the instruments used to build the composition. If the sketch is carefully done, the direction and color of the light will be apparent. If necessary, the designer will have prepared several sketches to show major changes in composition or color (Figure 1–1, page 2).

Such sketches, however, are only a start in the planning of stage lighting. Although a sketch represents an artistic concept, it must be technically sound to be properly realized. The floor plan and section that accompany the sketch give the first clues as to the credibility of

FIGURE 1–1
The Scene Designer's Sketch
The planning of stage lighting usually begins with the scene designer's sketch where the kind of illumination, its distribution, color, and general atmosphere are indicated. The sketch is for the opening scene of *Don Juan, or the Love of Geometry* by Max Frisch.

the designer's lighting ideas. Many a beautiful sketch has been based on a floor plan that revealed, on closer study, impossible lighting angles and insufficient space for the lighting instruments.

Ideally, a single person should design the entire production—scenery, costumes, and lighting—thus assuring a unified concept. But more often today we see a production design team made up of three designers and the director. Diverse ideas and views must be brought together into a single outlook or concept by active and open communication among all designers as well as strong leadership from the director.

STAGE LIGHTING

What is the magic of stage lighting? The demands on it are many. The costume designer, while considering period, silhouette, color, and character in choosing the fabric for a costume, also wonders how it will look *under the lights*. The scene designer, in selecting the colors of draperies and upholstery or deciding the scale of detail on the scenery, hopes they will show *under the lights*. The actor in the dressing room ponders if makeup will look right *under the lights*.

Good lighting—and there is much that is not good—should tie together visual aspects of the stage. The primary concern of stage lighting is, and will always remain, *visibility* (a rule that the designer must never forget). Yet, we will see that visibility is much more than simple intensity or brightness of light. The lighting designer must also be concerned with revelation of form, with the mood of the scene, and with the overall composition of the stage picture.

Scripts often call for startling effects such as an explosion, a fog, a flashing sign, lightning, or a hearth fire. Effects usually occur either to advance the plot or establish the mood for a scene and are most often the responsibility of the lighting designer.

Recent trends in stage design have given lighting such a conspicuous share of the total visual effect that it often is the basic element of scenery. The new scenic role of light can vary from the conventional use of a projected scenic background or shadow patterns (see Chapter 11) to extreme abstract forms.

The Lighting Designer

In contemporary theatre, the lighting designer is the newest member to join the design team. Except for a few scene designers who enjoyed lighting their own scenery, the lighting of most Broadway productions in the first half of this century was neglected and became, by default, one of the innumerable duties of the stage manager or stage electrician. It was inevitable that lighting specialists would eventually move into this neglected field and demonstrate with startling results what could be done if one person devoted his or her sole attention to the planning of lighting. This trend continued as lighting designers, inspired by the work of people like Jean Rosenthal, Stanley McCandless, and Abe Feder developed their art and craft.

Contemporary theatre training and awareness of total theatre on the part of the lighting designer have brought greater unity to the visual side of today's theatre. The lighting designer must have compassion for and understanding of the total design effort since he or she is the only design member who does not make an advance statement in visual terms of what is intended. The costume and scene designers submit a multitude of sketches, material samples, and models as visual examples of their intent. The lighting designer, on the other hand, simply submits a light plot and a verbal description. Fortunately, the lighting designer will most often have the advantage of seeing and discussing the work of the other designers and the director before the final plot is completed.

Training. Of course, there is no formula which outlines exactly what makes a good lighting designer—or, for that matter, a good lighting design. It is clear though that the student of lighting must seek, before all else, a well-rounded background in the art of the theatre. Ideally, he or she should know what it is like to be on stage before an audience, understand how a flat is constructed and why it is done that way, be aware of the choices the costume designer goes through in creating a design and in choosing fabric, and understand why an audience enjoys Shaw, how to feel the poetry of Shakespeare, and why O'Neill captivates an audience with hours of dialogue. The lighting designer should know what it is to back-paint a flat every bit as well as how to wire a pin connector. Only then can the young lighting person begin to learn what it is to design lights.

The mechanics of lighting design are fairly simple. The script is read (many times), conferences are attended, rehearsals are viewed, a light plot is drafted, instruments are hung and focused, levels are set and cues adjusted, and another production opens. While a more detailed examination of process will be found in later chapters, it must be understood at this point that the first thing the young lighting designer must concentrate on is learning to *see*. There is not a practicing lighting designer worth his or her salt who doesn't possess a strong visual memory. In order to develop a mental file of visual experiences, one must first learn to notice, to observe, and to analyze light and shadow. Light is a constant part of our lives. The lighting designer must enjoy neon for its uniqueness, realize the effect of mercury vapor, feel the qualities of fluorescence, and see the color of the noonday sun. Learning to see is an ongoing process, not one to be learned in a month or even several years. We are constantly seeing anew.

STAGE LIGHTING AND THEATRICAL FORM

Several factors have a great effect on the development of a lighting design and the subsequent plot. The production concept and resulting scene and costume design will influence color palette as well as style. Scenery will affect specific placement of lighting instruments. The style of the production as well as the script itself guides the lighting designer toward an approach. Finally, the physical form of the theatre will have significant impact on the lighting design.

Production and Lighting Style

While the term *style* is frequently subject to overuse and misunderstanding, we use it here in its broadest sense. At the most basic level, there are two styles of lighting: motivational and nonmotivational. Motivational lighting will attempt to reinforce a specific source or sources (the sun, a candle, a window, and so on) as well as be concerned with actual environmental conditions such as time of day, weather, time of year, and locale (Figure 1–2). Nonmotivational lighting will ignore the above rationale as a basis for color selection, instrument choice, and lighting angle. Instead, the lighting designer will make these choices as a result of the desired mood, compositional requirements, or simple "feeling" about a scene.

The young lighting designer should concentrate on motivational lighting but must realize that a nonmotivational approach can be quite as valid and sometimes more expressive and exciting. The production style will help the designer select an approach which will employ one or perhaps both of these two basic lighting styles (Figure 1–3, page 6).

Physical Plant

The shape of modern theatre has had an influence on the development of stage lighting. Beginning with the *proscenium theatre* and its

FIGURE 1–2
Motivational Lighting
This designer's sketch for a ballet version of Maxwell Anderson's *Winterset* indicates a motivational approach to the lighting.

Introduction to Stage-Lighting Design

FIGURE 1–3

Lighting Styles: Motivational and Nonmotivational

(*Top*) The documentary style of Brecht's *The Measures Taken* illustrates a highly motivational approach to the lighting. Designer—Frederic Youens. (Photo—Nelson) (*Above*) The symbolic style of *Owner of the Keys* lends itself well to a nonmotivational lighting approach. Designer—Josef Svoboda—Prague. (Photo reprinted from *The Scenography of Josef Svoboda* by permission of the Wesleyan University Press. Copyright 1971 by Jarka Burian.)

traditional audience and stage arrangement, lighting, for the most part, is essentially shadowbox illumination catering to theatrical realism or the illusory theatre. Lighting instruments are traditionally concealed behind masking on stage and in "ports" or "beams" front-of-house. Positions are often limited front-of-house, possibly to only a balcony rail. Worth noting is the fact that, scenery permitting, the proscenium stage is the most versatile form for side lighting positions.

The *thrust stage,* with its audience on three sides, minimizes the use of scenery and makes illusion a greater responsibility of the lighting designer. This new-old form of theatricality (popular in the sixteenth century) relies chiefly on lighting, costumes, and properties for its visual composition. Thrust staging requires full coverage (360°) lighting and is an exciting and challenging theatre form. The modern thrust theatre provides great flexibility in lighting positions both front-of-house as well as over-stage.

Arena staging surrounds the stage area with audience. The arena-theatre form increases the demands on stage lighting and virtually eliminates scenery. Like thrust, the arena requires 360° coverage but is usually a bit more restrictive in terms of lighting possibilities. A good arena theatre will be equipped with a lighting grid which covers the entire space and allows total flexibility in hanging position.

Theatre of total environment, the most recent form, not only brings back scenery elements but also expands the use of lighting to even greater dimensions by surrounding or immersing the audience in the atmosphere or environment of the play. The circle has been completed by returning to a proscenium form. The production, however, is not contained behind the frame, but is allowed to spill out and surround the audience.

Flexible or *black box staging* should not be neglected, for it is capable of achieving, on a small scale, any of the aforementioned audience-stage arrangements and even more. It is, by its sheer flexibility, a frankly impromptu form with its exposed lighting instruments and temporary seating arrangement.

It can be seen by now that, between the rapid expansion of imaginative theatrical forms and the numerous physical forms in the explosion of new theatres, lighting designers are facing demands on their skills that are totally different in taste and technical capabilities of only a generation or so ago. The opportunities are challenging. You by now may be asking, "Where does the study of stage lighting begin?"

Setting aside the technical aspects of electricity, instrument and control design, and the nitty-gritty of plotting, scheduling, and handling of equipment, the lighting designer is concerned first with the esthetics of light. To develop a sense of composition and taste in color, a lighting designer must start with qualities and limitations of the medium, light, itself.

Introduction to Stage-Lighting Design

QUALITIES OF LIGHT

Once light is created, whether it be from the sun or an artificial source, it has certain inherent qualities that become characteristic of the light medium. Just as paint has traits particular to its medium, so light conforms to its own set of attributes. The study of light in its application to stage lighting involves the qualities of intensity, distribution, and color.

Intensity

The first and most obvious quality of light is its intensity or brightness, which may be actual or comparative brightness. The actual brightness of the sun, for example, can be contrasted to the comparative brightness of automobile headlights at night. Spotlights in a darkened theatre offer the designer the same comparative brightness under more controlled conditions.

Varying intensity of a light source is achieved by means of a dimmer. Groups of dimmers working together can direct audience focus as well as alter the stage composition.

Distribution

Light rays follow an energy path which is known as distribution. The control of the distribution of light gives it direction and texture as a design feature. The various kinds of distribution begin with the general radiation of direct emanation through the more specific reshaping of the light rays by reflection or optics to the parallel rays of the laser beam. The sharp or soft-edged quality of the light beam coupled with its degree of brightness give texture to the light itself (Figure 1–4).

It is easy to see how the distribution of light can affect the ultimate design of a scenic form. The considered use of the direction and texture of light can introduce highlight, shade, and shadow into the composition. The angle or direction of the light that is illuminating the actor, for example, becomes very important in giving the actor a natural look as might occur under sunlight. Unnatural angles such as illumination from below distort the face with unusual shadows and misplaced highlights.

Color

The third property of light is its ability to transmit and reveal color. Color, in addition to being a forceful element of design in all phases of the visual side of the theatre, is often considered the most effective and dramatic quality of light. Setting aside the physics of color and its position within the electromagnetic spectrum (see Chapter 7) and turn-

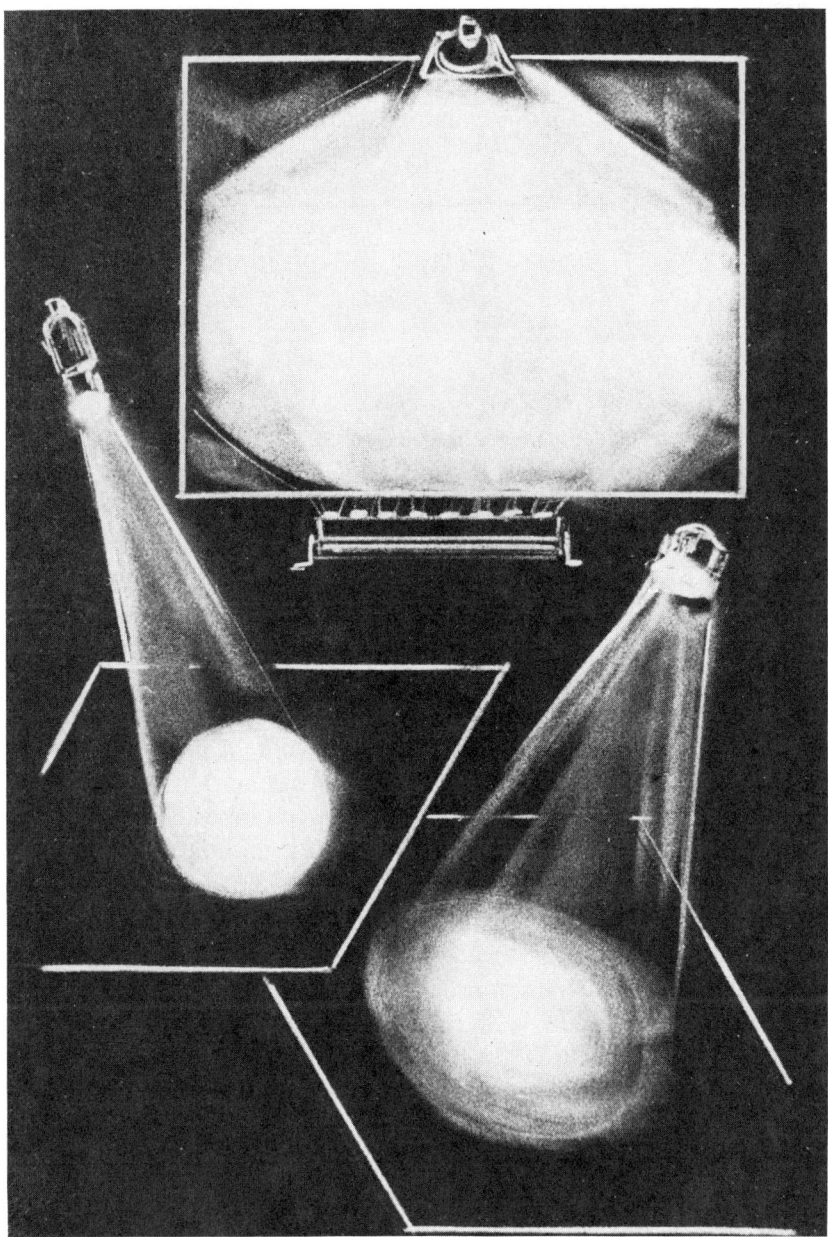

FIGURE 1–4
Distribution
Both specific and general distribution are illustrated from four different theatrical light sources.

ing to the design aspect of color in light, we find that its chief contribution is the transmitting of color or colored light. The modification of the local color of a scenic form by colored light is a design technique unique to the theatre. Color modification and the additive mixing of colored light are two rather basic concepts of color as a quality of light that has to be understood by all designers in the theatre. Both are discussed in detail later.

Introduction to Stage-Lighting Design

Movement. Movement cannot be categorized as a quality of light, yet its effect upon the theatrical use of color, distribution, and intensity is enormous. While movement implies change, it does not necessarily mean a change in focus or composition; it might be as subtle as the slow color shift from pre-dawn to daybreak.

STAGE LIGHTING AND THE FUNDAMENTALS OF DESIGN

Composition

The principles of composition are the same for the lighting designer as they are for the scene designer or any graphic or visual artist. Composition is the organizing of the visual elements of design into a unified form or arrangement of forms. The meaning attached to forms in a stage composition is, for the most part, a visual interpretation of the playwright's ideas. Lighting is the final unifying force of the stage composition.

Unlike a painting, a stage composition is not static but is an ever-changing arrangement of forms with a moving center of interest. More than any other design element, light is able to direct the audience's eye and control what is and isn't seen. Since light possesses the additional quality of incredible fluidity, stage composition can be altered with relative ease. Although light can have composition of its own (projected patterns, for example) its chief function is to reveal stage forms in the proper relationship to other forms and to the background. And here the complexity of compositional lighting begins.

Compositional lighting means lighting one form and not another; lighting two-dimensional forms to make them look three-dimensional; keeping shadows off the background; lighting three-dimensional forms to make them look three-dimensional (not as easy as it seems); and many other similar problems, the most important of which is the compositional lighting of the actor (Figure 1–5).

The Elements of Design

The role of the lighting designer as a member of a design team demands that he or she be acutely aware of the elements of design that affect the creative process of the scenery and costume designers.

The fundamentals of design can also apply to the composition of stage lighting as an integral force in the total visual composition, which of course includes the actor. The elemental factors that make up any visual form or arrangement of forms can be listed in the order of their importance to the creative process. They are: line, dimension, movement, light, color, and texture.

Line as an element of design defines form. Its force is present in a composition in many ways. Line can enclose spaces as outline creating shape (two-dimensional form), or as contour-line suggesting three-

FIGURE 1–5
Composition
Two photographs from *Summer Tree* by Ron Cowen illustrate the use of compositional light in a simultaneous setting. Set Designer—Richard Churchill. Lighting—Bertrand Cottine. (Photo—Nelson)

dimensional form. Strong backlighting, for example, would emphasize the silhouette or outline of a form while directional side lighting reveals its contour. Light has the power to deny, alter, or accentuate line (Figure 1–6).

Line can appear in a composition as real line in many different modes (straight, curved, spiral, and so on) or as suggested line simulated by the eye as it follows a sequence of related shapes.

Line as a path of action frequently assumes direction. A strong beam of light cannot help but establish direction. The linear shape of the beam coupled with a concentration of brightness creates a strong focus in the composition.

Dimension is the size of form. As an element of design, it is not only

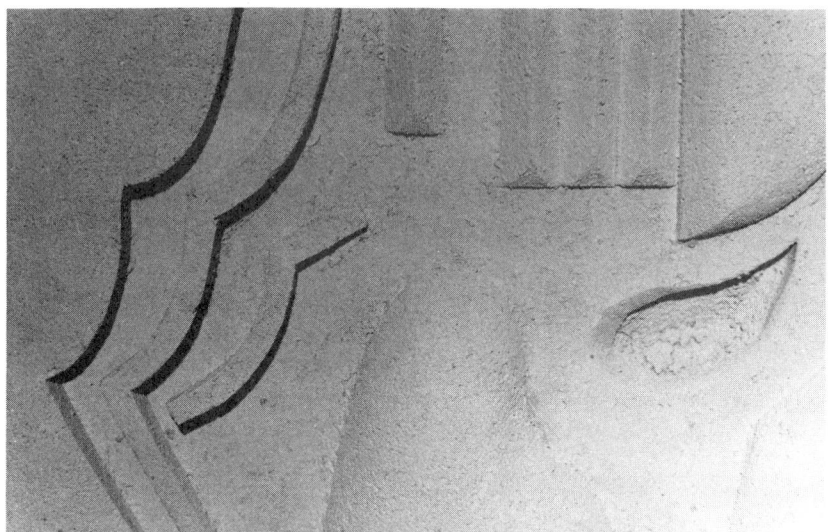

FIGURE 1–6

Textured and Low-relief Surfaces

Demonstrating the effects of angle and distribution of light on a highly textured surface or low-relief carving. (Top) A low-relief sculptural form lighted with a single source from the front. (Right) The same form lighted with two side-angle sources of different intensity or color.

Stage Lighting

concerned with the *size* of a shape or mass, but also with the relationship of the size of one shape to another—large to small, large to large, and so on. Hence the size of the interval has a definite effect on the apparent size or mass of a form and to its proportional relationship to other forms in the composition.

Control of light on either the form or the interval influences the dimension of one or the other. Light can reverse the feeling of dimension by making a two-dimensional shape look three-dimensional and vice versa.

Movement is the action of form. It is the kinetic energy of composition. Motion can exist in a stage design as real movement and as the movement of the eye or optical motion within a static composition.

The real movement of lights, of the actor, and on occasion, animated elements of scenery, are all very much part of a theatrical production. Any change of intensity, distribution, or color is the movement of light. The movement of a follow-spot beam, the change of a color on the cyclorama, and the raising or lowering of lights on different areas of the stage are a few examples of real movement.

Optical motion is the movement of the eye over a composition. When a form or arrangement of forms is static optical motion is dependent on the sequential arrangement of forms or elements of design. The movement of the eye can easily be altered through a shift in light intensity or composition. Strong directional light rays or the sequential arrangement of light sources are examples of the use of light as optical motion. The subtle gradation of one color and the vibration of two hue opposites are the extreme uses of color as optical motion.

Light reveals form. The dominant presence of light in all areas of stage design makes it imperative that light be considered as a basic influence in the beginning of the creative process and not something to be studied later. The early awareness of light as a design element is as important to the scenery and costume designer as the appreciation of all the elements of design is to the lighting expert to whom this book is devoted.

Color modifies form. As an element of design it is a powerful stimulus within the composition. It can change the dimension of form, reverse the direction of line, alter the interval between forms, and generate optical motion. Color in the theatre comes from two basic sources: pigment or dye colors present on the surface of the form, or colored light that modifies the color of the form.

Texture is the tactile aspect of form. It is the treatment of surfaces which is of interest to the lighting designer. Surfaces may be highly polished, rough-hewn, or rusticated, to name a few that may reflect light or cast interesting shadows. Real texture is best revealed by directional side light (distribution), while painted or simulated texture appears more real under a wash of light without a strong sense of direction (Figure 1–6).

In its simplest form, the texture of light is the product of a specific type of lighting instrument (Figure 1–4). Certainly one of the considerations in choosing the type of instrument to use involves the textural quality of its light. In addition, the designer can alter texture in light by adjusting focus or breaking up the light with specially designed patterns or frost media.

THE FUNCTIONS OF STAGE LIGHTING

Although visibility is the primary concern of stage lighting, the basic obligation of light on the stage is to give the actor or performer *meaning* in his or her surroundings and to provide an atmosphere in which the role may be logically interpreted. At the same time, stage lighting, like scene designing, has to bring to the audience the full meaning and emotions of the playwright's concept.

The lighting designer does not begin work until the setting has been designed but is guided by the same fundamentals of dramatic form as the set designer. Through the use of light in all its aspects—intensity, color, distribution and movement—the lighting designer assists in creating the proper environment for the play by helping to place the

FIGURE 1–7
Visibility
Illustrating the effect of four different kinds of visibility. (a) An object visible in silhouette only. (b) With front light added, the object is visible as a three-dimensional form. (c) With the addition of another angle of light, the object's detail becomes visible. (d) An example of detail and form becoming less visible as a result of too much light.

a					b

Stage Lighting

action, establish the mood, reinforce the theme, and stage the story of the play or related theatrical form.

Placing the Action

In some plays the designer may find that mood and theme are so much a part of the story line that it is hard to separate their functional differences. On the other hand, the action of a play is usually easy to isolate. Action, the designer soon discovers, can vary from a static, wordy, psychological study to a fast-moving farce or to the violent contact of a murder mystery. The physical action of a play or any theatrical performance is of prime importance to the lighting designer. We must know where the action has to be clearly seen, half seen, or not seen at all. For this reason and others, the process of viewing rehearsals is of utmost importance. In following the action, the designer frequently manipulates the intensity and distribution of light.

The placing of the action usually happens in the opening moments of the performance and can set the tone of the show. Whether it be a specific room in a house, a street in a village, a cabaret, or just action in limbo, it is still the place of the action that will set the proper environment for the rest of the scene.

Visibility. We cannot define visibility as a fixed degree of brightness or an established angle of distribution. It is the amount of light needed for a moment of recognition deemed appropriate for that point in the action of the play. "To see what should be seen" may mean the revealing of only the silhouette of a three-dimensional form, the solidity of its mass, or the full detail of all surfaces with decoration and texture. Each degree of visibility cannot help but take on an atmosphere or mood that will affect the action (Figure 1–7).

c

d

Introduction to Stage-Lighting Design

Establishing the Mood

The overall mood of a play or scene is the next important clue to the lighting designer. A color impression comes from the mood as well as a suggestion of the intensity and distribution of light. The word *mood* tends to suggest dark and gloomy surroundings, but bright comedy or nonsensical farce also indicates a type of mood.

Although an abstract or dramatic mood is more impressive and eye-catching than the realistic visibility of a conventional interior setting, it is also far easier to accomplish with light. How many times have the dancing shadows of an actor sitting in front of the single source of a hearth fire won more acclaim for the lighting designer than the hours of careful lighting of a realistic interior.

Reinforcing the Theme

The key word here is *reinforcing*. Because the visual expression of theme depends on the scene designer's interpretation of the playwright's message, the lighting designer is concerned with compositional revelation of the thematic forms of the setting. The theme-dominated play (Tennessee Williams' *A Streetcar Named Desire*, for example) asks the lighting designer to reveal the fragmented setting first as a

FIGURE 1–8

Theme

Tennessee Williams' *A Streetcar Named Desire* is an example of a theme-dominated play. The lighting designer is asked to support the theme with a distribution of light that follows the action in all areas within the apartment (below) as well as revealing the outside through transparent walls (page 17). Set Designer—Edward Pisoni. (Photo—Nelson)

16 *Stage Lighting*

structure having solid walls, then as a transparent, see-through skeleton; finally the designer is asked to illuminate the constantly moving center of attention from room to room, interior to exterior (Figure 1–8).

In the more extreme theme-oriented or documentary plays of Bertolt Brecht the theme is stressed by eliminating the theatricality of stage lighting and playing the show under a clear, uncolored wash of light. Lighting, however, is used to reinforce the theme visually through the use of projections. These take the form of propanganda pictures or subtitles and are used in place of scenic background.

Staging the Story

The story line of a play may be developed very simply as in a one-set, seven-character, domestic comedy or as in an extremely difficult, episodic marathon with a cast of hundreds. The narrative may require the cross section of a house or the establishment of many unrelated locales in a single-setting arrangement. The movement from scene to scene or from area to area requires logistical planning for the scene designer, while for the lighting designer it is an exercise in control of precise distribution and the delicate intensities of light. Movement or transitions within a scene or from scene to scene by lighting become a connecting or unifying factor in the production.

Introduction to Stage-Lighting Design

FIGURE 1-9
Lighting Style
Highly stylized motivational lighting is shown here from a production of *You Can't Take It With You.* Set Design—R. Craig Wolf. Lighting Design—Doug Grekin. (Photo—Mountain Mist)

DEVELOPMENT OF A LIGHTING DESIGNER

Designing for the theatre requires a great deal from an individual. Not only must one have artistic talent and technical knowhow, but the designer must also be able to communicate. The next few chapters will instruct the young designer in the nuts and bolts of lighting, but it must never be forgotten along the way that a *designer* is being nurtured. The importance of "learning to see"—of establishing visual memory—must always be in the forethought of the reader. Experimentation is essential: lighting instruments should be examined, dimmer systems operated, and colors mixed. The lighting designer can learn only so much from theory and example; he or she must have opportunities to put theory into practice. Since production space is always in great demand, a lighting laboratory becomes a tremendous aid to practical training.

But always remember, while wandering through the maze of technical information, pause now and then—and *look*.

2

Stage Lighting and Electricity

An understanding of electricity may seem nothing more than a bother to the lighting designer/*artist;* but such information is essential for the lighting designer/*practitioner*. At the very least, we must understand electricity and basic electronics well enough to make intelligent choices concerning usage and safety. Unfortunately, too many people believe that electricity is solely an electrician's concern and, as a result, a curious mystique surrounds electrical practice and theory. The fact is that electrical theory and basic electrical practice are simple and quite unmysterious.

ATOMIC THEORY

According to presently accepted theories, all matter consists of molecules, which are made up of atoms. Each atom is composed of a postively charged center called the nucleus around which are distributed a number of negatively charged bodies called electrons. The nucleus of an atom consists of protons and neutrons. Neutrons have no electric charge, but each proton has a positive charge exactly equal to the negative charge of an electron.

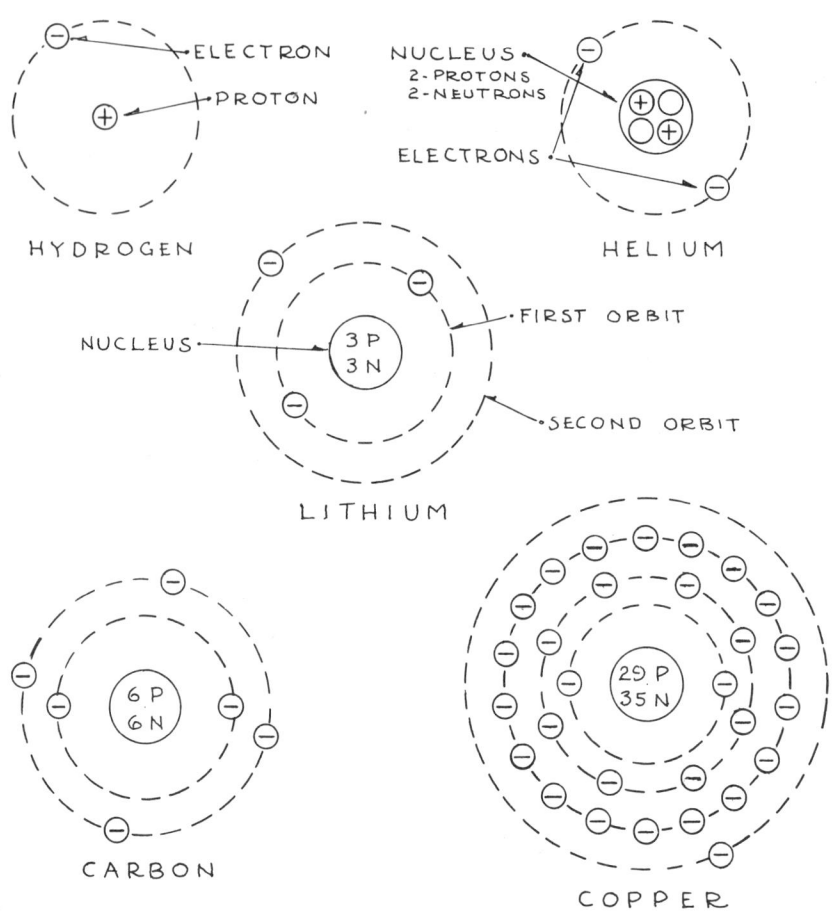

FIGURE 2–1
Schematic Diagram of the Structure of Certain Atoms

Every normal atom has as many electrons surrounding the nucleus as it has protons within the nucleus, and thus has an equal quantity of positive and negative charges. Thus hydrogen has one proton in its nucleus and one electron outside it; helium has two protons and two electrons; lithium has three of each, carbon has six, copper has twenty-nine, and so on up to uranium, which has the most: ninety-two protons and ninety-two electrons. It is thought that the electrons are in constant motion, revolving around the nucleus in orbits much the same as the planets revolve around the sun. Figure 2–1 shows a few examples.

In the atom of lithium, the lightest of all metals, the three protons are balanced by two electrons in the inner orbit plus one in the outer orbit. Carbon also has two electrons in the inner orbit, plus four in the outer orbit, to balance the six protons. Copper requires four orbits to take care of its twenty-nine electrons.

The various orbits are not all in the same flat plane, like a plate, but rather they are at angles to each other, somewhat like a number of rubber bands stretched haphazardly about a baseball.

Stage Lighting

The importance of all this is that the electron in the fourth and outer orbit of copper may be easily dislodged, providing a free electron, the basis of the flow of electrical current. The same is true of the outer electron in the lithium atom. In fact, all metals have electrons that can be readily dislodged and, therefore, are good electrical conductors.

CONDUCTORS AND INSULATORS

To allow electric current to move through circuits (established paths for electricity) of any kind it is necessary to provide a path through which the electrons may move as easily as possible. Materials made up of atoms that release free electrons readily also permit the movement of electrons through them and are known as conductors. Actually all materials will offer some resistance to such movement, but all metals are relatively good conductors, and silver is the best of any substance known.

Because of cost, the use of silver for extensive wiring is not very practical, and some less expensive material must be used. Copper is this material: its conductivity is almost as good as silver's, it is relatively inexpensive, and it is easy to work—to form into wires and other parts. Aluminum is coming more and more into use in some applications, and brass is valuable for large, permanent parts that need to be especially rugged. Other materials are also used for special purposes, but by and large when we think of electric wires, switch parts, and the like, we think of copper.

An important rule to remember is that electricity will always follow the path of least resistance. Some sort of insulation is necessary to prevent the electrons that are flowing in a conductor from short-circuiting—that is, escaping into other channels. This "short" may result in severe shock to anyone chancing to come in contact with the new and unprotected channel of flow. And because it may offer little resistance, this new channel may allow a higher current than the legitimate circuit was designed to carry, thereby causing damage to it.

Just as there is no material that is 100 percent conductive, so there is nothing that has 100 percent insulative properties, but there are many materials that can serve various practical purposes. Glass and ceramics are excellent for small permanent parts such as sockets and switches, slate for larger switch and fuse panels, and neolite where heat is involved. For wires and cables, rubber and fiber are used, while plastics are becoming increasingly common. The most useful insulator of all is dry air. If this were not so, every open socket or wall outlet would drain off current!

Permanent wiring such as stage circuits, which should be laid by a licensed electrician only, may have a solid copper core through which

Stage Lighting and Electricity

the current flows, but the temporary wiring cable used on the stage always has a core made up of a number of small strands of wire. This is to provide proper flexibility in handling and laying. Standard stage cable consists of two or three such cores, each surrounded by a strong rubber insulation. For physical strength, tough fiber cords are laid alongside, and the whole surrounded by either a rubber or a fiber sheathing.

National electrical codes now specify that all new electrical installations be grounded. Grounding requires that a circuit or cable have three rather than two wires. The third, the ground wire, is designed to offer an emergency path through which the current can flow in case of a short circuit. The wires of a stage cable or circuit are always covered with rubber insulation color coded as follows:

> black or red = "hot" line
> white = "neutral" or "common" line
> green = ground

Care must be taken in wiring plugs onto cable that the ground wire in particular is attached to the proper pin of the connector (see "Types of Connector").

Stage cable comes in different sizes, or gages, each of which is designed to carry a specific maximum current or amperage. These limits should never be exceeded. The most useful sizes are:

Size (gage number):	18	16	14	12	10	8	6
Capacity (amperes):	3	6	15	20	25	35	50

The most common (nearly standard) stage circuit will carry 20 amps. As a result, the most common cable will be #12, Type SO (rubber coated). Occasionally, for a very small load and a very short run, ordinary lamp cord (or zip cord), which has an 18-gage core, may be used, but this should be kept to a minimum and carefully guarded against abuse.

A final category of stage cable must be mentioned here because of its inevitable importance to a successful "put-in." The first members of this category are cables which allow the electrician to plug several lighting instruments into a single circuit. These cables may be called "two-fers," "Y-connectors," "spiders," or "three-fers"; all of them allow the electrician to plug two or three instruments into one circuit. One must remember that 20 amps is circuit capacity. Adaptors are the other type of special category cable. Simple adaptors are seldom more than 2 feet long, with one of various connectors on each end. Applications are endless, but an example of the use of an adaptor would be plugging a backstage work light equipped with a pin connector into an "Edison" or parallel blade socket.

SOURCES OF ELECTRIC CURRENT

Just as you cannot get water to flow out of one end of a pipe unless there is water being poured into the other end, so free electrons will not move through a conductor unless there is a supply of free electrons being introduced into it. Such a supply of electrons is known as voltage or as an electrical force (EMF). It can be established in a number of ways.

Battery

A common device for supplying an EMF is a battery, such as one consisting of a glass container filled with a dilute sulphuric acid solution into which are placed a strip of copper and a strip of zinc. If a meter is connected between these two strips, it will show a small electric current passing from one to the other through this connection (Figure 2–2). This is caused by the acid attacking the zinc, which dissolves into the solution and releases two electrons from each of its atoms. These electrons are left on the zinc strip, and because the acid will not permit them to return to their atoms, they flow through the wire to the copper strip.

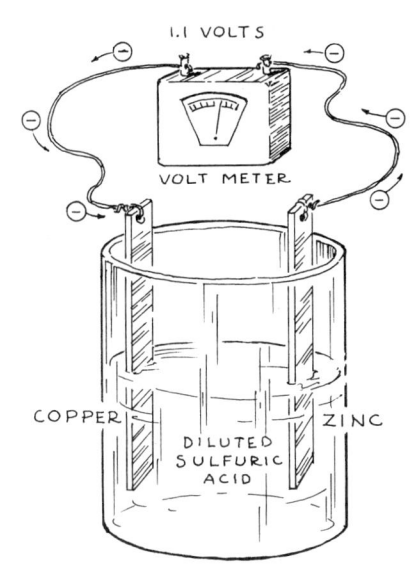

FIGURE 2–2
A Simple Copper-zinc-acid Battery

Other Sources

An EMF may be built up in a number of ways other than the battery. *Electrostatics* produces electricity by rubbing two dissimilar substances together. *Photoelectricity* is the action of sunlight on certain photosensitive materials. *Thermoelectricity* is the application of heat to the junction of two dissimilar metals that have been welded together. *Piezoelectricity* is the mechanical compression of certain crystals. New techniques to produce electricity are being developed, but the method most important to the stage electrician is that of *electromagnetism*: the creation of an EMF through a generator, powered by water, steam, or other means.

Generator

The principle of the generator is the relative movement of a conductor within a magnetic field. The conductor may be moved while the field is stationary, or the field may be moved and the conductor remain stationary. The latter is usual in very large installations, but it is somewhat easier to comprehend the operation by considering a moving conductor in a stationary magnetic field.

The two diagrams in Figure 2–3 show a highly simplified a-c generator, usually called an alternator. We see an armature in the shape of a single coil of wire being rotated through the magnetic field between the two poles of a magnet. This induces an EMF in the coil causing negative electrons to accumulate at slip ring 5 and flow off the

Stage Lighting and Electricity

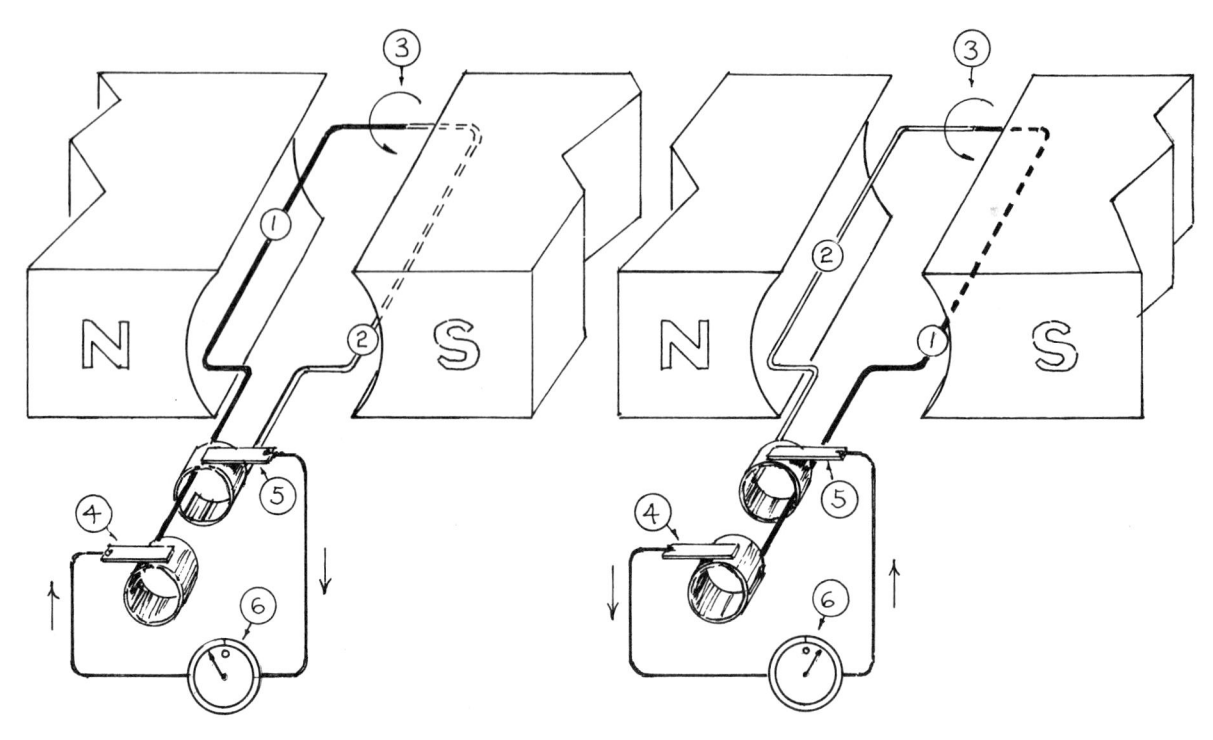

FIGURE 2–3
Simple A-C Generator (or Alternator)
(1) Side 1 of coil (2) Side 2 of coil (3) Direction of rotation of coil (4) Slip ring A (5) Slip ring B (6) Volt meter.

slip ring through the brush and thence along the connecting wire and through a voltmeter to slip ring 4, whence they reenter the coil. In the second diagram the sides of the coil have reversed positions and directions, so now the electrons will accumulate at slip ring 4, pass through the connecting wire and meter and reenter the coil at slip ring 5. Each complete revolution of the coil is called a cycle, so for one half of each cycle the electrons move in one direction and for the other half in the opposite direction. Thus the current is said to alternating (a-c).

In Figure 2–4 we see the construction of the sine curve that represents the variation of the induced EMF for any portion of the complete cycle of the armature through the magnetic field. At the exact instant that the armature is passing the 0-degree point in its rotation it is moving parallel to the magnetic field, not through it, and hence is producing no EMF at all.

As it reaches the 30-degree mark it is cutting into the magnetic field somewhat and hence is generating a small EMF as depicted by extending a line from the 30-degree point to a somewhat later point than the 0-degree reading of 0. At the 60-degree position, an EMF of greater magnitude is produced and at 90 degrees the maximum EMF. After this the EMF drops back to 0; then in an a-c generator it starts to build up in the opposite direction as depicted below the time line.

Stage Lighting

FIGURE 2–4

The Construction of an A-C Sine Curve

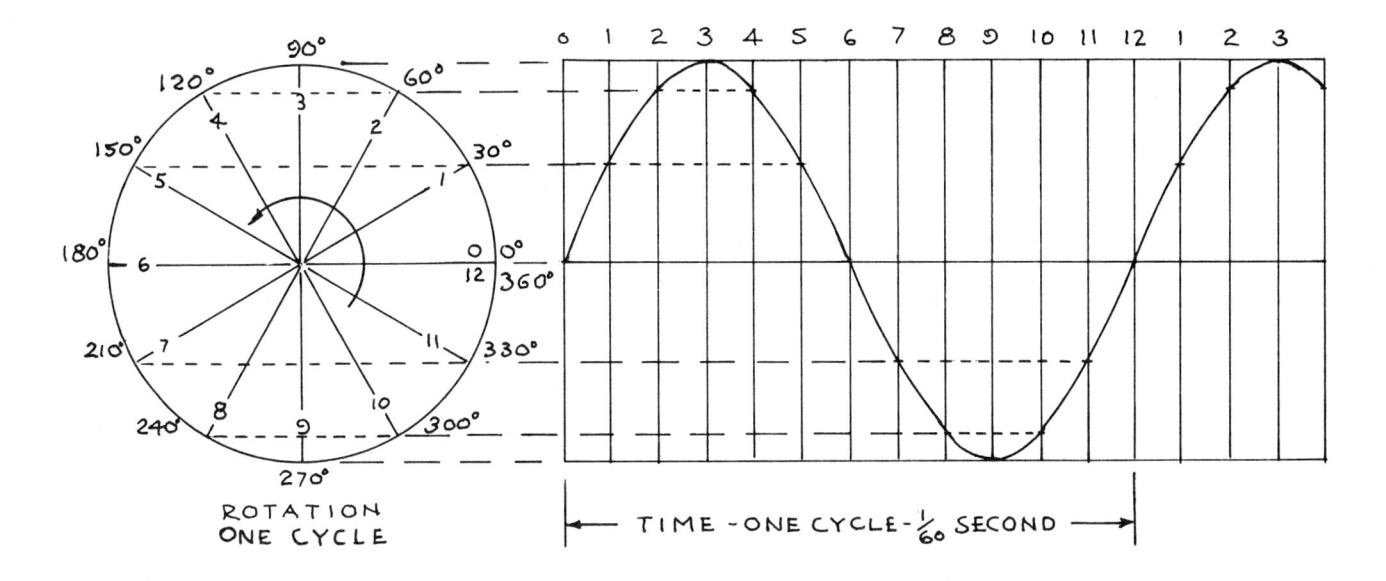

For the sake of economy it is practical to build not a single armature into a generator, but several of them. Because they must be at angles to each other, it is obvious that their respective EMFs will not reach any one point at the same instant, but rather they will produce sine curves as indicated in Figure 2–5. Here we see the very common arrangement of three armatures each producing its own curve. This is known as three-phase current and will be discussed later.

ELECTRIC UNITS OF MEASUREMENT

Four basic measurements can be made in any electric circuit. Their definitions and relationships are below.

Volt

The volt is the difference in electrical potential between two points in a circuit. Another way of putting it is to ask how many more free electrons are there at point A than at point B, to which they will flow if a path is opened for them. Voltage is also called electromotive force (EMF), and its symbol is E.

Voltage can be thought of as the pressure behind electrical flow, although this definition is not completely accurate.

Ampere

The ampere is the rate of flow of current through a conductor: how many electrons pass a given point in one second? The symbol for the ampere in mathematics is I (for intensity of current flow). Amperage is used to describe a stage circuit's electrical capacity. For instance, most theatrical circuits will carry 20 amps.

Stage Lighting and Electricity

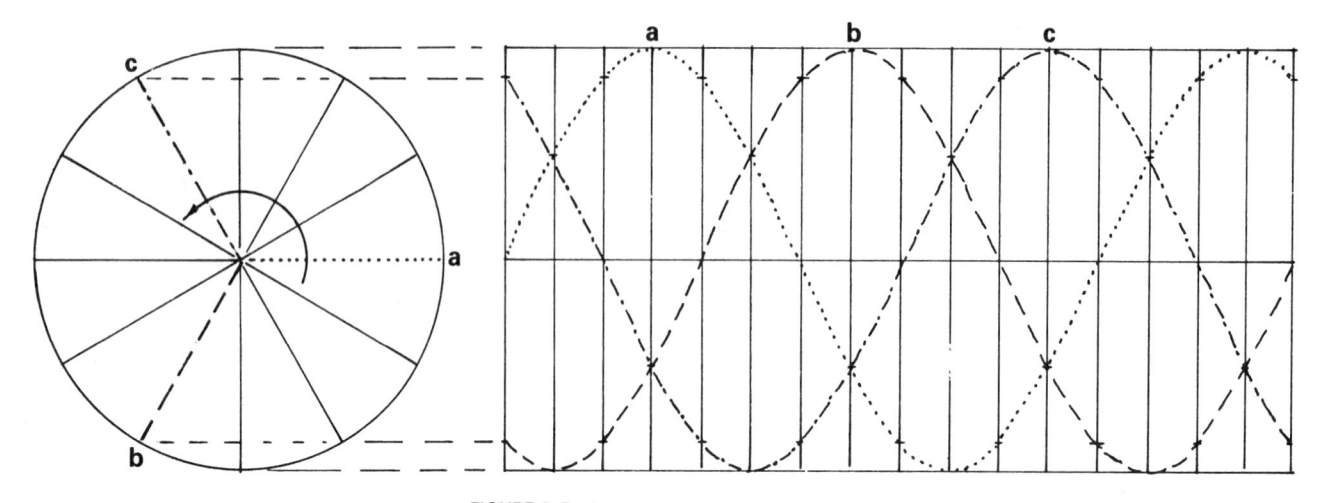

FIGURE 2-5

Overlapping Sine Curves Produced by an A-C Generator with Three Armatures at 120 Degrees to One Another

Ohm

Every substance offers some resistance to the flow of current; some, such as copper, offer very little while others, such as rubber, offer a great deal. The ohm is the measurement of such resistance and its symbol is R.

Watt

The watt is the rate of doing work, whether it is turning an electric motor, heating an electric iron, or causing a lamp to glow. Its symbol is P, for power. Wattage can be thought of as "consumption" of electricity, although one must be aware of the fact that flowing electrons are never actually consumed.

The Power Formula

The power formula is important to remember because it expresses the relationship between wattage (P), amperage (I), and voltage (E). It states that the rate of doing work (wattage) is equal to the product of current flow (amperage) and potential (voltage):

$$P = I \cdot E \text{ (Called the "pie" formula)}$$

or

$$W = V \cdot A \text{ (Using first letters of unit names—called the "West Virginia" formula)}$$

An application of the power formula might be to determine how many 750-watt lamps one could plug into a single 20-amp circuit.

Stage Lighting

$$W = 750 \text{ per lamp}$$
$$V = 120 \text{ (U.S. Standard)}$$
$$A = 20 \text{ (given)}$$

$$X \cdot 750 = 120 \cdot 20$$
$$X = \frac{2400}{750}$$
$$X = 3$$

A 20-amp circuit thus will carry three 750-watt lamps.

Ohm's Law

Ohm's law introduces resistance (R) into a useful formula. It states that amperage (I) will equal voltage (E) divided by ohms:

$$I = \frac{E}{R}$$

DIRECT AND ALTERNATING CURRENT

Before the recent development of new techniques, direct current was not an efficient way to transport electricity over long distances. However, it was the only way known in the early days of electricity, and for that reason was installed in the downtown areas of many cities, where it can still occasionally be found. Elsewhere it has almost entirely been replaced by the more versatile alternating current.

Alternating current has the great advantage of being easily changed from low voltage to high and from high voltage to low by means of transformers. A transformer consists of an iron core, frequently doughnut shape, about which is coiled two wires, the primary and the secondary. When an alternating current is sent through the primary coil, it sets up a magnetic flux in the iron core, and in turn this flux induces a new current in the secondary coil. It must be understood that there is no electrical connection whatever between the two coils, and that the voltage transformation is solely the result of fluctuating magnetic fields which surround any electrical conductor through which power is flowing.

If the primary has few turns about the core and the secondary has more, the voltage induced in the secondary will be higher than that in the primary, but if the primary has more turns than the secondary, then the induced voltage will be lower. These are known as "step-up" and "step-down" transformers, respectively.

Stage Lighting and Electricity

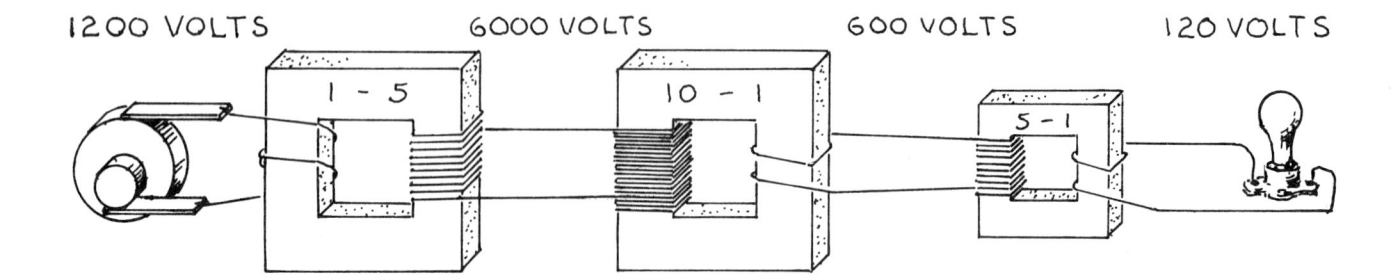

FIGURE 2–6
Schematic of A-C Transportation from the Generating Station to the Home

Figure 2–6 depicts a portion of a typical arrangement for a modest alternating-current service. At the left side we see the a-c generator station producing an EMF of 1200 volts. This is fed to the substation where a transformer boosts it to 6000 volts, because the higher the voltage the less loss there will be in transit (some high-power transit lines carry as much as 500,000 volts!). As the current nears the neighborhood in which it will be consumed, it passes through another substation where the EMF is reduced to 600 volts. This is sent out over a local wiring system until it reaches a house, where a small transformer on a pole by the highway reduces it still further to 120 volts for use in the home.

In this country the most common household service is 120 volts a-c at 60 cycles. Many foreign countries use quite different voltages, ranging from 105 to as much as 240, and these are usually at 50 cycles or even fewer.

ELECTRIC SERVICES

It is essential for the stage electrician to know which of several possible wiring systems (referred to as "service power") is carrying electricity to the theatre. This is especially true when a touring company moves into an unfamiliar building and must connect up its portable control board and other equipment. Let us glance briefly at the three forms of service in common use (Figure 2–7).

The first is the two-wire system, in which one line is said to be "hot" and the other "neutral." The potential between them is 120 volts.

It should be noted at this point that 120-volt service is often, in fact, closer to 115 volts and may drop as low as 110 volts. But today's portable lighting equipment will operate well on any of these voltages.

The second form of service is the three-wire system, in which the two outside (hot) wires usually have a potential of 240 volts between them. However, each hot wire has a potential of only 120 volts between it and the third wire, the common neutral. A familiar domestic application of this service is found in many homes, where the electric lights are on two or more circuits of 120 volts each, while the electric range operates on 240 volts. Great care must be taken when working

Stage Lighting

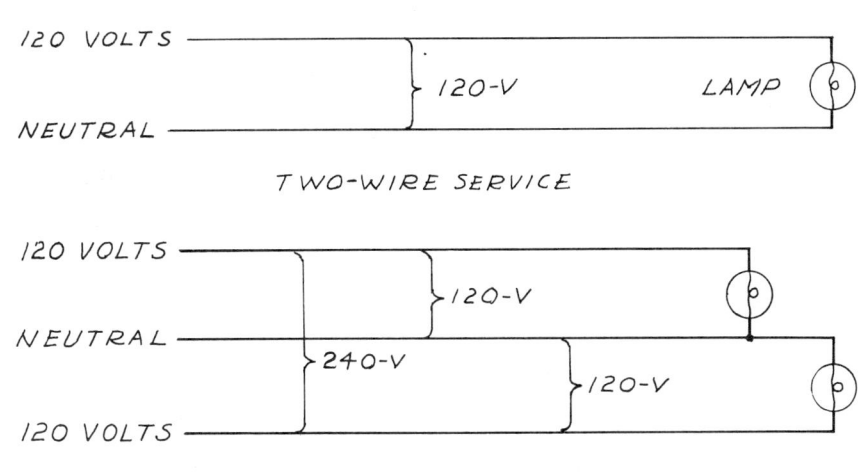

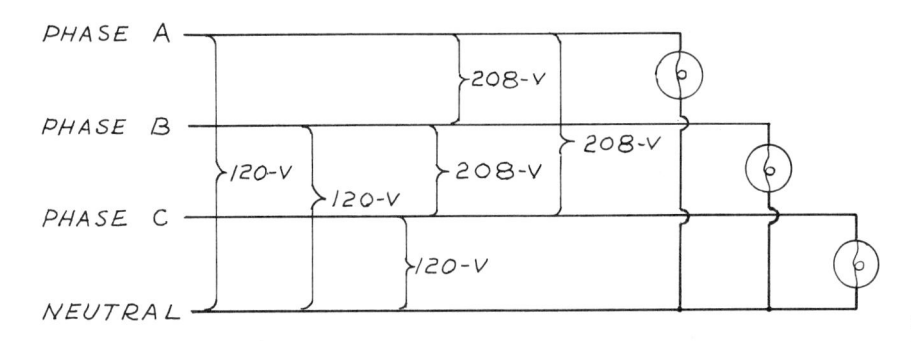

FIGURE 2-7
The Three Kinds of Electrical Distribution Service

with such a system to avoid connecting any apparatus designed for 120 volts across the two hot lines. The 240 volts will blow lamps at once, ruin other equipment promptly, and provide grave danger of fatal shock. The British, who use 240 volts for all their home lighting, must take precautions that would seem very irksome to us, who are used to our comparatively mild 120-volt service.

The third type of service, and one that is popular because of its efficiency in distribution, is the a-c 120–208-volt, four-wire system, also known as the three-phase system. The generation of these three phases is illustrated in Figure 2-5. The EMF produced by each phase is said to be at 120 degrees to the others. If the EMF in relation to a common neutral conductor is 120 volts, then any two phases will be 208 volts from each other, this being the product of 240 volts times the sine value of angle 120 degrees, or .8660. Many motors are built to run on this 208 voltage, but this is of little concern to us, except that we must be sure never to connect standard-voltage equipment between two hot lines of a three-phase system. This type of service is quite commonly found in theatres.

Stage Lighting and Electricity

SERIES AND PARALLEL CIRCUITS

Once the current has been received from the supplying mains in any location, regardless of how it reaches the building (by two-, three-, or four-wire systems), it is distributed in two-wire systems, similar to the one diagrammed in Figure 2–7. The various elements that work in these circuits—lamps, switches, dimmers, fuses, and the like—may be connected in either of two ways.

One is the series circuit, in which the flow of current passes through the various elements successively. In the top diagram of Figure 2–8 we see that the current must pass through each of the four lamps, one after the other, before returning by the neutral wire. But in the center of the diagram the same four lamps are connected "in parallel," and it is apparent that a portion of the total current can flow simultaneously through each lamp.

Almost all practical lighting circuits are a combination of these two. The bottom diagram of Figure 2–8 shows a typical example. The switch and fuse are in series, and they are also in series with each of the lamps. But the four lamps are in parallel with one another. Let the switch be opened or the fuse blown and all the lamps will be extinguished. One of the lamps may be removed, however, and the remaining three will not be affected. In other words, the series portion is used to control the circuit as a whole, while the parallel portion is valuable as a distributor of the current.

In stage lighting we find that switches and fuses are most often replaced by circuit breakers and that these breakers and the dimmers

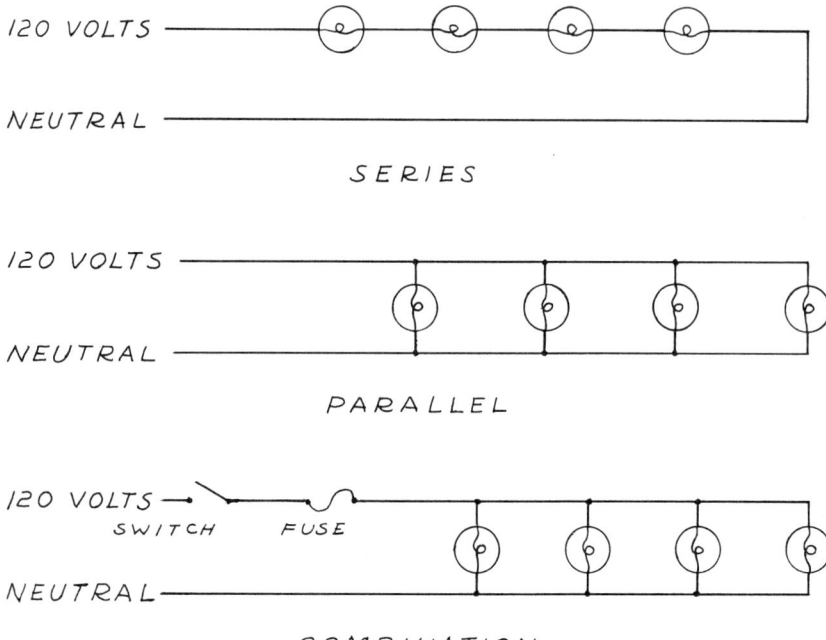

FIGURE 2–8
Types of Electric Circuits

Stage Lighting

are put in series with the stage lights for the sake of control. The circuit breaker can act as a switch, but its primary function is to protect the entire circuit against a short circuit or an overload that would result in a harmfully high flow of current.

The lights themselves are always in parallel, as several spotlights ganged on one dimmer or the lamps in one color circuit of a striplight. In each case they are simultaneously under the control of the dimmer and the circuit breaker, but each is independent of the other. If they were connected in series, none would burn at full brightness; and, like strands of old Christmas tree lights, if one lamp fails, no lamps can burn (the broken filament will act like a switch). One or more lamps in a parallel circuit may be removed, or, providing no overload is involved, one or more may be added in parallel, without affecting those already in the circuit.

A calculation of the utmost importance in parallel circuitry is to ascertain quickly the ampere flow in a circuit. This is usually necessary when several stage instruments are ganged together or several striplights are fed through each other.

Suppose we have four spotlights ganged on one circuit, each one burning a 500-watt lamp. We may invert the power formula ($P = I \cdot E$) to read $I = \dfrac{P}{E}$. Then:

$$I = \frac{4 \times 500}{120} = 16.67 \text{ amperes.}$$

If our circuit is fused at 20 amperes we are safe. But if we wish to change the lamps to the more powerful 750-watt variety, then:

$$I = \frac{4 \times 750}{120} = 25 \text{ amperes.}$$

This is too much for our 20-ampere circuit, so we must go back to the 500-watt lamps or put one or two of the spotlights on a different circuit.

STAGE CONNECTORS

Types of Connector

Lights on stage are temporary. They are moved after each production and even between scenes of a play. Thus, it is not wise to make permanent connections of the cables to the various lighting instruments. Devices that can be easily connected and disconnected are needed. Ordinary household plugs with parallel blades are used on some small stages, but because they are easily disconnected in error

Stage Lighting and Electricity

FIGURE 2–9
Connectors

(a) Female and male heavy duty parallel-blade plugs. (b) Female and male twist-lock connectors. (c) Female and male three-wire twist-lock connectors. (d) Male and female pin connectors. (e) Male and female three-wire pin connectors. (f) Full stage plug.

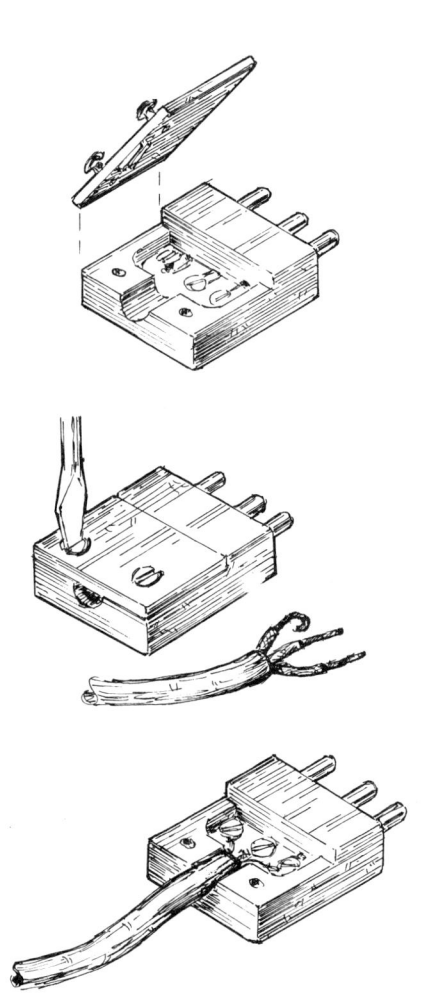

FIGURE 2–10
Steps in Wiring a Pin Connector

(a) Remove cover plate. (b) Wrap wire around screw terminal clockwise, making sure that the green or ground wire is attached to the center screw terminal. (c) Tighten screws and replace cover plate, making sure that the strain release is effective.

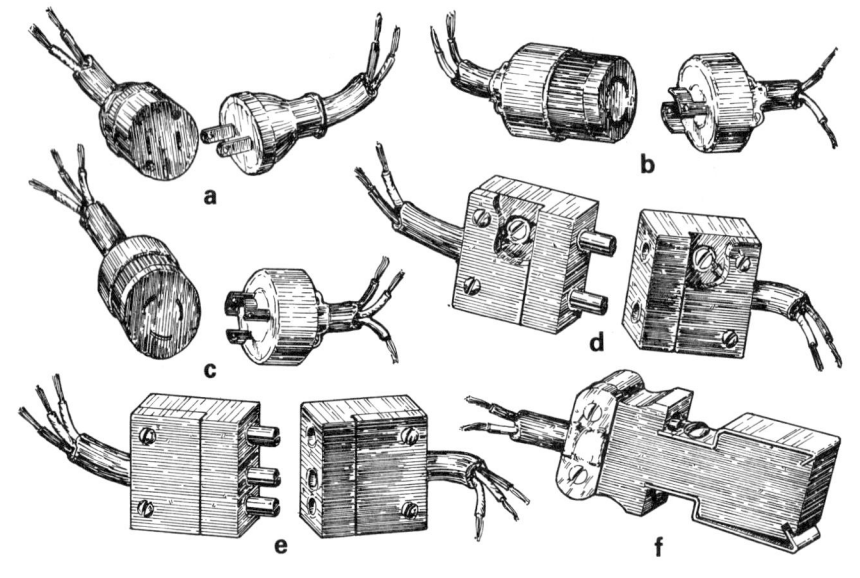

and have limited capacities, they are not advisable. A departure from this style that is in popular use is the twist lock, roughly similar in appearance to a heavy-duty parallel blade plug but with a design that permits the male and female caps to be locked together quite easily yet firmly (see Figure 2–9).

Beware!

Unfortunately, the electrical industry has seen fit to manufacture an amazingly large number of twist lock blade configurations. The most common stage twist lock is the 20-amp, three-prong variety, which, however, comes in several styles. The most significant difference among these styles is in the third or grounding blade, which will often have a part of the blade bent either toward the center of the plug or toward the outside. These two variations are commonly called "pin-in" or "pin-out," respectively, and cannot be used interchangeably.

When wiring a three-prong twist lock, always be sure that the grounding (green) wire is connected to the grounding prong (marked "G" or having a green screw head).

Pin connectors, heavy-duty fiber blocks with sturdy brass pins and sockets, are probably used as much as any other devices. They have the disadvantage of not always giving a firm electrical connection, and they can be easily pulled apart by mistake unless the two cables or connectors are tied together. Pin connectors have a "split" down the center of each brass male pin (hence the name split-pin connector). If a pin is not making a good connection, electrical arcing will occur and the connector will overheat. To avoid this, the individual pins can be "split" or slightly separated with a small knife blade.

Note that in pin connectors with three pins, the grounding pin is *always* the center pin.

Stage Lighting

As in the case with cables, all such connectors come in different sizes, each rated to carry specific maximum amperages. For the stage it is wise to settle on one size and one type of connector to avoid confusion and save time. The 15-ampere pin connector or the 20-ampere twist lock is the usual choice.

The connectors described above can all be used to join a lighting instrument to a cable, or two cables to each other, or a cable to a switchboard or cross-connect panel. There is also a nearly obsolete device, known as a stage plug, which is used solely to connect a cable to a switchboard or a plugging box designed to accept it. The stage plug is a block of hard wood with a strip of brass down each of its edges that fits into a porcelain receptacle of rectangular shape. The standard plug is about 1 inch thick and is rated to carry 50 amperes.

Wiring Connectors

Proper wiring of stage connectors is important to insure against short circuiting or loose connections which can result in arcing within the plug. Stage cable and "leads" from lighting instruments will consist of small strands of copper wire. The easiest method of wiring a pin connector is to twist the small strands together (forming a more cohesive single strand) and then wrap the exposed wire around the screw terminal (Figure 2–10). Be sure to take the following precautions: (1) Expose only as much bare wire as is necessary. (2) Always wrap the wire in the direction the screw will turn when being tightened down (clockwise). (3) Be sure that the connector's strain relief is effective. The strain relief feature of a stage connector will insure that any pulling tension is placed on the cable rather than on the connecting terminals.

Pin connectors are available for two different types of stage cable: rubber cable (Type SO) and asbestos leads from instruments. The rubber cable type will have a single hole in the back of the connector while the asbestos type will have two or three smaller holes. These two connector types should not be used interchangeably.

A better and safer technique of wiring a connector involves "tinning" the exposed copper wire. The tinning process simply requires soldering all the small copper strands together to form one stiffer strand. This tinned lead will then be connected to the terminal as explained.

A third technique involves the use of a small connecting device commonly called a "Sta-kon" (Figure 2–11). The "Sta-kon" is pinched onto the exposed wire with a crimping tool. The ring is then placed around the screw terminal of the connector. Make sure that the "Sta-kon" is the proper size for the wire and that the two or three "Sta-kons" cannot make contact with each other.

Perhaps it is obvious, but one should realize that a male connector must never be "hot" or "live." For example, leads from a lighting instrument will always terminate in a male connector so that the "live" shielded female connector will plug into it.

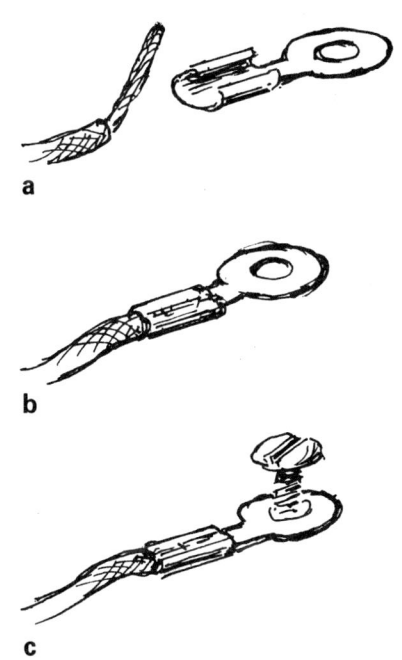

FIGURE 2–11
The "Sta-kon" Solderless Terminal
A special crimping tool is required to securely attach the copper wire to the "Sta-kon" terminal.

Stage Lighting and Electricity

SWITCHES

A switch is a device put into a circuit to interrupt and restore the flow of current as desired, or, in more familiar terminology, to open and close the circuit. There are many types of mechanical switches, from the familiar domestic wall type to great knife-blade arrangements that handle many hundreds of amperes. Like everything else electrical, the type and size to use depends on the duty the switch is expected to perform and the load it is intended to carry.

The "disconnect" box is a heavy-duty switch housed in a metal box which may also contain fuses (Figure 2–12). A disconnect may be permanently mounted in the theatre to receive temporary lighting-control equipment, thus allowing quick and easy access to a power supply. In addition, a disconnect box, fused to the proper amperage for a traveling control system or other electrical apparatus, might also be carried by a touring production. In this case, the disconnect (fused at 100 amps, for example) would be connected to a larger amperage power supply (perhaps another disconnect) in order to protect the touring equipment from a power overload.

A contactor is an electrically operated device in which a small switch, located at some convenient place on-stage, controls a magnet which operates a large-capacity switch in a remote spot. This has the double

FIGURE 2–12
Disconnect Box
Shown is a 300-amp three-phase disconnect. Power in at the top goes through knife switches (shown in off position) and fuses to copper buss bars. Touring "road boards" and auxiliary equipment are connected to the buss bars by means of lugs or bolts.

advantage of keeping the dangerously high current at a distance from the operator and allowing the heavy-duty portion, which is very noisy, to be placed where it cannot distract the audience.

CIRCUIT PROTECTION

No chain is stronger than its weakest link, and should an electric circuit suffer damage that causes a short circuit somewhere along the line, the ampere flow will increase to a point where *something* must burn out. The same thing will happen in the case of an overload—that is, if too many lamps are connected to the circuit. By using the power formula, we see that if six 500-watt lamps are connected to a 120-volt circuit, 25 amperes will flow through it. If 14-gage wire, which has a capacity for only 15 amperes, is used in the circuit, its limit will be greatly exceeded and again something must burn out.

To protect against such occurrences, fuses of suitable capacities are inserted to form the weakest link in the electrical chain. Then, should the current flow increase to dangerous levels, it will be the fuse that gives way, thus breaking the circuit and preventing more serious damage. The trouble is then located and corrected, and a new fuse is inserted with a minimum of trouble.

FIGURE 2–13
Fuses and a Circuit Breaker
a, b, and c are knife-blade cartridge fuses, capacities as indicated; d, e, and f are ferrule-tipped cartridge fuses; g is a typical circuit breaker; h and i are standard plug fuses; j and k are type-S plug fuses (note the difference in the threads as shown in the inserts).

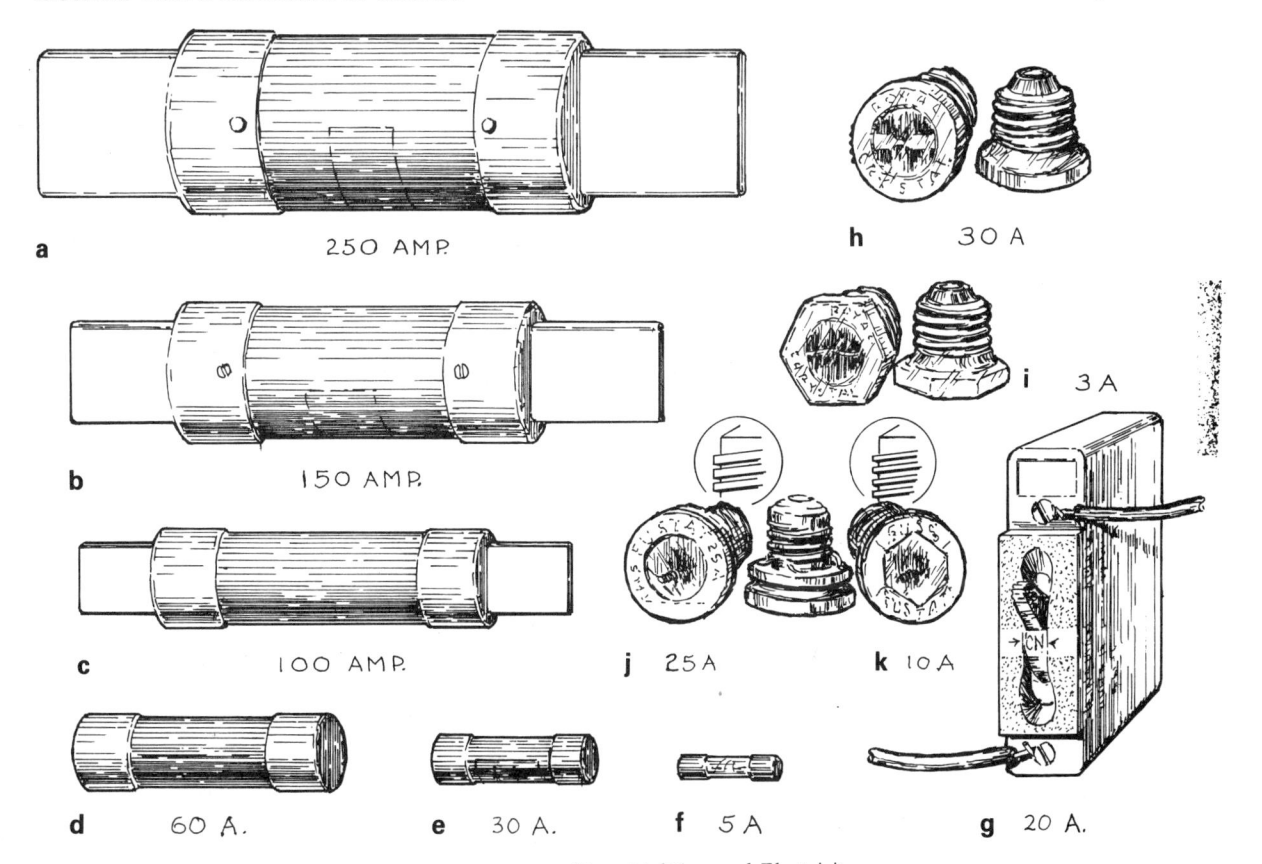

a 250 AMP.
b 150 AMP.
c 100 AMP.
d 60 A.
e 30 A.
f 5 A.
h 30 A
i 3 A
j 25 A
k 10 A
g 20 A.

Stage Lighting and Electricity

Figure 2–13 shows various forms of fuses in common use at the voltages usually encountered in stage-lighting circuitry. Everyone is familiar with the plug fuse which screws into a socket like a lamp. There is a special and very useful variation of the plug fuse known as nontamperable or "Type S," which has one thickness of threading for ratings up to 15 amperes and a different threading for those rated 16 to 30 amperes. The socket is designed to take either one threading or the other but not both. When wiring up a switchboard, for example, the electrician will install a socket that takes only the proper-capacity fuse, depending on the other elements in that circuit. Thus no one can change to a higher-capacity fuse, and the circuit is always protected.

A different shaped fuse is the cartridge, which is available in contact types, sizes, and ratings as listed below.

CONTACTS	LENGTHS	CAPACITIES
Ferrule	2 inches	up to 30 amperes
	3 inches	31 to 60 amperes
Knifeblade	5⅞ inches	61 to 100 amperes
	7⅛ inches	101 to 200 amperes
	8⅝ inches	201 to 400 amperes
	10⅜ inches	401 to 600 amperes

If fuses continue to blow whenever replaced, it is a sign that there is either an overload or a short circuit, and immediate steps should be taken to eliminate the hazard. Overfusing, or bypassing a fuse, is a dangerous and foolish practice that can cause a fire.

Circuit Breakers

Today, in many installations, the fuse is being replaced by the circuit breaker. This, briefly, is a form of switch that automatically opens when the current flow becomes higher than it should. For most installations the circuit breaker is a great convenience: it saves the trouble of keeping a supply of fuses on hand, it cannot be carelessly replaced by one of the wrong capacity, and it can also serve as a switch for the circuit.

TESTING EQUIPMENT

A stage electrician must have ready access to various testing tools in order to "troubleshoot" electrical problems which invariably arise precisely when time is most critical. These tools range from the simplest test lights to rather sophisticated meters. A test light such as the one shown in Figure 2–14 will indicate whether an electrical circuit is "live" simply by either lighting or refusing to light. Test lights should be inexpensive, easy to carry, and hard to break. The neon tester shown in the figure should prove most satisfactory.

FIGURE 2–14
Neon Test Light

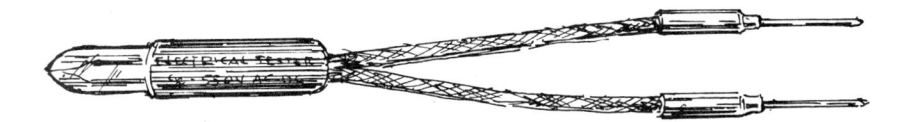

A fairly recent addition to the line of stage testing equipment is the compact continuity tester (manufactured by Frontal Lobe, Ann Arbor, MI). This simple female pin connector contains a small battery which passes a low-voltage electrical current through a connected circuit. If the circuit is complete (lamp good, connector good, cable good, and so forth), a small indicator lamp in the tester will light. This simple device eliminates the necessity of a circuit being live to test for a break. A continuity test, as its name indicates, will simply determine whether a circuit is complete.

More sophisticated testing equipment in the form of meters can read voltage, amperage, and resistance (ohms) in a circuit. Most meters will combine functions (such as the V.O.M.—volt-ohm meter), are fairly delicate, and are also fairly expensive.

ELECTRICAL SAFETY

Electrical safety, like most everything else, is a matter of common sense. If you don't know what you're doing, don't do it! Attention to the following points will be helpful:

1. Always remember that electrical current will follow the path of least resistance and that your body could be that path.
2. Insulation is a good thing. Tools should be insulated with plastic or rubber handles. Soles of shoes should provide good insulation.
3. Electrical fires are most commonly caused by heat buildup caused by arcing or a short circuit.
4. Know the locations of electrical (red) fire extinguishers.
5. Fuses and circuit breakers protect equipment and insure circuit safety. Never attempt to bypass them.
6. Never use a metal ladder for electrical work unless it is insulated with rubber foot pads on all legs. Wooden ladders are always safest.
7. Be particularly wary of damp or wet conditions. Water is a fairly good electrical conductor.
8. Strain relief in electrical connectors is important.
9. Green is ground.
10. Voltage kills.

Stage Lighting and Electricity

3

Light Sources

The development of even an adequate lighting design depends on a strong working knowledge of light sources and instrumentation: quality of light, distribution of light, intensity of light, color of light, and shaping or control of light. Obviously, much of this depends on the actual source of illumination. The theatre uses three basic types of light sources:

1. *Incandescence* Light given off by a glowing metal filament.
2. *Arc Light* Electrical arc that gives off intense illumination.
3. *Gaseous Discharge* Light production that depends on reaction of gases within an enclosure, but also requires an electrical arc.

INCANDESCENT LAMP

The most common source of light used on the stage today is the incandescent filament lamp: a gas-filled glass bulb containing a tungsten filament which emits light when an electrical current is passed through it. Tungsten is a metal which is relatively resistant to electrical flow. As a result, it will heat up and glow when a current is passed through it. The three important parts (Figure 3–1) of an incandescent lamp are the bulb (the glass envelope that encloses the inert gas), the base (to hold the lamp in position and to make electrical contact), and the filament (to pass the current, yet offer enough resistance to effect the transfer of electrical energy into light energy).

There are two basic categories of incandescent lamps: the standard incandescent lamp and the tungsten-halogen lamp. Thomas Edison developed the standard incandescent lamp in 1879, and it really hasn't changed much over the years. The tungsten-halogen lamp (also called the "quartz lamp," the "quartz-iodine lamp," and abbreviated "T-H") was developed in the 1950s and has become a popular theatrical lamp for reasons that will be discussed throughout the chapter.

Lamp Filaments

A passing acquaintance with optics (not a bad thing for lighting designers) tells us that a reflector of light wants to see as tiny a source as possible. The smaller the source, the more efficiently the reflector will carry out its job of gathering and precisely redirecting the light rays. Since almost all stage-lighting equipment uses reflectors of various types, the ideal lamp filament would be what we refer to as a "point source" (the size of a pinhead would do nicely). We have a long way to go toward achieving such a source, but attempts have been made to make tungsten filaments as compact as possible. The tungsten wire is often coiled (designated "C") and sometimes double-coiled (designated "CC" and called a coiled coil) in order to maintain as small a size as possible.

Among the standard incandescent filament forms used in stage-lighting equipment are the barrel (C–5) and the corona (C–7). These are designed to throw out their light equally in all directions. On the other hand, the monoplane (C–13) and the biplane (C–13D) emit most of their light in two opposite directions only, thereby permitting a larger proportion to be picked up and made useful by a reflector or a lens. The tungsten-halogen lamp uses a filament which is double coiled and tends to be a bit longer and narrower than the standard incandescent filament (Figure 3–2, page 40).

The LCL (light-center length) of a lamp is the distance from the center of the filament to some definite place in the base. With a screw-base lamp, the measurement is to the contact button at the end of the base (Figure 3–1). With a prefocus base it is to the fins, and with the

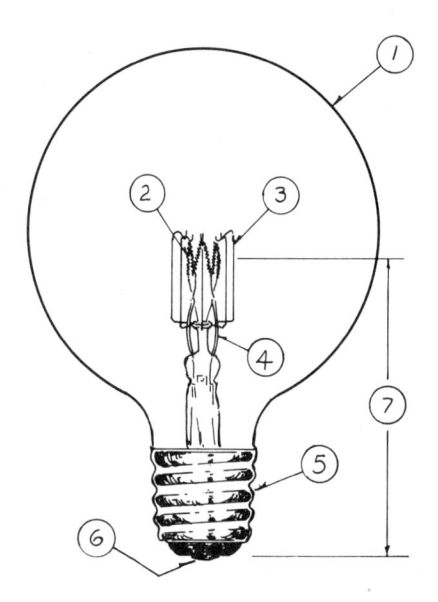

1. GAS-FILLED G-SHAPED BULB
2. BARREL FILAMENT
3. FILAMENT SUPPORTS
4. LEAD-IN WIRE
5. SCREW BASE
6. BOTTOM CONTACT BUTTON
7. L.C.L. (LIGHT CENTER LENGTH)

FIGURE 3–1
A Typical Standard Incandescent Lamp

Light Sources

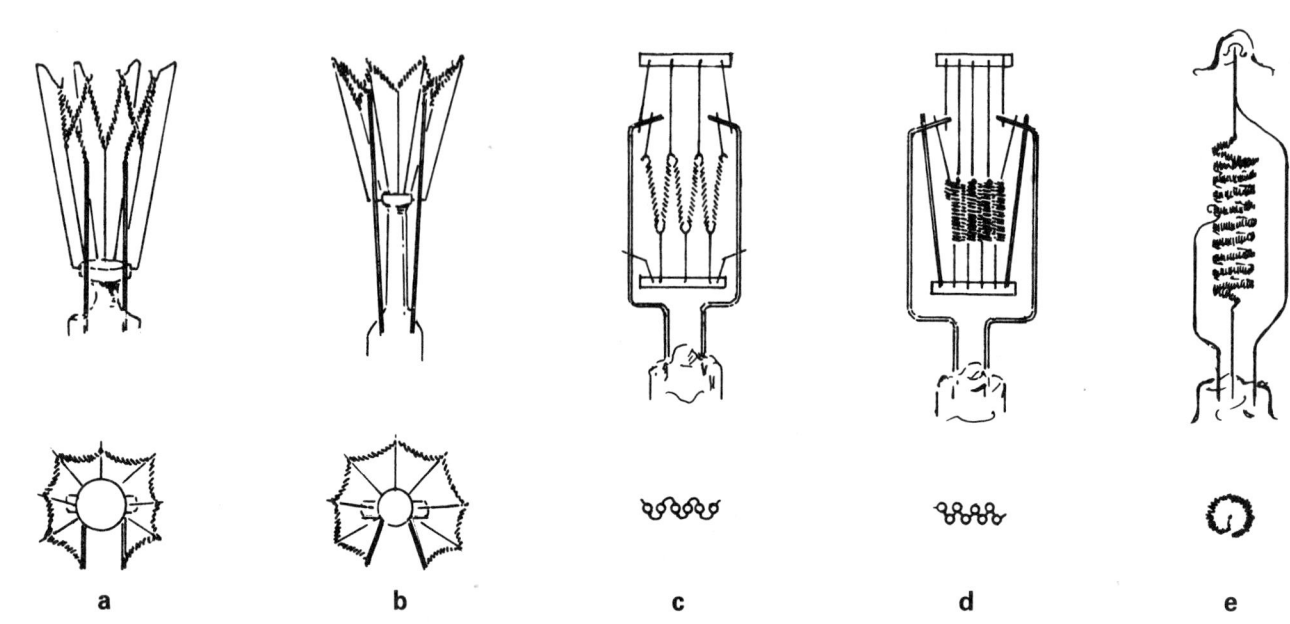

FIGURE 3–2
Filaments Frequently Used in Stage-lighting Instruments
The upper row shows a side view, the bottom row an end view of each. (a) The barrel. (b) The corona. (c) The monoplane. (d) The biplane. (e) The coiled coil.

bipost to the shoulder of the pins. It is particularly important to know the LCL when a lamp is to be used in conjunction with a reflector or a lens, for the center of the filament must be exactly aligned with the centers of such optical devices.

One important characteristic of the incandescent filament to remember is that when voltage to a lamp is reduced by using a dimmer, the color of light emitted is altered. This can be extremely important on the stage and also in color television, for the appearance of colored materials such as costumes and scenery, and even the faces of the actors, may be changed. This color shift will be discussed in greater detail later in this chapter.

Lamp Bulbs

The bulbs of standard incandescent lamps are made of ordinary glass, while the bulbs of tungsten-halogen lamps are made of the more heat- and pressure-resistant quartz glass. As a result, the standard incandescent bulb needs to be larger in order to dissipate the heat given off by the filament. The smaller envelope of the tungsten-halogen lamp has an important advantage over the standard incandescent lamp, for the size of a stage-lighting instrument is often dictated by lamp size.

Bulbs come in a variety of shapes, sizes, and finishes. The shape of a bulb is designated by a letter. The A (for arbitrary) and PS (for pear-shape with straight sides) are common forms seen in the general line of household lamps (Figure 3–3). Lamps used in stage-lighting in-

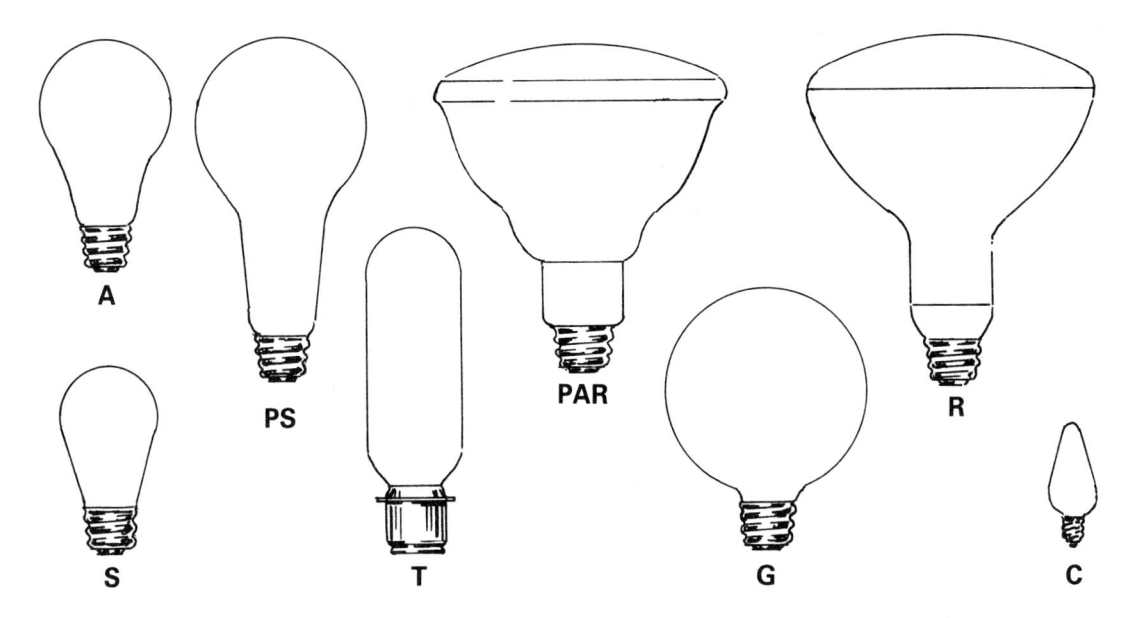

FIGURE 3–3

Typical Bulb Shapes

(A) Arbitrary designation. (S) Straight side. (PS) Pear shape, straight neck. (T) Tubular. (PAR) Parabolic aluminized reflector. (G) Globular. (R) Reflector. (C) Cone shape.

struments are usually either globe-shaped (G) to permit the even dissipation of heat or tubular (T) to allow the filament to be brought closer to some optical feature. There are a number of other shapes, some of which are purely decorative. Reflector lamps (R and PAR) will be discussed separately.

The size of a bulb is designated by a numbering system which may seem unnecessarily complex but which is, at least, standardized. The diameter of the bulb at its largest point is expressed in eighths of an inch, and this number is used to designate size. Therefore, a T–12 lamp (common in ellipsoidal reflector spotlights) means that the bulb is tubular in shape and $12/8$ of an inch (or 1½ inches) in diameter.

Bulb Finishes and Color. Lamps used on the stage usually are made of clear glass, which is essential for any source used in an instrument with reflector or lens. But the smaller wattage A and PS lamps are more readily obtained with an inner finish (called "frosting") that is intended to diffuse the light. If desired, these sizes can be ordered in the clear-glass style, but this is seldom necessary because they are rarely used in stage-lighting instruments of any precision. There are many kinds of finishes available, some purely decorative and others for some special application. The side-silvered showcase lamp that can be tucked away behind very little cover is often handy on the stage for throwing a little light in difficult corners. Colored-glass lamps are obtainable in the smaller wattages only and are not very useful on the stage except in the smallest installations.

Light Sources

Lamp Bases

The electrical contact part of the base of a lamp is generally made of copper, though aluminum is now being used for many of the smaller wattages. The base may be any of several sizes, but the medium size (as in common household lamps) with a 1-inch diameter and the mogul with 1½-inch diameter are the ones most commonly used in stardard incandescent theatre lamps. The tungsten-halogen lamp, because of its smaller size, will almost always have a smaller base.

Bases also vary in type, with the common screw base (which comes in all sizes) being the simplest (Figure 3–4). Occasionally this type is sufficient, but it is often necessary to provide some sort of locking device in the base so that the lamp and particularly its filament may be held in a precise relationship with optical features of the instruments in which it is designed to burn. This relationship is referred to as "lamp alignment." Standard incandescent lamps requiring specific alignment will usually have medium or mogul prefocus bases or medium or mogul bi-post bases. Smaller lamps such as the 100-150 watt, 3-inch Fresnel lamp may use the bayonet base illustrated in Figure 3–4. The prefocus bases and the medium bi-post base slip into the socket and require slight pressure downward and a turn before the lamp "clicks" into alignment.

Tungsten-halogen lamps will normally have special bases, although quartz lamps called "retrofits" are manufactured with standard incandescent bases so that the newer T-H lamps can be used in lighting instruments designed for standard incandescent lamps. Most T-H lamps have one of two types of bases: The bi-pin base or the double-ended recessed single-contact base (Figure 3–6). The bi-pin lamp slides straight into its socket and is held in place by a pressure plate. Excessive handling or jarring may cause this lamp to dislodge from its base, so care must be taken with instruments requiring the bi-pin lamp. The double-ended lamp is held in place by two metal contacts mounted so that they protrude through the reflector of an instrument. Depending on the design of the lighting instrument, these lamps can be difficult to get properly seated. Care must therefore be taken not to damage either the contacts or the seal of the lamp base, which is most often porcelain or glass. A fairly recent addition to T-H lamp bases is the small-size screw base called a "mini-can" (short for miniature candelabra) base. This base is extremely easy to use and seems to hold up quite well under the high heat conditions of the T-H lamp.

R AND PAR LAMPS

The R (reflector type) and PAR (parabolic aluminized reflector) lamps are discussed separately here because each is essentially a self-contained lighting instrument. Both the R- and PAR-type contain a par-

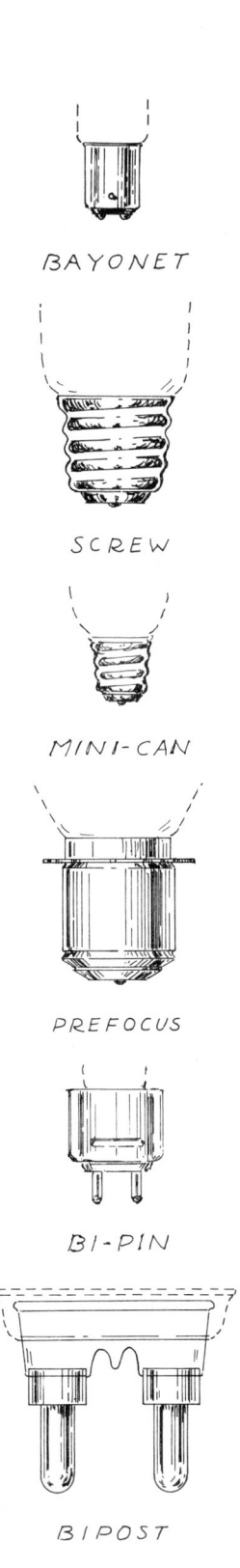

FIGURE 3–4
Common Base Types

abolic-shaped reflector, either a standard incandescent filament or a small quartz lamp and a sort of lens. Because much of the light emitted by the filament is reflected out of the lamps in a useful direction, and because the reflector is sealed into the bulb itself, R and PAR lamps are extremely efficient.

PAR lamps are made out of molded, heat-resistant glass and can be used outdoors without danger of cracking if snow or rain strike them while they are hot. They are a good deal heavier and sturdier than the Rs, which are made of blown glass and are light in weight and more fragile.

A PAR lamp costs more than an equivalent wattage R-type, but it will deliver a more powerful beam of light. However, the R-type lamps have a smoother pattern of light. Both lamps are available in spot and flood beam spreads from 75 to 500 watts; higher wattage PAR lamps are available in wide flood and in medium, narrow, and very narrow beams. The lower wattage R-type and PAR lamps have medium screw bases (up to 500 watts); R-type lamps above 500 watts have mogul screw bases; and the larger (300–1500 watt) PAR lamps have either side or end-prong bases (Figure 3–5).

Automobile headlights have used PAR lamps for years, but it took rock-concert lighting to introduce these high wattage lamps to the theatre. Quartz PAR-64 lamps are mounted in a very simple housing

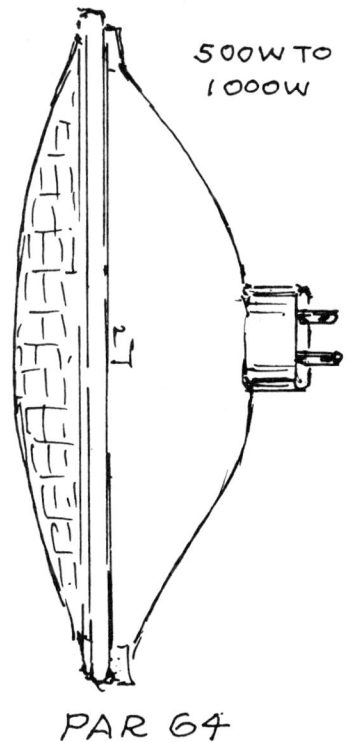

FIGURE 3–5
PAR-64 Lamp
Shown with extended mogul end prong base.

Light Sources

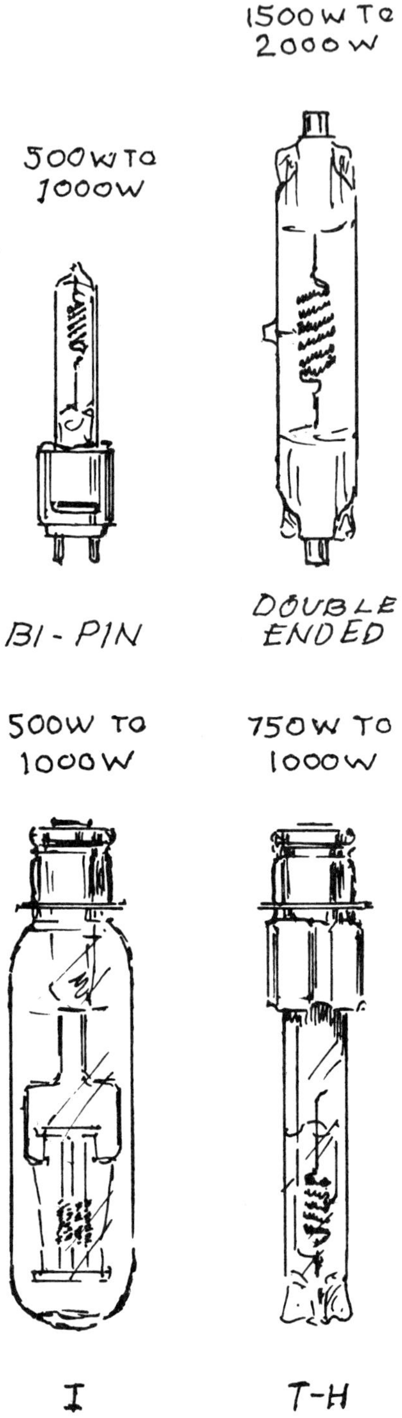

FIGURE 3–6
Tungsten-halogen Lamps
Top: Two common types. Bottom: Incandescent and tungsten-halogen lamp, both with medium prefocus bases.

(aptly named PAR cans) and have the ability to throw a highly concentrated beam of light over a considerable distance. The light has a very distinctive quality because of its nearly parallel rays and its sheer intensity. The beam from quartz PAR lamps is more oval than round because of the filament shape and has a very soft and fuzzy edge, making it easy to blend one beam with another. The direction of the oval beam is altered simply by rotating the lamp within the PAR can housing. The PAR lamp has one distinct disadvantage over more conventional stage-lighting instruments: It is nearly impossible to control and shape the beam. Therefore, the application of PAR lamps to theatrical lighting, although significant, has been limited.

Because of the great breadth of beam typical of R and PAR lamps, they can be very useful in striplights, where it is necessary to blend the light from different color circuits smoothly and at short range. Since the reflectors are sealed into the bulbs, there is no worry about dirt or corrosion affecting their surfaces. If the same type and size of base is used, it is a simple matter to change from type to type depending on the precise effect desired. For example, PAR spots may be used for a long, very intense throw and R floods for a short throw where smoothness is more important than brightness. It should be emphasized that the beam pattern from the R-type lamp is quite superior to that of the PAR, and, as a result, the R-type is a better general purpose striplight lamp.

Small wattage (30–75 watts) R-20 and R-30 lamps, often used in showcase lighting applications, are frequently useful in lighting tight spaces where a standard stage lighting instrument would be too large, heavy, or clumsy.

TUNGSTEN-HALOGEN LAMPS

The development of the tungsten-halogen lamp has led to significant changes in the lighting industry. The most important, perhaps, has been the creation of smaller and more powerful lighting instruments designed specifically for these new lamps, a development that has freed the lighting designer from the restrictions of relatively archaic equipment. Not only are the T-H lamps much more compact than standard incandescent lamps (see Figure 3–6), but they also have a much longer life and maintain initial intensity throughout their lifespan.

The secret of this significant innovation is the halogen-family gas introduced into the bulb. As a tungsten filament burns, particles evaporate from the filament and deposit themselves on the cooler glass envelope. The result of this process is a gradual darkening of the bulb and, consequently, a lessening of light output from the lamp. In the T-H lamps, however, the halogen gas gobbles up the elusive tungsten

Stage Lighting

particles and redeposits them at the hottest point within the bulb—the filament. (The lamp ultimately fails only because the halogen gas does not redeposit the particles evenly.) Because the desired reaction between the tungsten particles and halogen gas requires a great deal of heat, the glass envelope is made smaller and constructed out of strong quartz glass.

Naturally, the T-H lamp costs about twice as much as a standard incandescent lamp of comparable wattage; but its life is nearly two times longer and it is more efficient.

A significant disadvantage of the T-H lamp is that the quartz glass envelope cannot be touched by fingers. No matter how clean your hands happen to be, oil from your skin is deposited on the glass and will react with the quartz when it is heated. The result of this reaction not only weakens the envelope (possibly causing explosion) but also produces a frosted effect on the glass (if we had wanted frosted, we would have ordered frosted).

The tungsten filament found in most stage T-H lamps is probably more fragile than the standard incandescent filament. The only real explanation for this is poorer filament support within the envelope. As a result, many rental houses continue to use the older standard incandescent lamp, although they are now being forced to change over to quartz because of new instrumentation requirements. This unfortunate weakness in T-H lamps must be recognized, and all instruments equipped with them should be treated with great care. *Never* jar an instrument with the lamp burning, for the supple tungsten filament will almost surely break.

LAMP LIFE

The rated-average life for the common household lamp is usually 750 burning hours, but for many standard incandescent stage lamps it is only 200 hours. Rated-average life is determined by the manufacturer, who takes a number of lamps at random and leaves them burning under normal conditions until (1) they burn out completely or (2) their light output drops to 80 percent of what it was originally.

Rated-average life is presumed to apply under usual operating conditions. But a lamp's life may be shortened in a number of ways. It will give out more quickly if burned while enclosed in an excessively hot place such as one from which its own heat cannot escape (lighting instruments are specifically ventilated for this purpose). Rough handling may break some interior part, even though the outer appearance has not changed. If connected to a higher voltage than it was designed for, a lamp will burn out rapidly, even abruptly. And in the case of many standard incandescent lamps used in stage instruments, burning in the wrong position results in rapid failure. The correct burning position, if important, will always be marked on the end of the bulb and should be consulted if any doubt exists.

Standard incandescent T-12 and T-14 lamps are particularly susceptible to failure if they are burned in the wrong position. A nonquartz T lamp designed to be used in an ellipsoidal spotlight should be burned base up, or nearly so, for the filament is close to the end of the bulb, which would be melted by the heat if it accumulated there. On the other hand, the T-20 lamp intended to be used in a Fresnel spotlight should be burned base down or no more than 90 degrees from the perpendicular, for the filament is close to the base and if the heat should concentrate there it would crack the cement seal between bulb and base (Figure 3–7). All T-H lamps (except retrofits) are designed to burn in any position.

If a lamp designed to be used on 120-volt service is fed with only 110 volts, the lamp will last almost four times as long as it would on 120 volts, but there will be only about 74 percent as much light.

On the other hand, if this same lamp is fed 130 volts, there will be 31 percent more light, but the lamp will last only a third as long.

This relationship of voltage, intensity, and life must be kept in mind, especially when bargains in "lamps that burn twice as long" or the like are offered. It also explains why stage lamps often last far longer than anticipated: they have been burned at low dimmer readings.

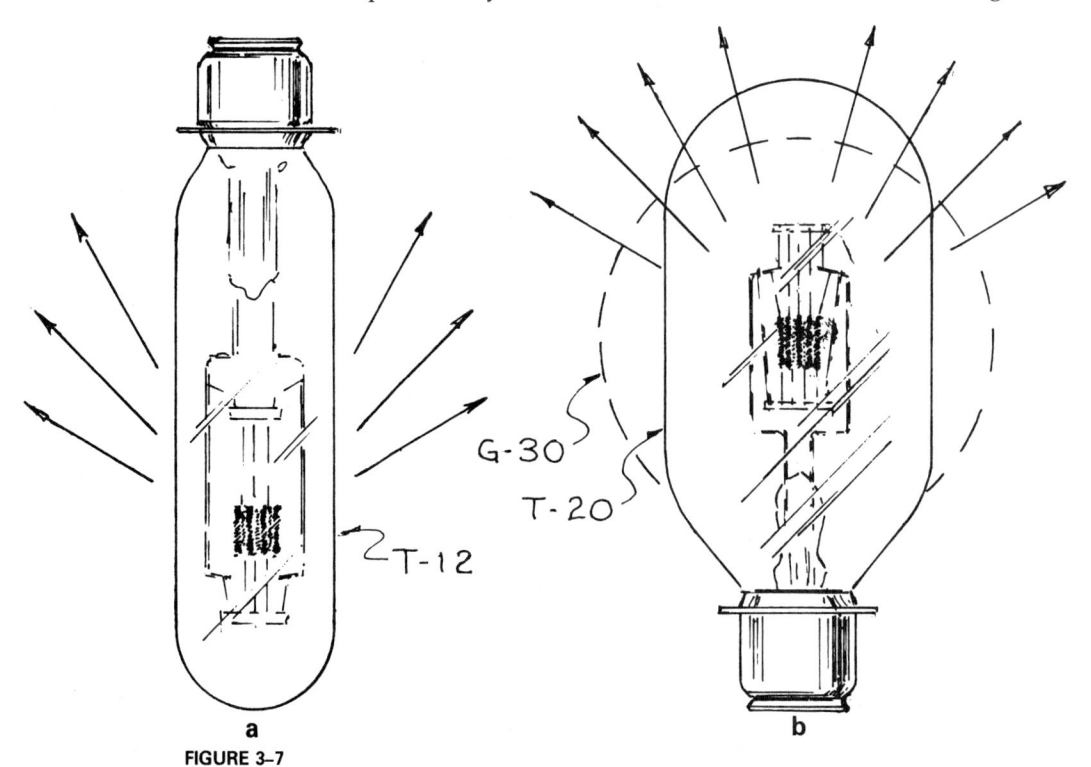

FIGURE 3–7
Dissipation of Heat from Incandescent Lamps
(a) A lamp designed to be burned base up. (b) Lamps designed to be burned base down.

Watts	GE Ordering Code	ANSI Code	National Stock No. 6240-00-	Std. Pkg. Qty.	Approx. Color Temp. °K	Approx. Hours Life	Approx. Initial Lumens	Lighted Length— Inches	Bulb Finish
1000	Q1000T6/CL	DWT	917-6915	6	3000	2,000	23,400	1	Clear
	FER-Q1000T6/4CL	FER	—	6	3200	500	27,500	3/4	Clear
1500	DVV-Q1500T8/4CL	DVV (11)	—	6	3200	500	42,700	1 1/4	Clear
2000	FEY-Q2000T8/4CL	FEY	231-0761	6	3200	300	59,000	1	Clear

FIGURE 3–8

Comparison of Wattage, Color Temperature, Life, and Lumen Output
(Table courtesy General Electric Company. Publication SS-123: *Stage Studio Lamps.*)

Wattage and Lumen Output

The general public has been taught by lamp manufacturers to equate the wattage of a lamp with its brightness. If our 75-watt reading lamp is too dim, we simply replace it with a 100-watt lamp. But, as we learned in Chapter 2, wattage is the rate of doing work and, therefore, is not necessarily an accurate measure of lamp intensity. Lamp manufacturers use a measure of intensity called the lumen to measure the light output of a lamp. Figure 3–8 shows how two lamps with identical physical specifications can be very different in brightness (compare DWT and FER). Note that as lumen output is increased, lamp life is significantly decreased.

IDENTIFYING AND PURCHASING LAMPS

The American National Standards Institute (ANSI) has established a system for identifying lamps by a three-letter code called the "ANSI Code." If one lamp differs in any way from another, it will be assigned a separate ANSI code (Figure 3–8). Although the three-letter codes are totally nondescriptive by themselves, they have greatly simplified the process of specifying lamps. One may now simply order a lamp by giving the supplier the ANSI code.

Of course, the wise electrician will also be familiar with all possible variations in lamp manufacture and will have access to up-to-date lamp catalogs. Not only are these catalogs useful when ordering spare lamps, but they also offer quick access to special application lamps such as flashbulbs, low-voltage lamps, and photo-floods. The two major lamp manufacturers in the United States are willing to supply you with their current catalogs. Write to either their regional sales offices or to the following addresses:

SYLVANIA

GTE Products Corp.
Lighting Center
Danvers, MA 01923

Light Sources

GENERAL ELECTRIC
General Electric Company
Lighting Business Group
Nela Park
Cleveland, OH 44112

In addition to its lamp catalogs, Sylvania publishes a short and easy-to-use book called *Sylvania Lighting Handbook* (currently in its seventh edition), which will be sent to you upon request.

COLOR TEMPERATURE

We tend to think of the light emitted from an ordinary lamp as being "white," but the fact is that so-called "white" light is relative, and the actual color of light given off by sources can vary greatly. The method we have to identify the color makeup of any light source is called color temperature and its measurement is in Kelvin (K) degrees. To standardize color notation, a light-emitting device called a blackbody was developed; when heated it emits light consisting of various color wavelengths. The blackbody responds to heat in much the same way that a tungsten filament does; it begins to glow a very warm red-yellow, moves toward "white" as more heat is applied, and will finally appear to approach blue when a great deal of heat is applied. The color wavelengths of light emitted by the blackbody are identified by a sophisticated meter called a spectrophotometer. Any color can thus be equated with the temperature of heat being applied to the blackbody, resulting in a meaningful Kelvin figure.

This is fairly important for a lighting designer to understand because theatre sources will typically range from standard incandescence, which is around 3000° K, to the much cooler arc lamps which can be as high as 6000° K. Obviously, the same color filter placed in front of two such different sources will project very different colors. For all practical purposes, no one will notice a source color difference of less than 200° K; but any more of a difference will be noticeable. The color temperature of stage lamps is often printed on their containers and is always noted in catalogs. A general rule to go by is the higher the color temperature, the cooler the light. And always realize that dimming a source decreases color temperature significantly.

LOW-VOLTAGE LAMPS

Low-voltage light sources are lamps designed to operate with less than 120 applied volts. Sealed-beam automobile headlights operate to full potential with only 12 volts, while aircraft lamps operate with 24 volts. The advantage of low-voltage lamps for theatre application is in the intensity and quality of the light they emit. The lower the voltage applied to a lamp filament, the smaller the filament can be. Therefore, low-voltage sources have filaments which really do begin to approach the much-desired point source of light. The more closely we approximate a point source, the better we can control the light through the use of reflectors and lenses.

Low-voltage lamps such as aircraft landing lamps (ACLs) deliver an incredibly coherent light that is intense and harsh in quality. To use such lamps on the stage, however, a low-voltage power source is necessary. A variable voltage transformer is a good equipment investment for an active theatre, but it can be fairly expensive. Two substitutes come to mind. The first is the continuous duty car battery charger, which is actually a step-down transformer from 120 to 12 volts. The second is the auto transformer, which functions as a dimmer by reducing the voltage to a lamp (not true of the modern SCR and other electronic dimmers). One can put a meter on the output of an auto transformer dimmer and set the reading to any desired voltage.

When using low-voltage sources, care must be taken not to overload a circuit or the transformer. The power formula tells us that, given the same-wattage lamp, as the voltage is lowered, the amperage is subsequently raised.

ARC LIGHT

The first electric light source to be used in the theatre was an arc light in the form of limelight. Blocks of calcium oxide (lime) were used in place of the more modern carbon rods in spotlights each requiring an operator. In fact, there are reports that the quality of limelight was so flattering that patrons bemoaned the installation of more modern incandescent light sources in many theatres. Arc light is impressive because of its brilliance—a streak of lightning during a thunderstorm is an example of arc light on a grand scale. The brief off-stage striking of an arc is a theatrical technique used to simulate lightning on stage.

Carbon-Arc

The carbon-arc light source became popular in the theatre because of its intense and high color temperature light. American taste in follow spotting, especially for Broadway-type musical productions, calls for a strong frontal source; and, because of physical restrictions on where one could place such a lighting instrument and operator in the typical Broadway house, an instrument with the potential of delivering a whole lot of light was developed. This instrument was the carbon-arc follow spot.

Two copper-coated carbon rods, about the size of pencils, are mounted within a housing along with a reflector and lenses. Electricity is conducted to the tips of the rods via the copper coating. The two rods are brought together to begin the flow of electricity (called "striking" the arc) and then backed off, forcing the electricity to jump the ¼ - ½ inch gap. This gap, which is air filled with a few flying carbon particles, offers a good deal of resistance to the electrical flow and, as a result, quite a bit of heat and light is generated. The arc is fairly small, so it works well with the instrument's optical system. As the carbons burn down (the life of a carbon should be at least 45 minutes), they are slowly fed into each other, thereby maintaining a constant gap.

A byproduct of carbon-arc combustion is carbon monoxide gas, a lethal substance. Never operate a carbon-arc follow spot or projector without proper ventilation.

The major manufacturer of carbon-arc follow spots in the United States is Strong Electric, a company well known for its Trouper and Super Trouper series of follow spots. While carbon-arc sources had a stronghold on follow spotting and projection for many years, recent developments in arc lamps will ultimately make carbon-arc as antique a light source as limelight.

Short-Arc Lamps

Two tungsten electrodes in a strong glass enclosure of gas under high pressure produce an intense light source when the current arcs between the electrodes. The result is a brilliant point source. Because the arc is shielded from the oxygen in the air, the tungsten electrodes do not burn up as do the carbons in the arc light.

Of the short-arc lamps currently available the xenon lamp is the oldest. The xenon lamp, which is filled with high-pressure xenon gas, burns with a brilliant, cool light. Its high efficiency and long life help to compensate for its high cost. Because of its efficiency and long life

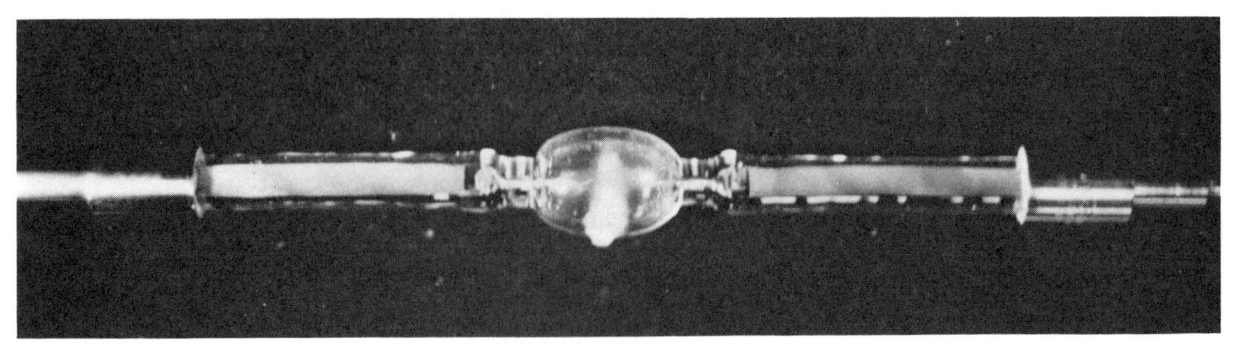

FIGURE 3–9
Short-arc Lamp
The HMI lamp, 2500 watts.

Stage Lighting

it has been standard installation in motion picture projectors and long-range follow spots.

The problem with the xenon lamp is that it has a tendency to explode because of the high pressure of the gas within the glass envelope. Several xenon lamp accidents (with small fragments of glass being propelled through the air at startling velocities) have prompted the enactment of safety regulations for the use of xenon sources. Among others, these include explosion-proof lamp housings that further increase the user's cost.

The more recent HMI lamp is constructed like the xenon lamp but with the gas under a much lower pressure. It is a good projector lamp, although the light has such a high Kelvin temperature that it needs a warm filter to correctly project the colors of the film or slide (Figure 3–9). HMI follow spots are becoming more common, and this trend will probably continue unless an even more acceptable high-intensity source is developed.

A final note: The major disadvantage of any arc source for theatrical applications is that it cannot be electronically dimmed.

GASEOUS DISCHARGE LAMPS

The most familiar form of gaseous discharge lamps is the fluorescent tube, which never achieved its promises of becoming a major light source in the theatre. Current passing through a pressurized mercury vapor causes a gaseous discharge, predominantly in the ultraviolet zone, which is absorbed by the phosphorous coating on the inside walls of the tube. The coating reemits the energy, becoming the light source itself.

Because the fluorescent tube is a line of light and not a point source, its uses in the theatre are limited to producing a wash of light on a cyclorama or backdrop. The shape of the lamp makes it difficult to achieve smooth color blending. The fluorescent hoods, however, can be installed with black light flourescent tubes to flood the stage with ultraviolet light for a black light effect.

A black light effect is the illuminating of a surface treated with fluorescent paint or dye with ultraviolet light (UV). The fluorescent surface becomes, in effect, the light source as it reemits the energy of the ultraviolet light.

The mercury vapor lamp with a UV filter is another effective instrument to produce black light. Both the black light fluorescent tube and the mercury vapor lamp require a ballast and warmup time and cannot be dimmed.

It should be also be mentioned that the arc-light follow spot can be equipped with a UV filter and be used for a black light effect.

Light Sources

SAFETY AND LIGHT SOURCES

A good electrician follows several simple rules when working with the various light sources found in the theatre:

1. Always unplug a lighting instrument before replacing a bad lamp.
2. Lamps are expensive, so be sure to treat them with care.
3. Unshielded arc light is bright enough to blind anyone looking directly at the source. A warning to contact lens wearers: An unshielded arc flash has been known to weld the lens (plastic type) to the cornea, resulting in blindness. (From the latest report of the Union [USA] Safety Study.)
4. Keep your fingers off quartz bulbs.
5. The envelope of a burning lamp gets too hot to handle even with the best of gloves.

4

Reflection and Refraction

When a beam of light passing through air encounters anything in its path, three things can happen. The light may be absorbed (for example, by a sheet of black material), it may be refracted (through a lens), or it may be reflected (by any opaque substance it strikes). Actually, none of these things will happen completely: a mirror or a lens will absorb a small portion of light, the blackest of materials will still reflect some light, a piece of colored glass will absorb certain light rays and allow others to pass through. All stage-lighting instruments use reflectors to increase the efficiency of a light source, and some use lenses to gather and redirect light from the source. By understanding the laws by which reflection and refraction operate, we can better understand how stage-lighting instruments work and why light behaves as it does when it strikes the stage and actors.

REFLECTION OF LIGHT

The law of specular reflection explains what happens to a light beam when it strikes a smooth, shiny surface, such as a mirror. It is reflected at an angle equal to the angle at which it struck, but in the opposite direction. (The angle of incidence is equal to the angle of reflection.) A moment's contemplation of a mirror will make this clear. Of course, if the beam strikes the surface head on, it will reflect directly back over the same path (Figure 4–1).

If the beam strikes a surface with slight irregularities, for example etched aluminum or foil paper that has been crumpled and smoothed out again, the same law applies. However, because there are now innumerable small surfaces rather than a single, perfectly flat one, the reflected rays will tend to be scattered but will not diverge too greatly from one basic direction. This phenomenon is known as spread reflection.

A piece of blotting paper or soft cotton cloth will produce a diffuse reflection because of the vast number and varied angles of the surface. In the case of these surfaces, there will be no single direction to the reflected light. Rather the whole surface will appear much the same from whatever angle it is viewed.

A combination of specular and diffuse reflection is known as mixed reflection. A piece of crockery with a high glaze will produce this: the rough surface of the ceramic will create diffusion, while the shiny glaze will act like a mirrored surface to give specular reflection. Furthermore, the diffused light will show the color of the material itself, while the other reflected light (or highlight) will have the color of the source.

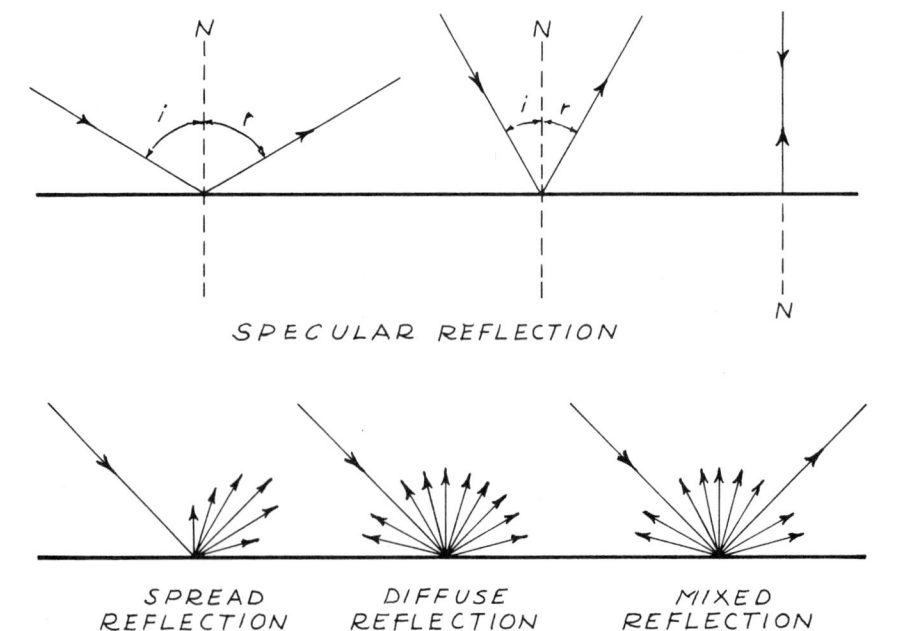

FIGURE 4–1
Types of Reflection

Stage Lighting

REFLECTORS

Early stage-lighting instruments used reflectors which were molded glass mirrors, but modern reflectors are constructed of a lightweight spun metal. After fabrication, this metal shell is given a highly reflective and durable surface treatment called the Alzak process. The Alzak reflector has become an industry standard.

Stage-lighting instruments use one of three reflector types or shapes:

1 *spherical:* found in the Fresnel-type spotlight.
2 *parabolic:* found in beam projectors and PAR- and R-type lamps.
3 *ellipsoidal:* found in ellipsoidal reflector spotlights (ERS).

As one would expect, the shape of the reflector determines exactly how it redirects light from a source.

Spherical Reflectors

If polished metal is made into a reflector in the form of a part of a sphere, and a source of light is placed at the center of the curvature of this form, each ray of light that strikes the reflecting surface will do so squarely. It will be returned through the source, thereby increasing the amount of light emanating from the source in the opposite direction (Figure 4–2, page 56).

Naturally, it is necessary for the source, say the filament of a lamp, to be located precisely in relation to the reflector, or its rays will not strike the reflector straight on but at various angles. Although not doubled, the efficiency of a light source in combination with a spherical reflector is increased significantly.

Parabolic Reflectors

The nature of a parabolic reflector is such that if a light source is placed at its focal center, or focal point, all rays that strike the reflective surface will emerge parallel to one another (Figure 4–3, page 56). This will naturally give a great concentration of light in a tight beam, rather than the spread effusion from a spherical reflector.

Moving the source from the focal point toward the reflector will spread the light, while moving it away from the reflector causes light rays to converge.

The only problem with the parabolic reflector in stage-lighting instruments is that in addition to the valuable parallel rays being reflected, the source also emits nonparallel rays out the front of the instrument. When we study the beam projector we will look at attempted solutions to this problem.

FIGURE 4–2
Reflection from a Spherical Reflector Under Different Conditions

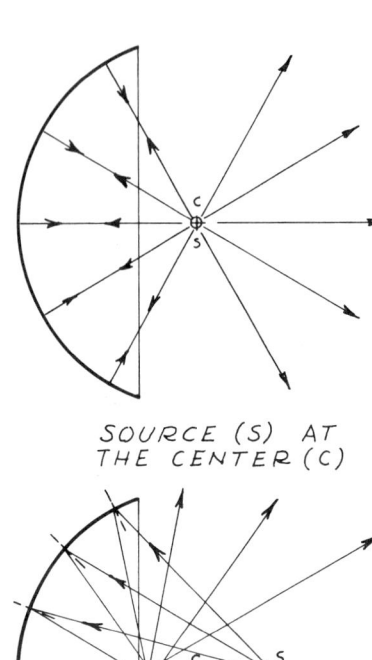

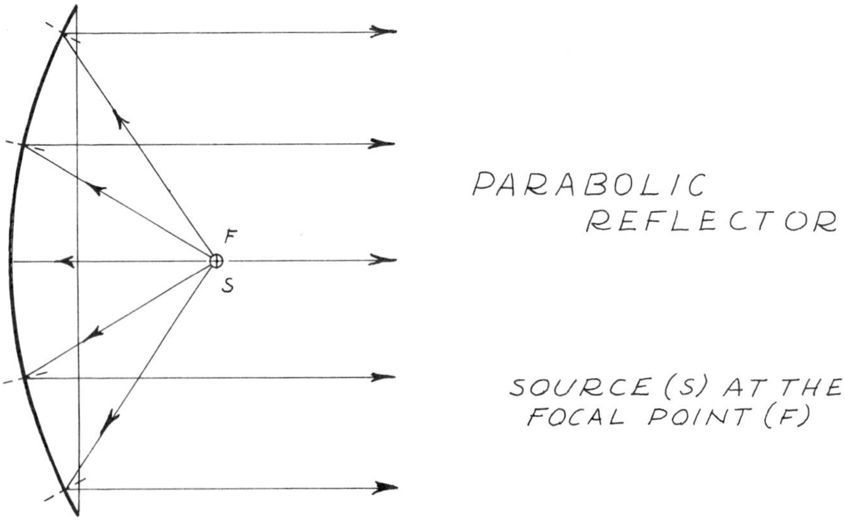

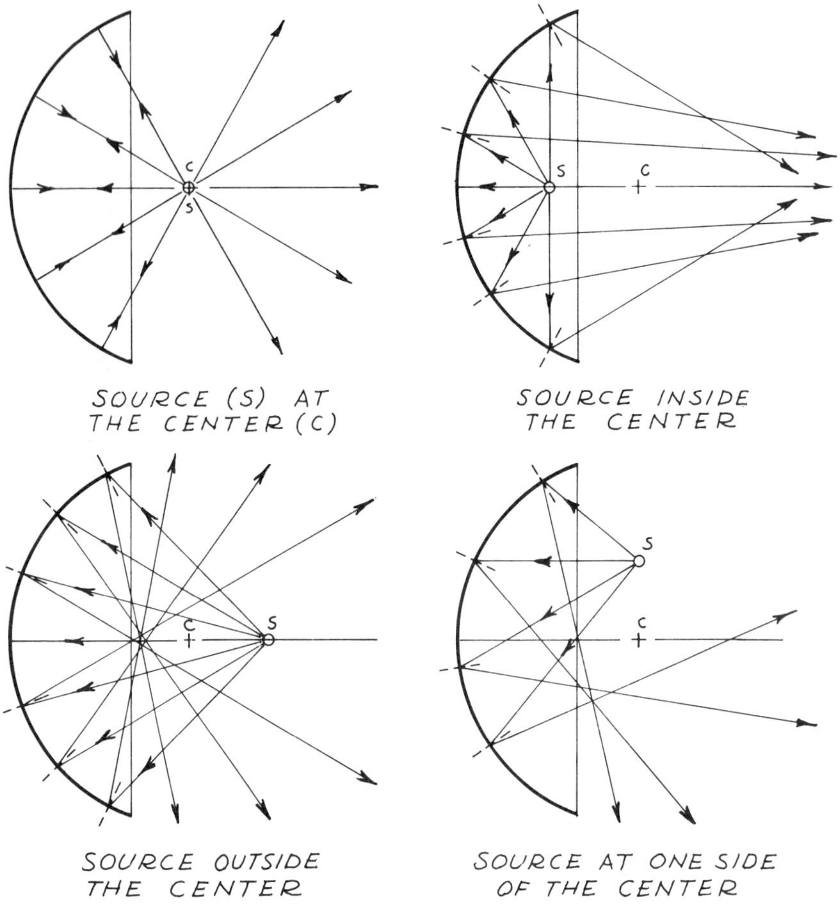

SOURCE (S) AT THE CENTER (C)

SOURCE INSIDE THE CENTER

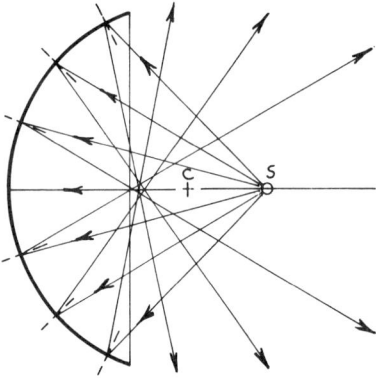

SOURCE OUTSIDE THE CENTER

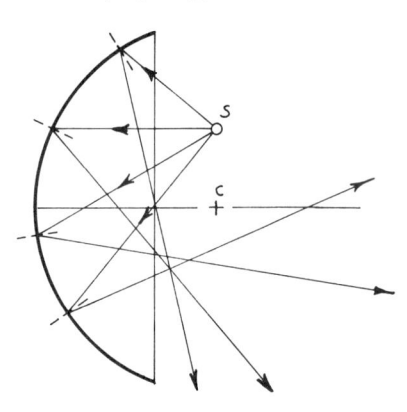

SOURCE AT ONE SIDE OF THE CENTER

PARABOLIC REFLECTOR

SOURCE (S) AT THE FOCAL POINT (F)

FIGURE 4-3
Reflection from a Parabolic Reflector

Stage Lighting

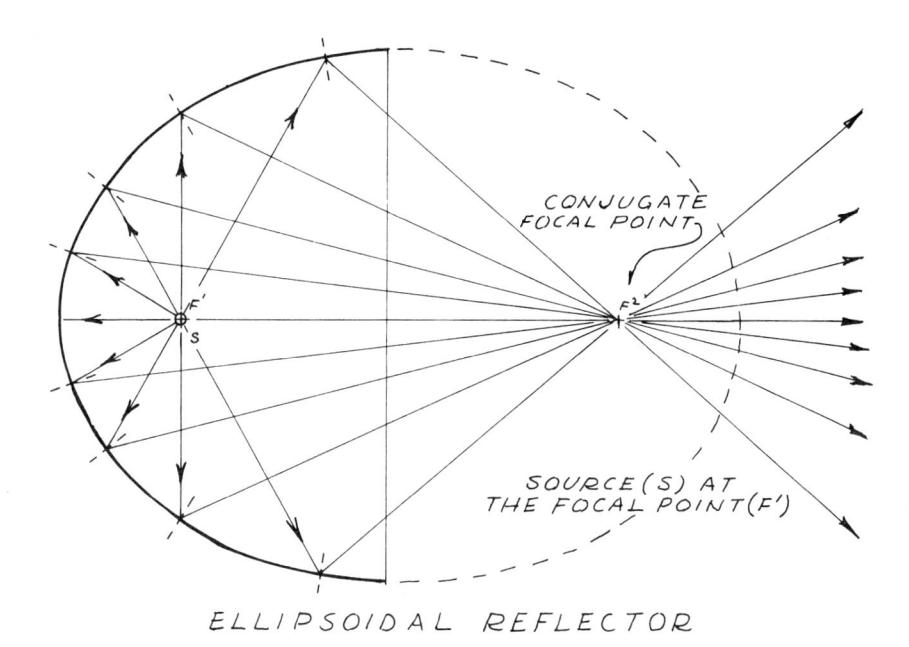

FIGURE 4–4
Reflection from an Ellipsoidal Reflector

Ellipsoidal Reflectors

The ellipsoidal reflector is more efficient than either the spherical or parabolic reflectors. By mathematical definition an ellipsoid has two focal points. When a reflector is constructed in the form of half of an ellipsoid and a source is placed at the focal point at that end, all rays of light that strike the reflector will be diverted through the second or conjugate focal point (Figure 4–4). The result is that an enormous percentage of the light from the source is directed in a manner that makes it easily usable, as we shall examine in Chapter 5 in the section on spotlights.

As we saw earlier, the ideal source of light is a point source; stage lamps only approximate such a source. Because of this, some ellipsoidal reflectors are not a continuous smooth surface, as expected, but are regularly broken up into small rectangles or facets. These facets tend to more precisely direct the light to the conjugate focal point of the ellipsoidal reflector. Such a reflector is called a flatted reflector (Figure 4–5).

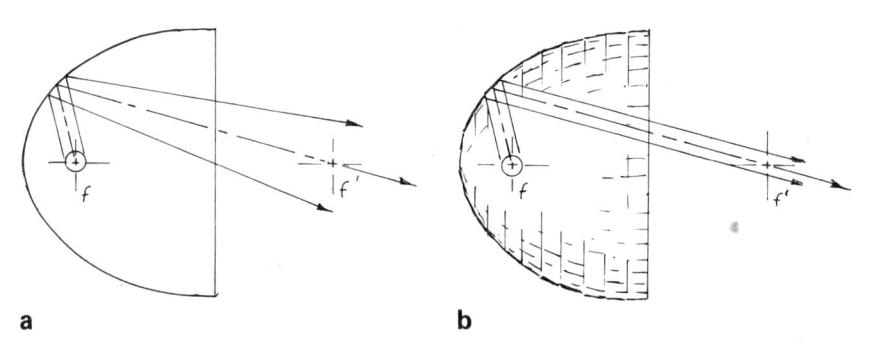

FIGURE 4–5
Double-flatted Ellipsoidal Reflector
(a) The interaction of an area light source with a nonflatted reflector. (b) How the same light source reacts to a flatted reflector.

Reflection and Refraction

Other Reflectors

Two other reflectors should also be mentioned: the combination reflector and the dichroic reflector.

The combination reflector unites the properties of all three reflectors discussed above and is more efficient. Light quality from this reflector is nearly identical to that from a normal ellipsoidal reflector but lamp efficiency is greater.

The most common example of a dichroic reflector can be found in the lamp and reflector assembly used in the Kodak Carousel slide projector (ANSI code: ELH). The term *dichroic* does not refer to a particular reflector shape but to the special properties of selective reflection. Put simply, the dichroic reflector will allow a great deal of heat to pass through it while still reflecting nearly 100 percent of the visible light. This is especially significant in projection equipment, where major efforts are taken to protect the slide or film from overheating.

REFRACTION OF LIGHT

Refraction is a phenomenon observed by anyone who looks into a pool of water and notices how a straight stick will seem to bend sharply as it passes beneath the surface. The law of refraction states that when a ray of light passes into a denser medium (for example from air into water), it is bent toward a perpendicular drawn to the surface at the point of entry; when it reemerges into the less dense medium, it is bent away from the perpendicular drawn at that point.

Plano-Convex Lens

If the two surfaces of a sheet of glass are parallel, the path of an emerging ray will be parallel to its entering path but slightly offset (Figure 4–6). But if the two surfaces are not parallel, then the emerging ray will take a different course depending on the angle at which it strikes each surface. This is the principle of all lenses, of which there

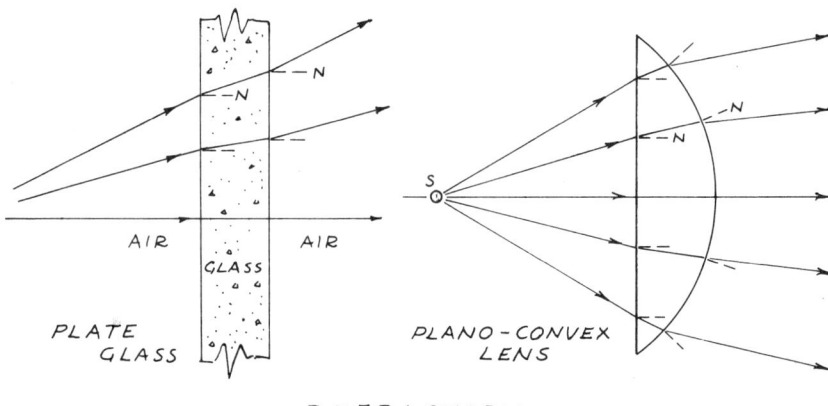

FIGURE 4–6
Refraction of Light
(Left) Refraction of rays of light passing through a sheet of glass. (Right) Refraction of rays of light passing through a plano-convex lens.

are many forms, but the plano-convex lens, with one flat side and one curved surface (or modifications of this) is the only one of importance to us. It is the simplest and least expensive lens for concentrating spreading rays into a compact beam of great brightness.

Focal Point and Focal Length

Every lens has a focal point. If parallel light rays (such as those from the sun) strike a lens, they will converge at the focal point. Conversely, if a source of light is placed at the focal point of a lens, all the rays of light that emerge from the lens will be parallel one to another.

Lenses are identified by two numbers. The first gives the diameter in inches, while the second gives the focal length (the distance from the focal point to the approximate center of the lens). Thus, a 6-by-9-inch lens (6 × 9) will have a diameter of 6 inches and a focal length of 9 inches. The greater the curve of the convex face, the greater the refracting power of a lens. Therefore, a thick lens will have a shorter focal length than a thin one.

It is usually desirable to know the focal length of a lens. However, because this information is rarely marked on lenses, a quick method of determining focal length is valuable. If the sun is shining, the lens may be carried outdoors and held, plano side down, so that the sun's rays are concentrated on the ground. Then, using a ruler, measure the distance from the ground to the focal plane. For lenses used in stage-lighting equipment the focal lengths are measured in even inches.

When indoor light is used, stand as far away as possible from the light source. The resulting measurement will be, in this case, somewhat longer than the true focal length but by less than an inch. So by simply eliminating the fraction, we can calculate the exact focal length quite accurately. For example, if the measurement is 11½ inches, we know the focal length is 11 inches; if we measure 9¼ inches, we know the focal length is 9 inches.

Figure 4–7 (page 60) illustrates how emerging rays diverge if a source of light is placed between the focal point and the lens. If the source is placed farther from the lens than the focal point, the rays will converge and eventually cross one another. Since the light from a stage-lighting instrument should spread in the shape of a cone, the lenses of the ellipsoidal reflector spotlight will cause the light to converge and cross at some point beyond the lens barrel.

Fresnel and Step Lenses

The thick glass of a lens with a short focal length has a tendency to crack because of excessive heat from the source. Ellipsoidal reflector spotlights often compensate for this deficiency by using a combination of two lenses rather than one. In this way, each lens is thinner and therefore less likely to crack from heat build-up.

Two other solutions have been developed, both using the technique

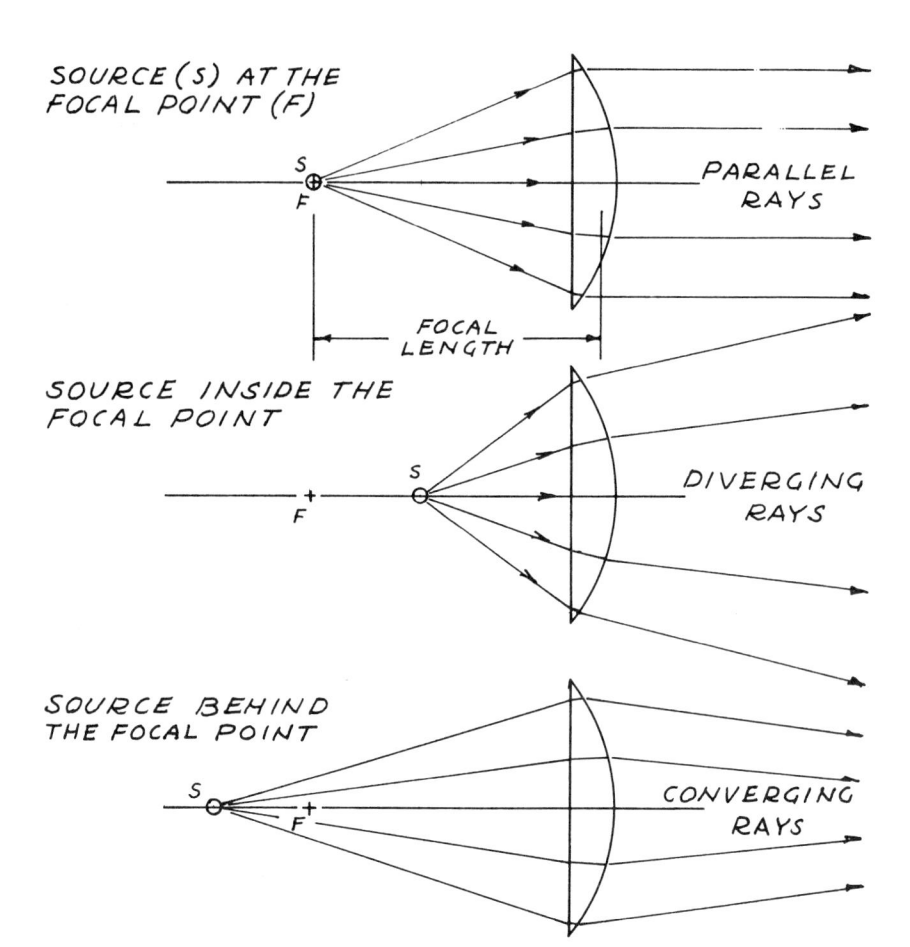

FIGURE 4–7
Refraction
Refraction of light passing through a plano-convex lens under different conditions.

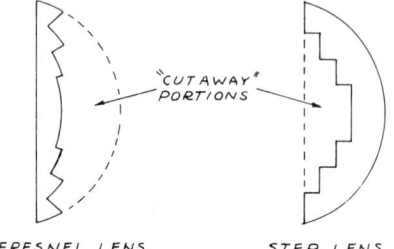

FIGURE 4–8
Simplified Diagrams Showing How Fresnel and Step Lenses are Derived from the Plano-convex Lens

of cutting away part of the thick glass yet retaining the basic relationships between the curved and the plano surfaces. The first of these is the Fresnel (pronounced Fre'nel) lens, in which the plano face is retained, but the curved face is cut back in steps. More recent is the step lens, in which the convex side retains its shape while the plano face is cut back (Figure 4–8).

The Fresnel spotlight derives its name from its lens. The plano surface of the lens is broken up by either a light frosting technique or by a series of dimples molded into the glass. This breaking up of the light results in the very smooth and soft illumination distinctive of the Fresnel spotlight.

The step lens was put to use in ellipsoidal reflector spotlights and became fairly popular because of its low cost and light weight. Yet, the light from a step lens simply is not of the same quality as that from a plano-convex lens. Disturbing ring patterns from the step risers are commonly projected by a step-lens instrument, and the light is never as clean or crisp in quality. As a result, instrument manufacturers have returned to the plano-convex lenses, using them in adjustable relationships to allow variable beam spreads.

Stage Lighting

Lenses in the Theatre

An ellipsoidal reflector spotlight will be designated either by its lens diameter and focal length (6 × 12, for instance) or by the spread of its light beam in degrees. Both designations are accurate, but the labeling by degrees is probably the most helpful. A general rule to follow is that the shorter the focal length, the wider the beam spread (given identical lens diameters). The following table illustrates some standard instrument designations and their respective field* spreads in degrees:

INSTRUMENT	FIELD SPREAD
6 × 9 ERS	40°
6 × 12 ERS	28°
6 × 16 ERS	20°
8 × 9 ERS	15°
10 × 12 ERS	10°

Always consult the specifications published by instrument manufacturers to determine the exact light-beam spread for a specific instrument.

The quality of light from a stage-lighting instrument greatly depends on its optical system. This not only involves the type of reflector and lens but also their condition. Mistreated or dirty lenses and reflectors can turn a very fine spotlight into little more than a lamp in a can. Keep lenses and reflectors clean; replace cracked or chipped lenses; and treat your spotlights with the care they deserve. You'll have a happier bunch of luminaries, and your work as a designer will be much more gratifying.

---

*The definition of, and distinction between, field and beam spread will be discussed in following chapters.

Reflection and Refraction

5

Distribution Control

Distribution is the first of the controllable properties of light we will discuss in depth. Recall that the term *distribution* refers not only to direction or angle of illumination but also to quality of light. Will the light be soft or harsh; will it be textured and broken up or coherent and smooth; will it have sharp, linear edges or a soft, rounded shape? The lighting designer must always go through a specific (although often subconscious) process of matching known instrument capabilities with specific requirements of a production. Assuming the designer has an image of the quality of light desired, the next step is to determine what lighting instrument will be most capable of delivering that specific feeling. Several factors will affect this determination:

1. Instrumentation available.
2. Physical (theatre) restrictions.
3. Quality of light.
4. Beam shaping and control.

Instrumentation Available

Choices of lighting instruments would be unlimited with a large budget; but the lighting designer is seldom in such an enviable position. Most often, the designer will be working with a limited and specific equipment list and with a restricted budget. It is always wise to confirm the accuracy of an equipment list before completing the design work.

Physical Restrictions

Physical restrictions invariably affect lighting possibilities. They include the throw distance (distance from lighting instrument to target), the amount (if any!) of offstage space for sidelighting positions, the adequacy of hanging positions both front-of-house as well as overstage, and the degree of restricted space to make a lighting "shot."

Quality of Light

The designer must now consider the quality of light possible. Perhaps an 8-inch Fresnel would be a better choice than a 6×12 ERS because of the softer quality of its beam. Perhaps an ERS is the only answer because we want to break up the light with a template. Perhaps a PAR can will best deliver the strong yet soft-edged illumination sought by the designer.

Beam Shaping and Control

The final consideration is a simple one: will the chosen instrument provide the desired beam shaping and control?

The following information on stage-lighting instruments will give the reader a basis for making intelligent decisions. Because stage workers have a habit of referring to whole classes of instruments by trade names or other slang terminology, there seems to be a bewildering complexity of such instruments. Actually, there are just a few basic types.

SPOTLIGHTS

The spotlight is by far the most important lighting instrument on the modern stage. Broadly defined, the spotlight is a metal hood containing a high-powered source of light which is made more effective by use of a lens and usually a reflector as well. The resulting beam of high-intensity light can be shaped by various means to forms that may be significant in the stage picture.

The Plano-convex Spotlight

The first incandescent spotlight, and for many years the only kind, was the plano-convex spot. In a simple hood a G-shaped lamp is mounted on a sliding carriage to which is attached a small spherical

Distribution Control

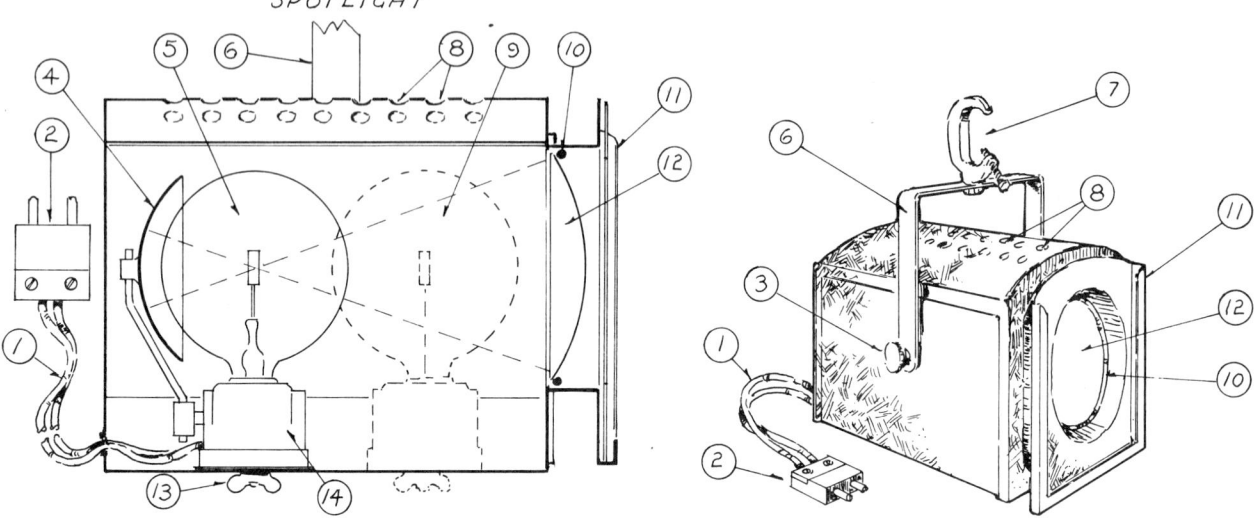

FIGURE 5-1

The Plano-convex Spotlight

(1) Asbestos-covered lead wires. (2) Pin connector. (3) Vertical adjustment knob. (4) Spherical reflector. (5) G-shape lamp. (6) Yoke. (7) Pipe clamp. (8) Ventilation holes. (9) Lamp in flood focus position. (10) Spring ring to hold lens in position. (11) Color-frame holder. (12) Plano-convex lens. (13) Focus-adjustment knob. (14) Movable lamp socket.

reflector that rides behind the lamp and is always in correct relationship to it (Figure 5–1). As was explained in Chapter 4, such a reflector sends all rays that strike it back through the original source, thus increasing output.

In front of the lamp and carefully aligned with its filament is placed a plano-convex lens which refracts all the rays that strike it and bends them into a comparatively narrow beam. When the lamp is close to the lens in flood position the percentage of total light that strikes the lens is quite high, but because this spreads into a wide angle after leaving the lens, there is no great intensity to the beam at any distance from the instrument. When the lamp is moved back toward the focal point of the lens, the angle of acceptance of the lens is less and the beam much narrower. So, although a smaller percentage of the light is utilized, the beam then has greater intensity because all the light is concentrated in the narrower shaft. The inside of the hood is painted a flat black to absorb all rays of light that do not strike the lens directly.

Spotlight Accessories. The lens of a plano-convex spotlight is held in place by a strong metal spring ring. Above and below the lens opening in the hood there are small troughs to hold color media frames. Every spotlight has some means of mounting, usually a yoke held in place on side studs by large nuts or set wheels and a C-clamp for attaching the instrument securely to a pipe. Ventilation must be supplied—above to allow hot air to escape and below to let cool air in. The ventilation holes or slots are fitted with baffles to prevent light spill. Some means of access permits the electrician to inspect the hood's interior and change the lamp without otherwise disturbing instrument or focus.

Plano-convex Spot Sizes. The P-C, as the plano-convex spot is frequently called, was manufactured in three sizes, the smallest and least powerful of which had a 5-inch lens and burned G-shaped lamps of 250 and 400 watts. It was useful for short throws, as on a very small stage and could be hidden in nooks where other instruments would prove too large. This small spotlight was usually referred to as a "baby."

Larger "brothers" were those with 6-inch and 8-inch plano-convex lenses. In general it may be said that the 8-inch type burned 2000-watt lamps while the 6-inch models ranged from 500 to 1500 watts, all of the G type.

While important in the minds and hearts of stage-lighting practitioners, the fact is that today the P-C is almost never found in everyday use. Because of their greater efficiency, the Fresnel and ellipsoidal reflector spotlights have replaced the P-C in nearly every application.

Fresnel Spotlight

The Fresnel is actually very close to the P-C in design and operation. The main difference between the hoods of the plano-convex and the Fresnel spots is that the latter are considerably shorter, because the short focal length of the Fresnel lens makes a long movement of the lamp unnecessary. The lamp and the spherical reflector move together from spot focus (narrow beam, source farthest from lens) to flood focus (wide beam, source closest to lens) by means of a worm screw or a thumb screw similar to that found on a P-C spotlight (Figure 5–2).

While internal beam shaping is not possible, accessories called "barn doors" can be placed in the color frame holder to effectively shape the beam by cutting it in a linear manner from either of four sides (Figure 5–3, page 66). It is wise to "safety" a barn door to the pipe or yoke of the instrument by means of a small chain or wire rope. This is particularly important for the larger Fresnels, whose barn doors tend to be heavy and are easily dislodged by scenery flying on an adjacent batten.

Another spotlight accessory which is particularly useful with a Fresnel is the "top hat" or "snoot." A top hat is nothing more than a tin can open on both ends, attached to a rectangular metal frame which fits into the color holder and is painted flat black inside and out. The top hat controls lens flare by absorbing stray light refracted by the risers of the Fresnel lens. If the lens is in audience sight, lens flare can be quite distracting.

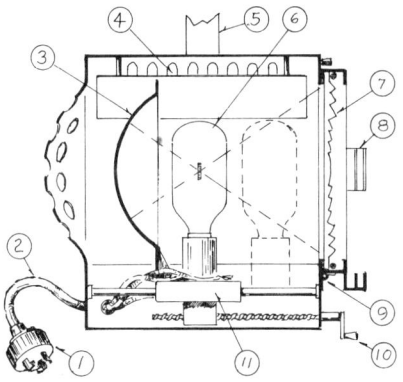

FIGURE 5–2
The Fresnel Spotlight
(Top) An 8-inch Fresnel that uses the tungsten-halogen lamp. (Above) Section. (1) Three-wire twist-lock connector. (2) Asbestos-covered lead wires. (3) Spherical reflector. (4) Ventilation holes. (5) Yoke. (6) T-shaped lamp, base down (tungsten-halogen or incandescent). (7) Fresnel lens. (8) Color-frame holder. (9) Hinged lens front for interior access. (10) Lead-screw drive for movable lamp socket and reflector. (11) Movable lamp socket. (Photo—Kliegl Bros.)

Distribution Control

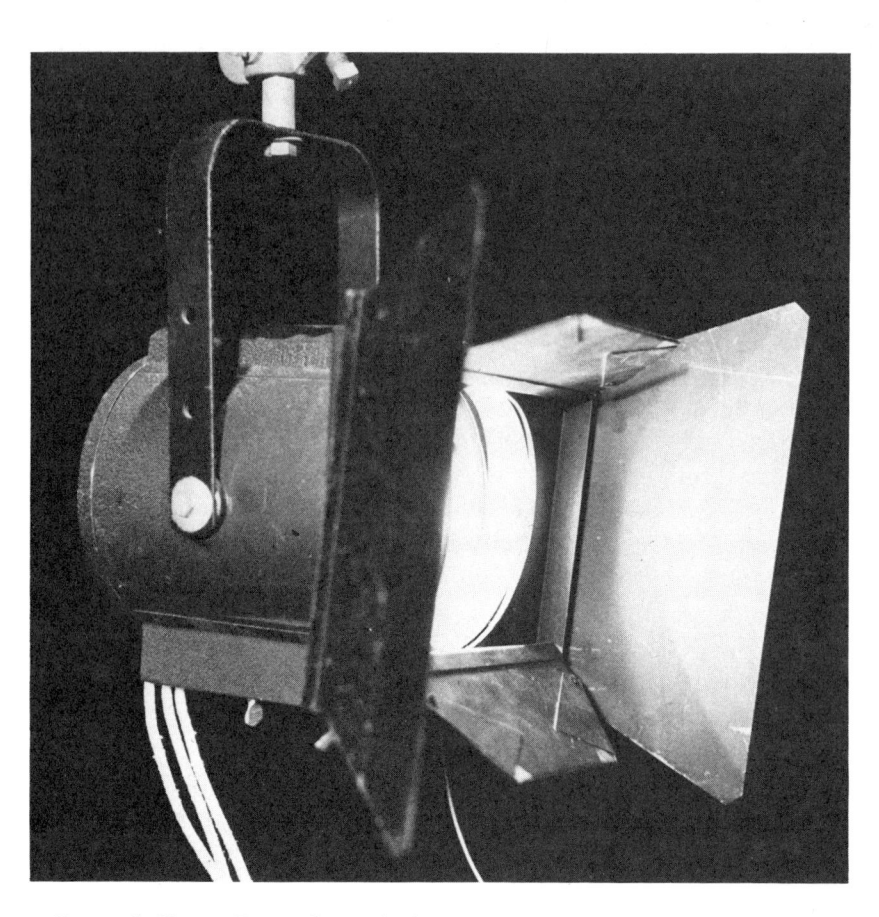

FIGURE 5-3
A Fresnel with Barn Doors

Fresnel Sizes. Fresnel spotlights come in a number of sizes, the smallest of which has a 3-inch lens and burns a 150-watt G-shaped standard incandescent or T-shaped quartz lamp. Fondly called an "inky," this little instrument, although not possessing much punch, is very handy for tucking into small corners.

The most common Fresnel is the 6-inch, burning 500- and 750-watt T-shaped lamps. This spotlight is a true workhorse, being invaluable for the upstage acting areas, where its soft-edged beam fades away on the scenery without leaving obvious and distracting lines and patterns. It throws a good punch with a typically smooth beam pattern. For the larger stage the 8-inch Fresnel can be almost as valuable and with its 1000- to 2000-watt lamps has a powerful beam that can be put to many uses.

The Fresnel spotlight is also sold with lenses from 10 to 20 inches in diameter. These have little importance for the conventional stage, being primarily designed for television and motion-picture studios. They might be useful in outdoor productions, where exceptionally long throws are often the rule. Another feature that has been introduced for television purposes is the Fresnel lens that throws an oval beam. This can be very useful on the stage as well, to spread the light laterally, making cross-stage blending easier.

Stage Lighting

Fresnel Beam Characteristics. The beam of light from a Fresnel is soft in quality, with a smooth, even field. The light will appear to "wrap around" a figure and shadows will be soft edged and not very harsh. Being a spotlight, the light from a Fresnel exhibits a good sense of direction, but it can also be used for wall washes or blending. In a proscenium theatre the Fresnel is limited, however, to use over-stage because of its scattered beam characteristics. Also, throw distance of even the 8-inch Fresnel is restricted for the same reason. The following table lists beam spreads for typical 6- and 8-inch Fresnels at both flood and spot focus:

	SPOT FIELD ANGLE	FLOOD FIELD ANGLE
6-inch Fresnel	16°	60°
8-inch Fresnel	14°	50°

While the Fresnel is an ideal instrument for some spaces and certainly a practical instrument for almost all spaces, the ellipsoidal reflector spotlight is a more versatile lighting instrument.

The Ellipsoidal Reflector Spotlight (ERS)

This is, unquestionably, the most important, useful, and common stage-lighting instrument today. In Chapter 4 we saw that if a source of light is placed at one of the focal points of a reflector built in the shape of half an ellipsoid, all the light rays that strike this reflector are diverted through the conjugate focal point. By placing a lens just in front of this secondary focal point a spotlight of great efficiency and power can be constructed. Such an instrument, properly called an ellipsoidal reflector spotlight (ERS) is also commonly referred to as a Leko or a Klieglight, the trade names of Strand-Century and Kliegl Brothers, respectively.

Most ellipsoidal reflector spotlights manufactured before 1980 will burn either a standard incandescent T-12 or T-14 base-up lamp or a quartz lamp designed to replace them (Figure 5–4, page 68). Nearly all newer ellipsoidals are designed to take only quartz lamps, usually in an axial-mount configuration (Figure 5–5, page 68).

Beyond the conjugate focal point, where the rays of light are starting to spread again, a lens (or lenses) is mounted to refract these rays into a comparatively narrow beam. In most ellipsoidal spotlights two thinner lenses are employed to get the effect of the one thick one, although a single step lens may also be used.

ERS Beam Shaping. Just before the conjugate focal point, where the various rays are still converging, is a metal baffle known as the "gate." This cuts off stray rays of light that are not useful in forming a well-controlled beam. It is an image of the opening in this gate, called the aperture, which appears as a round and reasonably smooth pattern

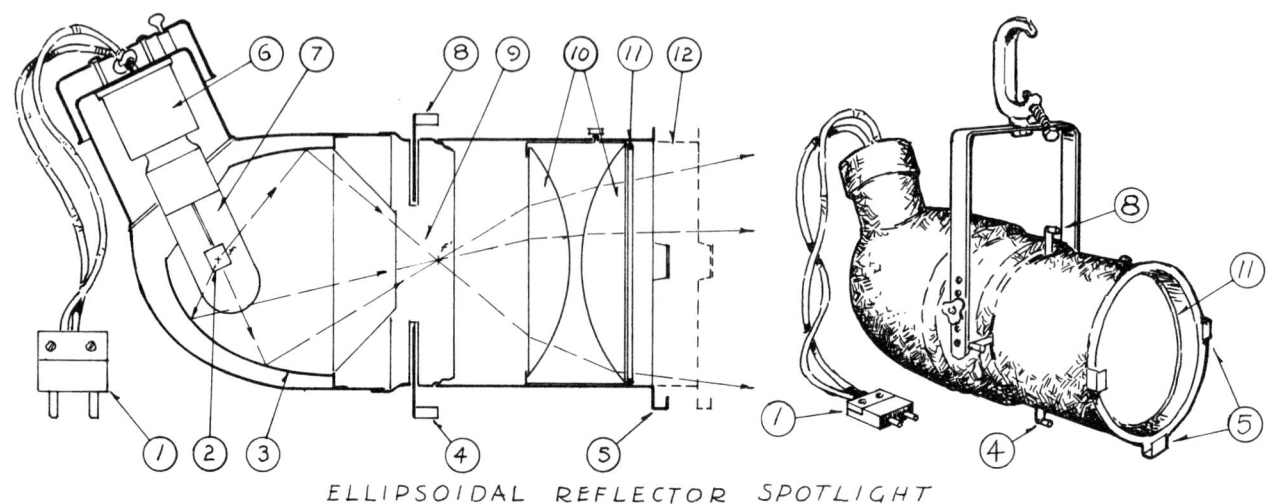

FIGURE 5-4

The Ellipsoidal Reflector Spotlight

(1) Pin connector. (2) Monoplane (or biplane) filament, with its center at the focal point, "f." (3) Ellipsoidal-shaped reflector. (4) Bottom shutter, which shapes the top of beam. (5) Color-frame holder. (6) Prefocus base socket. (7) T-shaped lamp, to burn base-up. (8) Top shutter, which shapes the bottom of the beam. (9) The "gate," with typical reflected rays crossing at the conjugate focal point, "f^1." (10) Two plano-convex lenses. (11) Spring ring, to hold lens. (12) Alternate position of lens system.

when the ellipsoidal spotlight is focused on a plain surface. Various other features to shape the beam may be placed at the gate, a standard device being four shutters which, by proper manipulation, can change the beam pattern into almost any simple linear shape. An iris is sometimes inserted here, allowing the circular form of the beam to be made smaller or larger at will, though this is most significant when the instrument is to be used as a follow spot.

A well-equipped ERS will also have a pattern or template holder located just in front of the four shutters. A template, commonly called a "gobo," is a metal plate with a pattern cut in it. When equipped

FIGURE 5-5

Axial Mount Ellipsoidal Reflector Spotlight

(1) Three-wire pin connector. (2) Coiled-coil filament. (3) Ellipsoidal reflector. (4) Bottom shutter which shapes the top of the beam. (5) Color-frame holder. (6) Axially mounted socket. (7) Tungsten-halogen lamp. (8) The "gate" with typical reflected rays crossing at the conjugate focal point. (9) Top shutter. (10) Double plano-convex lenses. (11) The lens barrel in alternate positions.

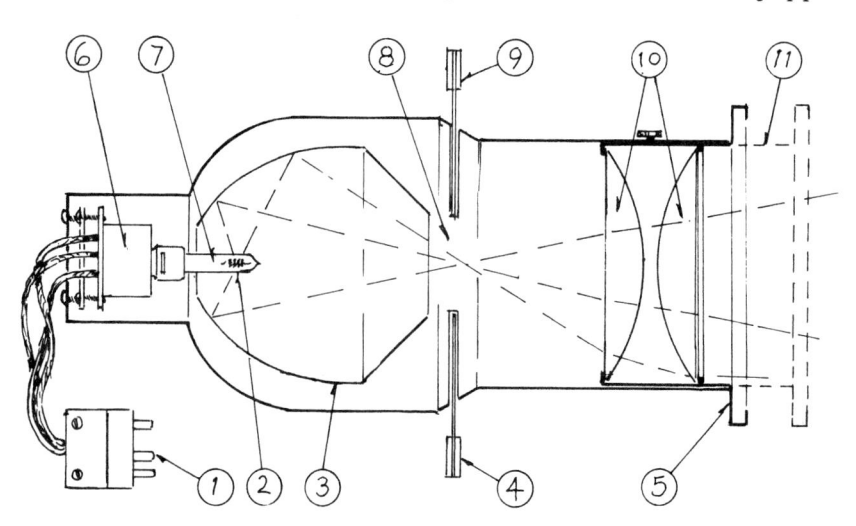

68   *Stage Lighting*

with a gobo an ERS can serve as a shadow projector. Light can simply be textured, or specific patterns can be projected on scenery, actors, or the stage floor. Stainless steel templates available in a large variety of patterns can be purchased, or homemade gobos can be cut out of pie tins or aluminum lithoplates. (You can probably get lithoplates free from a local printer.) In using a gobo, remember that the pattern image will be inverted because of the crossing of the light rays. Consequently, the gobo should be placed in its holder in an upside-down position.

ERS Beam Characteristics. The ellipsoidal reflector spotlight throws an extremely powerful beam of light capable of creating harsh and sharp shadows. An "edging" of light can best be achieved with an ERS, whose light is much more controllable than that of other theatrical lighting instruments. Because the lamp, reflector, and lens are in static relationship, there is no flood and spot focus as in plano-convex and Fresnel spotlights. But the lenses may be moved a few inches, allowing the beam pattern to be thrown out of focus and thus softening the hard, sharp edge of the field.

Because of the delicate relationship between filament and reflector, it is easy for the instrument to get out of adjustment, particularly if an inexperienced electrician tampers with the adjusting devices on the socket cap of older ellipsoidals. Sometimes the lamp base has not been properly seated in the socket. At other times it is necessary to focus the spotlight on a plain surface and manipulate the adjusting devices until a firm, circular field is found again. The better of the new axial-mount ellipsoidals will have the lamp socket (normally a bi-pin) mounted on a ball-and-socket type joint and attached to a "joy stick" handle or knob. This arrangement allows for rapid and simple lamp alignment.

ERS Sizes. The ellipsoidal reflector spotlight comes in several sizes, from one with a 3½-inch lens that burns 400- and 650-watt lamps and throws a wide beam, suitable for small stages and auxiliary use on large stages, up to a 12-inch model that uses a 2000-watt lamp for a very narrow and extremely powerful beam intended for long throws.

The workhorse of the ellipsoidal line is the 6-inch, which is available in a variety of focal lengths (see table on page 70). Older 6-inch units will accept either a 500- or 750-watt lamp, while the newer quartz units can be lamped to 1000 watts. The 8-inch and 10-inch ERS will provide a narrower beam as well as allow for higher wattage lamps, usually up to 2000 watts.

Beam and Field Angle. The table on page 70 lists typical beam and field angles for various sizes of ellipsoidal reflector spotlights. Note that these figures are approximate and may not correspond exactly to the performance of any specific unit. Consult manufacturer specifications before using.

When an ERS is properly aligned, its cone-shaped beam of light will

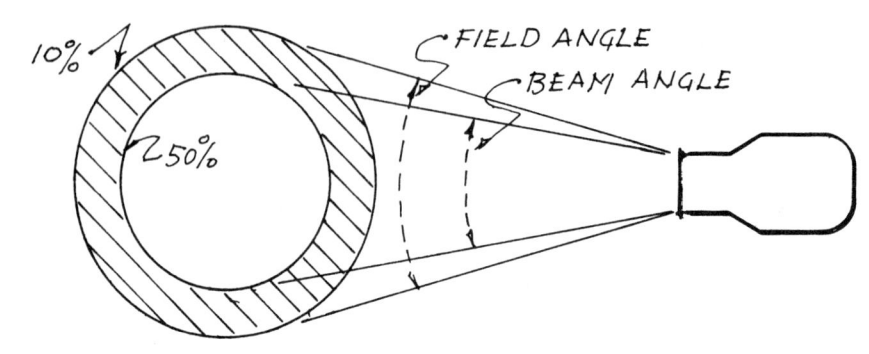

FIGURE 5–6
Beam and Field Angles

be most intense along the center line of the cone and drop off evenly toward the edge of the beam (Figure 5–6). If the intensity of light from an ellipsoidal is considered in terms of percentages, and the beam center line illumination is 100 percent, the beam and field angles are defined as follows:

Beam angle is the point where the illumination falls off to 50 percent.
Field angle is the point where illumination falls off to 10 percent.

ERS TYPE	BEAM ANGLE	FIELD ANGLE
3½ × 6	25°	32°
3½ × 8	18°	24°
3½ × 10	16°	20°
6 × 9	24°	40°
6 × 12	16°	28°
6 × 16	15°	20°
8 × 9	7°	15°
10 × 12	7°	10°

It is important to note, however, that many of the newer axial-mount ellipsoidals allow an additional adjustment of the lamp in respect to the focal point of the reflector. By moving the entire lamp housing either in or out, an electrician is able to change the field of light from an extremely "hot center" to a "flat" field. The hot center concentrates a greater percentage of the light into a small beam, while the flat field evens out the intensity through the beam. This adjustment does not alter the effective field angle but obviously changes beam angle considerably. Because of this new design feature, manufacturers have begun exclusively to use field angle degree designations for their ERS instruments.

New Silhouettes. The development of the tungsten-halogen lamp triggered new instrument design, particularly in the ellipsoidal reflector spotlight. The near point source, reduced size, and greater intensity of the lamp has increased the efficiency of the reflector and changed the hood design. The forerunners in new instrument design were Colortran and Electro Controls with its Parellipsphere, but Strand-Century and Kliegl have rapidly followed suit.

In addition to an improved hood design, the new ellipsoidals provide a variable focal length adjustment of the front lens system which increases the number of uses of an individual instrument. The Parellipsphere has a mechanism to change focal length (almost a zoom lens) as well as a new reflector design. As the name implies, it involves three surfaces. The basic shape of the reflector is ellipsoidal with a parabolic apex at the lamp position and an off-axis spherical reflector in front facing the lamp to redirect outside rays back into the ellipsoidal portion of the reflector (Figure 5–7).

The introduction of Colortran's mini-ellipse has made a significant contribution to the line of short-throw ellipsoidals. Like its bigger 6-inch counterpart, the mini has a three-position lens adjustment allowing beam spreads of 30°, 40°, and 50°. Its 500-watt compact quartz lamp delivers a great deal of intensity and is relatively inexpensive (Figure 5–8, page 72).

The new quartz ellipsoidals are already having a positive effect upon theatrical lighting design. The greater flexibility and higher intensity of these instruments has proved a tremendous aid to the lighting de-

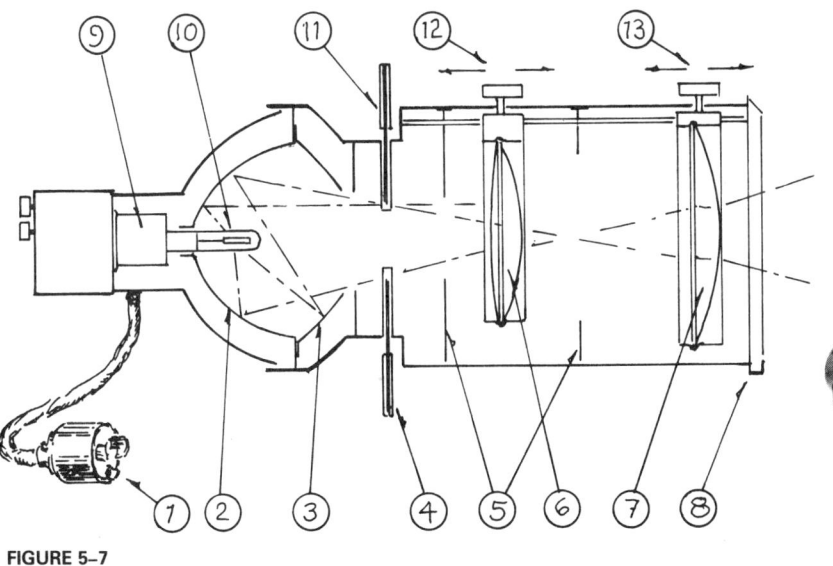

FIGURE 5–7

The Parellipsphere

Although basically an ellipsoidal reflector spotlight, the Parellipsphere has a more sophisticated reflector design and greater flexibility in the lens system. (Photo courtesy Electro Controls, Inc.) (1) Three-wire twist-lock connector. (2) Parellipse part of reflector. Apex of reflector is parabolic in action. (3) Kickback reflector with slight spherical configuration. (4) Bottom shutter. (5) Baffles. (6) Nonsymmetric biconvex lens. (7) Plano-convex lens. (8) Color-frame holder. (9) Prefocus medium base socket axially mounted. (10) T-H lamp. (11) Top shutter. (12) Lens adjustment knob to change focal length of objective system. (13) Knob to change beam spread.

Distribution Control

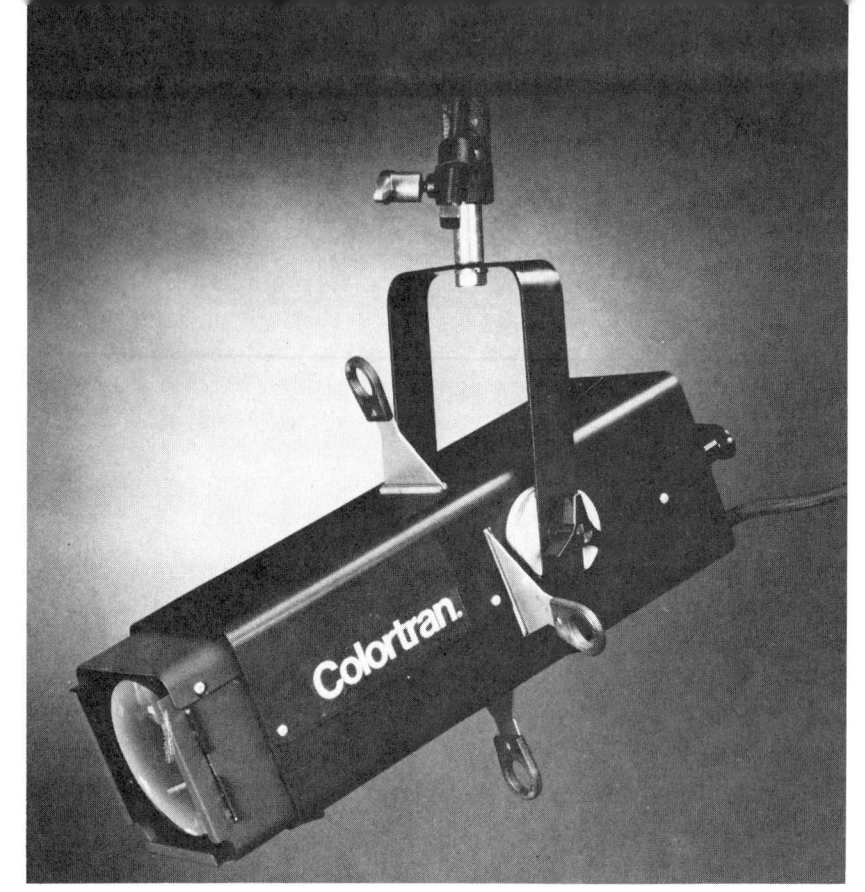

FIGURE 5–8
The Mini-ellipse
An efficient short-throw ellipsoidal reflector spotlight developed by Colortran. (Photo courtesy Colortran, Inc.)

signer in the transfer of a visual image in the mind's eye to reality on the stage.

BEAM PROJECTOR

Despite its narrow beam and intense output, the beam projector is not a true spotlight. It has no lens, and, more important, its beam pattern cannot be greatly altered from the small and very bright circle that is its characteristic. The lamp can be moved slightly in relation to the reflector, which results in a somewhat larger pattern but one which has a "hole" or dark spot in its center. In no case is the beam projector's pattern very smooth, and masking will not alter the shape in any way but instead dims it in an erratic fashion.

This instrument makes use of a parabolic reflector which sends all the rays that strike it forward and parallel one to the other. In order to eliminate diverging rays of light that would not contribute to the tight beam pattern, but would prove undesirable and distracting, a spherical reflector is often placed in front of the lamp to redirect such rays back to the parabolic reflector, from which they may augment the other parallel rays (Figure 5–9). In some styles of beam projector baffles or louvres serve to intercept and absorb such diverging rays. The beam projector is basically a searchlight adapted to the theatre.

Stage Lighting

FIGURE 5–9

The Beam Projector

(1) G-shaped lamp. (2) Parabolic reflector. (3) Concentrated filament. (4) Lamp socket, adjustable. (5) Pin connector and lead wires. (6) Spherical reflector. (7) Color-frame holders. Photo of 11-inch Kliegsun Beam Projector, 500–1000 watts. Also available in 15-inch, 1000–1500 watts. (Photo—Kliegl Bros.)

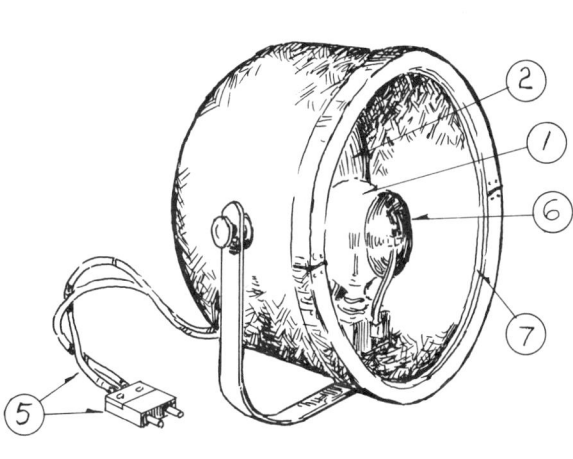

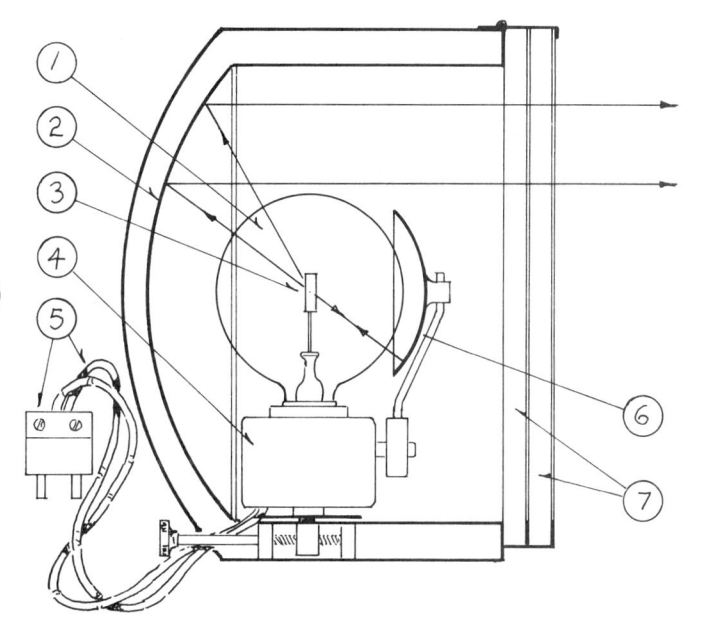

BEAM PROJECTOR

Its stage uses are largely limited to strong shafts of light of great intensity but confined to small areas, for example sunlight through a window. For musical comedy and the like, great banks of beam projectors may be employed, but for the modest stage this instrument has limited uses.

The beam projector comes in various sizes, from 10 to 30 inches in diameter. The 10-inch style may take a 250- to a 750-watt T-lamp, while the larger types use 1000- to 2000-watt lamps, either quartz or standard incandescent. Anything larger than 16 inches would scarcely be required for even a sizable stage. Because of the tremendous punch of the light, the beam projector is very hard on non-Mylar color media, burning the color out of some shades within minutes after replacement.

Distribution Control

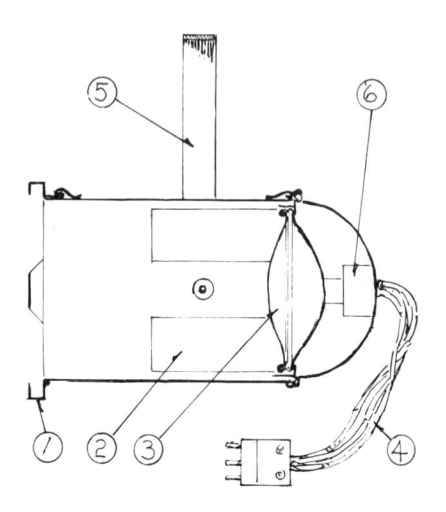

FIGURE 5-10
The PAR-64
(1) Color-frame holder. (2) Light baffle over air vent holes. (3) PAR-64 lamp. (4) Three-wire cord and pin connector. (5) Yoke. (6) Lamp socket.

PAR CAN

The parabolic aluminized relector (PAR) lamp was mentioned earlier in the chapter on light sources. Its housing, the PAR can or PAR head, and its applications for stage lighting will be discussed here. The extruded-metal PAR can housing simply secures its PAR-64 lamp in place by means of a large spring ring and absorbs immediate flare created by the built-in lens of the lamp (Figure 5–10). The butt of the housing hinges opens to allow access to the lamp and socket, and color frame holders are fixed to the front of the unit. The PAR-64 lamp is rated at 1000 watts and is available in the following beam spreads:

	ANSI CODE	BEAM ANGLE	FIELD ANGLE
Very Narrow	FFN	6° × 12°	10° × 24°
Narrow	FFP	7° × 14°	14° × 26°
Medium	FFR	12° × 28°	21° × 44°
Wide	FFS	24° × 48°	45° × 71°

The oval-shaped beam of light cannot be effectively altered or adequately controlled, but the quality of light is uniquely harsh, and the beam edge is fairly soft. Relative to other stage instruments, the PAR can is nearly indestructible, and the lamp life is long. Although not an ideal stage-lighting unit because of its lack of beam-shaping capabilities, the PAR can is economical and may be perfect in certain applications.

FLOODLIGHT

A floodlight is, as its name suggests, a device for throwing a broad wash of light over a wide area. For many years the so-called Olivette was the standard instrument for such a purpose. Large and unwieldy, burning a 1000-watt G-lamp, the Olivette reflected a smooth wash of light from its boxlike hood and white-painted interior.

The most common floodlight today is the ellipsoidal reflector floodlight (ERF), or "scoop." It has a matte finish that distributes the light smoothly and without a sharp edge to the beam. A single such instrument can be valuable for lighting a fair-sized window backing, while a bank of them may be used to illuminate a drop. They are especially useful for washing any curved surface, such as a cyclorama.

Most of these floodlights are about 15 or 16 inches in diameter and burn general-service PS lamps or quartz lamps of up to 2000 watts. There is also a small 10-inch model that uses 250- and 400-watt G-lamps, or, occasionally, gives good service with a 100-watt A-lamp when only a very low illumination is required.

STRIPLIGHT

One form of stage-lighting instrument that predates the invention of the incandescent lamp is the striplight, which produces the effect of a line of light by means of a number of sources—formerly candle or gas, but now electric—adjacent to each other. In its crudest form, the striplight can be found as footlights, a row of bare bulbs, sometimes as far apart as 12 inches, extending the entire width of the proscenium opening.

While permanently installed footlights are still fairly common, the more general approach today is to have striplights prepared in sections between 3 and 9 feet in length. These sections may then be placed about the stage, including the usual footlight position on the apron's edge or hung from overhead. This system allows far greater flexibility in the use of equipment than do permanently installed striplights.

Certain basic principles in striplight design must be understood. The lamps should be wired in several color circuits, three or four being the most common. Then, by using different colors in each circuit and properly controlling their respective intensities, practically any color or tint of light may be attained. Obviously, the lamps should be closely spaced, so that their various beams will blend together more readily.

Types of Striplight

For small and most medium stages, only one style of striplight is needed: that with PAR or R lamps on 6-inch centers (Figure 5–12, page 76). Color frames that will accept both color media and glass should be employed. Because the lamps have built-in reflectors, these strips do not need any of their own—a saving in money and time. The strips should be wired in three- or four-color circuits, depending on the preference of the producers; probably three is sufficient in the great majority of cases.

The 150-watt R and PAR lamps prove adequate for many stages, though occasionally the 300- or 500-watt R spots may be needed for extra punch, for example, in lighting a large cyclorama. The 150-watt PAR spots are also effective but throw too narrow a beam for anything but a sheet of light focused up or down a flat surface. For a very broad, smooth field of medium intensity the flood types of either R or PAR lamps are the most useful. Larger stages use striplights specially designed to take the 200-watt PAR-46, the 300-watt PAR-56, or the 500-watt PAR-64 lamps.

With the advent of the quartz lamp came a new design in striplights. Although each manufacturer uses a different trade name for its particular unit, they all use 1000- to 2000-watt double-ended quartz lamps and are available with one to four lamp compartments per section (Figure 5–13). Because of the reflector design, each color compartment

FIGURE 5–11
Floodlights
(a) Soft Lite, 2000 watts, double-ended, linear filament T-H lamp. Also available, 4000 watts. (Photo—Kliegl Bros.) (b) Ellipsoidal Reflector Floodlight. Often called ERF's or "scoops," 300–500 watts. T-H lamp. (Photo—Kliegl Bros.)

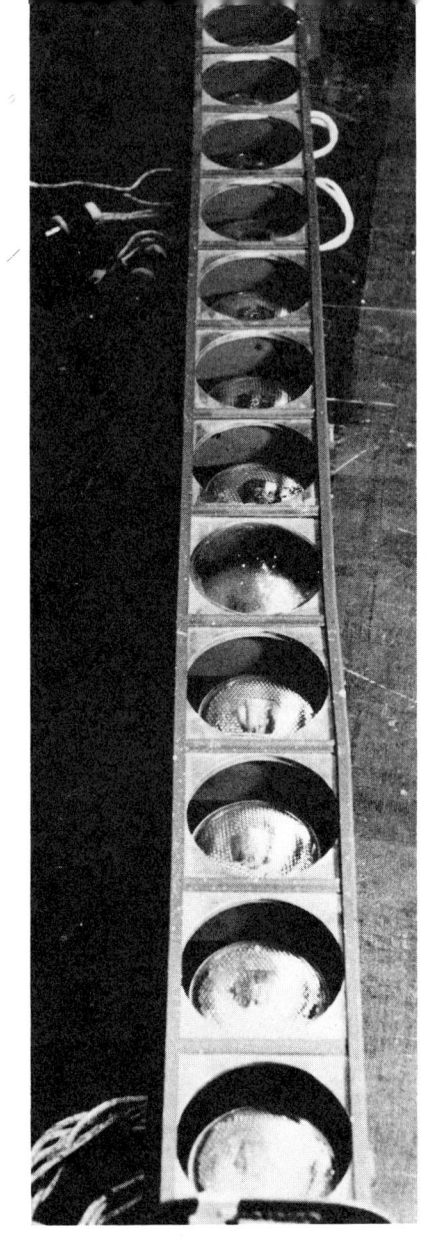

FIGURE 5–12
Striplight with R-type Lamps

FIGURE 5–13
The "Far Cyc" Striplight
An example of new-generation striplights manufactured by Colortran. (Photo courtesy Colortran, Inc.)

can be spaced as far as 8 feet apart and still maintain a smooth wash of light on a cyclorama or a drop. Quality of light as well as output is far superior to the older R and PAR strips for general wash applications. Roundels (glass color filters) are not made for the newer quartz strips, but the use of Mylar color media is perfectly satisfactory.

FOLLOW SPOTS

Carbon-arc light, discussed in Chapter 3, has been the traditional high intensity source for follow spots for many years. Although newer

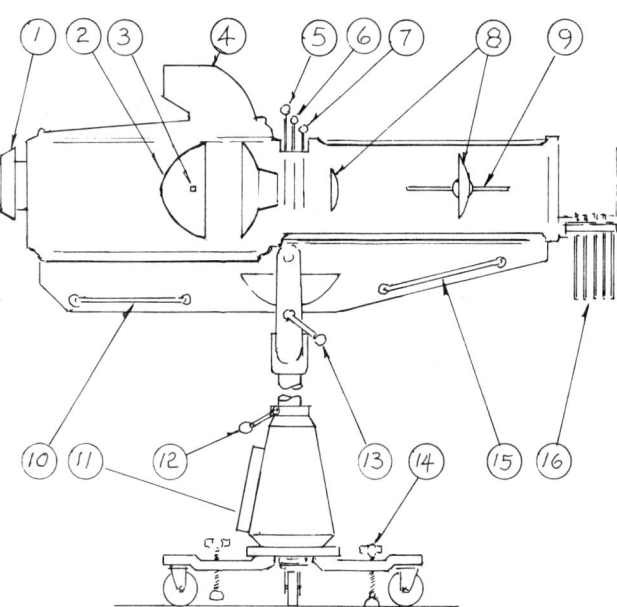

FIGURE 5-14
The Carbon Arc Follow Spot
(1) Lamp adjustment and changing assembly (arc lamp only). (2) Spherical reflector. (3) Light source: carbon arc or arc lamp. (4) Cooling and exhaust vent (carbon arc only). (5) Dimming control (Douser). (6) Horizontal shutter control (Damper). (7) Iris control. (8) Lens system. (9) Zoom track. (10) Rear pan/tilt handle. (11) Compact solid state switching regulator. (12) Pan lock. (13) Tilt lock. (14) Lock-down stabilizer. (15) Front pan/tilt handle. (16) Six-color boomerang. (Photo courtesy Colortran, Inc.)

and more effective sources are replacing carbon arc, the principle of the follow spot instrument remains the same (Figure 5-14). A spherical reflector is used to help direct the light to an aperture similar to that of the ERS. Mounted at the aperture will be an iris, a mechanism called a "damper" or curtain shutters which chops the beam of light horizontally, and possibly a mechanical dimmer called a "douser." Mounted in a long barrel in front of the aperture will be a lens or lenses which can be moved to adjust beam size and sharpness as well as a color boomerang which allows for rapid color changes.

In the carbon-arc follow spot, adjustments for the reflector and the arc source itself are found at the rear of the instrument. These adjustments move the carbon rods forward or back in relationship to the fixed reflector for better source alignment. They also tilt the reflector itself for more accurate focus. An arc source is desirable for throw distances of 75 feet or more, while one of the various quartz-lamp follow spots is sufficient for shorter throws.

The newer xenon and HMI sources (see Chapter 3) have stimulated change in the design of follow spots. More compact units which are generally easier to operate are currently available (Figure 5-15).

Distribution Control

a b

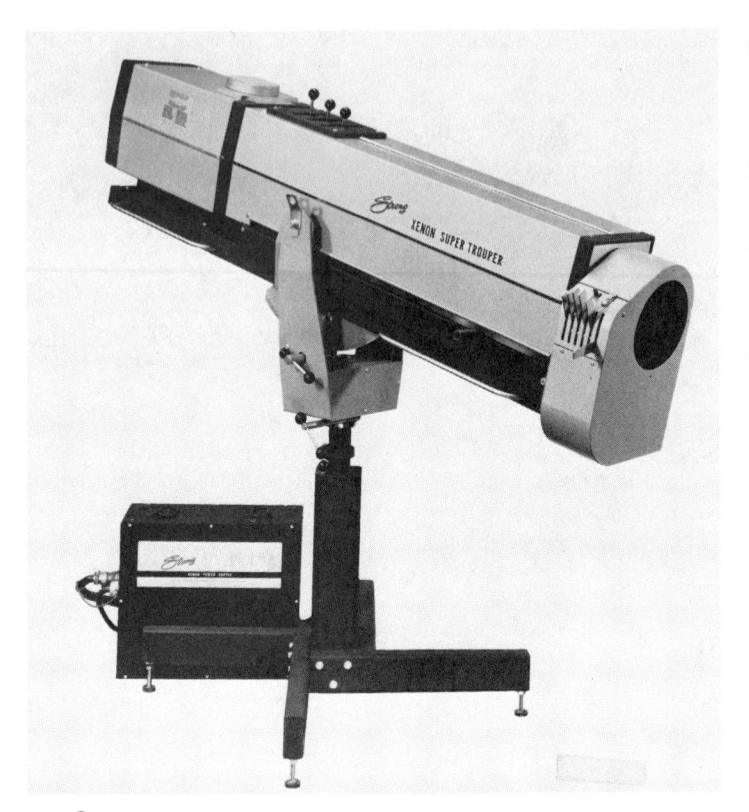

FIGURE 5–15

High Intensity Arc Lamp Follow Spots

(a) The Strong Xenon Super Trouper uses a xenon arc lamp for high intensity over long throws. (Photo courtesy Strong Electric) (b) The Long Throw Ultra Arc Followspot uses a G.E. Marc 350 projector lamp for high intensity and is one of the lightest followspots available. (Photo courtesy Phoebus Manufacturing)

AUTOMATED FIXTURES

Recent technology, good research and design, and the lighting industry's demand for more flexible equipment has introduced us to what may become the lighting instrument of the future: the automated fixture. Two remote control servomotors tilt and pan a lighting instrument to any position with accurate repeatability and variable speed. A third small motor may change instrument focus (lens adjustment) while yet another drives a color changer equipped with either dichroic or standard filters. The unit illustrated here (Figure 5–16) is manufactured by Strand Lighting and is currently available only as a PAR but will likeoly be marketed using an ellipisoidal reflector spotlight in the future.

Control of the automated fixture can be from a conveniently located station or built into the user's dimming system. Typically, various focus and color settings are stored into the memory of a control system as cues and then played back just as any other lighting cue would be. Currently the prime market for units like Strand's ParScan is not the theatre. One will be more likely to find them on tour with industrial shows or "rock" concerts or in television and film studios where one automated fixture might replace a dozen standard instruments—thereby saving time, space and ultimately money. However, theatrical appli-

Stage Lighting

cation is growing and as the automated fixture becomes quieter, less expensive, and more reliable it will find its way onto the stage.

CARE AND HANDLING

While standard practices will naturally vary from one situation to another as well as from one locality to another, there are good practices which should be observed everywhere. By far the most important concern should be with maintenance of equipment. Instrument hanging, circuiting, and focusing is made infinitely simpler if the equipment is in good condition.

The Hang

A definite schedule must be published at least a week before the actual "put in" of equipment. This is to assure adequate participation by crew members and minimize any space conflicts. Equipment must be ready and waiting to be hung. There are certain tasks that are best accomplished by a large crew and others that are more suited to one or two people. Preparing equipment (lamps, lens adjustment, color, gobos, cable, etc.) is best done by the head electrician and perhaps one assistant, while the actual hang requires a larger group of four to eight individuals. Therefore, the master electrician (M.E.) must have all equipment needed for the hang in good ready condition before the larger crew is called. This simple policy allows the M.E. a fighting chance of doing a good job as crew head.

Just as the goal of the preparation period should be to make the hang go smoothly, the goal of the hanging session should be to make the focus uneventful. It is most efficient to split the crew into groups of two or three people with a group leader reporting to the head electrician. In this way, one group can begin working on the booms (which always take a good deal of time), another on the first electric pipe, while a third starts hanging front-of-house. The M.E. coordinates all, checking from time to time on a crew's progress and seeing that everything is being done properly. A given hanging position should be completely hung before cabling is begun. C-clamps should all face the same way (bolts either up or down stage) so that the focusing electrician knows where they are. If the designer indicates focus on the light plot, instruments should be roughly aimed in that general direction—this also saves valuable focus time. Instrument adjustments for pan and tilt should be snug but not so tight that a wrench is required before setting focus.

Depending on the circuit layout of the house, cabling may be the

FIGURE 5–16
The Automated Fixture
Shown here is Strand Lighting's new "Parscan" Automated fixture (photo courtesy of Strand Lighting).

FIGURE 5-17
The Hang
An electric pipe flown in to working height is readied by the crew.

most time-consuming part of the hang. It is often better for the designer not to specify circuits, thereby allowing the electricians freedom to cable to best locations. If this is the case, a single person (designer's assistant) should be assigned the task of recording circuits onto the hook-up or instrument schedule. The only disadvantage of this system is that patching cannot be completed until circuiting is done and recorded. Begin circuiting as soon as each position is hung, with one or at most two electricians assigned to the task. It is best to allow one electrician to cable a hanging position alone due to the complexity of the work, unless the position is very large. Cable should be attached to the pipe with tie line (cotton sash card works well) using bow ties. Adequate slack must be left in the instrument leads, never cabling so taut as to prohibit free instrument focus. If a connection is loose, it should be taped or repaired at the time rather than later during focus. A quality electrician will constantly be anticipating the needs of the upcoming focus.

The Focus

A focus crew normally consists of the designer, two focusing electricians, the board operator, and one or two additional electricians. The production's master electrician has done a full checkout and completed all necessary repairs well before the focus crew arrives. With communications set up, general focus philosophy discussed, and coffee drunk, the focus begins. The designer will often focus two electricians simultaneously in the front-of-house position, and have the two focusing electricians take turns on the ladder over-stage.

A good focus team in action is wonderful and awe-inspiring to watch. Talk is kept to a bare minimum as the electricians keep ahead of the designer, anticipating his or her next move. The team works like a well-oiled piece of machinery and soon a pace is established and the job is done before anyone realizes that they are hungry or tired. On the other hand, an unprepared and/or unskilled focus team is dreadful to observe and even more painful to be a part of. Headsets do not work, lamps are burned-out, one instrument is discovered without a lamp in it at all, shutters stick, cables short out, barrels do not move, and three instruments are hung upside-down. By lunch time, 18 instruments have been focused with 108 left to do, and everyone is tired and feeling mean. The reality of the situation is that the good team is prepared and their equipment is well maintained while the poor team is sorry.

The Equipment

When not in use, cable should be neatly coiled in large coils (diameter approx. 2 feet), tied with tie line, and hung up for storage. It is a good idea to permanently attach a length of black tie line next to the female connector on all pieces of cable. Cable length marking codes should be maintained and connectors checked for strain relief periodically.

Older instruments can be valuable if they are used properly and taken care of. Do not attempt to increase light output of an older instrument by exceeding recommended limits with newer quartz lamps. These older instruments simply do not dissipate heat as well as newer equipment and they were made for lower wattage lamps—use them that way.

The single most important factor in instrument maintenance is keeping everything clean. Lenses can be washed in mild soap and water or with a good glass cleaner. Reflectors should be wiped with a soft cloth or washed with vinegar and water. Keep body parts as free of dust as possible. A clean spotlight will dissipate heat better, thereby increasing lamp life and decreasing warpage, and will also deliver more light. Commonly needed spare parts such as shutters, knobs, and lenses should be kept on hand so that repair is not delayed by waiting for a parts order. Be advised that most instrument manufacturers require a fairly large minimum charge for parts orders and, to add insult to injury, take forever to fill the order.

Safety

Once again, the best way to prevent accidents from happening is to keep your equipment in good operating order. Sticking shutters, bent bolts, and missing knobs or handles all frustrate an electrician and encourage mistreatment. A conservative estimate would be that 25 percent of all lamp "burn-outs" are caused by an angered electrician attempting to free a stuck part by giving it a tap with the old wrench.

Some houses require that lighting equipment mounted above the audience be secured to a pipe with a safety chain or wire in addition to the C clamp. While the likelihood of an instrument falling during a performance is slim, nothing could be more unnerving for a theatre patron than to have a 10-inch Leko fall from 30 feet and land nearby. To prevent accidents, the safety cable should ideally be attached to the instrument itself (as opposed to the yolk) and then around the pipe. A second cable clipped to the color frame will assure that it stays with the instrument. Other theatres may require that a wire mesh separate all instrumentation from the auditorium.

When working overhead, remember to carry a minimum of tools and always tie off your wrench. Take special precautions to avoid falling gel frames, pens and pencils, and gobo holders.

6

Intensity Control

Another one of the controllable properties of light is intensity, which refers to the brightness of a source. Intensity is controlled by the use of dimmers. To dim a tungsten-filament lamp, the voltage to the lamp is reduced and the metal will glow less brightly as well as give off a warmer light. The minimum requirement of any dimming apparatus is the capability of dimming a lamp completely to black in a smooth and even manner. When this is possible, dimmers can be used to alter the composition of the stage picture by dimming (up or down) one or a whole series of lighting instruments. Such movement of light can suggest time change, alter the mood or feeling of a scene, or shift emphasis from one area of the stage to another.

Huge advances in lighting control have taken place over the past ten years thanks to the electronic revolution and to the theatre's insatiable demand for better equipment. New control systems have been springing up so quickly that it is difficult to keep track of them all; but it is clear that electronic dimming (using the SCR) is here to stay, tape or disc memory storage systems will replace preset systems in nearly every application, and dimmer-per-circuit has become an economically viable system.

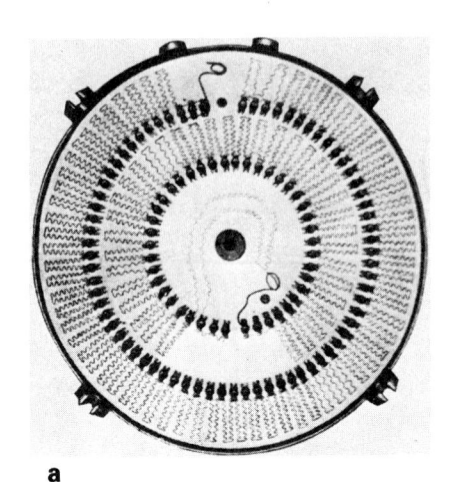

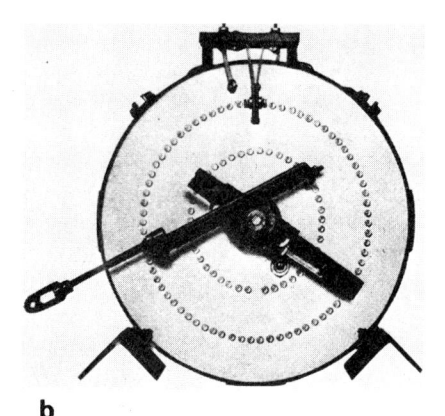

FIGURE 6-1
The Resistance Dimmer

(a) The plate of a two-wire, rotary resistance dimmer before the second coat of vitreous enamel has been applied over the concentric patterns of wire. (b) The same plate with the vitreous enamel covering the resistance wires. The arm coming in from the left is operated by the handle on the face of the dimmer board. Here is it geared to the rotary sweep which makes contact at both ends with the protruding studs. (Photo—Ward Leonard)

ARCHAIC FORMS OF DIMMING

The history of the use of dimming is a long one. On seventeenth-century stages cans on cords were lowered over the candles to vary the light; and in the eighteenth century candles in the wings were frequently mounted on vertical boards that could be revolved to turn the light away from the stage or back toward it. In the nineteenth century the gas table—a complex of pipes, rubber tubes, and valves—adjusted the flow of gas to the various jets about the stage and provided quite a complete control over intensities.

With the advent of the incandescent lamp, crude forms of dimming control were introduced almost from the start. These all utilized the principle of placing in series with the lamp some sort of resistance that could be varied at will. The carbonpile and salt-water dimmers were among these. But the most popular of all and one that only recently has been retired is the resistance-wire dimmer, often called a rheostat.

Types of Resistance Dimmers

The resistance dimmer is found in two standard forms. The less complex contains two coils of resistance wire placed parallel to each other and a short distance apart. The circuit enters at the top end of one coil and leaves at the top end of the other. A conducting shoe slides up and down between the two coils, making contact with each. When this shoe is at the top it bridges the gap in the circuit without introducing any resistance whatever. But when it has been moved to the bottom the full lengths of both coils have become part of the circuit. This so-called slider dimmer is quite simple in its operation but is so difficult to maneuver smoothly that the light tends to jump when its intensity is being changed. Further, it is impossible for one operator to manipulate more than two of these contraptions simultaneously.

The other form of resistance dimmer (called a resistance plate) has its wire in the shape of a multi-pointed star, or as two stars, one within the other. The wire is fastened to a circular vitreous plate and is sometimes baked into it with only taps showing at the surface. The shoe is on the end of a pivoted sweep (when two coils are involved there is a shoe at each end of the sweep) and the sweep is moved by means of a projecting handle. Various refinements such as a cutoff switch at the low end, provision for interlocking all the handles in a bank of them, and the like, were supplied with this type of rotary dimmer.

Disadvantages of the Resistance Dimmer

Because the resistance dimmer consumes full current as soon as it is switched on—whether the lamp burns full up or otherwise—it is extremely wasteful of electric power. And the heat generated by the coils can be quite overwhelming unless adequate ventilation is provided. But these are less important from the artistic point of view than

Stage Lighting

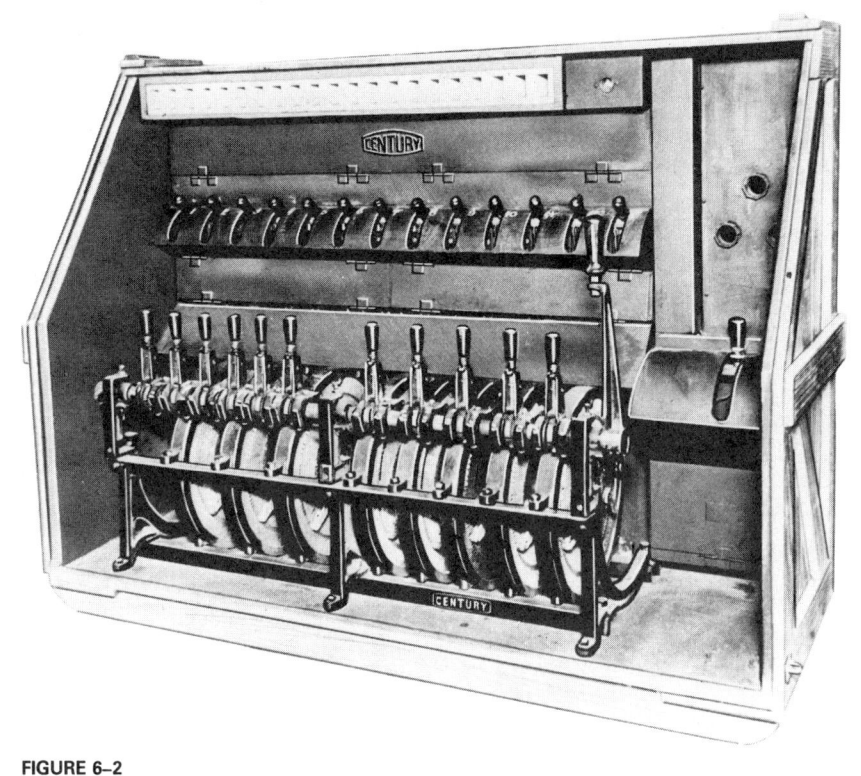

FIGURE 6–2
A Resistance Board
Example of an early switchboard, built into a box for travel. At the right end of the row of dimmer handles is the long interlock handle and beyond it the master switch, above which can be seen holes for a three-wire service. (Photo—Century-Strand)

is the problem of fixed capacity. The length of wire in each dimmer is determined by the exact wattage of the lamp it is expected to control. If a lamp of a smaller wattage is used instead, the dimmer will not put it out completely, and what dimming it does accomplish will be at a different rate from those lamps of proper size on adjacent dimmers. This must be corrected by the expedient of connecting, in parallel with the stage light, a second lamp or "ghost load" hidden offstage and of sufficient wattage to make the total load on the dimmer approximate what it was designed to control.

AUTOTRANSFORMER DIMMERS

Many complaints about resistance control were solved by the autotransformer dimmer. This device consists of lots of copper wire wound around an iron core. The wire is wound in such a manner that the magnetic fields created anytime electricity flows through a conductor are made to work against each other, causing a phenomenon called back-electro-motive force (back-EMF) or back-voltage. If the wire is arranged properly, a variable voltage will be available along the coil.

Intensity Control

By means of a sliding contact shoe called the "brush" moving over the bared turns of the coil, the exact voltage required is drawn off. Because this tapped-off voltage does not depend on a resistance relationship between the coil and the lamp, it will be the same regardless of what load is placed on it. Thus any lamp from the smallest to the highest allowable can be dimmed smoothly and effectively between full out and full up.

Because the only current drawn is that actually used by the load, the autotransformer is not wasteful of power nor does it create any appreciable amount of heat. Autotransformers were built in two styles. One of these has a rotating knob control and therefore is not suitable for stage use; the most skillful operator can handle only two at the same time and it is doubtful if even then they can be brought smoothly and correctly to exact readings (Figure 6-3). The more useful kind is somewhat akin to the rotary resistance dimmer in that it can be mounted with others in a bank and has a protruding handle that makes manipulation simple; this handle can be mechanically interlocked with those of its neighbors.

Mechanical Mastering

The simplest method of mastering autotransformer dimmers is by interlocking. A number of dimmers mounted side by side may have their handles locked to a shaft that runs the length of the dimmer bank. This is usually done by twisting the end of the handle and thus releasing a spring-loaded plunger which drops into a spline, or groove, cut into the shaft. By means of a long master handle (for leverage), the shaft is turned and all dimmers locked to it will simultaneously turn to the same reading. When a handle is twisted in the opposite direction, the plunger is withdrawn from the spline and the dimmer may be worked independently of the others (Figure 6-4).

The drawback is obvious. If we want one dimmer to stop at a reading different from the others, it will take some fast and dexterous work on the part of the operator to disengage the proper handle at the proper place. If several dimmers must be dropped off at different readings during a fairly rapid dim, the whole process becomes impossible. Further, those that are dropped off correctly will have reached their desired readings while the other lights are only part of the way to theirs.

Of course, the same thing happens in reverse when dimmers are set at different readings and the attempt is made to use the interlocking mechanism to take them to "out" simultaneously. Those dimmers that are set at the higher readings will start down first, and their lights will be partially out before dimmers set at lower readings are picked up by the revolving shaft. Although preferable to no master whatever, interlocking is an awkward, inartistic makeshift.

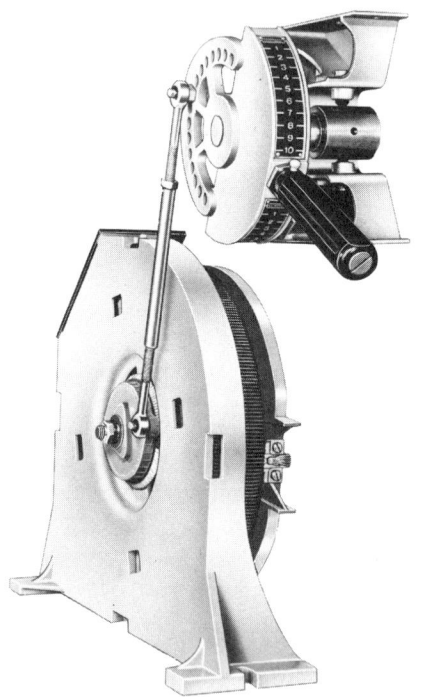

FIGURE 6-3
Autotransformer Dimmers
(Top) A 1000-watt capacity rotary autotransformer dimmer. At the top is the handle which revolves the contact within the coil below. Note the provision for two-, three-, or four-wire service and two- or three-wire output. (Above) A large capacity dimmer built in this shape to save space in a switchboard and to provide handle control and interlock possibility. (Photo—Superior Electric)

Stage Lighting

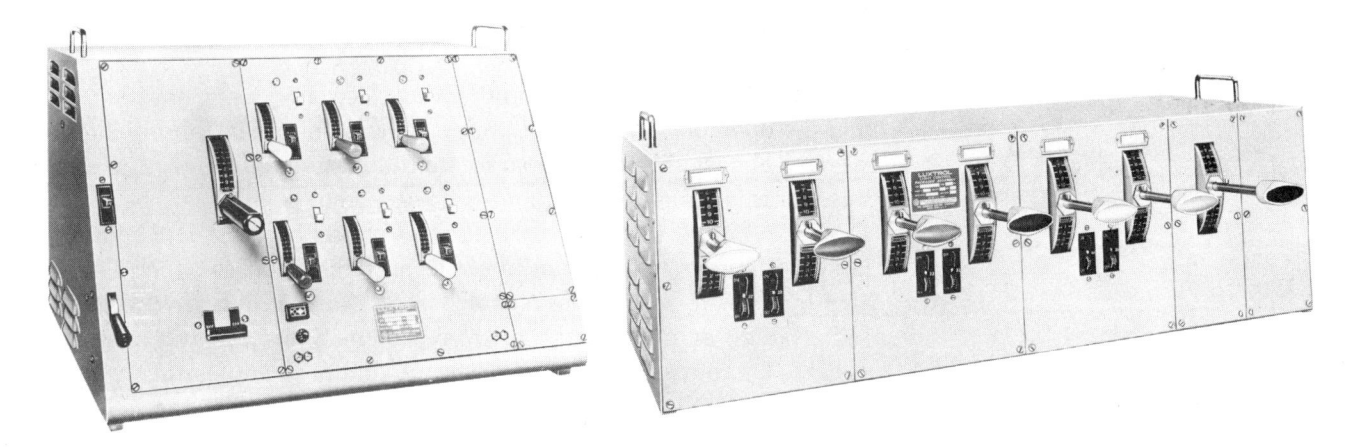

FIGURE 6–4
Autotransformer Package Boards
(Left) A package containing six 1300-watt autotransformer dimmers and one of 6000-watt capacity. By means of the white switches one or more of the small dimmers may be put under control of the large one, thus providing proportional dimming for up to a total of 6000 watts. Or the large dimmer may operate independently with its own big load and each small dimmer with its lesser one. Note the different color for each handle for easy identification, and the circuit breaker adjacent to each. (Right) A package with six 2500-watt autotransformer dimmers and an interlock handle to which several or all the others may be connected. Proportional dimming is not provided. This model was manufactured with three, four, five, or six dimmers. The interlock handle is optional, but even without it several handles may still be locked to the shaft and the handle of any one of them used as the master. In both models the plugging is on the rear face. (Photo—Superior Electric)

Electrical Mastering

In order to get truly proportional dimming, a master dimmer of large capacity may be employed to control a number of smaller ones and their respective loads. Obviously such a master must have a capacity equal to the total capacities of the lesser dimmers combined. And if these are resistance dimmers, all including the master must be loaded to full capacities for proper performance.

Autotransformer Package Boards

A "package board" is a relatively compact unit containing several dimmers, circuit breakers, and often a plugging panel (Figure 6–4). Although heavy, these boards were transportable and a popular means of control for a number of years. Figure 6–4 shows two styles of the package board, both manufactured by Superior Electric and called Luxtrol control boards. Several years ago the final Luxtrol package board rolled (or lumbered) its way off Superior Electric's assembly line—the electronic dimmer had finally and rightfully taken over the entire market of intensity control.

ELEMENTS OF ELECTRONIC CONTROL

The basic thing to understand about electronic control systems is that the operational or control part of the system can be (and in larger systems almost always is) separate from the actual dimmers. The way this works is quite simple: a low-voltage current (somewhere between 11 and 20 volts, depending on the system) is sent to the remotely located dimmers telling them what to do. This signal is either generated by a small fader called a controller or potentiometer in the "preset" system, or by a computer-stored intensity level in the memory system. Of course, the actual electronic dimmer handles full-voltage current (120 volts) and alters the flow of this current to the lighting instrument per instructions from the low-voltage control signal.

Aims of Electronic Control

Before taking a look at the various types of apparatus, let us consider briefly the advantages of electronic control over the older systems. It must be emphasized that the object of electronic devices is not mere gadgetry and certainly not complexity for the glorification of the technician. Rather their purpose is to free the artist from the tyranny of earlier crude mechanisms. Under the older methods a simple shift of emphasis in the stage lights required the designer to instruct (either directly or through a boss electrician) several operators, who probably could not even see the results, in what they were expected to do and coach them repeatedly and carefully on timing. If what was desired was executed correctly once out of five times, the designer would probably be considered fortunate.

With the low-voltage miniaturized control systems provided by electronics all facets of stage lighting, or any portion of it (sub-mastering or group mastering), can be mastered. Readings for future changes (presetting) can also be set up and can be brought into effect on cue and at whatever rate of speed is desired. The dimming devices are multicapacity: each dimmer will successfully control any lamp load from the top capacity of the dimmer down to the smallest load desired. And because the current is low in both amperes and volts, and the controls are miniature, the control panel is compact and may be located anywhere in the theatre that is practical rather than being pushed into a corner backstage. This allows the operator to follow the action on stage with ease and to make changes with accuracy.

Early Types of Electronic Dimmers

All electronic systems share basic elements. In most systems the same set of controllers, masters, and memories can be used, with slight modification, to control any of the dimmers used in the various systems.

Saturable-Core Reactors. Although not strictly a fully electronic device, the saturable-core reactor was the first attempt along these lines. It consists of a transformer built on a core shaped like the figure eight. The primary and secondary coils are wound around the opposite ends of the eight, and a low-voltage d-c control current coil around the common central bar. By varying the control voltage, the current flow in the secondary is affected, thereby furnishing the lamps with greater or lesser voltage.

There are a number of disadvantages connected with the saturable-core reactor which prevented it from receiving wide acceptance. First, the load current and the control current are related, so the reactor can operate effectively only in a comparatively small range close to its rated load. Secondly, the reactor itself is a ponderous piece of apparatus, and it dims ponderously, with a noticeable time lag between the giving of a control command and the resulting change of the light. However, saturable-core reactors were installed in a number of large houses during the 1920s.

Thyratron Tubes. The first truly electronic system was put into operation by George Izenour in 1947 at Yale University. The dimming device is a pair of thyratron tubes which are controlled by varying their grid voltages from the control panel. This results in a rapid switching on and off of the supply voltage which modifies the familiar a-c sine-wave form, thus feeding more or less voltage to the lamps.

The tubes are multicapacity, dimming any loads up to their top rating; the reaction time is instantaneous, and only current that is actually consumed by the load is drawn.

But thyratron tubes also have their disadvantages. They require a certain warmup time before loads may be placed on them, and they give off a good deal of heat that must be disposed of to prevent their early failure. The tubes have a tendency to "drift"—that is, to get out of adjustment—and therefore demand frequent and careful attention. And they do need replacement now and again, making maintenance a time-consuming and costly affair.

The Magnetic Amplifier. During the 1950s the magnetic amplifier seemed to be the answer to the electronic dimming problem. A refinement of the saturable-core reactor, the magnetic amplifier is multi-capacity, has a fast reaction time, needs no warm-up, gives off little heat, and has an unlimited, maintenance-free life. Its only disadvantages seemed to be its bulk, its weight, and its cost. But, soon after the magnetic amplifier became a reality, a new breakthrough in electronic dimmers was made: the silicon controlled rectifier. This little wonder quickly made all other dimmers obsolete.

Silicon Controlled Rectifiers

Usually referred to as the SCR dimmer, its name means "a silicon rectifier under control" and not "a rectifier controlled by silicon." A kind of large-capacity transistor, this device presents all the advantages of the magnetic amplifier but it is quite small and light in weight and is a good deal less expensive. The early SCRs were sensitive both to overcurrents and to high ambient heat, but special fusing and fans took care of these drawbacks. Another problem was that its rapid switching action often caused a distinct and annoying hum in the lamp filaments, requiring the addition of a special filter called a "choke" to correct it.

As indicated above, the SCR performs its dimming task by very rapidly switching on and off, thereby "chopping" the a-c sine wave. Two SCRs are required for a single dimmer, but the actual SCR is only the diameter of a nickel and is ¾-inch thick. These little "buttons" are mounted in metal finlike devices called "heat sinks" which dissipate the heat generated by the rapid switching. An entire SCR dimmer (never larger than a shoe box) will also include a circuit breaker and a printed circuit card which contains the other necessary electronic components (Figure 6–5).

A welcome result of the SCRs' gain in popularity was the steady decrease in cost to the point where today we are experiencing patch or interconnect panels being replaced by dimmer-per-circuit systems.

The Interconnect System

Figure 6–6 illustrates the flow of power from the service entrance of a theatre to a lighting instrument in a typical electronic system using

FIGURE 6–5

SCR Dimmer Plug-in

A modern SCR dimmer plug-in which contains two 2400-watt capacity SCR dimmers, circuit breakers, and printed circuit cards. The small jacks designated TP1 and TP2 are for testing purposes. (Photo courtesy Kliegl Brothers)

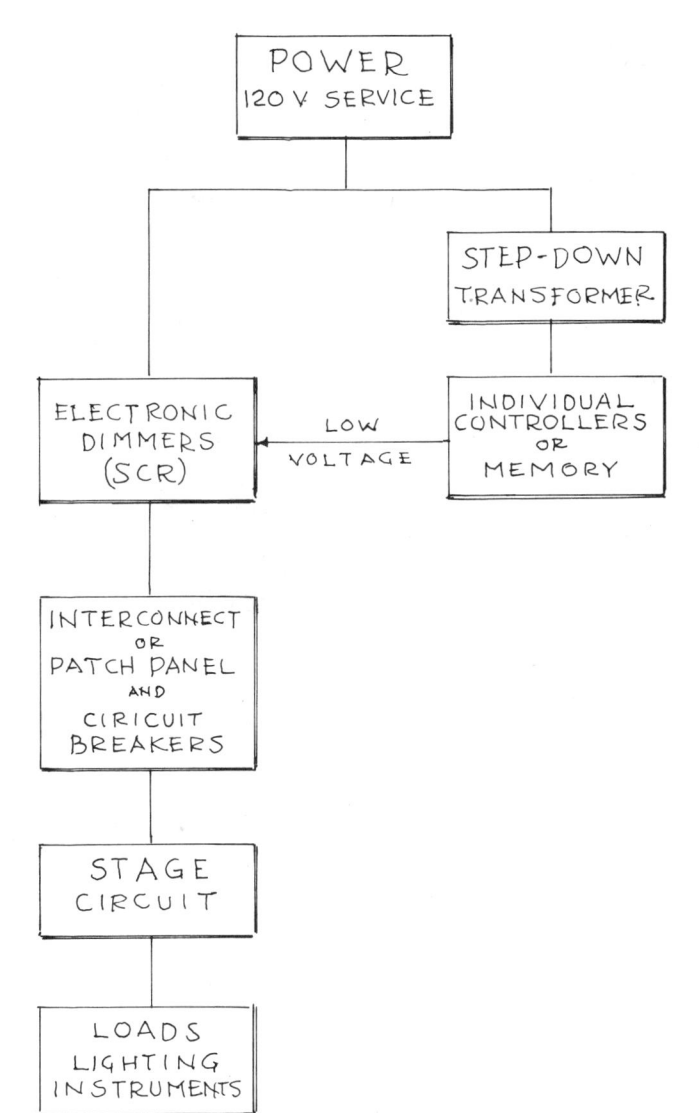

FIGURE 6-6
Typical Theatrical Power Flow
A block diagram illustrates the flow of power from the service entrance through control and to a lighting instrument.

an interconnect or patch panel. In all but the smallest theatres it is normal to have many more stage circuits than dimmers. In order to make possible the connection of any circuit to any dimmer, or indeed to place several lights under the control of a single dimmer of suitable capacity, flexible systems, variously referred to as interconnecting, cross-connecting, or patching, have been devised.

Possibly the simplest and most common form of cross-connecting panel is the type that has all the stage circuits terminating in plugs at the end of retractable cables, much like the old-fashioned telephone switch boards (Figure 6-7, page 92). The dimmer circuits end in jacks mounted in the panel. Any plug may be pushed into any jack; therefore any instrument may be under the control of any dimmer. Usually there are several jacks for each dimmer circuit, thus providing a simple way to gang several instruments on the same control if desired.

Intensity Control

FIGURE 6–7

Telephone-type Interconnect or Patch Panel

Single jacks representing each circuit in the theatre are plugged into one of several receptacles assigned to each dimmer. Circuit breakers for each individual circuit are located on the face of the panel below the jacks. Repatching during a show is often done by throwing the proper circuit breakers.

The "slider" patch is a full-voltage sliding contact system arranged on a grid. Stage circuits are normally represented by vertically sliding clips while each dimmer is assigned a horizontal buss bar. One need only align the slider (circuit) with the dimmer in order to complete the patch. This system eliminates the "spaghetti" of cable too often found in the telephone-type patch board, but several problems have surfaced with the slider patch:

1 The circuit-to-dimmer connection is not a sure one, and it is easy to make a poor contact.

2 Often the sliders are not built to take the rugged treatment and frequent use given nearly every patch panel.
3 It is quite simple to overload a dimmer by placing too many circuits on it.

A recent development in patch systems is the miniaturized low-voltage matrix patch, which looks much like a cribbage board and employs metal pins to make the low-voltage connection. This low-voltage patch in turn remotely activates a standard voltage connection. Have a good supply of pins on hand and keep dirt out of the holes.

The Dimmer-per-Circuit System

Although patch systems are still very common, new installations are frequently opting for the dimmer-per-circuit system. The dimmer-per-circuit concept has been with us for many years, but only recently with the introduction of high-density dimmers, computer control, and lower dimmer cost has this system been considered a truly competitive alternative to the interconnect system. Dimmer-per-circuit is exactly what its name implies: a system with an individual 2000- or 2400-watt dimmer assigned to every circuit in the house. Patching still exists, but it is of a different kind. Instead of patching a circuit into a dimmer, circuit and dimmer are patched electronically to a control channel at the console. This patch is totally flexible, allowing as many circuits and dimmers to be controlled by an individual channel as is desired. Note that a slight change in commonly used terminology is necessary with this system: no longer can a control channel be referred to as a dimmer, for the relationship between the two is no longer constant.

This system is an exciting one for the lighting designer because of its great flexibility—provided, however, that the number of stage circuits has not been compromised in the initial installation. Where this has occurred the theater would be better off with an interconnect system.

TYPES OF ELECTRONIC CONTROL

For all practical purposes, only two types of electronic control exist: the manual system and the memory system. The manual system always consists of at least one controller or potentiometer per dimmer as well as a master controller. It may be quite sophisticated, with a great number of possible presets, masters, submasters, and group masters.

FIGURE 6–8
Six-dimmer SCR Controller
A six-dimmer controller with master and circuit breakers; manufactured by Electronics Diversified. Each dimmer has a capacity of 2400 watts. Circuit plug-ins are located on the rear panel. A remote control unit is also shown. (Photo courtesy Electronics Diversified, Inc.)

Manual and Preset Systems

The simplest and least expensive of the manual electronic control systems provides one controller per dimmer and might very well be contained in a single housing (Figure 6–8). Although these systems are inexpensive and quite portable, they are also inflexible and can be poorly built. When considering purchasing such a control system, pay close attention to the following considerations:

1. Are the dimmers themselves easily accessible for repair?
2. Have the dimmers been properly protected from power surges?
3. Is proper dimmer ventilation provided?
4. Are chokes installed to prevent excessive lamp-filament vibration?
5. Is a master controller provided?
6. Do the controllers work smoothly and seem sturdy?
7. Finally, can the system be expanded?

The only advantage these systems provide over the older autotransformer package boards are in compactness, lightness of weight, and electronic mastering.

FIGURE 6–9

Two-scene-preset Console

The transparent disks with the white handles are the controllers for the thirty dimmers, one apiece for each preset. Below them is a row of off–on switches for each circuit. At the right end of the white plate may be seen the fader handle. The six switches to the left are for the non-dim circuits. At the extreme left is the master dimmer for houselights and a lock for the board. (Photo—George Izenour)

Presetting. Preset systems provide, in addition to the direct, manual control of each dimmer from the console, one or more additional sets of controllers. When only one duplication of controls is provided, it is usually identical to the manual control and located in the same panel. This is referred to as a two-scene preset board (Figure 6–9). The set of controllers energized at a given moment also acts as the manual control, while the readings on the other set of controllers are being adjusted as a preset that will shortly be used.

When there are several duplicate controls, usually five or ten, they are placed in a panel adjacent to the console, and an assistant sets the readings on them. In running the show with, let us say, ten presets already set up, the operator need only cross-fade back and forth from one preset to another at the speed dictated by the cues and the action. If a set of readings is not required again once it has been used, it may be erased and a new preset set up in its place. Thus as many as sixty or more complex readings may be utilized in desired sequence for a single performance. This is certainly a simple enough procedure and one not likely to cause confusion in the mind of the operator. Figure 6–10 (page 96) shows a multipreset board and its console.

FIGURE 6–10

A Ten-scene-preset Console

To the left is the preset panel with ten rows of forty-five controllers each, for the forty-five dimmers. The upper portion of the console desk contains the forty-five manual units, each with its reading indicator at the top, below which is the controller handle, and beneath this the transfer switch, which allows the circuit to be placed under either manual or preset control. At the left end of the desk are the selector buttons for the ten presets, plus blackout. There are two rows, one for the "up" and one for the "down" position of the fader, which is adjacent. When the fader is "down" (as in the picture) the preset "selected" in the bottom row is energized. As the fader moves toward "up," the preset "selected" in the upper row fades into prominence, cross-fading the former selection, until the handle reaches its top limit. When the "down" preset has been eliminated a new preset may be selected on the bottom row. At the right end of the desk is the master dimmer handle, which dims all circuits on manual control proportionately down or up. (Photo—George Izenour)

The presetting approach does create certain problems, however. A completely new preset is required for most lighting changes. It is sometimes possible to make a minor change in the preset panel itself, but this is frequently awkward and, in some models, impossible.

Further, all fades between presets must be linear; that is, if it is desirable to dim spotlight A from 10 (full up) to 0 (full out) while spotlight B is moving from 0 to 10, then when A reads 8, B will read 2, when A is at 5, so is B, and when A reaches 3, B will be at 7.

Split-faders (two cross-faders rather than one) help to solve this problem. One cross-fader is assigned to the preset first in use, while the second is ready to activate the next preset in order. The fade can then be nonlinear and two presets can even be active at the same time (a phenomenon called "pile-on").

Group Mastering. Another method of designing a control board does not depend exclusively on separate preset panels but divides the manual board into various groups and subgroups, each with its own master control. This system is known as group mastering. The groups may be used as presets independent of each other, operated together, or used to pile on new readings on top of the old ones, as well as other combinations.

Unfortunately, the operation of such a console can become extremely complex if a great many changes are needed in rapid succession. There are just too many things for an operator to keep track of in a swiftly moving play. But for fewer cues and with a tempo that permits careful checking and preparation for the next change, this type of system has much to offer.

A very distinct advantage of the group system is that the console may be run effectively with little rehearsal, a great boon for multipurpose auditoriums, while the preset system demands considerable preparation time to record the readings.

Combination Systems. The most desirable manual system obviously will combine the virtues of presetting with those of group mastering and sub-mastering. An incredible variety of such control systems exist today, each with its own idiosyncrasies. Although computerized memory systems have almost eliminated large preset systems from the market, smaller systems such as Strand Century's Mantrix and Colortran's Patchman have a great deal to offer (Figure 6–11). These manual control systems are equipped with a two- or four-scene preset, sub- and group mastering, matrix patching, and timed split cross-faders. They are economical, portable, and offer a good alternative to small computer memory control.

FIGURE 6–11
Two-scene-preset Control System with Sub-mastering
The "Mantrix" control system, manufactured by Strand Century. This system has twenty-four channels, eight sub-masters, split cross-faders, and a grand master. Also included is an electronic dimmer to channel patch (left side of board). (Photo courtesy Strand Century)

Computerized Memory Systems

The combination of the SCR dimmer, low-voltage control circuits, and miniaturized parts has led inevitably to computerized control of lighting. The ability of the computer to store information enables it to hold preset or cue information in whatever quantities a production situation might desire. A computer can be programmed with the digital information of a cue that is randomly recalled with push-button speed. The only limit to capacity is the size or number of storage elements in the memory bank.

Types of Memory Systems. Compared to those being manufactured today, early memory systems were generally large and bulky. They would often have a single set of controllers or potentiometers as well as a keyboard, and cue information could be stored in the memory by either means. A split-fader, often a timed-fader, and possible group and/or sub-masters were also standard equipment. The main memory storage was either disc or core, and only later was disc or magnetic tape "library storage" added as a standard feature. Q-File, developed by Thorne Electric of Great Britain and by Kliegl Brothers, was one of the first systems to eliminate a full set of controllers and add library storage (Figure 6–12). Autocue, maunfactured by the now-defunct

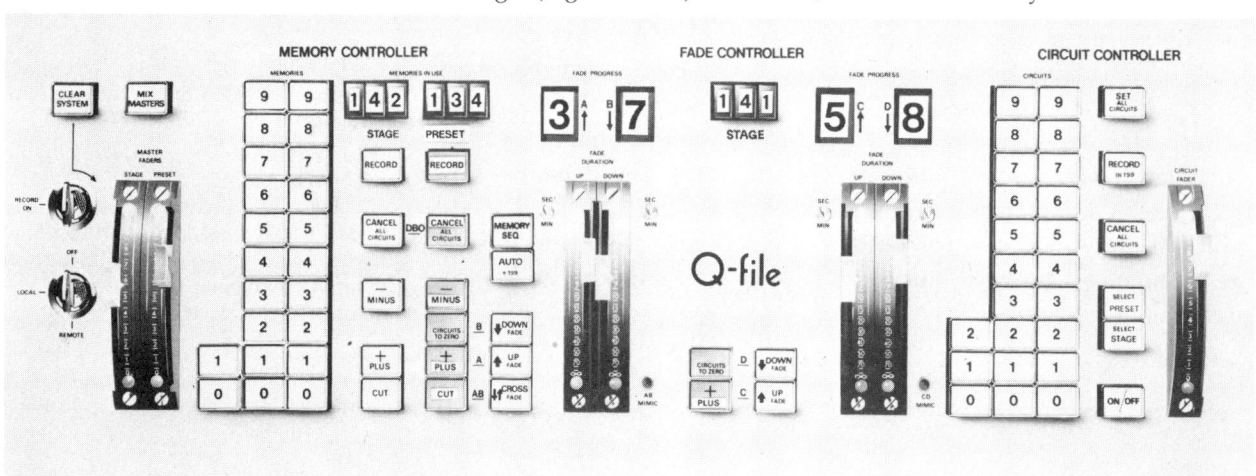

FIGURE 6–12

Q-file Memory System

The first successful preset memory system designed and manufactured by Thorn Electrical Industries, Ltd. Originally developed for television lighting control, it revolutionized theatre lighting control. The console has fingertip control of a keyboard of close to 400 lighting-control circuits with a Servo Fader to control levels of one or a group of dimmers prior to memory storage; for faders grouped in inverted pairs with time-controlled cross-fading capabilities; a keyboard for the selection of nearly 200 memory positions; a status display panel to tell the operator at a glance (1) the control channels that are energized in the stage mode and (2) the channels being held in the next preset mode, and a peg matrix or patch panel. Extra features include an auxiliary control panel, a portable remote-control panel, and a library device in which an entire show can be stored on standard tape cassettes for recall at a later date. (Photo Kliegl Bros.)

Skirpan Lighting Control Corporation, introduced the video monitor (a standard TV screen) to their control system. Although more complex than necessary, Autocue led the way to the development of current state-of-the-art equipment.

Kliegl took Q-File off the market and replaced it with their more sophisticated and less complex Performance system. Colortran introduced Channel Track, which has since been updated; and Strand Century developed Multi-Q and Micro-Q.

State-of-the-Art Control. Today's memory systems can be fairly easily categorized into two classes: the small, portable systems such as Strand Century's Mini-Palette, Kliegl's Performer series, and Colortran's Color Track (Figure 6–13), and the larger, more sophisticated

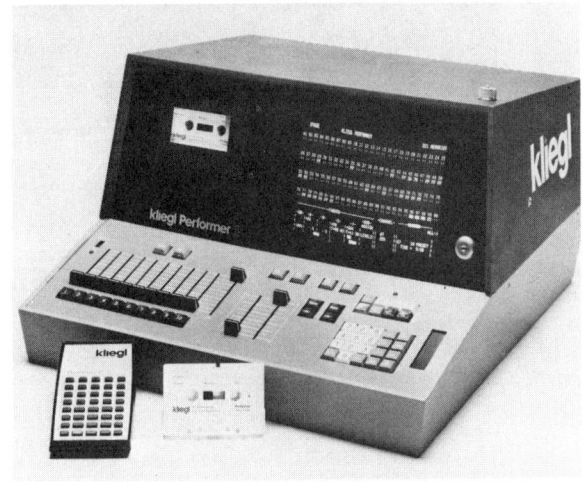

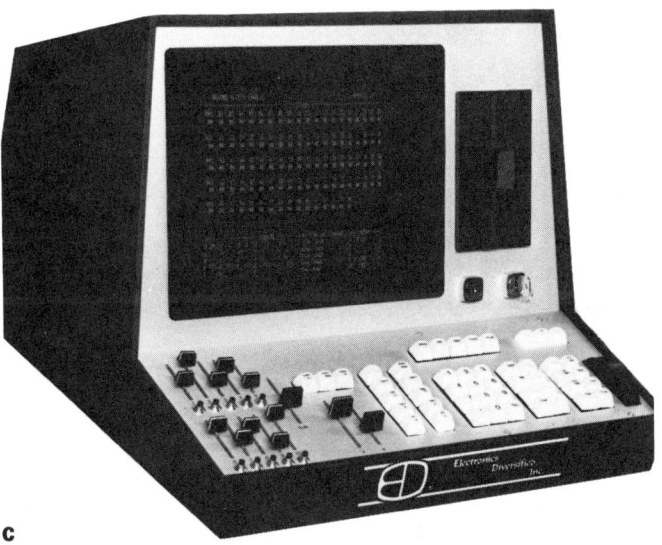

FIGURE 6–13
Small Memory Systems

(a) The Mini Light Palette has two video screens (one for dimmer levels and the other for cue sheet), rate wheel, group and sub-masters, and a split cross-fader. The slot at the lower left of the console is for disc memory. (Photo courtesy Strand Century) (b) The Performer II is a popular control system for touring productions. As indicated, its memory is provided by tape. Also shown is the hand-held remote control unit. (Photo courtesy Kliegl Bros.) (c) The EDI Mini-Memory Control Console (Photo courtesy Electronics Diversified, Inc.) Most of these units have similar features.

Intensity Control

console systems such as Kliegl's Command Performance, Colortran's Dimension Five, and Strand Century's Light Palette (Figure 6–14).

The smaller systems are all similar in that each will contain the following features or functions:

1. Library storage (either disc or tape).
2. A single video display able to inform the operator of various memory functions.

FIGURE 6–14
Large Memory Control Systems
(a) The Strand Century Light Palette has several specialized features not available on the Mini Light Palette. (Photo courtesy Strand Century) (b) Colortran's Dimension Five control system uses rate wheels and is equipped with color CRTs. (Photo courtesy Colortran) (c) Kliegl's Command Performance is another state-of-the-art control system. (Photo courtesy Kliegl Bros.)

3 Timed split cross-faders.
4 Group or sub-masters.
5 Key pad access to memory.

These units will typically have limited memory and are ideal for small to medium facilities as well as touring.

The larger console systems generally have greater memory capacity, are more flexible, and offer more features:

1 Remote control console and keypads.
2 Hard-copy printers.
3 Greater number of group and sub-masters.
4 Two video displays.
5 More sophisticated memory backup systems.
6 A greater variety of control functions.

Designing with Memory Systems. When Tharon Musser, one of America's most outstanding lighting designers, insisted on a Light Palette control system for her Broadway production of *Chorus Line*, it became obvious that even New York was going to have to accept memory lighting control. There is no doubt that lighting designers can achieve a higher level of artistry with the help of the computer. Cue writing is simplified, the potential for more complex and sophisticated cues is greatly expanded, and changes are made quickly and accurately—every time. The systems offer the designer a choice of manual or automatic operation with manual override (the operator simply presses a "go" button), simultaneous fades, channel tracking, electronic patching, and a variety of more specialized functions. In effect, these memory systems have passed the artistic "buck" back to the designer. No longer does a control system place severe limitations on what can be achieved. New levels of creative lighting design are being reached every day with the help of computerized control.

THE OPERATOR AND REMOTE CONTROL

As we have pointed out, the low amperage and low voltage used by the control system permit the operator to be placed at any distance from the stage and in any location that seems appropriate. Of the practical places, the rear of the main floor of the auditorium is unquestionably the best. It is a good place from which to run the show, the view of the stage is satisfactory, and the operator and light designer are, during rehearsals, in easy and direct communication with director, scene designer, and others. It is inexcusable to place the control panels backstage, although the cross-connecting system should be there, while the actual dimming apparatus can be tucked away in the basement or other convenient location. This applies equally to a permanent installation consisting of console and preset panels and to the controller units of a portable board.

It would not be wise to leave the subject of electronic dimming without speaking of the person who will operate the controls. This is a very different task from that presented to an electrician standing backstage and manipulating several large handles, heavy with friction, under the direct supervision of a stage manager or a chief electrician.

A console operator is usually in a booth out in the house. Cues may be taken from the stage manager, but if the show is being called from backstage, the operator should take sight and sound cues from the stage action itself. Often the control apparatus is delicate and complex, not at all like a bank of simple and rugged resistance or autotransformer dimmers. An error could very well result in every light on the stage assuming the wrong reading. Nothing is more agonizing than watching an operator fade to a blank or totally incorrect preset in the middle of a subtle stage moment. While a good memory control system will lessen the chances of operational error, a highly competent operator is still essential.

A good operator will have confidence, a cool head, and enough understanding of the control system to rectify an error before it gets out of hand. In addition, the operator must know the show and fully understand the lighting designer's intentions. He or she *must watch the stage*.

Perhaps, most of all, the operator requires a sensitivity and sense of timing akin to that of an actor's. In a very real sense, the operator is also an actor. An operator does not merely snap lights on, but dims in gently, with feeling, perhaps at a varying pace to suit best the action on the stage. If the actors are fast in their pace one night, an adjustment must be made to the new tempo. Many highly competent electricians cannot adjust to this sensitivity. They may understand, but the delicacy of feeling isn't there: their lights are always a trifle off cue, a bit jerky on the fade-up, a little slow on the dim, a trifle rushed on the cross-fade sequence. A lot of sensitivity and a little know-how is a good formula for a successful operator of today's control systems.

7

Color and Light

Color is a dominate force in a stage composition. It can be subtle or dramatic, decorative or atmospheric and, by its very absence, call attention to itself. Color in light animates the scene. The energy of light reveals, brightens, and adds color to inert forms thereby increasing their vitality.

There are, however, many definitions of color. The chemistry and physics of color are the most familiar because they directly influence the use of color in the theatre. But we must not overlook the fact that the eye sees color and the brain interprets the color experience. Also, within the physiology of the eye are phenomenons of color vision that should be considered by all designers in the theatre.

Although lighting designers as well as costume and scene designers desire a knowledge of color, they have slightly divergent interests. The lighting designer, for example, is more involved with the physics of color, while costume and scenery designers are interested in the painting and dying of color as well as the manipulation of colored materials. A beginning lighting designer, though seeking to be accomplished in the physics of color, should be aware of color in pigment and dye because often they interrelate.

COLOR AND LIGHT

Although we see color in nature all around us, our basic knowledge of color begins with light. Without light there would be no color. Everyone has seen in some form or other the breaking up or refraction of sunlight into a spectrum of color such as the refraction of sunlight through a bevel-edged window or in a rainbow. The physicist with more precise laboratory prisms can produce an accurate spectrum with wavelength values for each hue.

The Visible Spectrum. Color and light are the visible wavelengths of the electromagnetic spectrum (Figure 7–1). The visible portion of the spectrum measured in nanometers (one-billionth of a meter) is a minute section falling in the vicinity of 400 to 700 nanometers in length. The shortest, 390 to 430 nanometers, produces what we call violet light. The next length is blue followed by green, yellow, orange, and finally (between 630 and 700 nanometers), red light. The wavelengths shorter than 390 nanometers are called ultraviolet (beyond violet) and those longer than 700 nanometers are infrared (below red). From the six easily identified hues and the intermediate hues, twelve spectral hues can be separated as a palette for light and pigment in the theatre (Plate 7-1).

The Language of Color. To describe a new color or analyze an old one, designers in the theatre use a language of color terminology. The variants of color are the most familiar terms used to communicate or identify a specific color. The three variants of color in pigments and dyes are *hue, value,* and *chroma*. Since color in light is mostly transmitted, *intensity* is a term closely synonymous to *value*.

Within the framework of these variants a specific color can be described in simple terms by refering to its hue (red, yellow, and so on), chroma (freedom from neutralization), and value or intensity level (light to dark relationship).

Hue. The position of a color in the spectrum determines its hue. The number of hues that can be separated or identified as principal hues is arbitrary. Six easily identified hues are red, orange, yellow, green, blue, and violet. To expand the number of hues would depend on their ultimate use or application in a color theory or system of notation. The use of color by the artist, for example, is linked to the medium of paint or dye and therefore might desire a larger selection of hues. Light, on the other hand, is colored by passing it through stained glass or plastic. Because of the purity of the color mediums it is possible to establish light primary hues and work with a smaller palette.

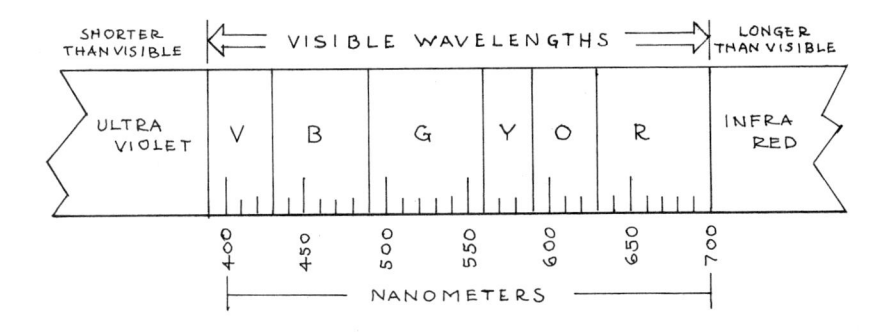

FIGURE 7–1
The electromagnetic spectrum.

A primary hue is a basic hue that is suitably located in the spectrum to mix secondary colors (See Additive Mixing). Red, green, and blue are light primary hues.

Value. The light to dark relationship of a hue or mixed color is its value. The lighter values, nearer white, are known as *tints* and the darker values, approaching black, are referred to as *shades*. Both represent a variation from the true hue.

In colored light, the light to dark comparison is primarily a product of *intensity*. A tinted surface reflects more light and conversely, a tinted color filter transmits a brighter light. Although similar, the difference between value and intensity is within their respective methods of mixing color. In paint, to raise or lower the value of a hue affects its chroma because of the use of *black*. In light, black is merely the absense of light. To change the intensity of a color does not affect its purity or chroma. The only exception is when a change in intensity is accomplished by dimming in which case the filament emits a warmer color (approaching orange) and in turn modifies the chroma of the filter.

Chroma. The instant the purity of a spectrum hue is modified by mixing, the change is referred to as a change of chroma. Chroma changes are more in paint than in light because of subtractive mixing. Chroma changes in light happen in the color filter (dye) or by overlapping color filters. Both are a product of color mixing.

COLOR MIXING

Hue, value, and chroma are the variables of color. Color is varied by mixing. The two methods of mixing are *additive mixing* and *subtractive mixing*. While both methods affect hue changes, additive mixing also noticeably alters value, and subtractive mixing modifies chroma.

Additive Mixing. The mixing of colored light from two or more sources is additive mixing. It can be demonstrated by the overlapping of sharply defined fields of two or more spotlights each with a separate color filter (Figure 7–2). A single filter such as red, for example, absorbs

Color and Light

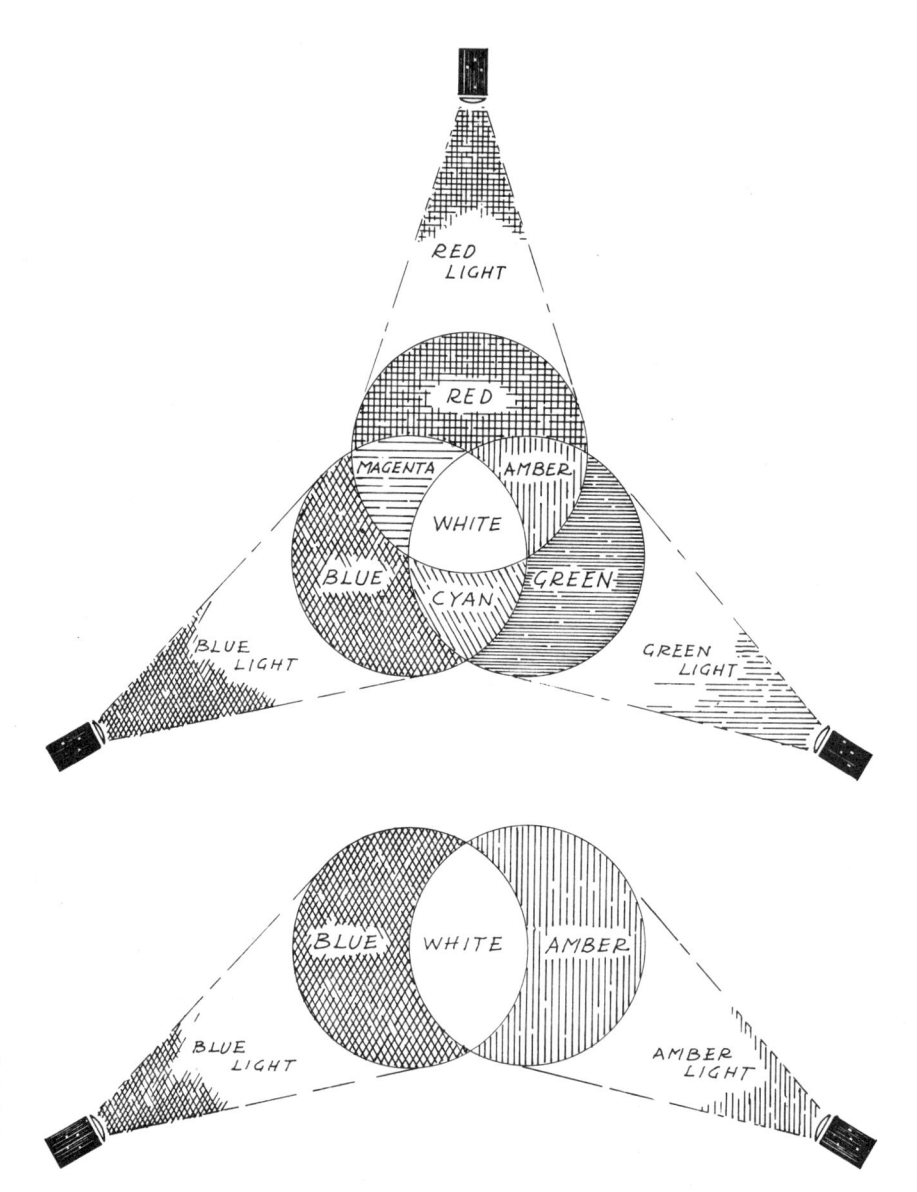

FIGURE 7–2
Additive Color Mixing
(Top) The three primary colors which, by overlapping, produce the secondaries (any two) and white (all three). (Below) A primary and its complementary secondary produce white.

all other hues from the spectrum and transmits only red. When the red rays overlap or are added to the light from the blue filter the result is a red-violet or magenta color. A hue produced by additive mixing is always lighter in value.

The most spectacular example of additive mixing is the combination of two contrasting colors, red and green. Their mixing produces a yellow, which is not too surprising when it is noted that yellow and yellow-orange hues fall between red and green in the color spectrum.

Mixing Primaries. The additive mixing of the three primaries in light produces a synthetic white light. When the field of each primary color is partially overlapped it is possible to see the forming of secondary

Stage Lighting

colors. The secondaries are hue-opposites to the primaries, which are referred to as complementary colors. Blue and amber, for example, are complementary colors. Their mixing produces white light (Figure 7–2).

Primary and secondary hues in lighter values (tints) are frequently used to light the actor. Tints of the complementary hues, yellow and blue, for example, are often used from opposite sides of the stage or in pairs from one side to light the actor. The additive mixing of the two colors model the actor in flattering white light that can be warmed or cooled by changing the intensity of one of the spotlights (Plate 7-2).

Subtractive Mixing. The opposite of additive mixing is subtractive mixing. In light it is the crossing or combination of color filters in front of a single light source. Figure 7–3 illustrates the merging of a magenta and amber filter (secondaries) to produce red light. The magenta absorbed or subtracted all spectral hues but red as does the amber filter. If two primaries are crossed, such as red and blue, all hues are subtracted and no light is passed. For examples of subtractive mixing in both light and pigment, see Plate 7-3.

Color Reflection. The eye sees the color of a surface by reflection. To a degree, the same absorbtion of color happens when we observe a colored surface. An orange surface, for example, absorbs all spectrum hues except yellow, orange, and red to reflect to orange color we see (Plate 7-4).

The Color Wheel. Sir Isaac Newton, who first observed the phenomenon of refraction and the spectrum, was also the first to bring

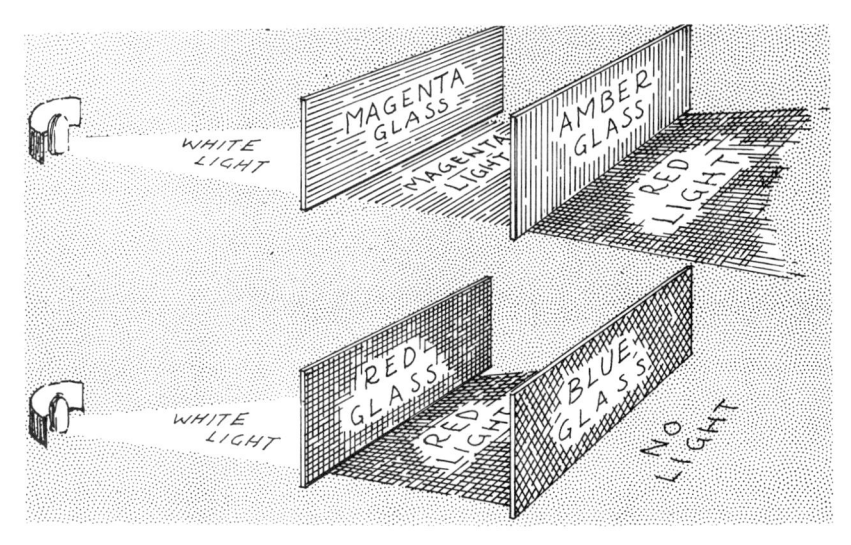

FIGURE 7–3

Subtractive Mixing

(Top) White light, when filtered through two secondaries, produces a tint of their common primary. (Bottom) Light, when filtered by two primaries, is completely absorbed so that no light whatever emerges.

Color and Light

the ends of the spectrum together into a continuous circle or *wheel*. The circular arrangement of hues brings into view the diametric and adjacent correlation of the twelve spectrum hues and thus provide designers a schematic view of primary and secondary hue relationship in both pigment and light (Plates 7-5, 7-6).

The subtractive mixing in the pigment wheel neutralize complementary hues to the gray in the center. In the light color wheel the additive mixing of diametrically opposite hues produces the white in the center.

The location of the light primaries in the light wheel represents more accurately their spectral hue. Red, for example, is red-orange (RO); blue, blue-violet (BV); and green, yellow-green (YG).

With some latitude light primaries can be described in terms of Roscolux color mediums (Rosco Laboratories, Inc.) as (1) a red with some orange content (Roscolux No. 26, light red) designated as Ro (small orange). (2) A blue containing some red (Rv) Roscolux No. 47, light rose purple plus No. 65, daylight blue, is very close to primary blue. (3) The remaining primary, green, is obtainable by combining No. 89, moss green, and No. 12, straw. These primary hues are close enough to be thought of as red-orange (RO), blue-violet (BV), and yellow-green (YG) as they appear in the pigment color wheel.

The light secondaries are the result of the additive mixing of the primaries. They are complementary colors and are located directly opposite each primary in the pigment color wheel. Yellow-orange (YO) is opposite light-primary blue-violet (BV) and can be produced in light by doubling Roscolux No. 03, dark amber. Blue-green (BG), across from primary (RO), is near Roscolux No. 71, sea blue; and red-violet (RV), the complement of primary (YG), is almost the same as Roscolux No. 48, rose purple. Note that the light secondaries are lighter in value than their corresponding pigment hues because of the additive mixing that formulated them.

COLOR VISION

The source of color can be scientifically expained; the mixture of color can be diagrammed; and all the variants of color can be arranged in a system of notation. However, what the eye sees and the brain interprets is an individual and personal color experience. Although the eye functions very much like a camera, it is not a scientific instrument. It receives light through its lens, which focuses the image of impression onto the layers of the retina in the inner eye. The innumerable nerve endings (rods and cones) of the retina culminate in the optic nerve, which carries the impression signal to the brain for interpretation. The impression is registered in terms of color and intensity (brightness), which in a sense is another way of saying hue and value. The eye sees value differences because of the variation of reflected intensities. Lighter pigment tints, for example, reflect more light (intensity) than do lower value shades. A few people can only distinguish value difference and not variations of hue. Because the greatest differences in hue fall in the middle of the value scale, most color-blind individuals cannot see the difference between reds and greens.

Intensity and Color. The chroma of colors in light (and pigment) are influenced by the intensity of the light that is reflected by, or transmitted through their respective surfaces. A saturated hue (full chroma) has an inherent brightness or intensity level within the compar brightness of the twelve spectral hues. A deep amber filter (orange), for example, transmits more light than a deep blue filter. Any change in the relative intensity of the source behind one color or the other would change the comparative value of the hue. If, for example, the fields of two clear spotlights side by side on a blue wall were of different intensities, the brigher spot would appear to be a lighter value of blue. The opposite is true of a *blue* spot of light on a blue surface. Under blue light a blue surface is more brilliant in hue because, within the lighted area, more blue wavelengths are being reflected in comparison to the rest of the surface (Plate 7-7). Many intensity differences on the stage are achieved by higher or lower wattage or by the *distance of throw*. Remember that light falls off in intensity at the rate of the square of the distance between the source and the object being illuminated (the inverse square law). If a light is moved twice the distance away from a surface, four times the intensity will be needed to achieve the same brightness. This can be a critical factor in projected scenery when the designer is trying for example, to balance color and brightness from two different slide projectors.

COLOR PERCEPTION

Knowledge of *how* we see color is perhaps of greater interest to the lighting designer than to other designers in the theatre. An understanding of the physiology of the eye as it relates to color vision gives the designer some indication of how the audience reacts to both intensity and color.

The eye's sensitivity to high or low levels of light affects the color we see. Since the rods of the retina, for example, produce most of the low-level or night vision, their sensitivity to green-blue would tend to add a greenish-blue cast to all hues seen under a low level of light. Moonlight, for example, though it is the reflection of the sun greatly reduced in intensity, appears to have a blue tint. However, blue tint, as far as the brain is concerned, is a *color impression* a designer has to consider within a stage composition. The high-intensity vision of the cones in the retina are more sensitive to yellow; the sun at noon,

Color and Light

although a brilliant white, appears to have a yellowish tint. In a stage composition, however, there is a less apparent shift of color under high intensities.

Intensity and Color Overload. The retina of the eye assimilates light energy. When it is saturated it is said to be *bleached*. Hence after any sudden change of intensity or color, the retina has to regenerate itself. This process takes palce over a noticeable period of time. Since the rods are sensitive to intensity, and the cones are sensitive to both intensity and color, there is a difference in the times it takes the eye to readjust to a sudden intensity change and to a color change. It takes the eye about 1 to $1\frac{1}{2}$ minutes to adjust in a blackout, for example (rod regeneration), while a color change (cone regeneration) may take as long as 5 minutes.

After-image. The time lag the eye experienced after a sudden change of color explains *after-image*, a phenomenon of color vision. Until the eye has recovered, it retains an image of the object and a color impression long after the object has been removed or changed. The after-image, however, is in the *complementary hue* of the original image color.

A theatrical demonstration of after-image was present in the productions of Diaghilev's Ballet Russe *Le Coq d'Or* with décor by Natalya Goncharova. The first scene, a garden, is dominated by a brilliant red-orange tree. During 20 minutes of dancing the eye was saturated with an unbalanced color scheme; upon changing to the next scene the audience was plagued by a blue-green after-image of the first-scene tree floating ethereally about the stage. The impression was in the eye, of course; the tree was not on stage.

The Color of Cast Shadows. The phenomenon of after-image or the color-balancing tendency of the eye is present in other forms. The shadow cast from a colored light source, for example, appears to the observer to be in a complementary color. Plate 7-8 illustrates the pale red-orange shadow cast from a blue-green light which is not there in reality but is an optical illusion or color impression within the eye. It should be mentioned that the shadow has to be faintly illuminated with a colorless light to accomplish the demonstration accurately.

The Interaction of Color. How a color reacts to an adjacent hue or to its background is known as the interaction of color. Certain reactions are painfully obvious while others are extremely subtle. The juxtaposition of hue opposites such as colors blue-green and red-orange seem to vibrate in violent interaction. To experience the same interaction in light it is necessary to compare surfaces that are independently colored by two or more light sources. It is a condition where colored light is not mixed but is viewed side by side. An example of the interaction of color in light is illustrated in Plate 7-9. The angled position of the surfaces separate the contrasting colors from the two right and left sources. The third softer tint in the center seems bluish as it interacts with the blue-green on the left and has a reddish cast when influenced by the red-violet on the right.

DESIGNING WITH COLOR

Both color mixing and color filtering are extremely important in stage lighting, and it seems that the use of color is one of the areas in which the young designer feels most insecure. Of course, we all make numerous color choices in the course of our everyday lives, but the average human being will make many or most of them on a subconscious level. The interior designer, fashion designer, and theatre designer must force such choices to the conscious level and begin to analyze how and why specific color determinations are made.

First of all, the term "white light" is heard a great deal in the theatre when talk turns to color. The fact is that so-called white light is relative, and our eye will accept an astonishing range of colored light as "white," depending on the circumstances. For this reason, the term "no color" (abbreviated N/C) is preferable to "white" when one discusses color and filtering. The concept of color temperature (measured in degrees Kelvin, or K) is also valuable to a discussion of color. Refer to Chapter 3, "Light Sources.")

Most stage-lighting instruments deliver a light which we consider "white" rated at approximately 3200° K. Unfortunately, the only practical means of significantly altering this color is by interrupting the beam of light with a filter. Clear glass vessels containing red wine and other colored liquids were once employed as filters, but we have advanced into the age of modern technology and now use colored plastic. This method of altering the color of light, however, is really quite inefficient, for any filtering will decrease light transmission; in fact, highly saturated filters, such as primaries, may allow as little as 5 percent light transmission.

Mixing occurs anytime two colors of light are used on the same area. The resultant color depends on colors and angles of the two light sources as well as the surface on which they fall. If two light sources strike a surface from different angles, and if the surface is three-dimensional and sculpted (an actor's face, for example), many interesting things happen. First of all, one source will cast shadows which will be filled or partially filled by the other source's light and color. Second, an overall even color mix won't be achieved because the sources are coming from different directions. What will be seen, instead, is a heavy coloration from one source that merges gradually to an even mix with the second color and finally moves into the color of the second source. Such coloration adds to the three-dimensionality of a figure on stage and can help establish a direction of light.

Another form of color mixing involves the placement of two or more light sources very close to one another so that they effectively act as a single source. The most common example of such mixing in the theatre is the use of striplights on a cyclorama or backdrop. But this technique is also employed for area lighting using spotlights placed very close to one another. The point of this is to give the designer a large range of color options through mixing while only using two lighting instruments. Of course, this type of mixing depends on dimming, and therefore each instrument must have separate control.

The designer chooses colored light for one of four reasons:

1. The light is motivated by a specific source (the sun, a lamp, the fireplace), and colored light will help convey that motivation.
2. The mood of a scene is reinforced by the light, and color will heighten the effect.
3. A visual contrast between light sources is desirable, and color will increase that contrast.
4. Change or dramatic effect for its own sake is desired.

Distribution and Position. As indicated earlier, successful designing with color depends on taste, knowledge, and experience. Let us begin with a technique developed by Stanley McCandless, a man who more than any other might be considered the founder of lighting design in the United States. McCandless suggested that one way to achieve the most *natural* look when lighting the actor on stage is to position lighting instruments to each side of the actor at an angle of approximately 45 degrees (Figure 7–4). Two complimentary colors will then be placed in the instruments—say a light blue in one and a warm amber in the other. The amber will act as a "key" or primary source light while the blue will read as a "fill" or reflected light. The colors mix with each other on the actor's face and body front to a shade which will be read as white. This technique is a basis of modern lighting design.

Warm and Cool Colors

In general, most people will consider the color red as bloodlike, typifying anger and war. Amber is likely to be perceived as sunlight, warm and comfortable. Blue will typify restraint and coolness, while green may be seen as restful. These and similar identifications must always be taken into consideration when a designer selects stage colors. But for us there is no advantage in going deeply into the psychology of color, about which there are many (often contradictory) theories.

There is one psychological aspect, however, that cannot well be ignored: the matter of the relative warmth and coolness of colors. Few

FIGURE 7—4

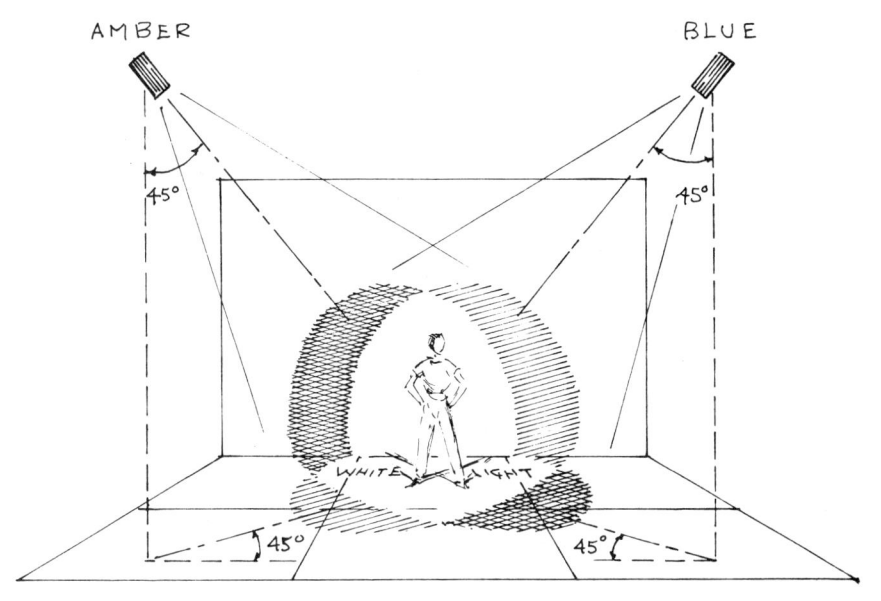

45°-45° Color Mixing

A stage-left blue and a stage-right amber will mix toward white light at the center of the actor's body (See Plate 2).

people would deny that a bright red-orange suggests warmth; most would agree that a brittle blue-white gives an impression of coolness.

Given samples of twenty different tints and shades, rarely will two people list them in exactly the same order from most warm to most cool. But in general we can say that the reds, oranges, and ambers are considered in the warm group, while the blues, violets, and greens fall within the cool range. Some mixtures of hues from the opposing groups seem on the border line, and the particular effect they give at any moment is in contrast to whatever other color is seen in relation to them (Interaction of Color).

As a matter of fact, the precise feeling given by most tints is purely a matter of contrast. A pale blue that seems positively icy in contrast to a strong amber will appear quite warm when placed next to a stronger shade of blue. Pink and lavender are frequently used on the stage as freewheeling tints whose effects we can reverse merely by changing the hues used in association with them.

Two other factors in the use of colored light, one psychological and the other physiological, are important to note. The first has to do with colors which appear to recede or move away from the viewer and those which seem to accede or move toward the viewer. The cool colors (blues and greens) fit into the former category of those that recede, while the warmer colors (reds and ambers) tend to accede. This phenomenon may be put to use by the lighting designer only in specific instances but is one that should always be kept in mind.

Our eyes tire of a constant color, especially if it is at all saturated

Color and Light

and tending toward one of the primaries (blue is a good example). A stage picture washed only in blue light will soon lose its color quality because of this fatigue effect. Color contrast or variation will counter fatigue and maintain the intended look.

Unfiltered light may also seem to have warm or cool characteristics. Opposite a cool color, such as the palest of blues or greens, uncolored light will appear quite warm. But when it is opposite a pink or pale amber, white light will definitely be on the cool side in contrast.

Remember that as dimmer readings are changed the color of light produced by a source changes. A low dimmer level will generate a very warm light compared to a reading at full intensity.

Colored Light and the Actor

In a later chapter, we will suggest specific colors to use in different situations, but here we will consider general effects desired in various portions of the stage picture. For acting area front light, for example, it is best to stay clear of saturated and unnatural shades that will adversely affect the faces and costumes of the actors.

Preserving color integrity of costumes can be a difficult task. Often the acting areas are lighted with tints of pinks and ambers, flattering enough to the human face, but deadly to green materials. Because the scene may definitely call for such colors in the light, the lighting designer should be in contact with the costume designer sufficiently ahead of time to prevent later distress.

Knowing what will happen to a given costume under colored light is simplified by breaking down the colors into primaries. For example, let us assume a yellow dress will be lit by a cool blue light from one angle and a straw or cool amber from another. The cool blue contains some mix of green and blue, the cool amber is made up of both red and green, and the yellow dress is going to reflect red and green. The conclusion, reached by simply noting the preponderance of green, is that we are probably going to be in trouble. A warmer blue or a lavender and a warmer amber light might be a better choice.

Beware of Green! Green light has limited use on the acting areas of the stage. Green on the human face is extremely unbecoming, muddying the natural healthy colors of cheeks and lips, deadening blonde and reddish hair, and exaggerating to the point of grotesqueness the slightest blemish in the complexion.

This does not mean that green should never be used. It is an extremely useful color, expecially for the enrichment of costumes and scenery. But it should be handled with considerable care, unless, of course, a distorted effect is actually desired.

Colored Light and the Scenery

Always operate on the assumption that the scene designer has painted the settings the way they should appear. Thus, for a lighting designer to attempt to improve on the scene designer's artistry would be impertinent. Enhance it, yes, but strictly in accordance with the scene designer's wishes. Ideally, of course, the scene designer should light settings, and many of the finest do just that. At other times, close collaboration between scene and lighting designers is crucial. The result will usually be that nearby scenery, such as the walls of an interior setting, will, like the acting areas, receive tints of light only. Strong colors, as we have made clear, will tire the audience and will alter the appearance of the painting. Furthermore, being so close to the acting areas, it is almost impossible to separate light on such scenery from other portions of the stage.

A good rule of thumb for a lighting designer to begin with is "If you are debating whether or not to light the scenery—don't." Generally, light on scenery such as flats and drops will cast unwanted shadows and possibly create a situation where the walls and the actors are competing for focus. On the other hand, color washing the scenery can help to create some very nice and useful effects. Nearly any scenic or costume color can be made to appear warmer or cooler—more or less inviting—through the use of colored light. A scene designer may, in addition, actually paint the set in several different colors which can be selectively accentuated or deemphasized by colored light.

Color Modification

Designers in the theatre not only have to consider the colors of a painted background, costumes, and other materials of a set, but also the colors of the lights that will reveal them. This is especially true if the lighting for the scene is unusual, such as a romantic moonlit scene or the flooding of the stage with red or green hues to provide an unnatural effect.

Fortunately, color modification is not quite as complicated as it seems. The effect of colored light on a colored surface is a result of subtractive mixing. In other words, if a red light is thrown on a yellow surface, the yellow is modified into orange tones (Plate 7-10).

The modification of a color in a costume or on scenery by colored light is a theatrical example of the joining of two color media, pigment and light. Designers in the theatre are constantly aware of how colored light and pigment influence each other. They are always prepared to compensate in either medium to create a natural effect or to deliberately cause dramatic reversals of color.

Color on the Sky

At some point a lighting designer will be called on to use color on a sky drop or cyclorama. Specific lighting techniques are discussed later, but the use of color deserves some comment here. Careful consideration and experimentation must be given before choosing a color to light a backdrop. The color of the drop itself will affect the lighting choice, for sky drops can vary from numerous shades of white to blue.

Is it better to select a single color medium that gives the exact hue desired or is a blending of several colors preferable? Of course, if there is to be a color change during the scene, then more than one color must be provided. More delicate and precise shadings can also be achieved if several different colors are blended into one.

Mixing of the three primaires is a traditional method of achieving variable color on a sky drop, and striplights will commonly be supplied with glass color filters (roundels) in the three primary colors. Remember, however, that light transmission from primary colors is extremely low, and pale tints usually are too pale for a sky drop. Therefore, colors closer to the secondaries are often the best solution.

Selecting Color

Experimenting with color mixing is especially important for the young lighting designer. Colors projected by stage-lighting instruments can be seen in the theatre or in a lighting laboratory—in fact any place that has dimmers. However, a useful tool for experimentation outside the theatre is the color mix-box (Figure 7–5). Three-inch Fresnels and three common household dimmers are used in the mix-box shown. The box

FIGURE 7–5
The Color Mix-Box
Three Fresnels on dimmers allow the designer freedom to mix colors in a space other than the theatre.

PLATE 7-1

Spectrum Hues

The breakdown of sunlight through prism refraction into first six and then twelve spectrum hues.

PLATE 7–2A
Additive Mixing

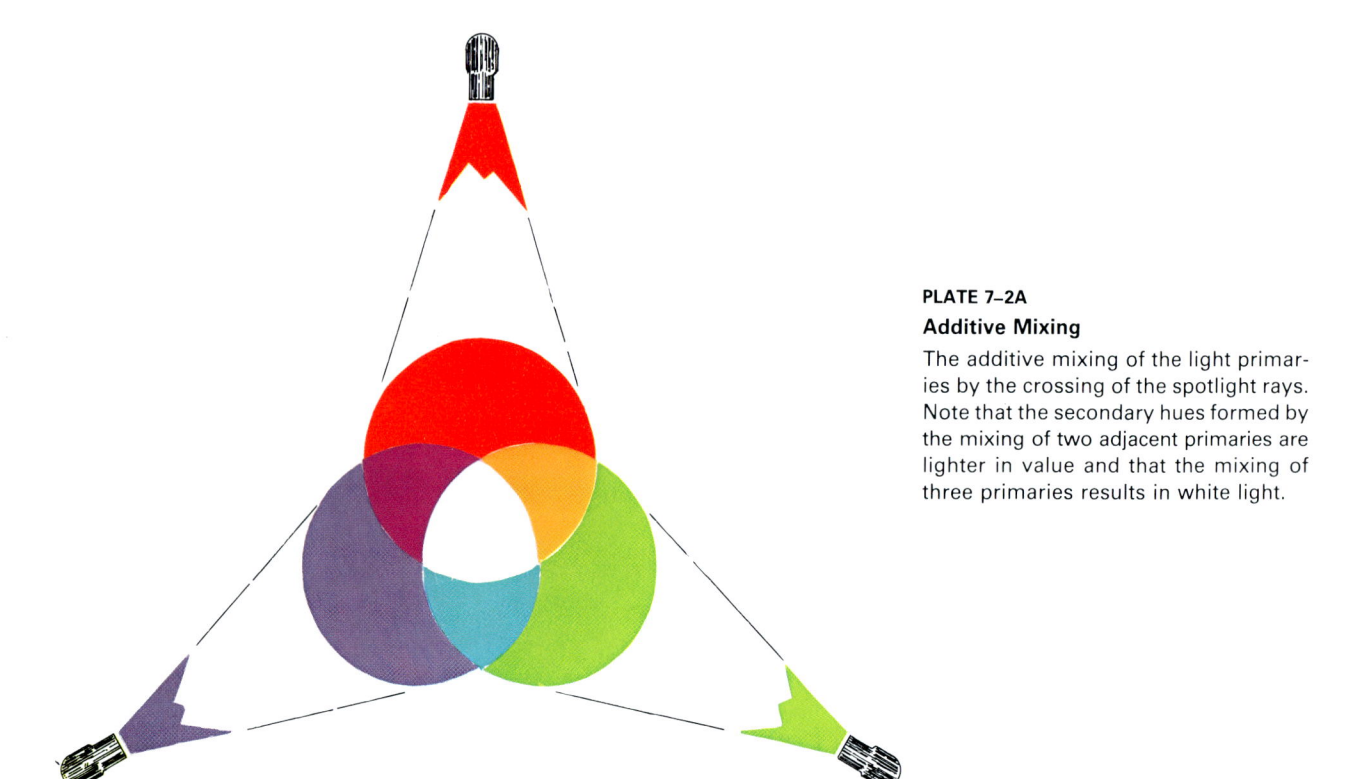

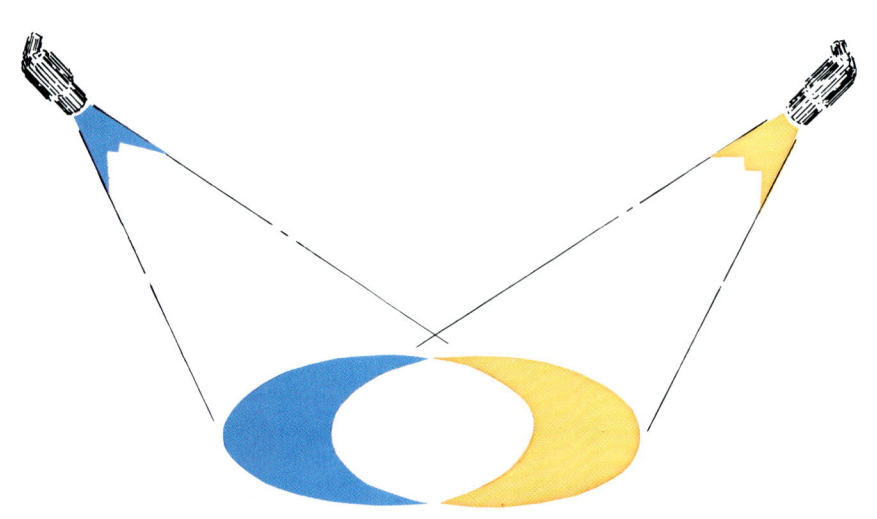

The additive mixing of the light primaries by the crossing of the spotlight rays. Note that the secondary hues formed by the mixing of two adjacent primaries are lighter in value and that the mixing of three primaries results in white light.

PLATE 7–2B
Application of Additive Mixing to Stage Lighting

The simple mixing of complementary colors to produce white light in an acting area. The white light can be "warmed" or "cooled" by altering the intensity of one side or the other or by moving the choice of color medium slightly off a true complementary scheme. (Left) Steel Blue, Roscolux No. 64, spectrum hue blue raised in value. (Right) Medium Straw, No. 14, a lighter value of spectrum hue orange.

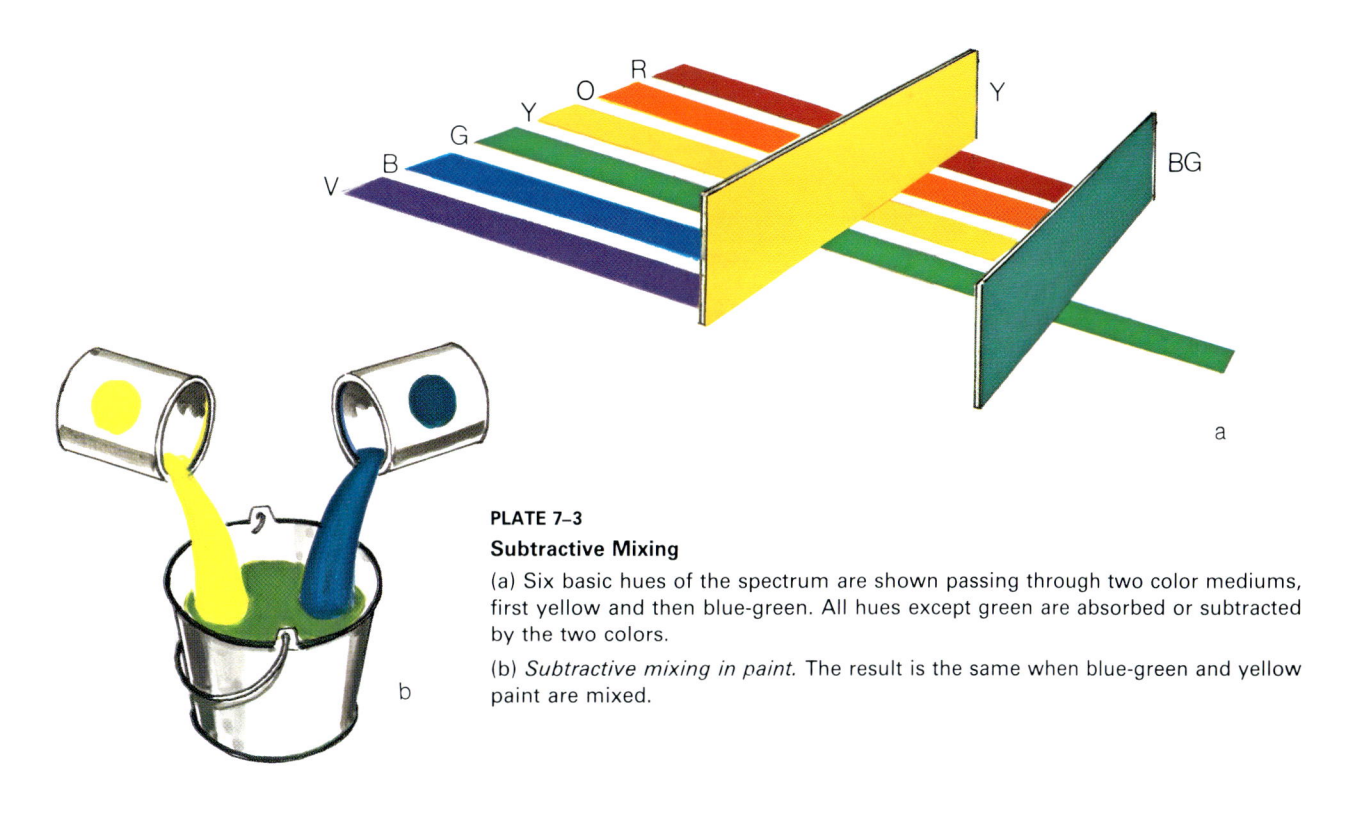

PLATE 7–3
Subtractive Mixing
(a) Six basic hues of the spectrum are shown passing through two color mediums, first yellow and then blue-green. All hues except green are absorbed or subtracted by the two colors.

(b) *Subtractive mixing in paint.* The result is the same when blue-green and yellow paint are mixed.

PLATE 7–4
Color Reflection
The horizontal orange strip represents an orange-colored surface. It appears orange under sunlight because only the red, yellow, and orange hues of the spectrum have been reflected. The other hues have been absorbed.

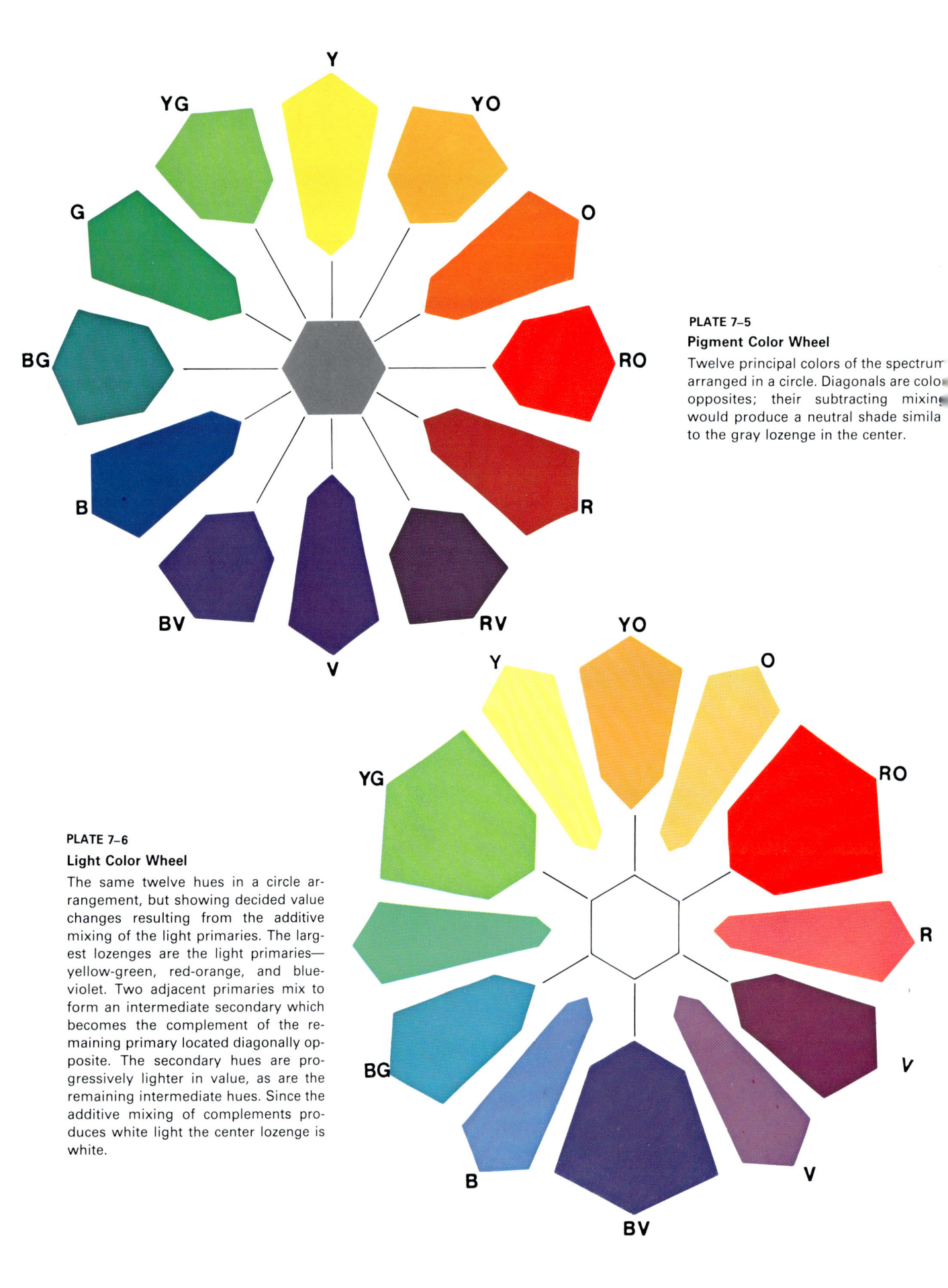

PLATE 7–5
Pigment Color Wheel
Twelve principal colors of the spectrum arranged in a circle. Diagonals are color opposites; their subtracting mixing would produce a neutral shade similar to the gray lozenge in the center.

PLATE 7–6
Light Color Wheel
The same twelve hues in a circle arrangement, but showing decided value changes resulting from the additive mixing of the light primaries. The largest lozenges are the light primaries—yellow-green, red-orange, and blue-violet. Two adjacent primaries mix to form an intermediate secondary which becomes the complement of the remaining primary located diagonally opposite. The secondary hues are progressively lighter in value, as are the remaining intermediate hues. Since the additive mixing of complements produces white light the center lozenge is white.

PLATE 7–7

Intensity and Color

A blue-green background seen under a low level of illumination. (Right) The field of a spotlight with higher intensity raises the value of the background color. (Left) The field of a spotlight with matching blue-green filter enriches and deepens the background color.

PLATE 7–8

The Color of Cast Shadows

A cast shadow takes on a color that is complementary to the hue of the light source. The color of the shadow becomes a more positive tint when it is illuminated with a subtle secondary light source. In the diagram the major light source is blue-green. The shadow is a red-orange tint, the hue opposite of blue-green.

PLATE 7-9

Interaction of Color in Light

Two pylons, three colors of light, yet the center tint seems to be two tones of lavender. The left is bluish, the right reddish. This shows the interaction of the brilliant blue-green and red-violet washes from the right and left that is sometimes referred to as the push-pull effect.

PLATE 7–10

Color Modification

A demonstration of the subtractive mixing effect when a colored surface is modified by a colored light. (a) Yellow surface under red light. (b) Green surface under red light.

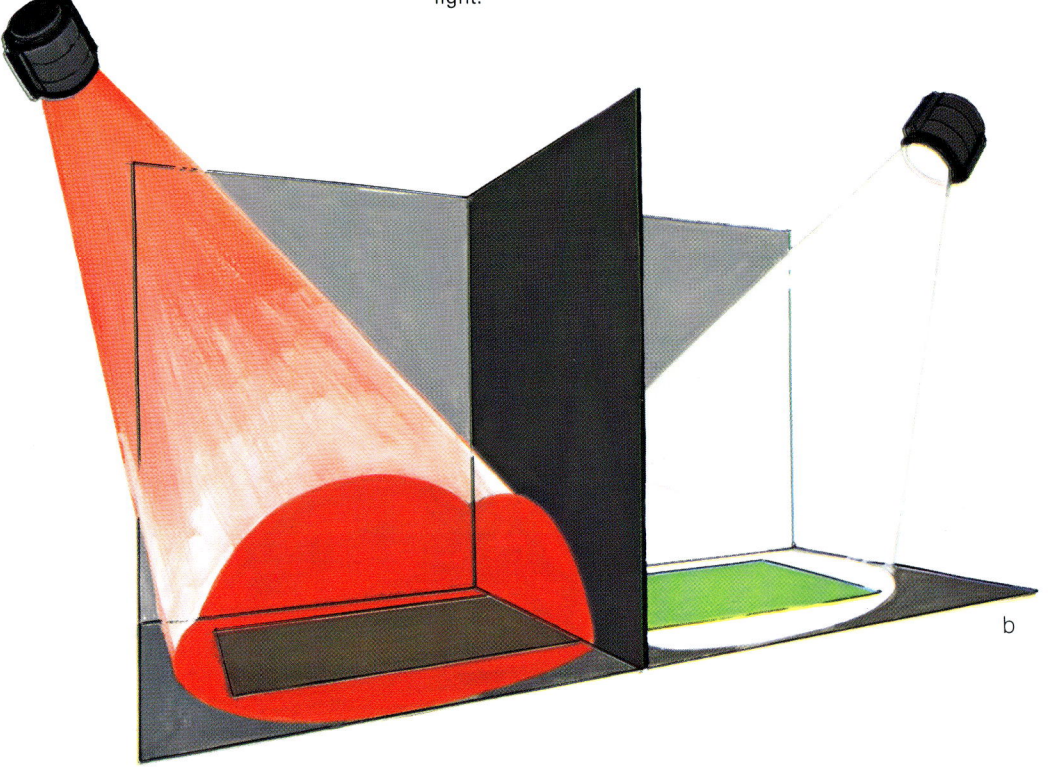

is portable and can be plugged into any household circuit. With the mix-box, the task of color selection is made easier and more convenient.

COLOR MEDIA

In order to use a mix-box, a lighting designer must have available a file box of color media that contains a frame-size cut of every color the designer may need. There are three kinds of color media in use today.

Gelatin

The least expensive of the color media, gelatin comes in the form of very thin sheets and in a considerable range of colors. But its disadvantages are numerous. It has to be cut with care to prevent tearing, it dries out and becomes brittle with age, and it loses all form when dampened, drooping like a wet dishrag in folds that adhere to each other and can never be separated. Some of its shades, particularly the blues and pinks, fade quite easily and must be replaced in the instruments frequently—sometimes after a single performance. The only remaining manufacturer of gelatin in this country is Rosco Laboratories, and their product is called "Roscogel."

Plastic Media

Two types of plastic color media are available: acetate and Mylar. While acetate is less expensive than Mylar, it too will fade and even change color over a period of time. Both plastics are waterproof and considerably more durable than gelatin and come in a wide range of colors.

Acetate. Two acetate colors are in common use in the United States: "Roscolene," manufactured by Rosco Laboratories, and "Cinemoid," manufactured by Rank Strand in Great Britain. Unfortunately, the high cost and unreliable availability of Cinemoid is forcing it out of the American market. The colors in most Cinemoid color reference (or "swatch") books will be numbered from 1 on into the 70s, but for identification it is a good idea to use the 500 series which is common to Great Britain. This practice eliminates any confusion with other brands of color which also begin their numbering with 1.

Mylar. Mylar was marketed several years ago for use with the hotter quartz stage-lighting instruments. Like acetate, Mylar is available in sheets (approximately 21" × 24") but also comes in rolls. It is extremetly durable and may be reused. Three companies supply Mylar filters in the United States: Lee ("Lee Filters"), Colortran ("Geletran"), and Rosco ("Roscolux"). Lee Filters are numbered in the 100 series and spill over into the 200 numbers. Both Roscolux and Geletran begin their numbering at 1. Use an *R* prefix before Roscolux numbers and a *G* prefix before Geletran number for clarity.

Most often the choice between acetate and Mylar is simply a matter of durability. Mylar is now available in a wider range of colors than acetate, but its higher cost can be prohibitive. However, the use of Mylar is recommended in the following situations:

1. In sky drop or cyclorama lighting, particularly if the lighting instruments are placed on the floor shooting up.
2. When using high-intensity lighting instruments with lamp ratings of over 1000 watts.
3. In scenic projection or follow spotting.

Handling Plastic Media. A new piece of plastic may, when placed in the heat of a light beam, give off considerable steam for a period. This effect, which appears to be smoke, can be quite distracting, if not alarming, to the audience. It is wise, therefore, to test new plastic well before curtain time and, if it smokes, leave the instrument switched on to dry it out before the show starts.

To allow the heat of an instrument to escape when acetate is used as its color medium, it is a good idea to perforate it with numerous small holes. These will not affect the performance of the plastic in any way, except to prolong its life, nor will the holes appear in the beam pattern. An ice pick, nail, or awl may be used for this purpose, but the neatest and easiest method is to run a pounce wheel several times over the full sheet before cutting it to size.

Colored Glass

The most expensive medium of all is glass. While gelatin and plastic may be cut to any size or shape desired, glass must be ordered for exactly the purpose required. It comes in few colors, is heavy and bulky to store, and although it never fades, is rarely affected by heat, and stands up well under ordinary usage, it can be smashed. Glass has two great advantages: it is heat resistant, and it can be molded into markings and prismatic lines that will spread light.

Roundels can be obtained with the following features:

Plain   For color filtering only.
Stippled   For color and also to diffuse the beam.
Spread   For color and also to spread the beam laterally, so that the various colors will blend more readily.
Stripped   Very thin glass in narrow strips to color the light from extremely hot-beamed instruments.

Diffusion Material

Diffusion material, often called "frost," diffuses light from an instrument and softens or even eliminates a shutter cut or beam edge. Although not a color medium, it is manufactured by the companies that produce color media, is listed in their swatch books, and is commercially available in sheets. Frosts have been with us for a long time, but recently Rosco Laboratories has greatly increased its selection of such media (in part due to the efforts of lighting designer Gilbert Hemsley).

Color Manufacturers

It is good practice to replace swatch books every two or three years to avoid faded color samples and keep aware of newly added colors. For a variety of reasons, a manufacturer may not be able to match exactly the color of a filter from one batch to another. Rosco has taken to adding a letter suffix to the number of a color filter that was not able to be adequately matched (R35A).

Finally, never trust the color names which the various manufacturers assign to each color. Names are assigned to aid in communication and to make a particular color easier to remember, but one need only compare Cinemoid's "Steel Blue" (517) with Roscolene's "Steel Blue" (854) to fully understand why such labels are meaningless.

To obtain color swatch books contact your local color media supplier or write the following manufacturers:

ROSCO: Rosco Laboratories, Inc.
36 Bush Avenue
Port Chester, NY 10573

LEE: Belden Communications, Inc.
534 West 25th Street
New York, NY 10001

GELATRAN: Colortran
1015 Chestnut Street
Burbank, CA 91502

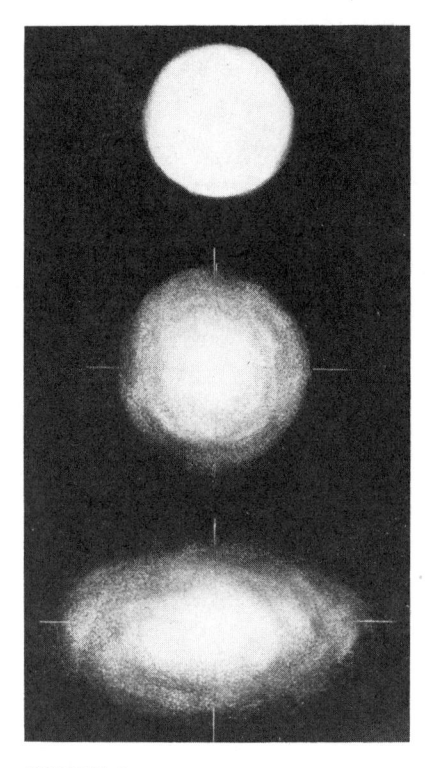

FIGURE 7-6
Diffusion Material
The effects of three different diffusion materials. (Top) A light frost. (Middle) A heavy frost which keeps a hot center. (Bottom) A spread frost such as Roscolux R104.

8

Stage Lighting Practice

The young lighting designer should first study motivational lighting. Accordingly, the early part of this chapter will lean toward a discussion of the types of light from those sources with which we are all familiar: daylight, night light, and light from artificial sources.

LIGHTING THE ACTOR

Actors must be seen in proper relationship to their backgrounds. This relationship, of course, is different for each play or dramatic situation. In general, the designer must vary the intensity, distribution, and color of light to solve the problem. Distribution is of primary importance because it involves the angle and direction of light that reveals the actors, especially their faces, in natural form.

The expression "in natural form" is the clue. It means the actor's face should be seen as it appears under natural lighting. Our eyes have been schooled by a lifetime of seeing one another under sunlight or interior lighting coming from above. We are so accustomed to seeing the features of a face disclosed by light from an overhead direction that to light it from below, for example, produces for us an unnatural look.

Anyone who has done outdoor photography knows how to maneuver a subject into a position where the sun will reveal the face most favorably. Overly bright sunlight from a single direction will cast such deep shadows that visibility of the face will be reduced. In the diffused light of shade or of an overcast sky the face appears in full visibility, although it is missing the dramatic accent of the brilliant sunlight.

Through the elaborate control of intensity and distribution possible in stage lighting, the face of the actor can be lighted to appear the way it does in nature.

It has long been a practice of artists and architects to render their drawings as though light were falling on the subject from over the artist's shoulder at an angle of about 45 degrees. The lighting designer adopts the same concept. Using spotlights, the beams may be directed on the actor at a 45-degree angle above and at 45 degrees from the right and left. To give the face an accent of brightness or color difference on one side, the intensity or color of the right or left spotlight may be varied. The face is then disclosed by a *fill-light* on one side and an accent or *key-light* on the opposite side. This slight difference in color and intensity not only improves the visibility of the face but also adds interest to the composition.

Back Lighting. A third angle also can be employed to further define the actor: lighting from overhead and behind. Back lighting is a stratagem borrowed from movie and television lighting. Because of the need to separate an actor from the background, back light is necessary in television lighting. (The tendency of the TV camera is to flatten or shorten distances appearing on the reception screen.) The use of back lighting on the stage to separate an actor from the background adds another dimension to the stage composition. It allows the lighting designer to put a brighter light on the background than would otherwise be possible, and it permits the scene designer to use colors without fear of failure to bring the actor's face into relief. Back lighting produces highlights on the head and shoulders of the actor that give a halo effect if the light is too intense. When it is kept in proper balance with the front lights the actor is etched clearly against the background.

Because back light tends to "rim" an actor, stronger colors than those used in front lighting may be employed. Such creative use of color can help to establish an overhead motivational source or simply color and texture the stage floor for a specific mood or effect. Back light will normally require a more intense source than front light. Care must be taken to keep back light from shining into the first row of audience seating. This often presents a problem, and the lighting designer may be tempted to compromise the back angle, making it more of a top or down light. Top light is not at all the same as back light, for it tends to "squash" rather than rim an actor.

Side Lighting. Side lighting gives the designer additional flexibility. Both color and angle add variety as side lighting is used in combination with frontal sources. Side lighting comes from the wings or tormentor positions and is best when directed parallel to the apron. A great variety of vertical angles, however, are available to the designer—from the low, straight-side angle of dance lighting to a high side that rims an actor from the side (Figure 8–1).

FIGURE 8–1
Sidelight

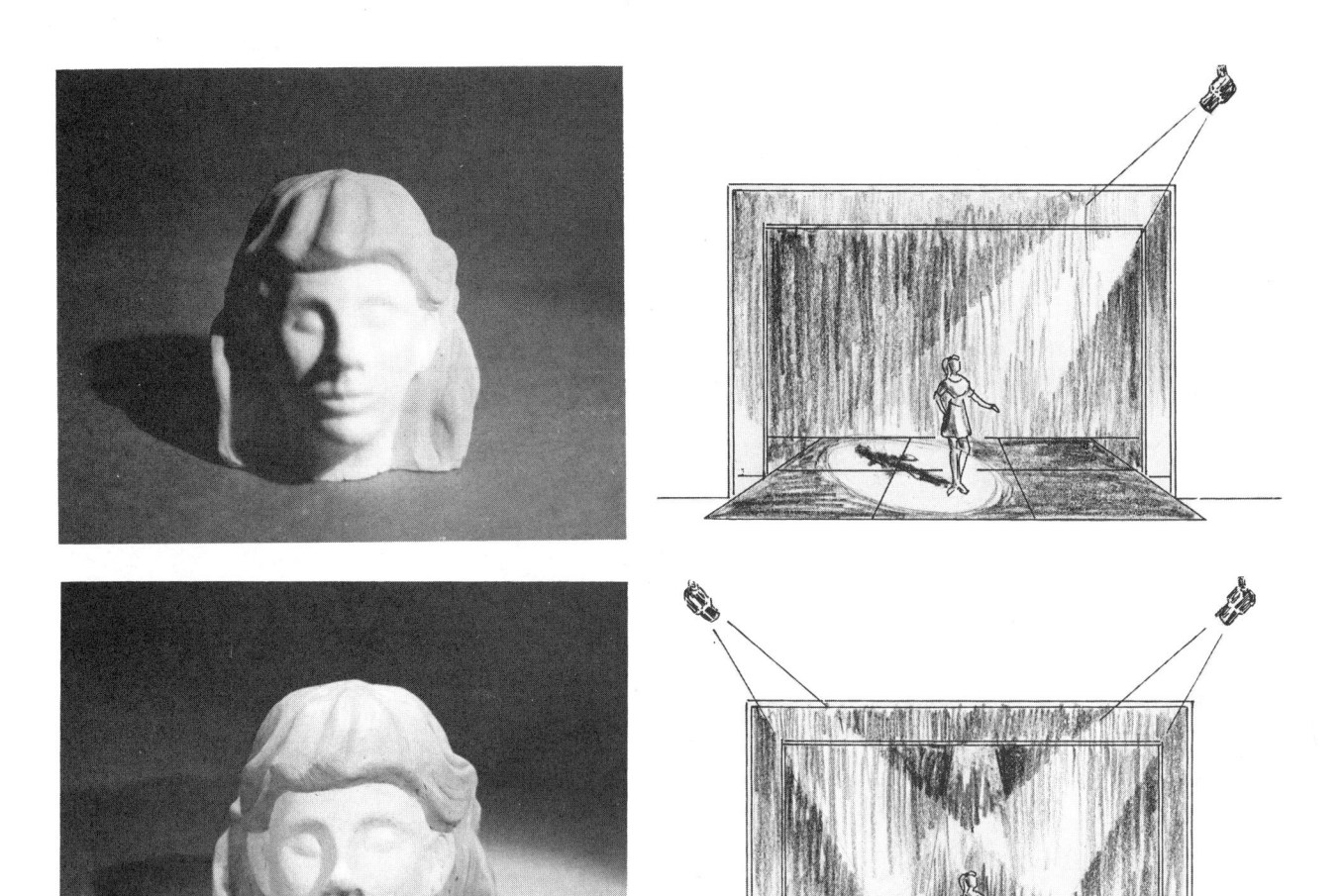

FIGURE 8–2
Lighting the Actor
The photographs through page 126 illustrate the effect of the angles of light on the composition of the face. (Top) Front light from stage-left, 45-degree angle. Lack of visibility on the dark side of the face. (Above) Front light from the left and right, 45-degree angle. The right side of the face has a higher-intensity light suggesting the direction of the motivating or "key" light.

Because side lights hit the actor from the extreme right and left, their color need not be as unsaturated as the front lights. They may be used with more chromatic colors to accent costumes or to add colored highlights to white or neutral costumes. Strong side lighting is frequently used for musical production as a part of this more presentational style of theatre.

Like back light, side light also can be used to establish a motivational source through color, angle, and intensity. In addition, such light is more apparent to the audience simply because it will "read" side light more readily than back light. Thus, dramatic lighting effects can be established through the creative use of strong side light.

Stage Lighting Practice

Lighting the Actor
(Top) Side light from the right, 45-degree angle. (Center) Side light from the right, 30-degree angle. (Bottom) Side light from the right and left, 30-degree angle. Note the shadow in the center of the face.

124 *Stage Lighting*

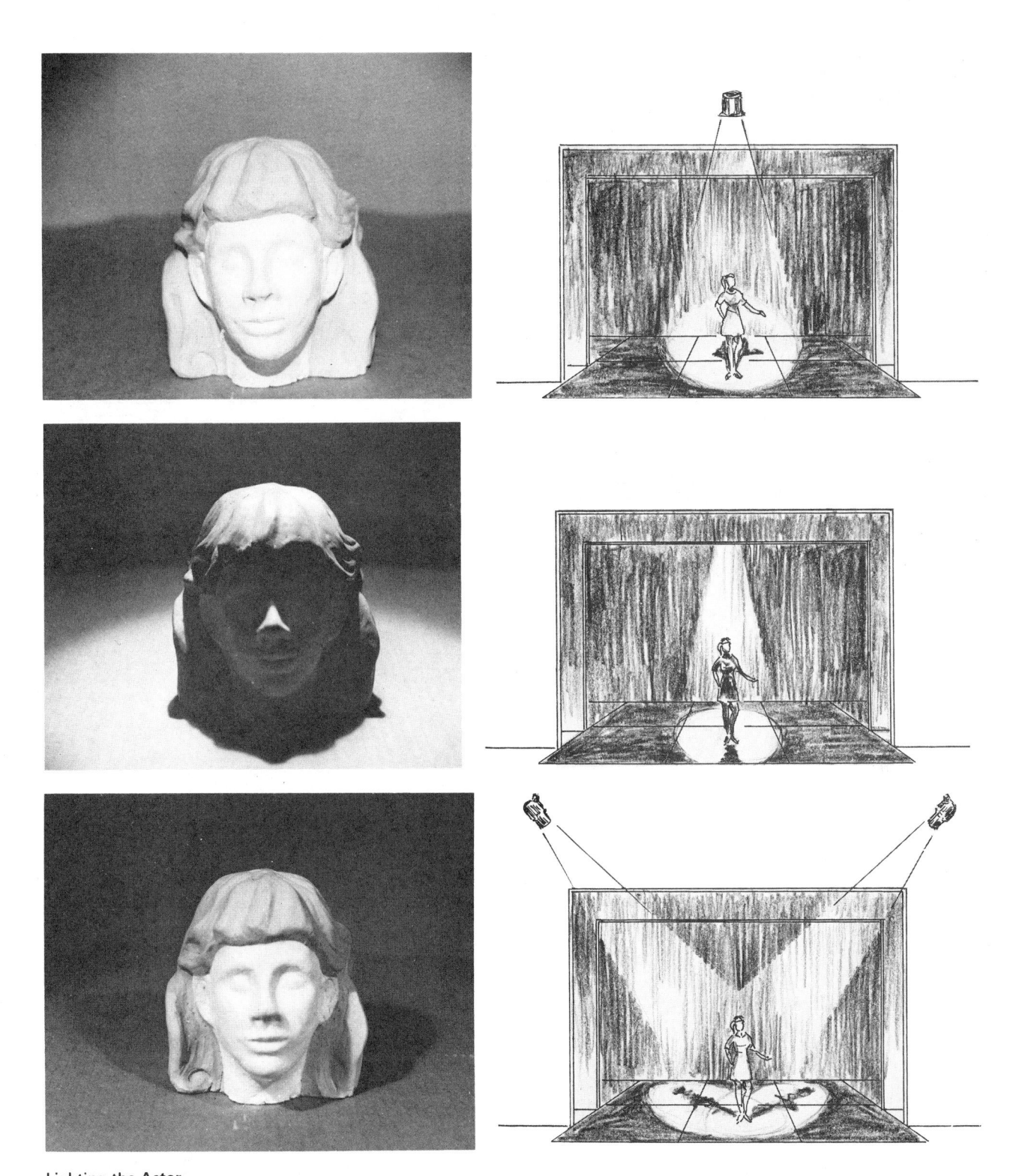

Lighting the Actor

(Top) Full front light. Note lack of definition. (Center) Backlight producing a halo or "rim" effect. (Bottom) Three angles: right and left front light and back light. The key light is from the left from a 45-degree angle, fill light from the right front and rim light from the overhead rear.

Stage Lighting Practice

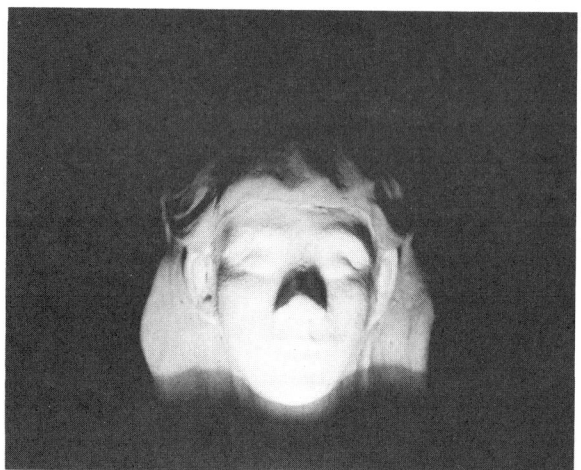

Lighting the Actor
(Top) Downlight or "pool," 90-degree angle. (Bottom) Upward angle from the footlights or apron. An unnatural, though dramatic, angle.

Lighting the Acting Area

Lighting an actor from various positions and angles is, of course, easy if the subject is posed or remains in a fixed position on stage. The actor, however, usually moves. Therefore, to produce the same uniformity of coverage as on a stationary figure, the lighting designer must constantly duplicate the focus of spotlights on many similar areas over the entire playing area.

By dividing the playing portion of the setting into convenient areas and then lighting each area with the same number of spotlights, the acting area is covered with a balanced illumination. The area method of lighting the actor, which was first developed by Stanley McCandless in the 1930s, has proved a very efficient and systematic technique. As scenery style has changed and lighting instrument design has improved, the method has been modified and expanded. The original

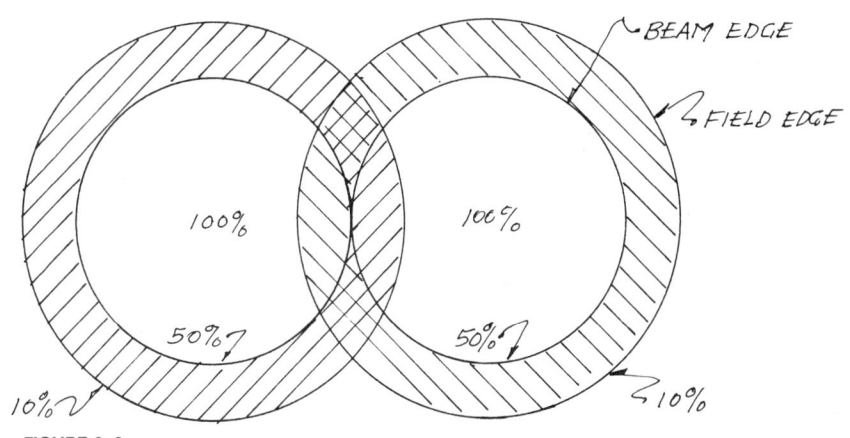

FIGURE 8–3
ERS Beam Alignment for a Smooth Field

concept of providing a smooth coverage through the use of a minimum of instruments has given way to double and triple hanging in the name of greater flexibility in color control and distribution. The resulting number of lighting instruments used in some shows is staggering. Although the area method was first developed for the proscenium theatre it has been readily adapted to other theatre forms such as thrust and arena (see Chapter 10).

In using the area system, one of the things a designer learns is that areas must overlap considerably or the actor will pass through dark spots ("dips") in lighting when moving from one area to another. A general rule of thumb for this overlap is to align adjacent instruments beam edge to beam edge, thus producing 100 percent light throughout (Figure 8–3). Ideal lighting angles often must be compromised. An example particular to lighting the proscenium stage is illustrated by the placement of instruments 1-L and 3-R in Figure 8–5, page 129. Since the desired 45-degree angle is impossible to maintain bacause of the proscenium arch, these instruments must be shifted toward center until they adequately cover the area.

The placement and choice of the number of areas are the lighting designer's decision and, of course, vary with the size and shape of the setting (Figure 8–4, page 128). However, in general, areas will vary from 6 to 10 feet in diameter, with 8-foot areas being a good average. Of course, area size is determined by beam spread along with throw distance of a given lighting instrument. The young designer should consider making up a beam and field spread template for each of the instruments in common use. Such a template, drawn to scale on drafting or tracing paper, can be used as an overlay on a sectional view of the theatre and will quickly show approximate area coverage.

The action of the play or the staging of the production also helps to determine the number of areas and the distribution of the coverage.

Stage Lighting Practice

FIGURE 8–4

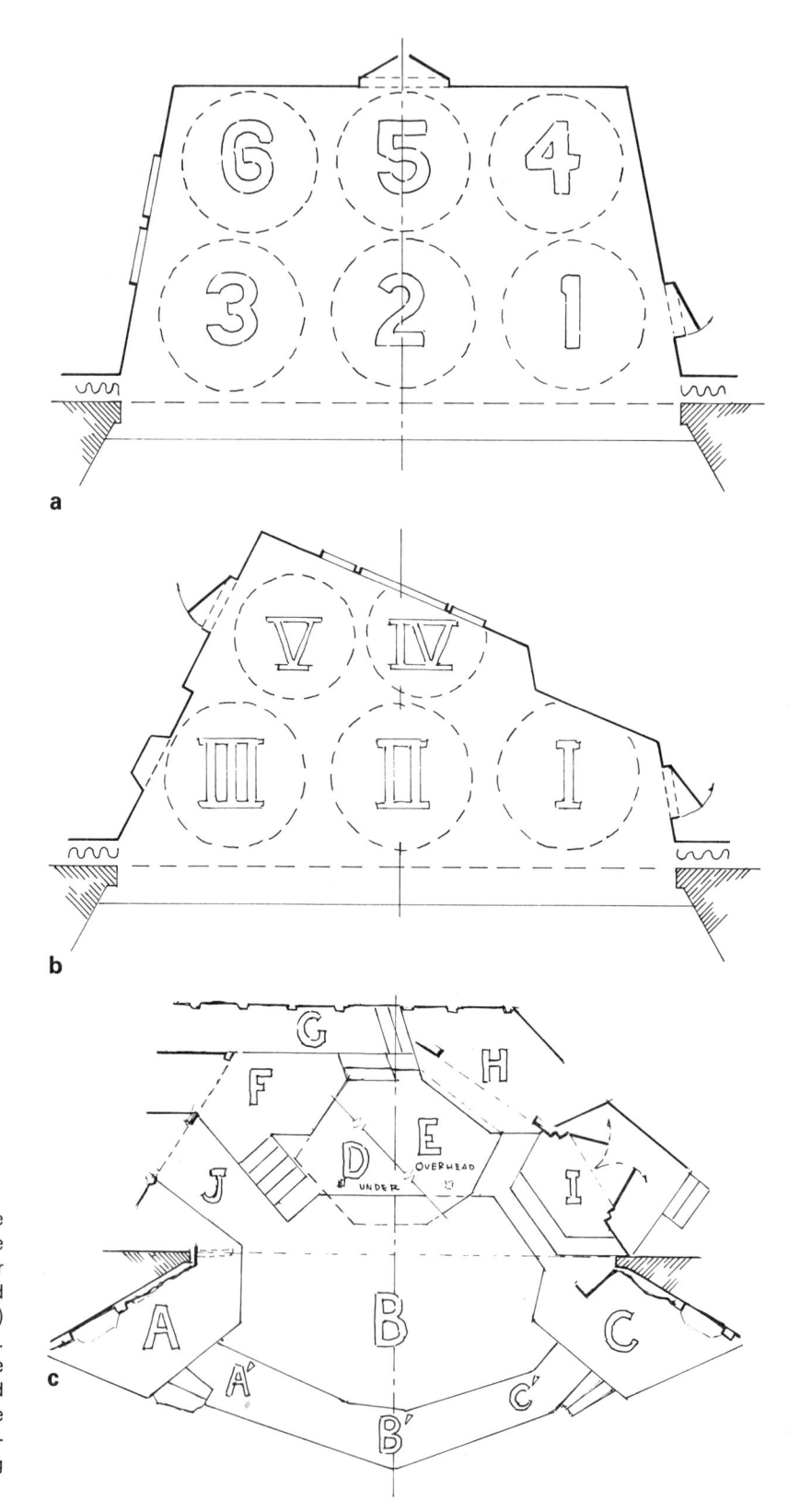

The Acting Areas

(a) A conventional box setting. Note the numbering of the areas from down-stage left to up-stage right. The total number of areas will vary with the shape and number of settings in the production. (b) An irregularly shaped interior setting. Some designers prefer to designate the areas with Roman numerals to avoid confusion. (c) A complicated set. For ease of communication, the director may establish areas and labels and the lighting designer may use the same system.

Stage Lighting

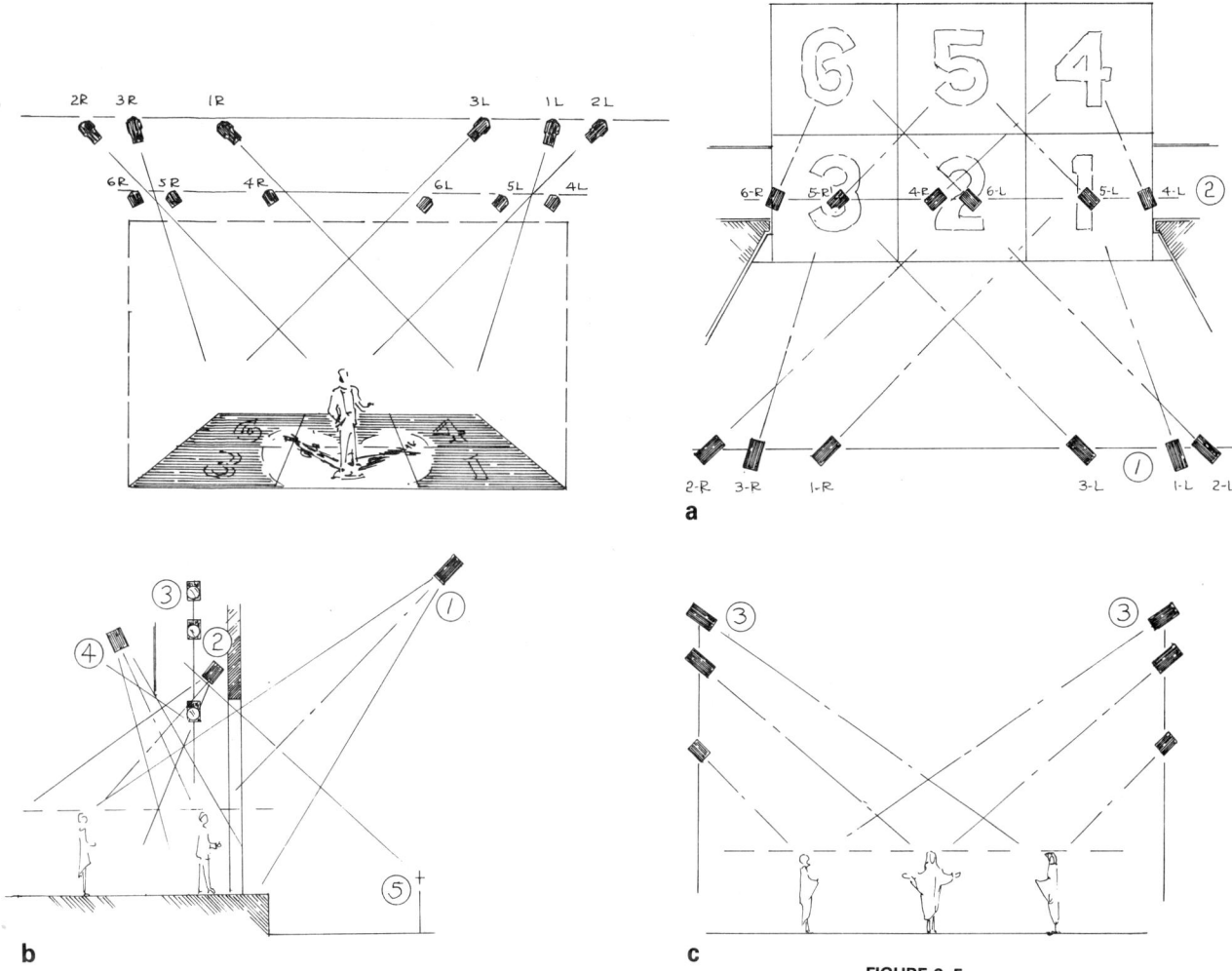

In a multiscene production some of the areas can be planned for use in more than one set, providing the floor plans are close to the same configuration.

One bit of advice: Most directors and actors have a tendency to love center stage (actors have been known to be attracted to center stage much like moths to a flame), so the prudent lighting designer should be sure to have a controllable center area.

Area Flexibility

The demand for greater and greater flexibility in area lighting stems from the trend toward increasingly complex staging, more frequent repertory organizations (where several shows are kept in rotation), and high labor costs that force the elimination of unnecessary handling or manual operation of equipment. It is cheaper, for example, to hang a few extra instruments than to pay an electrician to be present at each performance to change a color medium.

FIGURE 8–5

Lighting the Acting Areas

(a) The area system with a minimum of spotlights for each area. (1) Beam or ceiling position in front of the proscenium covering the downstage areas, 1, 2, and 3. (2) Teaser position. Spotlights on the first pipe batten upstage of teaser or proscenium opening are focused on the upstage areas, 4, 5, and 6. (b) A sectional view of the area system. (1) Beam spots. (2) Teaser spots. (3) Side lights and (4) back lights are additional angles that can be added into each area. (5) Extreme vertical sightline. (c) Front view showing the angle of side lighting for areas 1, 2, and 3.

Stage Lighting Practice

129

Double Hanging. To improve the limited flexibility of simple cross lighting the designer can hang two more instruments, right and left, as additional lights for each area (Figure 8–6a). By duplicating the area coverage on each side, several possibilities for color control are created. The designer can (1) change the warm-cool accent from left to right; (2) change the area color by independently mixing the colors from either the right or left; or (3) flood the stage with only one of the two area colors. If the setting is open enough to permit it, the back lights can also be double hung, providing even further flexibility.

Triple Hanging. A third spotlight may be added to each position lighting an area (Figure 8–6b). The extra light can given further dimension to color control, increase the intensity of the area, and provide greater flexibility of distribution for the area. An area, for example, can have both tight and wide coverage. To achieve tight coverage, the two extra spots are focused onto a smaller portion of the stage so that the focus on the scene is more concentrated.

Distribution Flexibility. Double and triple hanging offer the designer excellent color control, but an additional degree of flexibility can be achieved by varying the angle and direction of light. If side lighting (either from the wings or from a more frontal side position such as the traditional box booms) is added to area lights, the designer can then alter color as well as direction. For example, front-of-house right instruments can work with the stage-right side lights.

High side can be hung in addition to low side to create a different quality and color tonality for a given scene. Low-angle front-of-house sources called "washes" are often hung on a balcony rail and can be subtly used to change color tonality as well as the texture of a scene. However, care must be taken in using this rather flat angle in order not to lose dimensionality and lighting quality.

The possibilities are endless, and the more a lighting designer ex-

FIGURE 8–6
Double and Triple Hanging
(a) Double hanging on the stage left side. Only the downstage areas, 1, 2, and 3, are shown. The stage-right beam spots are cool in color while the spots on the left are both warm and cool to allow a color selection in the acting areas. (b) Triple hanging on area 2, double hanging on areas 1 and 3. The center area has a tight and open focus as well as a selection of color and direction of key light in each area.

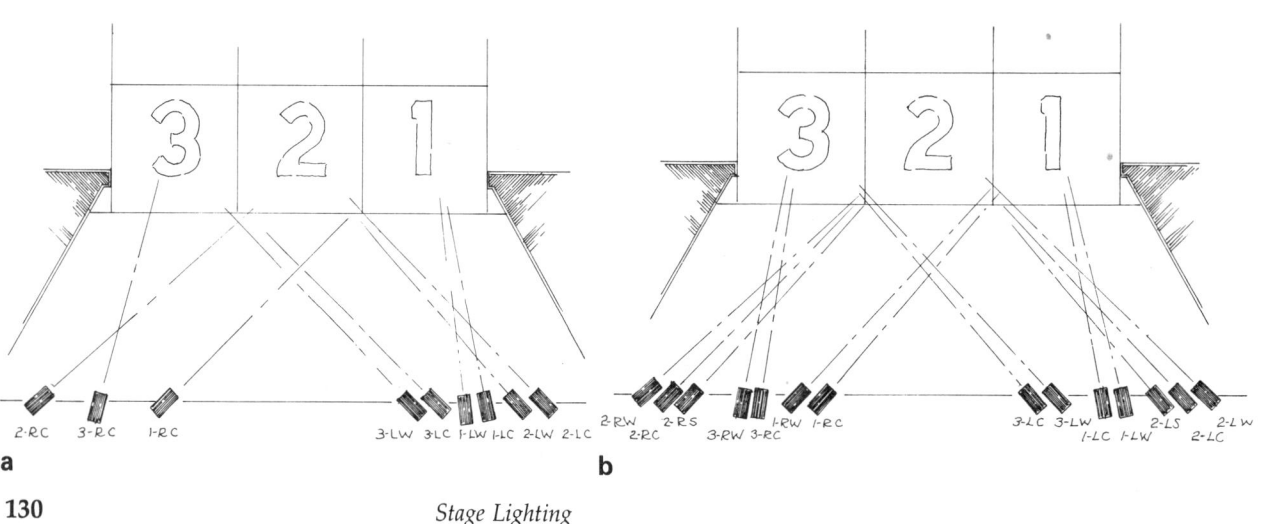

Stage Lighting

periments with area flexibility, the more diverse and exciting the product can be.

Area Specials and Special Visibility

Area specials are a variation of regular area lighting that uses instruments to specifically define or emphasize a part of the setting or draw attention to an actor at a given moment and in a certain position on the stage. Examples include a door special, an extra spot carefully framed to catch an actor in the doorway; a couch special, extra punch on the couch or settee where an important scene takes place; or a pin spot, a narrow beam of light on an actor's face that is held a moment longer than the rest of the stage lights on a final dim-out. Area specials influence composition by pulling the eye to the center of action.

Special visibility deals with the moving actor under more arbitrary or abstract conditions. The movement of light can be achieved in one of two ways. The actor can be covered by a series of carefully focused spotlights on the path of movement that dim up and down at the proper moments. The more traditional method is to use a follow spot. The movement of the actor is followed by a single freely mounted spotlight. The follow spot has long been in use in musical comedies, revues, and other presentational productions, where realism is of minor importance. It usually appears as a sharply defined, brilliant circle of light outshining all the stage lights.

Another form of follow spotting, often referred to as "European follow spotting" after the practice of placing follow spots and operators on a first light bridge, has become fairly popular for more dramatic productions. Unlike American Broadway musical follow spotting, the goal of European follow spotting is subtlety. A soft-edged incandescent follow spot is used to highlight the action unobtrusively. A vertical angle closer to 60 degrees than 45 degrees is preferable in order to mininize shadows around the actor. With good operation European follow spotting can be an extremely effective lighting technique.

Area Control

We now must touch on the tricky problem of control. Unless fortunate enough to be working in a situation offering unlimited dimmer control (such as that provided by dimmer-per-circuit installations), the designer must soon face the task of assigning instruments to dimmers. Color control is normally a high priority; seldom will it be desirable to have two sets of instruments of differing colors on the same dimmer. Area control is the next priority; which stage areas should be controlled individually and which "ganged" or grouped together? The latter is a critical decision, for the designer must work with the chosen control flexibility throughout the production. Before a choice is made, the designer should view rehearsals and discuss questions of control with the director.

Although there will never be absolute rules of control priorities, the following is suggested as a beginning:

1. Control of the front-of-house "visibility" area lighting is most important.
2. Area control of side-lighting sources, although of secondary importance, is still important.
3. Area control of back or top light is of least importance unless the stage floor and its composition are visible to the majority of the audience.

Of course, most specials require their own control channel but can be re-patched at an intermission in many instances. Don't forget to assign control for practicals, house lights if necessary, and curtain warmers or stage toners. Also, it is always good practice to save a couple of dimmers as spares in case of dimmer failure or additional control requirements are made during final rehearsals.

LIGHTING THE BACKGROUND

The mood of the environment surrounding the action of the scene is often so fully expressed in the intensity, color, and distribution of the area lighting that, except for special occasions, the area lights provide the major portion of the illumination of the setting.

In the case of a conventional interior or box setting, the area light will usually suffice to light the walls of the set. However, several precautions are necessary to make such wall illumination successful. Too often we see a box set with the stage-right wall a totally different color from that of the stage-left wall. This appallingly common mistake, a result of poor color mixing from the frontal-area instruments, can be corrected by making sure that all frontal colors hit the walls with relatively equal intensity. Instruments lighting the walls of a box set should be put into soft focus if they are ellipsoidals in a front-of-house position. Over-stage instruments should be Fresnels or frosted ellipsoidals.

Shadows from actors or furniture are a problem that may be difficult to solve. The best solution is to change the angle of light causing the shadow, but at times this may not be possible. Instead, a wall wash, using 6-inch Fresnels, or even strip lights, will help (but not solve the problem completely).

Background areas and backings, however, are a different matter. Many times the lighting problem may be small, for example the backing behind a doorway, rarely seen for more than a moment at a time, and then not directly by most of the audience. Not very elaborate equipment is needed to give these backings enough illumination so that an actor, when leaving the stage, does not seem to be retiring into a dark closet.

Backings can assume greater proportions, for example a section of exterior seen through a large window which might contain groundrows of distant hills or hedges and a section of sky. Rooftops or the exterior walls of an adjoining building may also be seen in a more detailed backing. Such backings usually demand greater attention to distribution and color control (to perhaps simulate different times of day) than would the simple doorway backing.

For the most complicated backgrounds, such as vast areas of sky sometimes with a painted scenic vista, large backdrops or cycloramas are usually used. These require rows of high-wattage instruments, both from above and below, in order to give the proper amount of light as well as even distribution and blending of color over the entire surface. Greater control of color is required if the mood of the background is expected to change with the time of day. Changes in distribution can also occur, especially if the backdrop is partly translucent, allowing a cross-fading from front lighting to back lighting furnished by an additional bank of lights behind the drop.

Scrim is a particularly useful material because of its capability to appear either opaque or transparent. Scrim in front of a backdrop or cyclorama will add the somewhat hazy quality of distance to the backing. The scrim itself can be lit, or, better yet, the drop behind the scrim may be illuminated (Figure 8–7c). Scrim may also be used alone as a drop, in which case the designer will most certainly need to pay close attention to the light that falls directly on as well as behind the scrim. A high-angle top light is the best means to create an opaque scrim. To

FIGURE 8–7
Lighting the Background

Various methods of lighting the backdrop and background arrangements. (a) Painted backdrop (1) lit from above and below. (5) Floor striplights behind a groundrow. (6) Overhead strip behind a border. (b) Painted backdrop (1) lit only from above. (c) Translucent drop (3) is illuminated by backlight reflected off a reflecting drop (2) lit by floor strips (7) and overhead strips (8). Frontlight comes from a second overhead strip (9). (d) A translucent drop upstage of a scrim. The drop has front and back lighting to change its quality or time of day. The scrim has front lighting to add depth and atmosphere. (10) Floor strip. (11) Overhead strips for backlighting. (3) Translucent drop. (12) Floor strip. (13) Overhead strip for front lighting. (4) Scrim. (14) Overhead strip for frontlighting scrim.

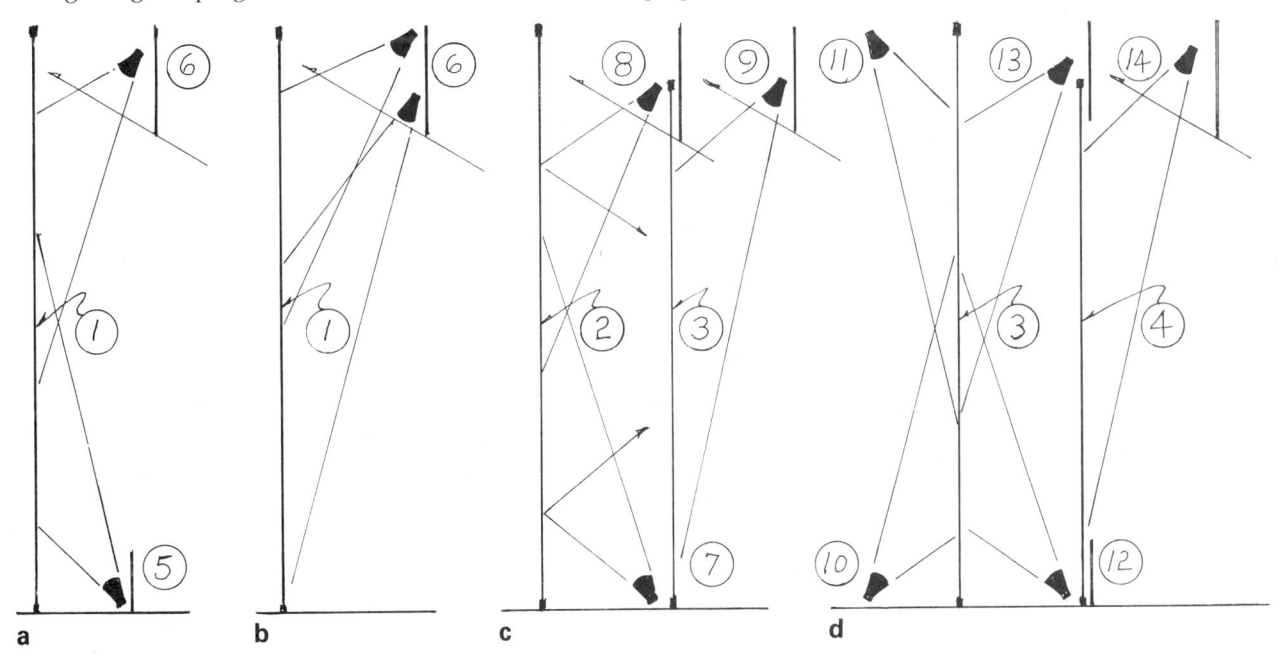

Stage Lighting Practice

make a scrim transparent, keep as much light as possible off the scrim itself while illuminating objects behind it.

Successful background lighting depends on the close cooperation of the lighting and scene designers. All too often the scene designer does not leave enough space between groundrows and the backdrop or between borders and the cyclorama to allow sufficient distance for proper distribution of the striplights. Backgrounds representing distant fields are sometimes so close to a window or door that it is impossible to keep the area lights from casting shadows on the background, thereby destroying any illusion of distance.

DESIGN DECISIONS

The designer is constantly making decisions concerning type and position of instruments, color filtering, and dimmer readings. We have discussed many of the technical considerations in making decisions about lighting design and now will look at the aesthetics of such decisions. The lighting designer must be equipped to make choices involving instrumentation, angle, color, and finally, dimmer readings.

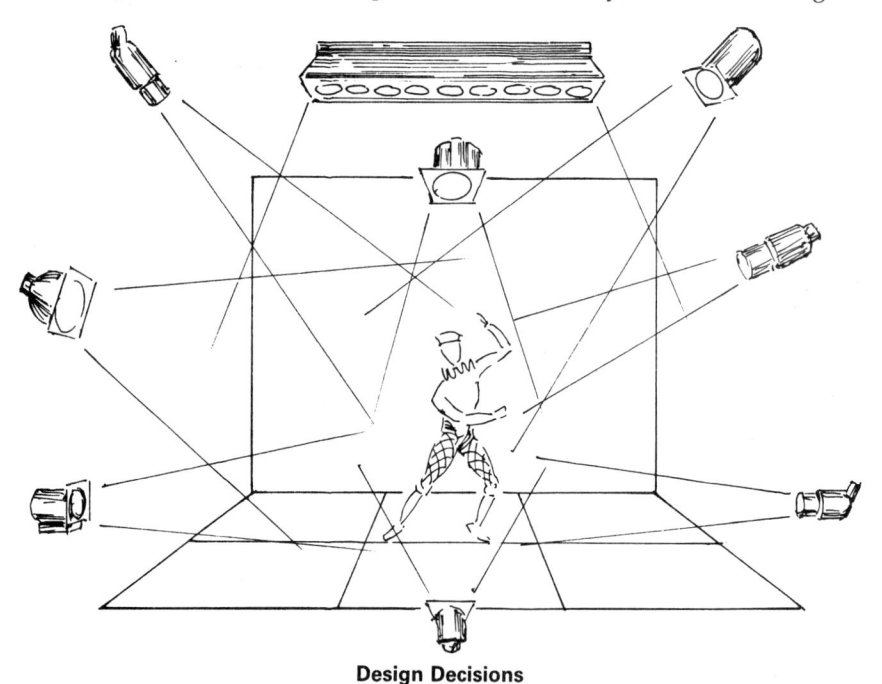

Design Decisions

Choice of Instrument Does it support an incandescent or fluorescent; practical, daylight, sunlight, moonlight, etc.?
Choice of Angle What is best position for the actor, director, costume, or set designer? View from balcony
Choice of Dimmer Reading(s) Intensity, movement, focus, nonverbal communication.
Choice of Color Motivation, nature, or optional. Brilliance, atmosphere, style.

**FIGURE 8–8
Design Decisions**

Choice of Instrument

As previously noted, a particular stage-lighting instrument will be chosen because it comes closest to satisfying requirements of intensity, coverage, and quality of light. Adjustability of beam spread and field quality of most of the new ellipsoidal reflector spotlights (ERS) along with increased light output certainly make this instrument the most valuable for the lighting designer (Figure 8–9). While the ERS is the logical choice for front-of-house, this workhorse of a unit also serves well backstage and should be considered along with the Fresnel, beam projector, and PAR can.

The Fresnel delivers a soft light whose beam blends very easily and therefore is ideal for upstage areas of a box set (Figure 8–10). Fresnels, having a tremendously variable beam spread, can be used over a wide range of throw distances: the 6-inch Fresnel lamped at 500 or 750 watts is effective to somewhat more than 20 feet, and the 8-inch Fresnel with lamps up to 2000 watts can be useful up to 40 feet. The soft light of a candle, the quality of dusk or an overcast sky, or the scattered, almost shadowless light from fluorescent tubes will all be most closely reproduced by using the Fresnel.

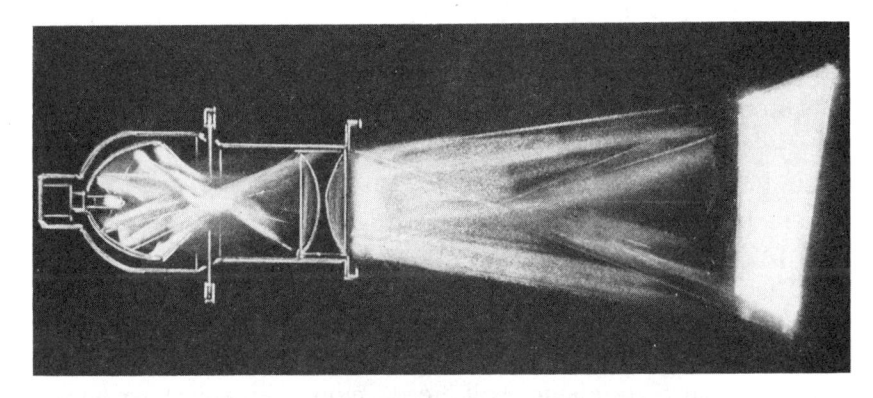

FIGURE 8–9
Ellipsoidal Reflector Spotlight

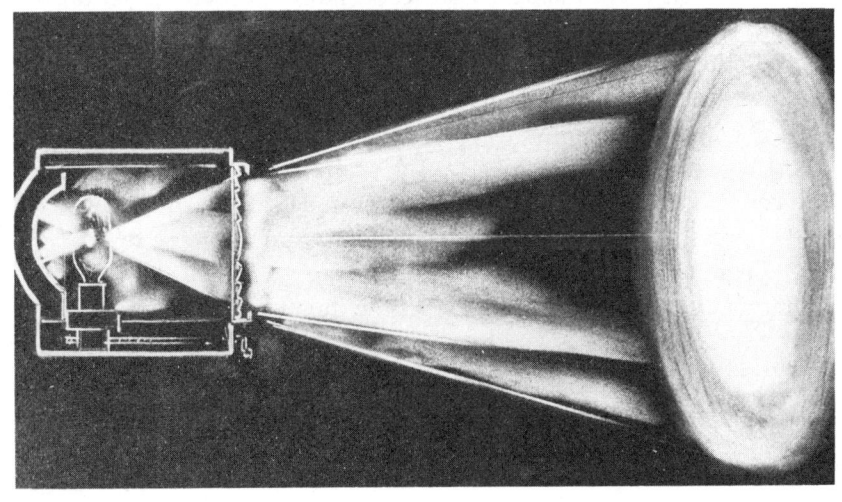

FIGURE 8–10
Fresnel Spotlight

Stage Lighting Practice

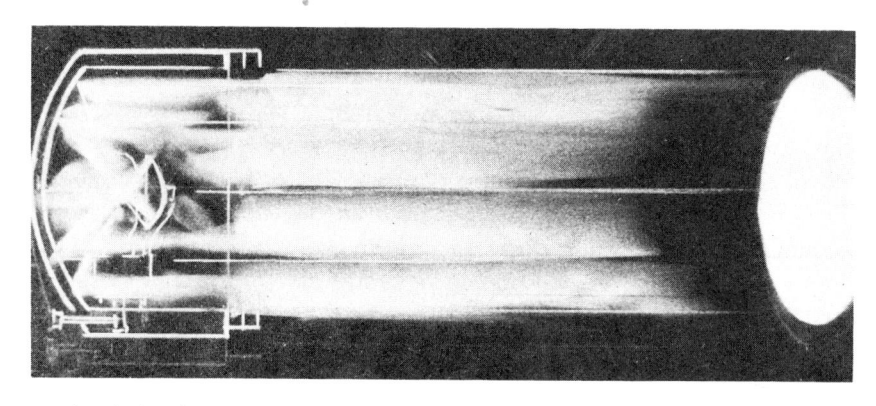

FIGURE 8-11
Beam Projector

The light from a beam projector cannot be shaped, but its near-parallel rays come closest to those of the sun (Figure 8–11). This quality can serve as a motivational source, whereas Fresnel and even ERS light will act as fill or bounce. Banks of beam projectors have been employed as "walls" of light shooting from an over-stage batten.

The PAR can, like the beam projector, has a parabolic reflector, but the lens of its lamp breaks up the light enough to cause a softer-edged beam than that of a beam projector. Yet, the PAR still delivers a sharp and intense light, harsh in quality. Remember, its beam is oval and cannot be shaped. PAR cans make good back lights and deliver a nice quality of light for dance.

Choice of Angle

Angle and color are probably the two most difficult choices for the young designer to make.

The purpose of two front lights at angles of 45 degrees each, rather than a single unit straightaway, is to add dimension to the actor's body and face. As the angle of front light is lowered, it tends to flatten features more and more. As the angle is raised, features become sharper and sharper, with deeper and deeper shadows. Remember that front light is what the audience will "read" more than any other angle of light.

Whether it be a bit frontal or straight out of the wings, side light is an exciting angle for both variety and revelation of form. A low angle side, such as that commonly used in dance lighting, will light the entire height of the body fairly evenly. The problem is that it is quite difficult to control. Therefore, a slightly higher angle side (from 30 degrees to 60 degrees) is often used in the theatre. Here is where the designer can begin to use richer and more expressive colors in order to establish a motivational source or simply set the mood for a scene.

Choice of Color

Color selection requires experience—experience in observing traditional theatrical usage (blue = night), experience in color mixing, as well as experience in knowing how a given color will act on stage. The lighting laboratory and color mix-box will help, but the lighting designer ultimately has to do some experimenting with the real thing. A masterful use of color can be one of the most exciting elements of stage lighting, but it takes time and taste.

Try to analyze color by feeling as well as seeing—how does sunlight feel? Then translate the feeling into color. This is why a visual memory is so important, for we tend to store feelings more than angstrom units. Why does the warmth of sunlight *feel* different than the warmth of a fireplace fire? It has something to do with color.

Throw distance tends to affect the intensity or saturation of a color—colors appear more saturated over shorter throw distances.

Choice of Dimmer Readings

Setting dimmer levels for the first time will probably be a painful and time-consuming experience, but be assured that it gets easier. Force yourself to write your dimmer levels "blind" several days before actually seeing them on stage. Take the time to think through each preset or stage picture: Which sets of instruments should be reading highest and which control areas should take focus? Write the levels on your "cheat sheets" (more information to come) and have your board operator transfer them to standard preset sheets or directly into the memory of a computer system. You will find that this process of writing blind takes a good deal of time, but it ultimately results in a better-looking product and can cut hours off a technical rehearsal.

In general, it is best to write and design for the highest dimmer levels to be between 80 and 90 percent. Then, if more light is required, you have room to maneuver. Depending on the curve of your dimmers, a reading of 10 percent will barely warm the filament, and a reading of 20 percent will just begin to deliver light. Keep in mind the saturation of color filters, for the more saturated filters will cut down light transmission significantly. Finally, always remember that the perceived intensity of light is relative.

THE LIGHT PLOT

The light plot and its accompanying paperwork (the instrument schedule, hookup, and section) forms the link between the designer's ideas and the reality of theatrical production. The importance of this piece of paper cannot be overstated. It must be 100 percent accurate and complete so that the "put-in" (hang, circuit, focus) can proceed in an orderly and rapid fashion. The simple process of executing a plot enables the designer to discover and eliminate many artistic as well as technical problems well before ever setting foot in the theatre.

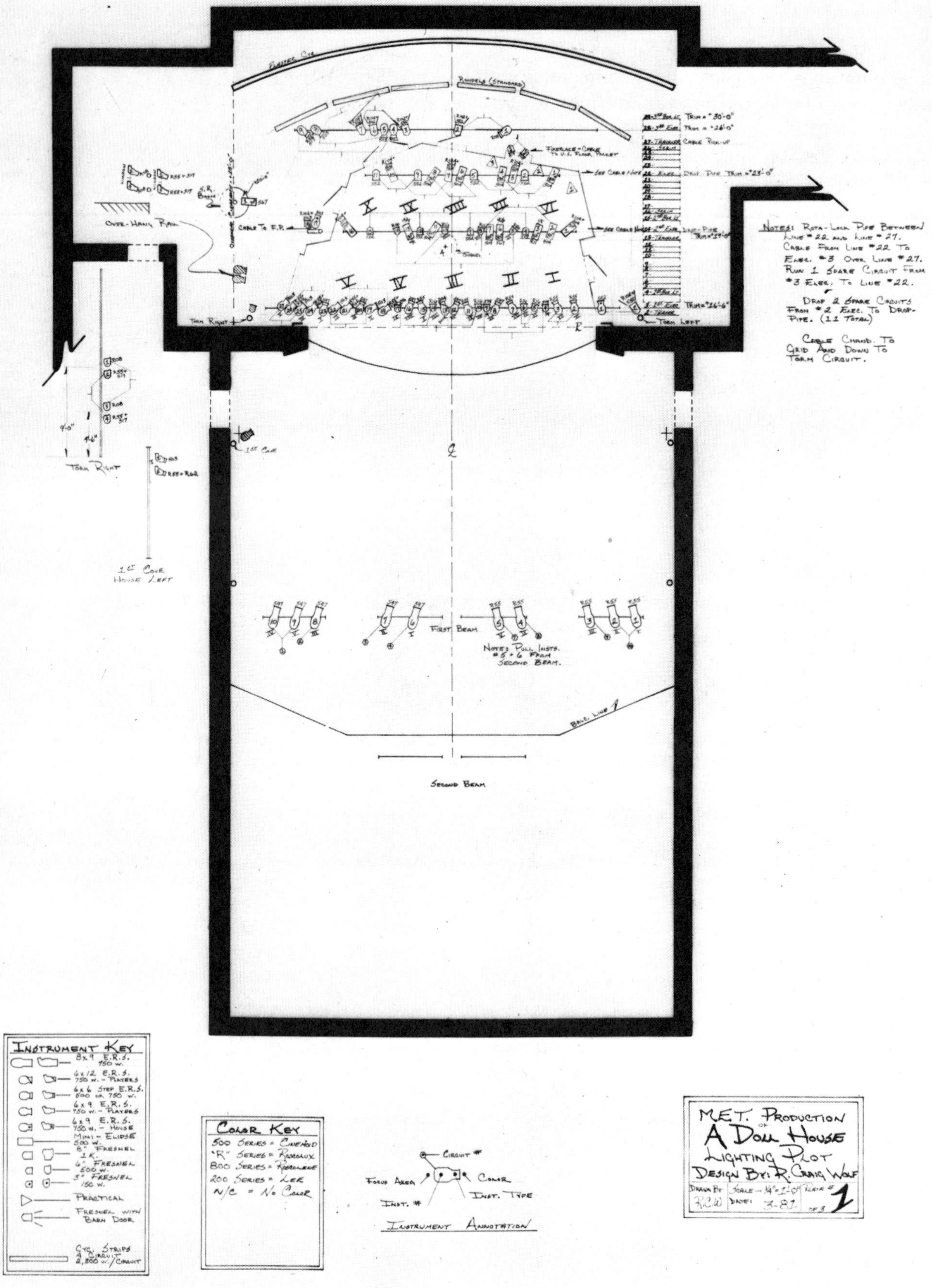

Notes: Rota-Lock Pipe Between Line #22 and Line #27. Cable From Line #22 To Elec. #3 Over Line #27. Run 1 Spare Circuit From #3 Elec. To Line #22.
Drop 2 Spare Circuits From #2 Elec. To Drop-Pipe. (11 Total)
Cable Chand. To Grid And Down To Torm Circuit.
Over-Hang Rail
Cable To F.P.
Torm Right
Torm Left
1st Cove
1st Cove House Left
First Beam
Note: Pull Insts. #5 + 6 From Second Beam.
Balc. Line
Second Beam
Instrument Key
8x9 E.R.S. 750 w.
6x12 E.R.S. 750 w. - Players
6x6 Step E.R.S. 500 or 750 w.
6x9 E.R.S. 750 w. - Players
6x9 E.R.S. 750 w. - House
Mini - Elipse 500 w.
8" Fresnel 1K.
6" Fresnel 500 w.
3" Fresnel 150 w.
Practical
Fresnel with Barn Door
Cyc. Strips 4 Circuit 2,300 w./Circuit
Color Key
500 Series = Cinemoid
"R" Series = Roscolux
800 Series = Roscolene
200 Series = Lee
N/C = No Color
Circuit #
Focus Area
Color
Inst. #
Inst. Type
Instrument Annotation
M.E.T. Production of
A Doll House
Lighting Plot
Design By: R. Craig Wolf
Drawn By: R.C.W.
Scale — 1/4" = 1'-0"
Date: 3-81
Plate # 1 of 3

Working on the premise that some standardization is desirable for any communicative tool, the light plot should include the following:

1. A plan of the theatre drawn to scale (preferably ½ inch—*never* ⅛ inch) showing and labeling all lighting positions.
2. A plan of the stage setting drawn to scale in light weight lines.
3. The lighting areas indicated by Roman numerals in heavy weight lines beginning down-stage left, working stage right and then up-stage.
4. Exact instrument placement, type and size, color and number.
5. Title block in lower right-hand corner, instrument key, instrument annotation key, and color key.

The Theatre Plan. This plan should show all rigging for the production, including masking, flying scenery and drops, as well as electric pipes. Critical audience sight points must be included. It is permissible to show distance to front-of-house lighting positions in a smaller scale, but this deviation should be noted. A lighting position is indicated by a single, solid line of medium weight. All positions must be clearly labeled.

Some designers prefer to include a plaster line scale and sometimes an up- to down-stage scale in order to facilitate hanging and placement of instruments. Refer to Figure 8–12 for examples.

The Stage Setting. The lighting designer's set plan need not be as complete as the scene designer's floor plan, but it should include elements of importance to lighting such as walls, doors, major levels, large pieces of furniture, and so forth. Plaster line and center line should be included. If the production requires several sets, the lighting designer may use transparent overlays of each set.

Instrument Annotation. One of the several available lighting instrument templates should be used to trace outlines of the various instruments (Figure 8–13, page 140). Templates can be ordered in either ¼- or ½-inch scale as well as in plan or sectional view. These outlines must be bold enough to stand out from all the other information on the plot. While the lighting instrument should intersect the lighting pipe, the pipe should never be drawn through the instrument. In most situations, instruments are numbered by position beginning house-

FIGURE 8–12

The Light Plot

A light plot for Michigan Ensemble Theatre's production of Ibsen's *A Doll House*. The theatre is a fairly typical proscenium with limited front-of-house lighting positions. Visibility instrumentation front-of-house is colored in R55 and 547. Double-hung back light is 504 and 552. Double-hung high side motivational sources from stage right are colored with R55 and R62 in one instrument and 503 in the second. A ½-inch-scale hanging plot was developed in addition to the ¼-inch-scale plot shown to clarify circuiting and distribution. Scene design by W. Oren Parker; lighting design by R. Craig Wolf.

Stage Lighting Practice

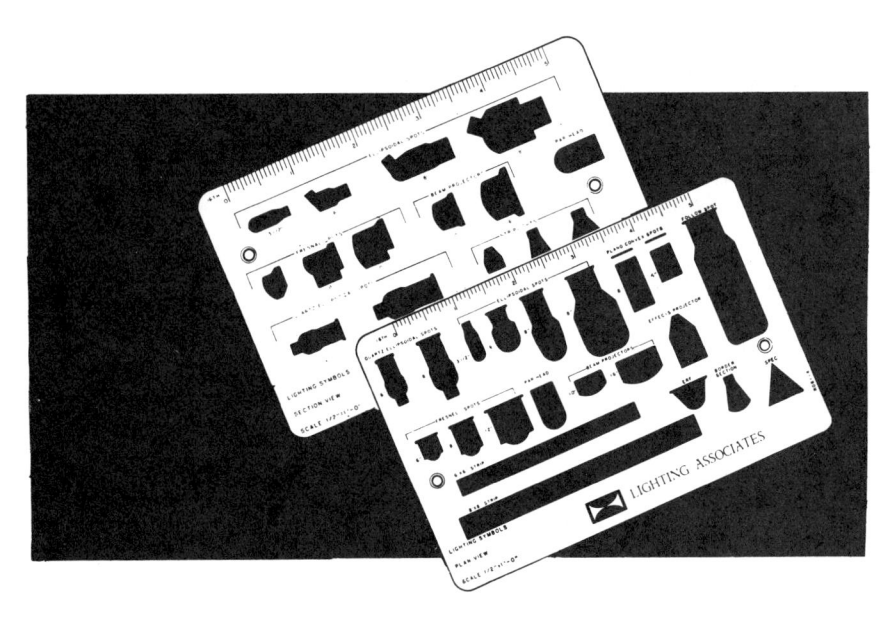

FIGURE 8–13
A Standard Lighting Template

right at the rear and working on-stage. Numbering by position means that all instruments in each position are numbered consecutively beginning with one (Figure 8–12). Some situations, however, may make numbering by position rather confusing (for example, a flexible theatre with a full overhead lighting grid). In such cases, *all* instruments should be numbered consecutively.

The instrument annotation shown in Figure 8–14 is recommended, although some designers might prefer not to include circuits, dimmers, or focus area on the plot itself.

The accepted method of indicating *type* of instrument is to crossmark the barrel, as illustrated in Figure 8–15.

Of course, all notation is explained in the instrument key.

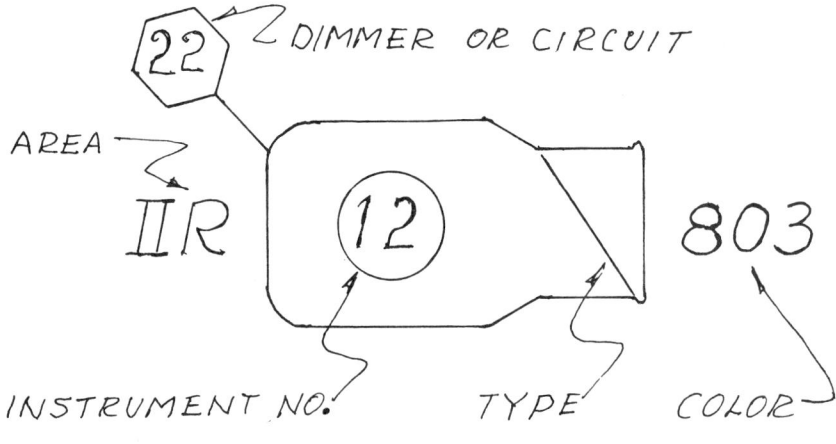

FIGURE 8–14
Instrument Annotation

Stage Lighting

Instrument and Color Keys. The instrument key indicates exactly which symbol the designer is using for a specific instrument. This key, which should include the wattage as well as the focal length or beam spread of the instrument, is normally located in the lower left corner of the plate.

The color key explains what numbering and lettering system the designer is using for each brand and type of color medium. For example:

"R" Series = Roscolux
800 Series = Roscolene
500 Series = Cinemoid
100 and 200 Series = Lee
"G" Series = Geletran

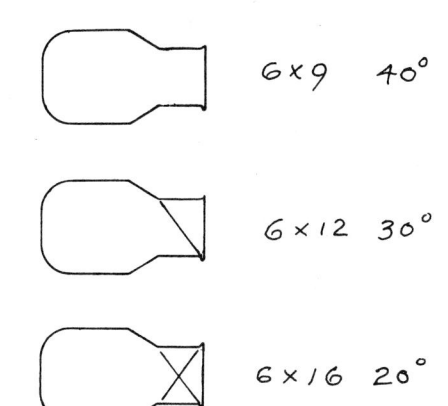

FIGURE 8–15
Instrument Types

Instrument Schedule and Hook-Up

Both these documents provide additional instrument information to an electrician, but each has a different purpose. The instrument schedule lists all instruments by location and instrument number and contains the following information in the following order:

1. Location and instrument number
2. Instrument type (specific)
3. Wattage/lamp designation
4. Color number
5. Use/focus area
6. Circuit
7. Dimmer/channel
8. Remarks

This schedule is simply a list of complete information about any given lighting instrument, some of which might not be included on the plot (Figure 8–16, page 142).

The hook-up lists instruments by dimmer number. The first column of this schedule should contain dimmer number, followed by circuit number, location and instrument number, type, focus, and color (see Figure 8–24, page 155).

Both documents are seldom necessary; the designer's preference as well as specific production requirements will determine which one is best to use.

The Lighting Section

The center-line section is important to the lighting designer as a tool to help assure plot accuracy. An electrician need never see the section, but the designer will consult it for vertical slightlines, throw distances,

Stage Lighting Practice

M.E.T.' Production of "A Doll House" Lighting "Instrument" Schedule — R.C.W. 3-'81

Instrument Location and Number	Type	Watt	Color	Use	Circuit	Dimmer	Remarks
Beam #1 1	6x9 ERS	750	R55	I	10	2B	"Y" w/ #2
2	—	—	R55	II	10	2B	"Y" w/ #1
3	—	—	R55	III	9	2A	
4	—	—	R55	IV	8	M2	
5	—	—	R55	V	7	M2	
6	—	—	547	I	4	1C	
7	—	—	547	II	3	1C	
8	—	—	547	III	2	1B	
9	—	—	547	V	1	1A	"Y" w/ #10
10	—	—	547	IV	1	1A	"Y" w/ #9
Cove #1 H.L. #1	6x6 ERS	750	503	I		5	
2	—	—	R55 R62	I		6	
Torm Left #1	8" Fres	1K	R102 552	Door Back		3B	Barn Door
Torm Rt. #1	6" Fres	500	R08	Window Back		5	"Y" w/ #3
2	—	—	R55 517	—		6	"Y" w/ #4
3	—		R08	—		5	"Y" w/ #1
4			R55 517	—		6	"Y" w/ #2
Elec. #1 #1 1	6x9 ERS	750	552	Door Back		3B	
2	6x6 ERS	500	R55	VI		2E	"Y" w/ #3
3	—	—	R55	VII		2E	"Y" w/ #2
4	3" Fres.	500	575	Mama Sp.		H1*	*Act I Only "Y" w/ #9
5	—	—	R16	VI		M3	"Y" w/ #6
6	—	—	R16	VII		M3	"Y" w/ #5
7	6x6 ERS	500	R55	VIII		2D	
8	—	—	547	VI		M1	
9	6" Fres	500	575	Mama Sp.		H1*	*Act I Only "Y" w/ #4
10	—	—	R16	VII		3E	"Y" w/ #14 + #17
11	6x6 ERS	—	R55	IX		2C	
12	—	—	547	VII		M1	
13	6x12 ERS	750	204	Door Sp.		H2	
14	6" Fres.	500	R16	VIII		3E	"Y" w/ #17 + #10
15	6x6 ERS	—	R55	X		2C	
16	—	—	547	VIII		1E	
17	6" Fres.	—	R16	IX		3E	"Y" w/ #10 + #14
18	6x9 ERS	750	R55 R62	II		6	"Y" w/ #21
19	—	—	503	II		5	"Y" w/ #22
20	6x6 ERS	500	547	IX		1D	
21	6x9 ERS	750	R55 R62	III		6	"Y" w/ #18
22	—	—	503	III		5	"Y" w/ #19
23	6x6 ERS	500	547	X		1D	
24	6x9 ERS	750	R55 R62	IV		6	"Y" w/ #26
25	—	—	503	IV		5	"Y" w/ #27
26	—	—	R55 R62	V		6	"Y" w/ #24
27	—	—	503	V		5	"Y" w/ #25

Instrument Location and Number	Type	Watt	Color	Use	Circuit	Dimmer	Remarks
Over-Head Rail S.R. #1	6x9 ERS	750	R55 517	[illegible]		6	"Y" w/ #3
2	—	—	R08	—		5	"Y" w/ #4
3	—	—	R55 517	—		6	"Y" w/ #1
4	—	—	R08	—		5	"Y" w/ #2
Elec. #2 #1	Mini 50°	500	R104 204	Scrim		4E	
2	—	—	504	Sconce Back		4A	"Y" w/ #7
3	—	—	R11	Tarr. Sp.		H1*	*Act II Only
4	6" Fres.	—	552	Sun Back		13*	*Acts I+II Only "Y" w/ #9, 12, 15
5	—	—	R16	Chand Support		3D	"Y" w/ #8, 10, 14
6	Mini 30°	—	567	Act III Sp.			
7	Mini 50°	—	504	Sconce Back		4A	"Y" w/ #2
8	6" Fres	—	R16	Chand Support		3D	"Y" w/ #5, 10, 14
9	—	—	552	Sun Back		13*	*Acts I+II Only "Y" w/ #4, 12, 15
10	—	—	R16	Chand Support		3D	"Y" w/ #8, 5, 14
11	Mini 50°	—	504	Sconce Back		4B	
12	6" Fres	—	552	Sun Back		13*	*Acts I+II Only "Y" w/ #4, 9, 15
13	Mini 30°	—	N/C	Act II Sp.		14*	*Acts I + II Only
14	6" Fres	—	R16	Chand Support		3D	"Y" w/ #5, 8, 10
15	—	—	552	Sun Back		13*	*Acts I+II Only "Y" w/ #4, 9, 12
16	Mini 50°	—	R104 204	Scrim		4E	
17	6x9 ERS	750	503	Door Back		7	"Y" w/ #18
18	6" Fres	500	R102 503	—		7	"Y" w/ #17
S.R. Boom #1	Mini 30°	500	567	Door Back		8	
Line #22 #1	Mini 30°	500	504	Sconce Back		4A	"Y" w/ #4
2	8" Fres	1K	552	Sun Back		12*	*Acts I+II Only "Y" w/ #5
3	Mini 50°	500	R104 204	Scrim		4D	
4	Mini 30°	—	504	Sconce Back		4A	"Y" w/ #1
5	8" Fres	1K	552	Sun Back		12*	*Acts I+II Only "Y" w/ #2
6	Mini 30°	500	504	Sconce Back		4B	"Y" w/ #8
7	Mini 50°	—	R104 204	Scrim		4E	"Y" w/ #10
8	Mini 30°	—	504	Sconce Back		4B	"Y" w/ #6
9	8" Fres	1K	552	Sun Back		12*	*Acts I+II Only "Y" w/ #11
10	Mini 50°	500	R104 204	Scrim		4E	"Y" w/ #7
11	8" Fres	1K	552	Sun Back		12*	*Acts I+II Only "Y" w/ #9
Fire-Place #1	3" Fres	150	505	Fire		9	"Y" w/ #2
2	—	—	819	Fire		9	"Y" w/ #1
Practicals #1	PS Type	25	N/C	Piano		M4	
2	PS Type	—	N/C	Sconce		4C	"Y" w/ #3
3	—	—	N/C	Sconce		4C	"Y" w/ #2
4	T Type	125	N/C	Chand		3C	

Instrument Location and Number	Type	Watt	Color	Use	Circuit	Dimmer	Remarks
Elec. #3 #1	6x6 ERS	750	R08	Door Back		3A	"Y" w/ #2
2	8" Fres	1K	R102 552	—		3A	Barn Door "Y" w/ #1
3	—	—	R102 552	—		11*	*Acts I+II Only "Y" w/ #7 Barn Door
4	6x6 ERS	750	504	Night Doors		10	"Y" w/ #9
5	—	—	503	Day Doors		11*	*Acts I+II Only "Y" w/ #8
6	8" Fres	1K	R102 502	Night Door Back		10	Barn Door
7	—	—	R102 552	Day Door Back		11*	*Acts I+II Only "Y" w/ #3 Barn Door
8	6x6 ERS	750	503	Day Door		11*	*Acts I+II Only "Y" w/ #5
9	—	—	R55 517	Night Door		10	"Y" w/ #4
Cyc Strips #1	PS	2300	Blue	Cyc		11*	*Act III Only
2	—	—	Blue	—		12*	*Act III Only
3	-	-	Green	-		13*	*Act III Only
4	-	-	Red	-		14*	*Act III Only

NOTE: * Indicates Repatch.

FIGURE 8–16

The Instrument Schedule

The instrument schedule for *A Doll House* (Figure 8–12). Instruments are listed by position and number. Complete circuit information was added to the schedule during the put-in.

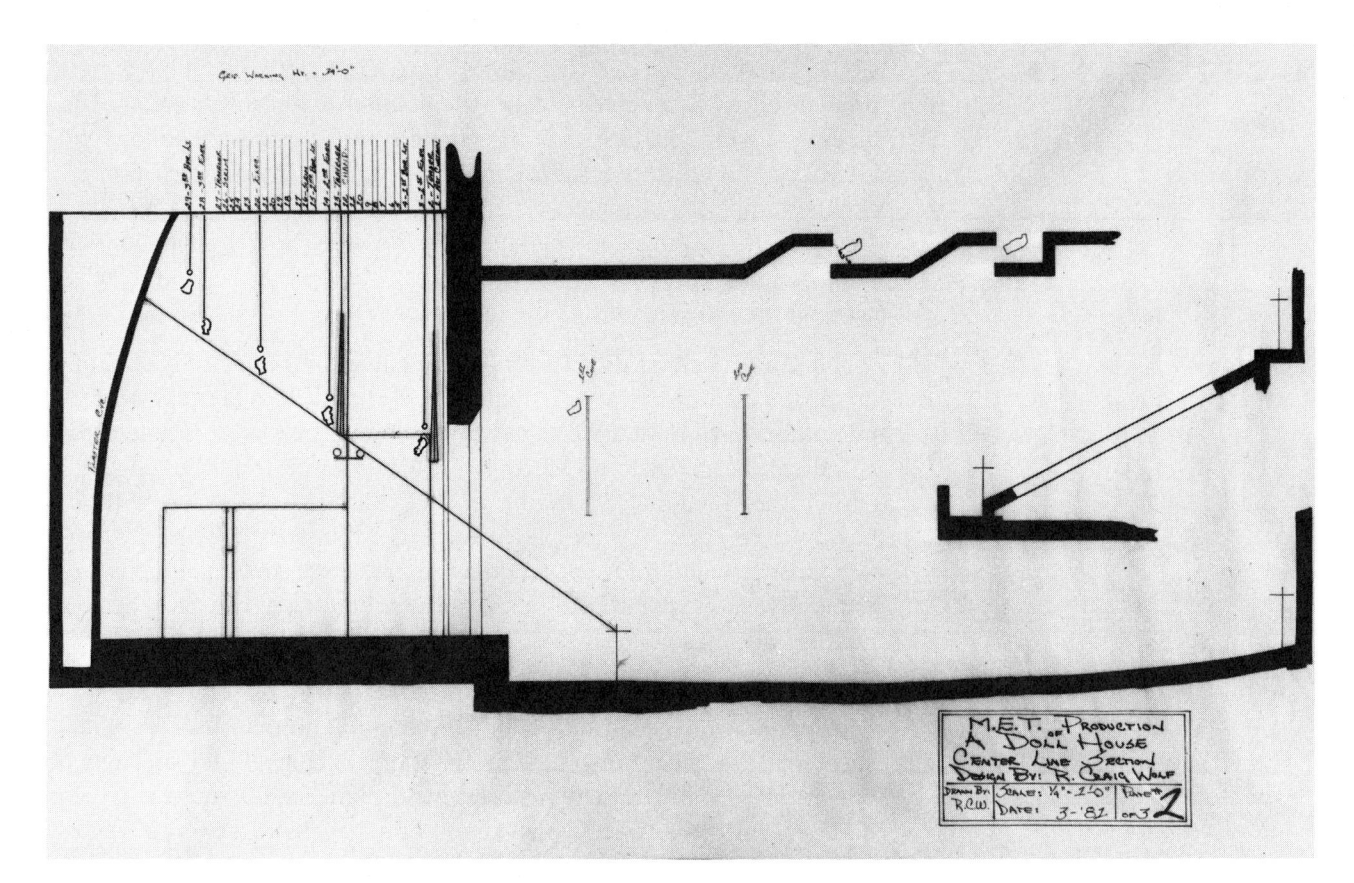

FIGURE 8–17
The Section
The center-line section for *A Doll House*. Note that the only masking is on lines number 2 and 13, forcing the up-stage electric pipes quite high.

acting levels above or below stage height, and accuracy of lighting angles (Figure 8–17).

The scene designer provides the lighting designer with a center-line sectional view of the stage that includes horizontal masking at trim height, critical audience sight points, as well as scenery placement. Occasionally various supplementary sectional views will be necessary; they can be easily and quickly drafted by the lighting designer.

Additional Paperwork

It should be fairly clear by now that the better prepared a lighting designer is before a production moves into the theatre, the easier the design will be realized. In fact, many professional designers would argue that preparation is as important as the design or artistic work. As a result, a variety of additional types of paperwork have been developed by designers in order to simplify the put-in and the execution of the design.

Batten Tapes. To expedite hanging and circuiting the electric pipes, the designer may wish to prepare batten tapes for each hanging po-

Stage Lighting Practice

sition. These consist of rolled pieces of paper or cloth which have been premarked with center-line and specific instrument information. The tapes are simply attached to the batten and electricians follow the instructions on the tape. Information may include instrument number, circuit number, instrument type, color, and even focus. Tapes eliminate any measuring and chalking of the battens and, in combination with hanging cardboards, could eliminate the necessity of an electrician ever having to consult the light plot.

Hanging Cardboards. Hanging cardboards are pieces of stiff paper or cardboard onto which a single location and its respective instrumentation have been transferred from the master plot. A single cardboard can be given to an electrician during the put-in, allowing him or her the freedom of hanging and circuiting the position without having to refer back to the plot. Hanging cardboards will usually contain more detailed information than the plot and, like batten tapes, are especially useful for touring situations, where they can be reused a number of times.

The Cheat Sheet. The designer's cheat sheet (Figure 8–18) was developed as an aid in setting and adjusting lighting levels. The cheat sheet will list all dimmers, their function, and levels for any given preset. This information then allows the designer to find quickly which dimmer controls a specific instrument or set of instruments as well as its intensity. As mentioned earlier, board operators can record prewritten dimmer readings from the cheat sheet onto standard preset sheets or into a computer memory. In the latter case, the cheat sheets act as "hard copy" in the event of memory loss or board malfunction. Obviously these sheets must be kept up-to-date as levels are adjusted—a good task for an assistant.

The Magic Sheet. Another aid to the designer while setting levels, magic sheets are arranged to indicate which dimmers control a specific set-up or stage picture. These sheets may take a pictorial form similar to the color key shown in Figure 8–19, or they may simply be listings of dimmers involved in a set-up. For instance, one section of a magic sheet might indicate which dimmers control the high-side blues, while another section might show how the warm front lights are controlled.

The Color Key. The color key (not to be confused with the plot key of the same name) is a communication device for the designer. This representational drawing will indicate which instruments (and therefore colors) are playing for any given stage picture.

Figure 8–19 shows a typical lighting area with front light of R09 at a level of 80 percent, R55 at a level of 60 percent, and side light from stage right in R04 at 90 percent. This key initially was developed as an educational tool offering a student designer a quick, nonverbal means of communicating lighting intentions.

Virginia Shakespeare Production Of: OTHELLO

Cue #			Preset #			Count:					
Dim #	1	2	3	4	5	6	7*	8*	9	10	11	12
Use	S.L. Zone 1	HI S.L. C.S. Zone 2	SIDE C.S. Zone 2	204 S.R. Zone 2	S.L. Zone 3	S.R. Zone 3	204 SIDE ABOVE	B-B-O HOUSE BACK	S.R. Zone 1	HI S.L. Zone 2	SIDE C.S. Zone 2	117 S.R. Zone 2
Level												
Dim #	13	14*	15	16*	17	18	19	20	21	22*	23	24
Use	117 S.L. Zone 3	117 SIDE ABOVE	117 Zone 4	Council Chamber	BACK Zone 1	WARM S.L. Zone 2	C.S. Zone 2	S.R. Zone 2	Zone 3	Hearld Sp.	BACK Zone 1	COOL S.L. Zone 2
Level												
Dim #	25	26	27	28*	29*	30*	31*	32*	33*	34*	35*	36*
Use	BACK C.S. Zone 2	COOL S.R. Zone 2	Zone 3	TORCH SL	CH CS	R55 SR	R55 SL	ABOVE SR	WARM SL	ABOVE SR	COOL SL	ABOVE SR
Level												
Dim #	37	38	39	40	41*	42*	43*	44*	45	46	47	48
Use					GOBOS DS	WALL US	WASH MAUVE	CYC. BLUE	CYC. RED	TOP BLUE	GR.	AMB.
Level												

Micro-Q:

Dim #	1	2	3	4	5	6	7	8	9	10	11	12
Use	F.O.H. D.S.L.	H.R. D.S.C.	R55 D.S.R.	S.L.	C.S.	S.R.	U.S.L.	U.S.C.	U.S.R.	FAR U.S.	H.L. D.S.L.	WARM D.S.C.
Level												
Dim #	13	14	15	16	17	18	19	20	21	22	23	24
Use	F.O.H. D.S.R.	H.L. S.L.	WARM C.S.	S.R.	U.S.L.	U.S.C.	U.S.R.	FAR U.S.	F.O.H. D.S.C.	H.L. D.S.C.	COOL D.S.R.	S.L.
Level												
Dim #	25	26	27	28	29	30*	31*	32*				
Use	F.O.H. C.S.	H.L. S.R.	COOL U.S.L.	U.S.C.	U.S.R.	TUNNEL SL	PIT SR	STEPS				
Level												

FIGURE 8–18

The Designer's Cheat Sheet

This production of *Othello* used two dimmer boards: one with 48 dimmers and the second with 32 dimmers. A given lighting picture or preset is written on such a sheet, given to the board operator to transpose to running sheets, and later serves as reference for the designer in correcting levels. Lighting Design by R. Craig Wolf for the Virginia Shakespeare Festival.

FIGURE 8–19

The Designer's Color Key

This particular color key indicates a stage-right side light source colored with R04 and running at 90 pecent of intensity, a front-of-house left source colored with R55 and running at 60 percent of intensity, and a front-of-house right source colored in R09 and running at 80 percent intensity. Color keys can be a simple method of indicating basic lighting intentions for a given lighting picture or preset.

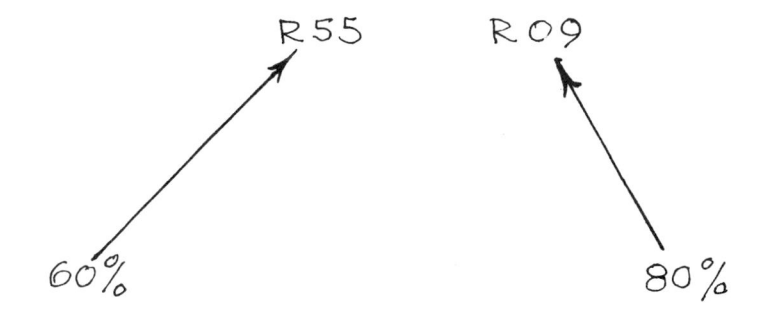

Stage Lighting Practice

REALIZING THE PLOT

The final step in lighting a production is, of course, realizing the plot. This process may be as short as two or three days or as long as two weeks and is always the most challenging time for the lighting designer. Let it be said one more time that any preparation completed before move-in will pay off tenfold while in the theatre.

Final Preparations and Put-In

Cues. Writing lighting cues is one of the most simple tasks for the lighting designer, although at first this might not seem to be so. The *rhythm* of a production will tell an observant designer where most of the cues belong. (The designer must be sure to attend several rehearsals and to concentrate on things other than blocking.) It is a good idea to note cue placement in the script during one of the final run-throughs before move-in. Cues can then be numbered and presets written. Cues should be numbered sequentially, with inserted cues having a letter suffix (Light Cue 12A) or decimal (Light Cue 12.1).

The cues and their placement, of course, must be given to the stage manager, who runs the show. This cue-writing session should take place at a sufficiently early date before the technical or first lighting rehearsal and ideally should include both the stage manager and the board operator. Set aside enough time for an uninterrupted discussion of the cues with both people so that they understand why a cue happens. Make sure that both know counts or cue times and, finally, make sure that your stage manager understands that the placement of some cues will most certainly change during the rehearsal process.

Cues should be called as follows:

"Warning Light Cue 12" (approximately 30 seconds before "go")
"Ready Light Cue 12" (approximately 15 seconds before "go")
"Light Cue 12 . . . Go"

The Put-in. The lighting designer should be present during the put-in, if for no other reason than to be available for questions. The lighting put-in should be carefully scheduled with the technical director in order to coordinate lighting and scenery, and step-by-step procedures should also be discussed with the head electrician. The designer should not take a major role in physically hanging the show. This is the crew's job and a designer's energy is best spent elsewhere.

Focus. Lighting focus takes concentration. If at all possible, electricians should have the stage to themselves during focus hours. Be prepared for the focus: be alert, have a dimmer list or cheat sheet with you, and work in a logical order. Front-of-house is often focused first. Learn to focus two electricians at once. Learn to focus with your back to the light, looking at your shadow. Learn to focus fast. And don't forget to give your crew periodic breaks.

Technical and Dress Rehearsals

The first time a show's director sees the product of the lighting designer's work will probably be at the technical or lighting rehearsal. This should *not*, however, be the first time the lighting designer sees his or her work. The ideal situation is to look at presets during the final run-through before the technical rehearsal, explaining to the cast and director that you will be adjusting a few levels and will most probably not be in sequence with the action on stage. This gives the designer a good chance to see the lighting on actors without the added pressure of a technical rehearsal.

The technical and dress period is most crucial to the lighting designer, for this is when the majority of design decisions are made. This is the time when the lighting designer is working the hardest. Accordingly, the designer *must* be fresh and alert—one can't see or think for very long with only four hours of sleep.

Technical rehearsals are infamous for being long and laborious affairs, hated by technicians as well as actors. If proper and thorough preparation has been done and if someone keeps things moving, the rehearsal can be relatively painless. Good judgment must be used in determining when to stop and fix something and when to keep going. Tactless people must be banned from technical rehearsals.

It is a good idea for the stage manager to call this rehearsal from the house rather than an isolated booth somewhere. He or she will be in better contact with the director, the designers, the technical staff, as well as the actors. Always make sure that headsets have been carefully checked out well before the technical rehearsal begins. Nothing is more frustrating (and, unfortunately, more common) than communications problems during a technical rehearsal.

The purpose of a technical rehearsal is to solve technical problems—*not* constantly to adjust light levels, and *certainly not* to write lighting presets. If presets are not complete before the technical rehearsal, the rehearsal should go on without lights. Remain objective, observe time deadlines and, above all, be sure that your operators and stage manager understand and record changes as they are made.

A production will normally have two or three dress rehearsals, with the first primarily devoted to costumes. Level changes have to be made during the dress rehearsal process, but the performance must not be stopped except for an exceptionally serious problem. Second and third dresses must never be stopped. The fewer changes made during dress rehearsals, the better your stage manager and operators will learn the show. Remember that the director's attention is divided among a great number of equally important things during this stage of a production. Never leave after a dress rehearsal without first talking to the director, the stage manager, and your operators.

Stage Lighting Practice

FIGURE 8–20
The Lighting Laboratory
Shown is the Lighting Laboratory at Carnegie-Mellon University with a makeup area (below) adjacent to the lab.

THE LIGHTING LAB

Preceding chapters have discussed the importance of the lighting laboratory as a teaching tool. More and more institutions that are genuinely committed to training lighting designers are seeking and finding the space and equipment for such laboratory work. The light lab comes in many sizes and forms; most exist in found spaces that have been equipped by students and faculty with a limited budget. The available equipment is often ancient and may be less than useful in an actual production. However, the lab is also the place for experimentation with state-of-the-art instrumentation; many facilities select for purchase one or two new pieces of equipment each year to be used in the lab.

Ideally the light lab will be on a human scale, with a grid somewhere between 12 and 15 feet high. It should have its own control system and circuitry, although neither need be elaborate. The lab shown in Figure 8–20 is a particularly intelligent arrangement, for make-up instruction which often requires stage lighting can take place in one area of the space. Lab exercises vary from reproduction of light in a painting to demonstrations of angle and quality of light.

An excellent example of the use of a large-scale model in the lighting lab is seen in Figure 8–21. Note the various uses of light angle for texture and composition.

LIGHTING FOR THE COMMERCIAL THEATRE

In the not-so-distant past we saw an amazing rebirth throughout the country of professional theatre, too long confined to New York

FIGURE 8–21
Using the Lighting Lab
In lieu of the training advantages of actual production lighting, a well-equipped lighting lab offers a simulated but parallel experience. The student lighting designer can reconstruct lighting angles and position of any stage—proscenium, arena, or thrust—and discover hands-on some of the compositional properties of light. In this exercise the scenic form purposely contains a variety of surfaces. Sweeping curves, sharp corners, openings, and texture lend interest. The photographs show some of the effects.

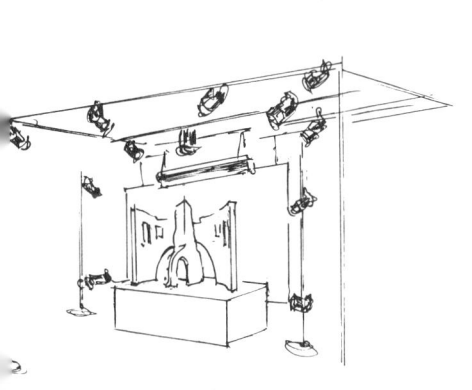

Stage Lighting Practice

and a few other large centers. Now it is a rare city that does not have its repertory or stock theatre, run by professional producers and directors and employing professional actors and designers.

Nearly all of these regional theatres (often called LORT houses after the type of Equity contract issued the actors) run apprentice programs which seldom pay much but which offer exceptional experience and valuable professional contacts. Theatre Communications Group (T.C.G.) publishes a complete list of theatres and programs which is available by writing to T.C.G. More and more college graduates, and even college students, are working in these theatres, on full- or part-time bases. This section is intended to give such people a picture of lighting practices and limitations of the commercial theatre.

BROADWAY PRACTICES

Broadway, for better or worse, is the ultimate in commercial usages and restrictions. Many of these pertain as well to resident professional theatres in other parts of the country, with considerable and unpredictable variations among localities.

Equipment in a Broadway Theatre

Most people would be surprised to learn that no commercial theatre on what is commonly referred to as Broadway has any lighting equipment of its own beyond the few items here listed: There will be a dimmer for the house lights; there will be a company switch furnishing considerable power, to which a show's dimmers may be connected; there will be current at appropriate locations for the use of follow spots; and, a fairly recent addition, there will be wiring in conduit to the front of the balcony and to the box booms, vertical pipes erected on either side of the auditorium in the upper boxes closest to the stage. Occasionally there will be conduit to a second balcony, if one exists.

This means that everything else must come in with the show: all the instruments and their accessories, the dimmers and plugging boxes, cable sufficient to connect all instruments to the dimmers, booms for offstage instruments, asbestos cloth to protect flying scenery from lights hung above the stage, work lights, all special rigging devices, everything!

The Broadway Lighting Designer

Before being permitted to light a show on Broadway, the designer must become a member of the United Scenic Artists Union (U.S.A.). To be admitted to this organization, the applicant must pass a difficult examination given once a year in either New York or Chicago.

The lighting designer is hired, often at the suggestion of the director or the scene designer, by the producer of the play. Under the rules of United Scenic Artists he or she must receive a minimum fee, although established designers ask for and get a great deal more than this minimum. It is not uncommon for a well-known designer to receive, in addition to a straight fee, a royalty based on a percentage of the gross receipts.

Hiring Equipment and Electricians

Because all expenses related to the play must be approved by the producer or business manager, the light designer must work within the figures that they have in mind. All the equipment is rented, the usual contract calling for a down payment of 10 percent of its price for the first three-week period, a lower charge for the next three weeks, and a reduced rental for the balance of the run of the play. Some producers make a practice of asking for competitive bids from the few companies that are engaged in the rental of lighting equipment for the stage; others always work with the same company. Some accept recommendations of the lighting designer to deal with a certain firm.

These bids are based on an equipment list called a shop order which must be drafted by the lighting designer or assistant well before the production moves into the theatre. For this reason, the Broadway lighting designer must complete the plot several weeks earlier than is required of a designer working primarily with in-house equipment. The shop order must carefully specify every piece of equipment to be rented or purchased (Figure 8–22, page 152). This includes instruments, cable, mounting equipment, connectors, lamps, dimmer boards, color, and even tape and tie line.

Even more important than the equipment costs are the wages paid to the electricians who set up and run the show. In New York these people must be members of Local No. 1 of The International Alliance of Theatrical Stage Employees, commonly called the IA. IA electricians are paid a substantial hourly wage and prudent use of their time is imperative. The fact is that labor costs on Broadway have recently become so high that they are frequently a limiting factor of design artistry.

Some electricians are far better than others, and a good chief electrician can help the designer immeasurably. For this reason a designer well established in New York will probably have in mind someone with whom he or she works well and will recommend that the producer hire this person. But the beginner must ask around to locate the best person available.

The chief electrician estimates how many people will be required to run the show, based on the number of instruments and type of control used and the number and complexity of the cues. If the show has electrical sound effects, the sound person is also under the jurisdiction of the chief electrician.

```
CYRANO                                          Equipment List

                      A Richard Gregson - Apjac Production

                      Lighting - Gilbert V. Hemsley, Jr.  608-836-1197

                      Electrician - Joe Monaco              914-949-6587

                      Company Manager - Victor Samrock  212-751-1290

                      Load out to Toronto  Feb. 15 or 16, 1973

                      Load in to Toronto   Feb. 18, followed by a possible
                      stand at the Colonial in Boston, and the Palace
                      in New York.


Balcony Rail   (This will be split between 2 Balconys in Toronto)

     24        750w 8 x 12 Lekos CC and CF

     16        750w 8 x 12 Lekos T and S, CC and CF

     12        750w 8 x 16 Lekos CC and CF

      6        500w 6 x 6 (Step Lens Wide Angle) CC and CF

               4 L.S. Units (Will come from Minn.)

     20        Twofers

      2        Threefers

               Rehearsal Worklites

               Cables and Jumpers   (CK with Royal Alex, Colonial, and Palace)

Box Boom Left

     24        750w 6 x 12 Lekos (Would prefer 6 x 16"s) CF

               Palace 12 Long Side Arms 2 T Joints Each (Same for Colonial ??)

               Royal Alex Possible C Clamps Ck with House

     12        Twofers

               Cables and Jumpers, ck with house
```

FIGURE 8–22
The Shop Order
The first page of the equipment list for the Broadway production of *Cyrano de Bergerac,* prepared by Gilbert Hemsley, Jr., the lighting designer. Abbreviations used: "CC" = C-clamp, "CF" = color frame, "T" = template (or gobo), and "S" = shutters.

PLANNING THE LIGHTING

After reading and rereading the script, the lighting designer consults the playwright, the director, the scene and costume designers, and others. Sometimes a producer will hold meetings at which the lighting designer can exchange views with these co-workers, but on other occasions they must be sought out. The designer must study the color renderings of the scenic designer and visit the shop where the scenery is being built to note the painting. He or she will wish to see samples of fabrics to be used in the costumes, and will consider the make-up to be worn by the actors. Most important, the designer will discuss with the director the visual effects desired for each scene of the play and the nature of all changes and cues that affect the lighting. At all times the designer must remember that he or she is part of a team, each member of which is striving to make the production a success, and all of whom have opinions that merit respect and consideration.

Of course, right from the start the designer has attended rehearsals to see how the director is interpreting the script and the style of the final presentation. And toward the end of the rehearsal period the designer will want to have learned the movements and positions of the actors, the timing of the cues, and any variations in approach that the director is taking.

The lighting designer will visit the New York theatre in which the play is to open and inspect it as to mounting positions and their distances from the stage, any possible difficulties in placing instruments exactly where desired, and all physical aspects that could affect the lighting of the play.

As mentioned earlier, the shop order is due well before move-in (at least one week and, more normally, two or three), therefore the plot may have to be completed before the designer has had a chance to attend to everything mentioned above. Nonetheless, late rehearsals must be attended—for cueing if nothing else.

It is accepted practice in New York to draw one's plot in ½-inch scale (Figure 8–23). This probably means that the scaled distance from front-of-house positions to the stage will be inaccurate.

Pre-Move-in. One week before the rented lighting equipment is to move out of the contractor's shop, the chief electrician and first assistant must carefully inspect and test everything ordered, rejecting all items that are not in satisfactory condition. They must also frame the color media, label the bundles of cable, prepare any special effects, and otherwise organize matters as far as possible.

The lighting designer also visits the shop and checks over the colors to be sure there will be no surprises when in the theatre. The designer will also check with the electrician to make sure that wall brackets and chandeliers are properly wired, and with the scene shop to be certain that the scenery on which lighting fixtures are to hang has been adequately braced. Electrification of turntables and other electrical devices should be checked. Lens systems for projections must be correct. Nothing is left to chance; whatever is delivered to the theatre must be exactly what is required.

Several days before move-in, the designer's time will be devoted to writing preset levels and giving cue placement to the stage manager.

Stage Lighting Practice

154 Stage Lighting

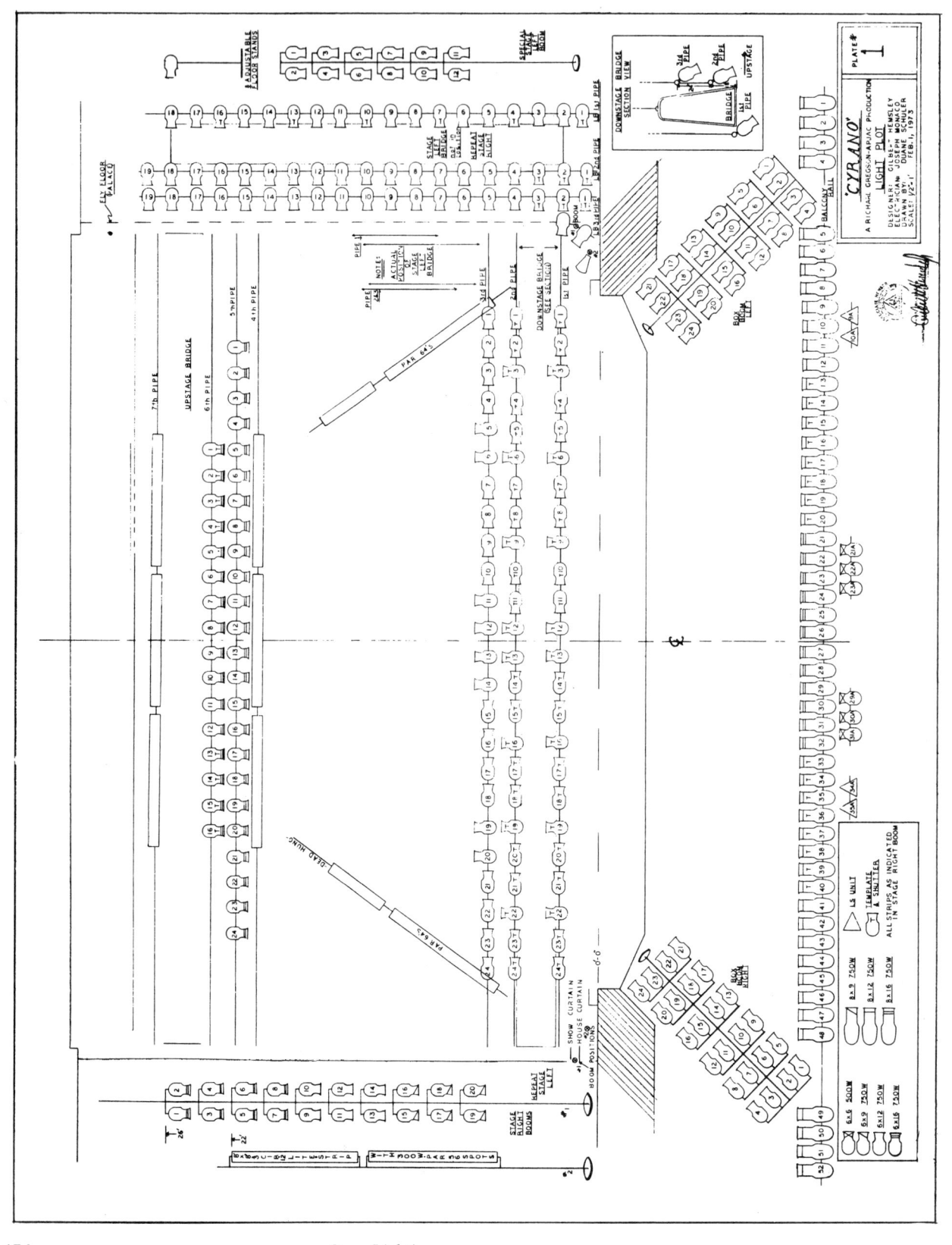

FIGURE 8–23

Professional Lighting Layout

Page 154. A lighting layout for the Broadway production of *Cyrano de Bergerac* by Gilbert Hemsley, Jr. Unlike most layouts, there is no floor plan of the setting. Because there are several arrangements of scenery it is difficult to show a composite of floor plans without causing confusion. In such cases the lighting designer frequently prepares a layout on transparent paper or plastic which is then placed over each floor plan in turn. In any event the layout is not a representational diagram but is a schematic working drawing for the lighting designer and crew.

CYRANO — BOARD #1

SWITCH	POSITION	TYPE	FOCUS	COLOR
1	Box Boom L 9·10·11·12	4-750w 6×12	L AREA 1	½ C.B.
2	Box Boom R 1·2·3·4	4-750w 6×12	R AREA 1	½ C.B.
3	Box Boom L 5·6·7·8	4-750w 6×12	L AREA 2	½ C.B.
4	Box Boom R 5·6·7·8	4-750w 6×12	R AREA 2	½ C.B.
5	Box Boom L 1·2·3·4	4-750w 6×12	L AREA 3	½ C.B.
6	Box Boom R 9·10·11·12	4-750w 6×12	R AREA 3	½ C.B.
7	#1 Boom L 16-18 / #1 Boom R 4-6	2-750w 6×9 / 2-750w 6×16	AREA 1	½ C.B.
8	#1 Boom L 10-12 / #1 Boom R 10-12	2-750w 6×12 / 2-750w 6×12	AREA 2	½ C.B.
9	#1 Boom L 4-6 / #1 Boom R 16-18	2-750w 6×16 / 2-750w 6×9	AREA 3	½ C.B.
10	#1 Boom L 15-17 / #1 Boom R 3-5	2-750w 6×9 / 2-750w 6×16	AREA 4	½ C.B.
11	#1 Boom L 9-11 / #1 Boom R 9-11	2-750w 6×12 / 2-750w 6×12	AREA 5	½ C.B.
12	#1 Boom L 3-5 / #1 Boom R 15-17	2-750w 6×16 / 2-750w 6×9	AREA 6	½ C.B.
13 M 131/132/133/134	Bal. Rail 21/22/31/32	4-750w 8×16	SPECIALS	½ C.B.
14	Bal. Rail 21A/22A/23A 29A/30A/31A	6-500w 6×6	FRONT CURTAIN WASH	911

1 OF 20

FIGURE 8–24

General Hook-up

A portion of the hook-up for the Broadway production of *Cyrano de Bergerac*. This organizes the nearly three hundred instruments of the layout into a scheme of control by designating the hook-up of each instrument to a dimmer in one of the system's six switchboards, ten auxiliary preset boards, or five auto transformer boards used for group mastering. The schedule also indicates the hanging position and type of instrument, its focus and color.

Stage Lighting Practice

Setting up the Lighting

Move-in and Set-up. On move-in day all the rented equipment is delivered to the theatre. Because there is a vast amount of work to be done, and done fast, the chief electrician will have called for such additional hands as needed to get the instruments mounted and cabled. Under the electrician's direction, and following the designer's layout, this work proceeds while at the same time the scenery is being erected on the stage. Usually, to avoid conflict with the carpenters, the front-of-house lights are the first to be put in place, with the onstage equipment following. Great cooperation is necessary at this time between the two departments; it is at this stage that a competent electrician can prove of great value to a production.

Focusing and Setting Cues. By the time the lights are in reasonably good shape—hung and connected to the dimmers—the light designer, who has been observing the work and double-checking the position of the instruments, takes over. It is normal to start with the front-of-house spotlights, sometimes while the upstage equipment is still being hung. The light designer will not have the exclusive use of the stage, but must carry on the work of focusing despite all manner of confusion, possibly even before all the scenery is in place.

If a regular technical run-through is scheduled, the designer may rough in the dimmer readings and cues. But all too often these delicate operations must be done under the most frustrating conditions, sometimes even with the houselights and stage work lights ablaze! And it is important that all be finished quickly, so that the regular crew will not run into overtime and the extra hands hired for the set-up may be let go. The job must be done right the first time, for if it becomes necessary to send someone up a tall ladder at a later time, a ladder crew of four people must be hired for the minimum of half a day just to adjust one poorly placed instrument.

During rehearsals the lighting people continue their work, adjusting dimmer readings, sharpening cues, and taking copious notes for refocusing, rehanging, matting, masking, changing color media, and the like. The designer frequently has an assistant to help with the paperwork and to keep in touch with the stage manager, and perhaps with any follow-spot operators, by means of a telephone or a headset system.

In this manner adjustments are made right up to the moment when the curtain rises before an audience, and once the play has started the designer will continue to make notes during this and subsequent previews. All changes are passed on to the chief electrician and stage manager, the people who henceforth are in charge of running the show.

It must be emphasized that the lighting designer never goes backstage during either rehearsal or performance, regardless of any temptation to do so. Instead notes are delivered after the final curtain.

According to union regulations, under no condition whatever may the light designer or an assistant handle any lighting equipment, but must request one of the electricians to do so. This applies to even such innocent actions as handing a wrench to its owner, or steadying a ladder on which an electrician is working.

After the Opening. It has long been a custom to open Broadway shows out of town, usually with a short run in one of the cities along the Atlantic seaboard such as New Haven, Boston, Philadelphia, Washington, and then to move it on to another city, polishing the play as it goes, before the official opening on Broadway. When these tryout runs are scheduled, the first of such openings pretty much follows the procedures that have been described above. Occasionally the lighting designer will stay with the show through all its wanderings to New York. More often he or she will leave it at its first stop, possibly dropping in later in another city, or, most likely, not seeing it again until New York. Meanwhile the chief electrician and the stage manager are responsible for the lighting.

Recently it has become popular not to venture a play out of New York at all, but to run only a series of preview performances in the theatre in which it is scheduled to open. The audience at such previews understands that the play is not yet in its final form but is undergoing continual revisions. Such revisions include the lighting, of course, thus giving the designer ample time to experiment and make changes, bringing concepts to perfection at comparative leisure.

But no matter how the play opens, it is advisable for the designer to drop in every once in a while during its run. Often things will start to slip a little from what had originally been set.

Going on the Road

If, after its Broadway run, a show takes to the road—or a national company is formed to troup about the country—it is necessary for the designer to work out a simplified plot. The road production will almost always carry less equipment. If the show is to play in schools, municipal auditoriums, or other than conventional theatres a simplified light plot is all the more essential.

Various techniques have been developed to make setting up and focusing as easy as possible. For one example, the original production may have used a great battery of beam projectors for back lighting the actors. For the road, large striplights burning high-wattage PAR lamps may be substituted; such units can be hung and focused in a fraction of the time.

Today when a show goes on the road its scenery, properties, costumes, and lighting equipment are always moved by truck. The lighting instruments frequently are left right on their pipes, and the whole unit is placed aboard the vehicle, where it is hung safely and securely until the next city is reached. More and more, instead of pipes, so-called tracks are used, to which instruments are hung and in which their cabling is enclosed. The use of either pipe or track permits many shortcuts in the remounting of instruments in the next theatre.

REGIONAL THEATRES

Many of the professional practices which apply to lighting design on Broadway are also standard for the country's regional theatres. However, accepted practice in the regional theatres will vary a great deal from theatre to theatre. Production schemes, from repertory to stock, will influence how a lighting designer approaches his or her work. Local union rules and regulations will differ; in-house equipment will probably exist, but will be radically different from house to house; and technical production practices will be unique to each situation.

Designing for Repertory

Traditional repertory production generally requires a daily changeover from show to show and may involve as few as two or as many as eight individual productions. The lighting designer will develop a repertory plot which acts as a basis for all shows and then add special instrumentation for each individual production. Repatching and sometimes color changes may take place during changeovers, but extensive refocusing should be avoided in repertory situations. As might be expected, a repertory design will require much more equipment than normal, and often an individual show's demands must be compromised for the sake of the entire production scheme. The repertory experience is an extremely valuable one in the developmental process of any young lighting designer.

Designing for Stock

The vast majority of regional theatres will produce their shows in a stock arrangement, running each production continuously for a period of two to six weeks. (Summer stock productions may run only one week.) Such a scheme requires rapid changeovers from show to show and normally a new lighting design for each production. The stock designer must be able to work quickly and efficiently, remaining one step ahead of the production schedule at all times.

Those theatres which run a production for more than three weeks will most often job-in their lighting designers for each production, while those operations with shorter runs may very well employ a resident lighting designer. Either way, the lighting designer is always under a great deal of time pressure. Like repertory production, the stock experience is invaluable for the young lighting designer.

Regional Production

Some regional theatres will hire only designers who are United Scenic Artist members, while others pay no attention to requirements of union membership. There currently exist only two U.S.A. "locals": 829, the New York local with jurisdiction over Broadway and the East Coast; and 350, located in Chicago and having jurisdiction in the Midwest. Designing on the West Coast is through a reciprocal agreement with the IA.

Most cities have their own IA local. Rules and regulations will vary radically from local to local as will quality of workmanship. This fact is of particular concern to the regional designer, for he or she can only be sure of the quality of any local membership by previous experience or word-of-mouth. It is wise to carefully evaluate the potential work force in addition to local rule idiosyncrasies well before a production is mounted.

Stage-lighting rental houses have grown in numbers along with the spread of regional theatres across the country. Some of these local businesses will be surprisingly efficient and well-stocked, while others are woefully ill-equipped and lacking in knowledgeable personnel. The designer must anticipate the possibility of having to go to New York or some other major center for equipment needs, a situation which will surely affect budget and time considerations.

More important than commercial usage is the quite different matter of professional standards. No one should consider for a moment going into any level of commercial theatre unless he or she plans to devote total energy and ability to the routines and the problems that present themselves. It is no place for the casual enthusiast or the dilettante, nor for the easily discouraged, the supersensitive, or the noncooperative.

Stage Lighting Practice

9

Lighting for the Proscenium Theatre

This and the following chapter will investigate lighting layouts for different types of production in a variety of spaces. Certainly the proscenium remains the most common type of performance space today. The designer will surely encounter a great variety of production styles within this space. We will consider four typical but quite different sorts of presentation: a realistic interior, a realistic exterior, a wing-and-border setting, and unit or simultaneous approaches.

The following examples have been greatly simplified for clarity and ease of presentation. The lighting layouts are deliberately designed to show the minimum number of instruments necessary to achieve acceptable lighting in each case.

Let us assume that the theatre we are using is of medium size. The stage will have a 30-foot proscenium opening. There will be ample provisions for hanging scenery and instruments above the stage. About 20 feet from the proscenium line will be a beam for mounting front spotlights.

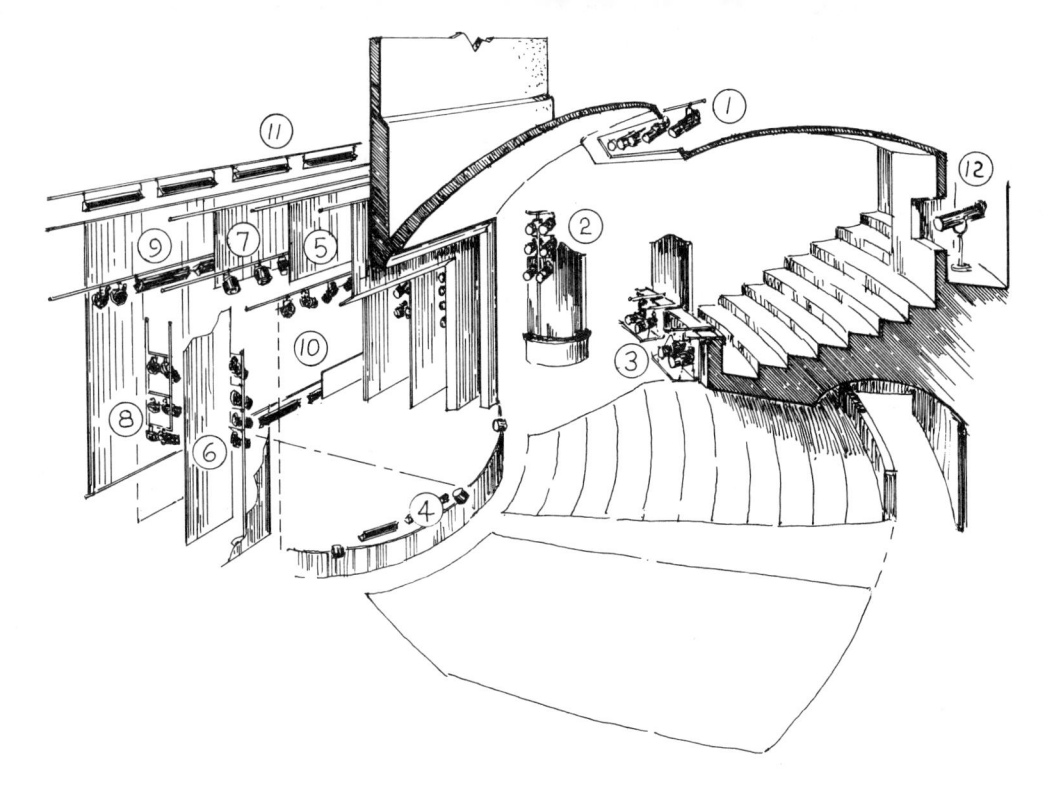

THE REALISTIC INTERIOR

A realistic interior usually calls for some variation of the conventional box setting, either with or without a ceiling piece. As one might expect, the existence of a ceiling will have a great effect on lighting possibilities. The primary interest is within the walls of this set, while the backgrounds seen through windows and doors are of less importance. The lighting is often motivated by apparent sources; in practically all cases it is realistically plausible.

Figure 9–2 shows such a setting. On the stage-left wall is a door leading to some other room or passage. In the up-left corner a flight of stairs comes down into the room from off left. In the center of the upstage wall is an archway opening into a corridor with an entrance at the stage-left end.

FIGURE 9–1
Lighting Positions in the Proscenium Theatre

(1) Ceiling beams. (2) Box booms or house-slot position. (3) Balcony front. (4) Apron or footlight. (5) Teaser. (6) Tormentor boom. (7) Midstage backlight position. (8) Wing ladder. (9) Backdrop or cyclorama lights. (10) Cyclorama base or horizon lights. (11) Translucent drop backlight. (12) Follow spot.

FIGURE 9–2
Sketch of a Realistic Interior Setting

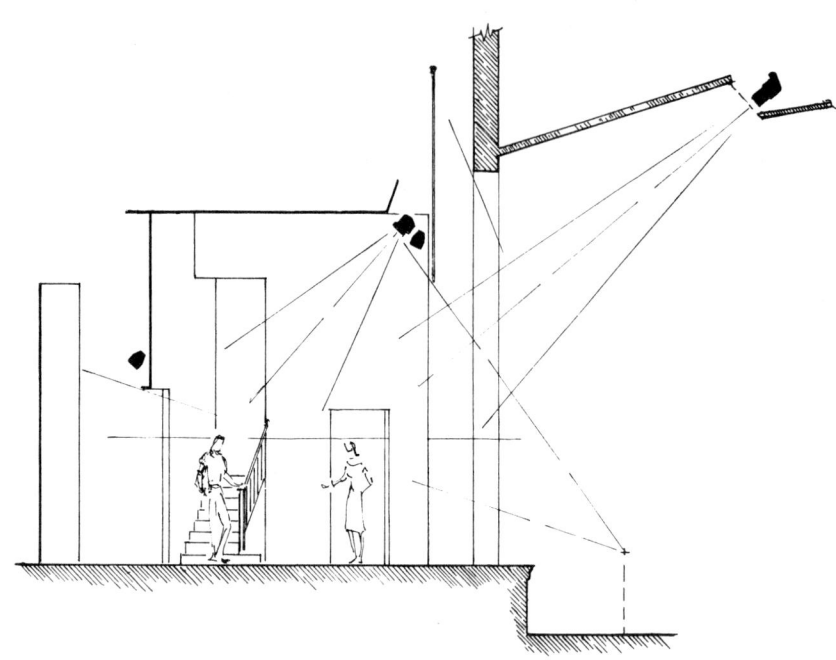

FIGURE 9–3

The Realistic Interior

This and the following lighting layouts are simplified to demonstrate the basic instrumentation for some typical proscenium-type productions. They are illustrations and should not be considered professional lighting layouts. For professional planning techniques see Chapter 8. A lighting layout, instrument schedule, and center-line sectional view are included.

a

No.	INSTRUMENT	LOCATION	PURPOSE	LAMP	COLOR	REMARKS
1	6" Ellips'l-Ref'r Spotlight	Beam - L	Area 2L	750T12	848	
2	" " " "	" "	" 1L	"	848	Frame off return
3	" " " "	" "	" 3L	"	848	
4	" " " "	Beam - R	" 1R	"	803	
5	" " " "	" "	" 3R	"	803	Frame off return
6	" " " "	" "	" 2R	"	803	
7	6" Fresnel-Lens Spotlight	1st Pipe - L	Area 4L	500T20	848	Mat top
8	" " "	" - C	" 5L	"	848	" "
9	6" Ellips'l-Ref'r Spotlight	1st Pipe - C	Stair Special	750T12	803	Frame to Stair
10	" " " "	" "	Arch Special	"	803	Frame to Arch
11	6" Fresnel-Lens Spotlight	1st Pipe - R	Area 5R	500T20	803	Mat top
12	" " " "	" "	" 4R	"	803	" "
13	6" Ellips'l-Ref'r Spotlight	Stand - L	Stair Backlight	750T12	810	
14	10" Flood Light	Scenery - L	Door Backing	250G30	810	High on scenery
15	" " "	Fireplace	Fire Glow	100A21	818	Gang with #24
16	16" Beam Projector	R - Stagewall	Sunlight	1000G40	—	High as possible
17	6" x 6'-0" Striplight	1st Pipe	X-Rays	150R40	Red	
18	" "				Bl. White Amber	
19	6" x 4'-6" "	Floor - R	Sky Backing	"	Red, Blue, Amber	
20	6" x 6'-0" "	Behind Arch	Hall	"	Red, Blue White, Amber	
21	Special	Fireplace	Fire Effect	2-60A21	Varied	Gang with #15
22	Desk Lamp	UL Corner	Lamp	150A23	—	Shield top & side
23	Wall Sconce	L of Arch	Wall Fixture	15FC/V		⎱ Gang - Candelabra
24	" "	R of Arch	" "	"	—	⎰ Socket Adapters

b

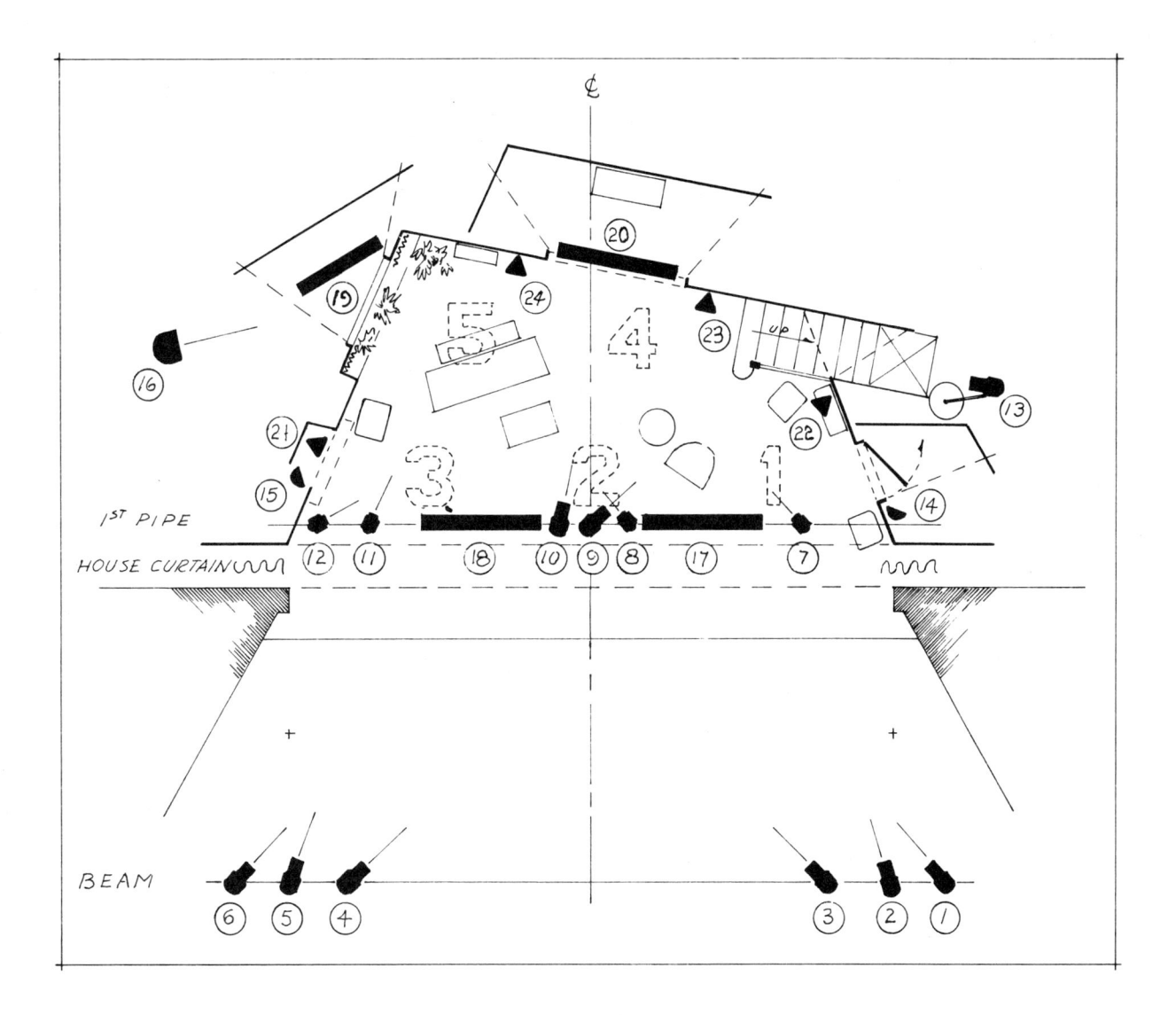

The stage-right wall contains a window and a fireplace. Through the window is seen a backing with painted sky and a scene of distant hills. This set has a ceiling piece which covers from the up-stage wall nearly to the first pipe position.

Two scenes are involved. In Act I bright sunlight streams in through the window. In Act II it is dark night outside and a fire is burning on the hearth.

Downstage Areas

In dividing the stage into acting areas, we find that the conventional three will be needed across the downstage zone, but only two will be required upstage. To cover areas 1, 2, 3, we mount 30° or 6 × 12 ellipsoidal reflector spotlights in our front beam position. We select the ERS over the Fresnel because the latter, though quite powerful,

Lighting for the Proscenium Theatre 163

has such side spill that we would have light all over the proscenium wall. For a longer throw than the one we have assumed for this theatre, we would naturally use the 20°, 6-by-16 or 8-inch ERS with their narrower and more powerful beams. For a shorter throw we could use one of several instruments: the 40° ERS, a 6-by-9 ERS, or one of the variety of smaller instruments such as the Mini-Ellipse.

In choosing the mounting positions for these instruments we attempt to achieve the ideal 45-degree angle, but note that we must mount the Area 1L instrument (number 2) somewhat in from the end of the beam in order to reach the extreme downstage-left corner of the stage without being cut off by the proscenium. In like manner, the Area 3R instrument must come somewhat nearer the center.

Therefore, we have sacrificed to some extent the ideal angle, but this is a necessary compromise. The remaining four instruments can be placed just about where we prefer them. All six instruments are carefully framed so as not to spill distracting light on the face of the stage apron, on the overhead teaser, and, in the case of numbers two and five, on the proscenium.

Upstage Areas

To cover the upstage areas we will use 6-inch Fresnels mounted on the first pipe. Fresnels are picked for this location because the soft edge of their beams makes blending between the areas much easier, and no sharp, distracting beam patterns will appear on the walls of the set. Numbers 7, 8, and 12 can be focused at close to the 45-degree angle for their respective areas, but number 11, focused on Area 5R, must move in a little in order to keep spill light off the stage-right wall.

All five areas must be consistent in regard to colors. Because in both acts warm light (sunbeams and fireglow) seems to come from the right of the stage, we can use a warm filter in instruments 4, 5, 6, 11, and 12. The opposite side of the room would need a relatively cool color for contrast in instruments 1, 2, 3, 7, and 8. Roscolene No. 803 (Pale Gold) and No. 848 (Water Blue) make an excellent combination for such a situation without appearing too strong in either shade.

The Stairway

Of course, the stairway must not be overlooked. But rather than consider it another area, it is preferable to handle it as a special problem because of its different levels. To light it properly, yet avoid spilling, we use an ellipsoidal reflector spotlight in soft focus from the first pipe, framing its beam to the stairs themselves and only high enough to cover the actor moving up and down. This would be instrument 9 (a 6-by-9), and because its beam is substantially at the same angle as the other stage-right instruments, its color should agree with these: a No. 803. To light the stairway from the other side, and particularly to

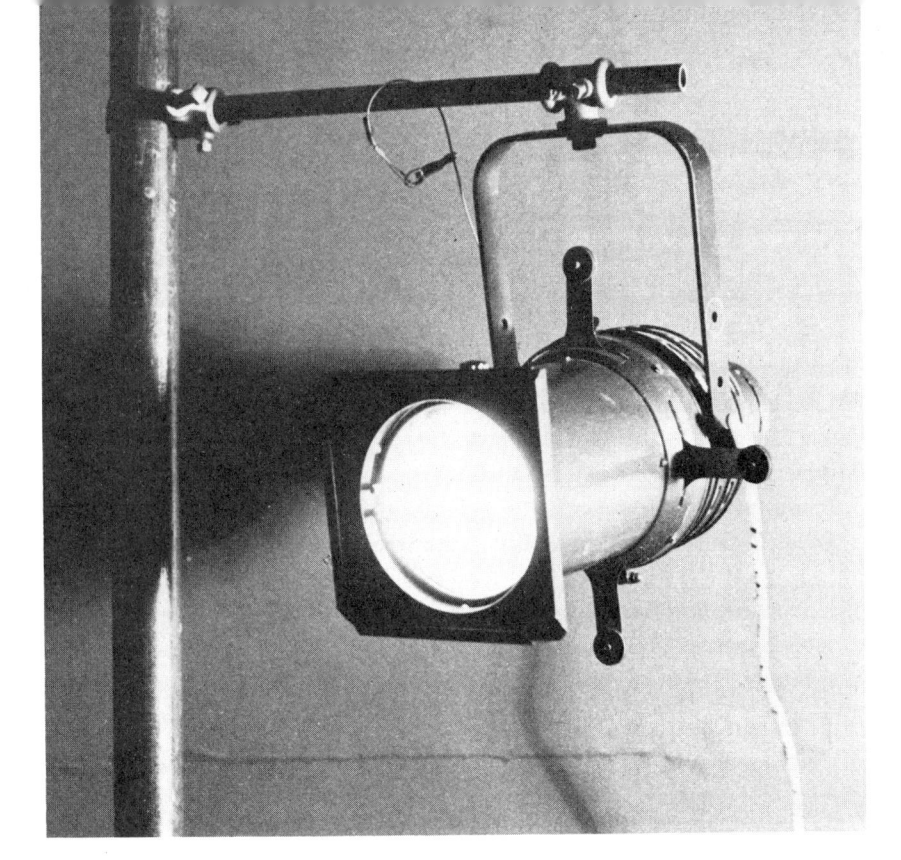

FIGURE 9-4
Lighting Instrument with Side-arm Mounted on a Boom

catch the face of an ascending actor another ellipsoidal spotlight (13) can be mounted on a boom (or from an overhead line) at the head of the stairs, about 8 feet offstage. The beam from this instrument may be presumed to come from a hall light at the head of the stairs, and a No. 810 (No Color Amber) filter could be used here for realism.

Booms. A brief word about floor stands or booms is necessary at this point. A boom normally consists of a heavy metal base into which screws a length of 1¼- or 1½-inch black pipe. Any length of pipe may be used, but booms of any great height must be tied off above for safety. A lighting instrument is then hung off the boom by using a cross-pipe or "side-arm" (Figure 9-4).

The boom can be represented on a light plot in one of two manners:

1 Drawing the pipe at scaled length and at an angle of 45 to 60 degrees directly out of its base. The various instruments are then shown in relationship to their boom pipe (Figure 9-5a). This is similar to an isometric view.
2 Showing the boom base and pipe in plan view, but without instrument specifications, with an additional elevation of the boom placed on the side of the drafting plate. The elevation will specify instrumentation (Figure 9-5b).

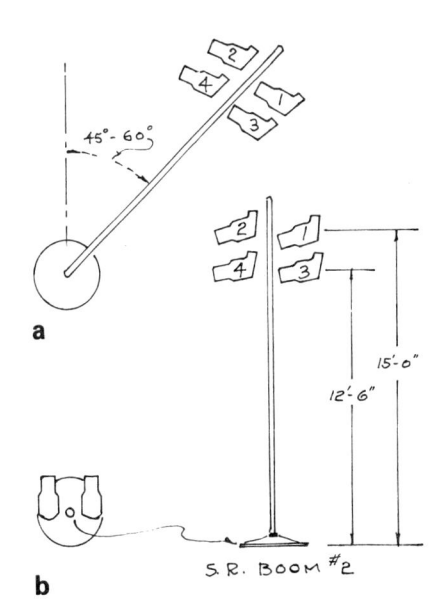

FIGURE 9-5

Representing a Boom on the Light Plot
(a) The isometric method shows the boom base in its actual position on stage. (b) The plan and elevation method is often desirable when space on the plan is tight.

Lighting for the Proscenium Theatre

165

The Archway

The acting area immediately beyond the archway is of utmost importance. Here the most vital entrances are made, and the actor must be well lighted as he or she prepares to come into the room. In fact, the director may even play brief but important scenes in just this location. To cover this area, instrument 10 (another 6-by-9) may be mounted in the center of the first pipe and framed to the opening of the archway.

Floodlights

Having listed the spotlights, we should next see what floodlights are desired. Two of the small, 10-inch variety are useful. Instrument 14 is placed behind the downstage-left door to throw illumination on the backing so this will not appear as a dark hole whenever the door is opened. This flood is placed at least 10 feet high on the scenery to throw its light downward as from a ceiling or wall bracket. A 250-watt G-30 lamp will give ample illumination, and a No. 810 filter will provide a color that resembles the warm light usually associated with such household fixtures. However, the choice of color will depend somewhat on the painted color of the masking flat behind the door.

Instrument 15 has a very different use: it is placed in the fireplace to throw a warm glow over all who approach it. It should not be too brilliant (and hence distracting), so a 100-watt A-21 is all that is necessary, with a No. 818 filter (orange), a more realistic color for fireglow than the traditional red.

Sunbeams

A large spotlight might be used for the strong beams of sunlight entering the window, but a beam projector is better because of the powerful punch of its parallel rays. No. 16 should be mounted well offstage, if possible even farther than our layout indicates. A producing group with ample equipment would use two or more instruments for this purpose. The height above the floor would depend on the hour of day as expressed by the script; a great height for near midday, a low, flat, angle for dawn or late afternoon. The color used would also depend on the time. Sunlight is often thought of as having a strong amber hue, but actually this is the case only in the late afternoon. For such a scene a No. 815 (Golden Amber) could be used. But noonday sun is much closer to white, and for such an effect it is probably wise to use no color medium at all.

X-rays

Borderlights have also been hung: two 6-foot strips on the first pipe, spaced slightly apart to allow certain spotlights to be mounted between them. A little more punch is needed for these "x-rays," so we have used 150-watt R-40 lamps in instruments 17 and 18, with the circuits being designated as red, blue-white, and amber. Considering that these lights are to blend and tone an interior, we need not bother with greens or very strong blues; the cheerful warmth of the amber will be useful in both our sunlit and firelit scenes.

Backing Strips

Instrument 19 is a 4½-foot striplight placed on the floor before the sky backing and focused on it. Considerable variation in color is desired here, so the 150-watt R-40 lamps would be in red, blue, and amber. The amber and blue mix will make a light blue daylight sky, while a rich night sky can be obtained by adding a small amount of red to the blue. If people in the rear of the auditorium can see this striplight through the low window, or if there are balcony spectators who would surely see it, the better technique would be to hang the instrument overhead and focus it down on the backing.

A 6-foot strip, instrument 20, is hung behind the header over the archway to light the passage and its back wall. Again the 150-watt Rs can be used, but these may well be amber, blue-white, and red lamps as a more useful combination for this interior corridor.

Note that different length strips are employed for these two backings because the area that can be seen by the audience varies: about 9 feet in one case, and 15 in the other. Such an analysis is always essential and is plotted carefully on the layout from the worst seat on each side of the auditorium (indicated by + on the plan) through the extreme limits of the openings to the backgrounds. For illustration purposes these sight lines are shown as dashed lines in the plan shown in Figure 9–3.

Specials

With the regular instruments cared for, we can turn to the specials. Instrument 21 is a fire effect: two 60-watt lamps hidden behind two or three logs. Their light will be seen through pieces of colored glass, or crumpled gel, to give the effect of glowing coals. Although this will be seen by only a small segment of the audience, it is a worthwhile device to give the fireplace a touch of realism and warmth.

In the corner between the wall and the stairs is another special, instrument 22, a conventional desk lamp with cord running offstage to connect with the regular stage cable. Because its shade has been made more dense by use of a brown-paper lining, a 150-watt lamp may be used to throw a strong downward light.

Finally, on the upstage wall are two sconces or wall brackets, instruments 23 and 24, one on either side of the arch. These have unshaded lamps, therefore ones of small wattage must be used to prevent glare uncomfortable to an audience. The 15FC/V lamp, a flame-shaped decorative style, is employed. Because these have candelabra-sized bases, adapters must be placed in the regular sockets of the sconces, unless these are already of the proper small size.

Control

Modest as our hypothetical layout is, it would still require no fewer than twenty dimmers to control the lights properly. There are twenty-four listed instruments, but the two sconces can be ganged, as can the fire glow and fire effect. On the other hand, the striplights each have three color circuits, each demanding its own control. The largest loads would be 1200 watts for each circuit of the borderlights.

If the control board could not furnish the necessary circuits, some ganging would have to be done. Great ingenuity is often displayed in doing this, but a truly artistic use of lights and color values could not be maintained with many less than twenty dimmers.

Losing the Ceiling

Figure 9–6 illustrates a lighting layout for the realistic interior with-

No	INSTRUMENT	LOCATION	PURPOSE	LAMP	COLOR	REMARKS
1	8" ELLIPS'L SPOTLIGHT	CEILING-L	AREA 2L	750 T12	R02	
2	8" " "	"	" 1L	" "	R02	
3	8" " "	"	" 3L	" "	R02	
4	8" " "	"	" 4L	" "	R02	
5	8" " "	"	SPECIAL	" "	R02	SOFA
6	8" " "	CEILING-R	AREA 1R	" "	R60	
7	8" " "	"	SPECIAL	" "	R60	SOFA
8	8" " "	"	AREA 2R	" "	R60	
9	8" " "	"	" 4R	" "	R60	
10	8" " "	"	" 3R	" "	R60	
11	6" ELLIPS'L SPOTLIGHT	1ST PIPE	AREA 9L	500 T12	R02	
12	6" FRESNEL SPOTLIGHT	"	" 5L	500 T20	R02	
13	6" " "	"	" 6L	" "	R02	
14	6" ELLIPS'L SPOTLIGHT	"	SPECIAL	500 T12	02	STAIR & LANDING
15	6" FRESNEL SPOTLIGHT	"	AREA 9L	500 T20	R02	
16	6" " "	"	" 7L	" "	R02	
17	6" " "	"	" 5R	" "	R60	
18	6" ELLIPS'L SPOTLIGHT	"	SPECIAL	500 T12	R02	UPPER LANDING
19	6" FRESNEL SPOTLIGHT	"	"	" "	R02	WINDOW SEAT
20	3½" ELLIPS'L SPOTLIGHT	"	"	300W TH-L	R60	FRAME ON TROPHY
21	6" FRESNEL SPOTLIGHT	"	AREA 6R	500 T20	R60	
22	6" ELLIPS'L SPOTLIGHT	"	SPECIAL	500 T12	R02	AREA 9-FRAME TO ARCH
23	6" FRESNEL SPOTLIGHT	"	"	500 T20	R02	WINDOW SEAT
24	6" " "	"	AREA 7R	" "	R60	
25	6" " "	"	" 9R	" "	R60	
26	8" FRESNEL SPOTLIGHT	2ND PIPE	1-L BACK LT.	1000 G40	R09	MAT OFF SCENERY TOP
27	6" " "	"	STAIR - LEFT	500 720	R02	" " " "
28	8" " "	"	2L BACK LT.	1000 G40	R02	
29	8" " "	"	1R " "	1000 G40	CLEAR	
30	6" " "	"	AREA 8L	500 720	R02	
31	8" " "	"	3L BACK LT.	1000 G40	R09	
32	6" " "	"	STAIR RIGHT	500 T20	R60	
33	6" " "	"	AREA 8R	" "	R60	
34	8" " "	"	2R BACK LT.	1000 G40	CLEAR	
35	8" " "	"	4L " "	" "	R09	
36	3½" ELLIPS'L SPOTLIGHT	"	SPECIAL	300W TH-L	CLEAR	FRAME ON TROPHY
37	8" FRESNEL SPOTLIGHT	"	3R BACK LT.	1000 G40	"	
38	8" " "	"	4R " "	1000 G40	CLEAR	
39	6" " "	1ST BOOM #1	KITCHEN LT.	500 T20	"	
40	6" " "	16' #2	HALL+UPPER	" "	R02	
41	6" " "	"	LANDING	" "	R02	
42	8" " "	SPOTLINE PIPE #2	STREET LTS.	1000 G40	R62	
43	8" " "	"	" "	" "	R62	
44	8" " "	"	" "	" "	R62	
45	SPECIAL	SPOTLINE PIPE #1	PORCH LIGHT	100 W	CLEAR	
46	"	"	" "	"	"	D.S. FIXTURE IN VIEW
47	14" ELLIPS'L R. FLOOD	"	WINDOW WASH	500 PS	R02	
48	9" " "	HALL	WALL WASH	250 930	R02	
49	SPECIAL	HALL	CEILING FIXTURE	3/40W	CLEAR	
50	"	S.R. WALL	WALL FIXTURE	2/40W	"	
51	"	STAIR	" "	2/40W	"	

Stage Lighting

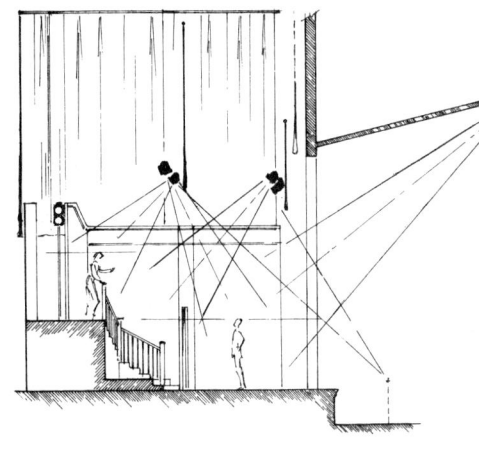

FIGURE 9–6
The Realistic Interior Without Ceiling
Present-day staging frequently omits the ceiling of an interior setting to facilitate the lighting. Shown are the instrument schedule, the sketch of the setting and a layout of lighting instruments, and a section.

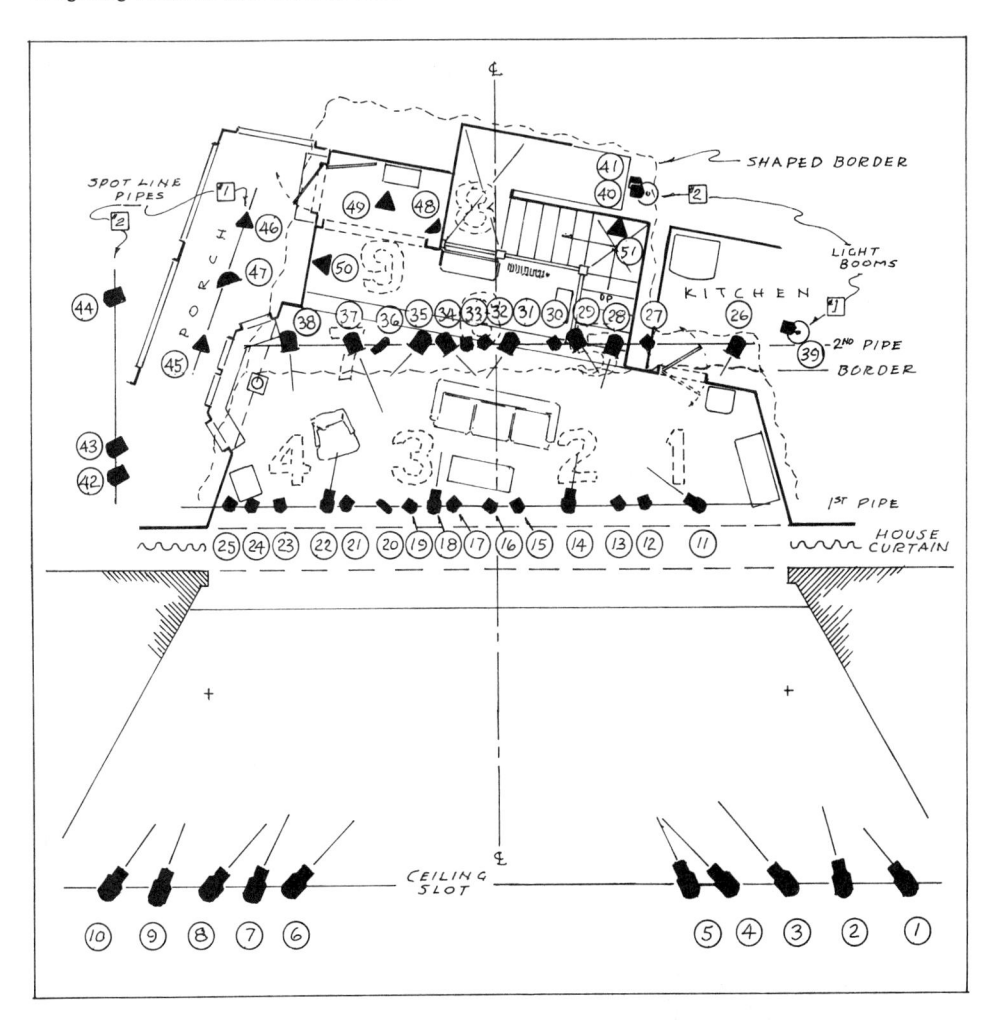

out a ceiling. Although losing the ceiling allows the designer a great deal more flexibility and variety, it may force trim heights up a good deal, depending upon masking. Additional high side lighting from stage right would be possible to support the bay windows. The color indicated is Roscolux.

REALISTIC EXTERIORS

The realistic exterior setting is one of the most difficult to light effectively because of the many maskings needed to prevent the audience from seeing into the wings or up into the hanging space. These maskings—flat surfaces painted to resemble natural objects—are never very convincing and tend to catch stray, unwanted beams of light.

An exterior setting almost always includes a large sky area or a painted scene in the background that needs special attention. Apparent motivation is necessary for all the lighting.

An Exterior Setting

Figure 9–7 (pages 172, 173) shows a typical exterior setting including many of the features frequently encountered. On stage left three sets of woodwings, painted as tree clusters, serve to mask the wings on that side of the stage. On the right there is a cottage which masks that side. In connection with the downstage woodwings, leaf borders cross the stage to mask overhead. Across the back of the playing areas is a ground row, 3 feet high in its lowest portion and representing hills in the middle distance.

The backdrop consists of a translucency, the lower portion of which is painted with opaque media to represent rolling hills and woods; above this the translucency is painted with dye colors to permit the light to pass through from the rear for greater luminosity and depth.

There are two scenes involved. In the first scene brilliant sunshine pours in from stage left. In the second, moonlight floods the set from the same direction.

Area Spots

The front lights are placed substantially as they were for the realistic interior, but because the sunlight and moonlight make two different effects necessary, the stage-left instruments are double hung; that is, there are two instruments focused on each area from this side. One set works in the first scene, the other set in the second. Or they might be used together at different intensities.

The three upstage areas are handled the same way, but because the first leaf border will hang so low, the usual first pipe location cannot be used. Instead this pipe is moved behind the leaf border. Great care must still be taken to prevent stray beams from touching corners of the second cloth border. Although Fresnels are indicated, a 6-inch ERS would be a possible substitute from the first pipe in order to keep light off the border. Careful use of the section will help to determine exact instrument placement and trim height.

Double-Hung Spotlights

The stage-left instruments that will work when the sun is shining are called the left-warms and they have No. 808 (Medium Straw) filters to give the effect of warmth on that side of the stage. Opposite them, in the stage-right spotlights, we use No. 842 (Special Lavender), a medium gel that will appear quite cool opposite the warm No. 808. But in Scene Two the left instruments contain No. 856 (Light Blue) which is so very cool that the lavender actually seems warm in contrast. This use of a neutral filter on one side of the stage to work alternately against a warm and a cool on the other is a device that is often of extreme value when instruments or control circuits are not too abundant.

Instead of lavender, many people would use no color at all. While it is true that the so-called white light from an ungelled spotlight is actually a trifle on the warm side of the spectrum, if used opposite a definitely warm color, such as amber, it will appear quite cool. Of course, opposite a cool color, it will seem even warmer than before.

Because the space just beyond the fence would be frequently used, especially for entrances, we are considering it a seventh area, with instruments (numbers 19, 20, and 21) mounted behind the second border. To make sure that an actor leaving or entering at stage right is completely covered, we place an additional spotlight (22) off right. The sunlight and moonlight coming in from stage left (as explained below) will take care of that side of the stage.

Sunlight and Moonlight

For a completely realistic effect, a great many powerful instruments would probably be needed for the sunlight and moonlight. But to keep our example within proper bounds, we will use only four for each. Because the moonlight need not be as bright, we have used 8-inch Fresnels, which give a much smoother and broader beam. Numbers 23 and 24 would be placed behind the first woodwing with their focuses overlapping across the stage. The remaining Fresnels, 25 and 26, would be mounted one each behind the other two wings. No 853 (Middle Blue) would give quite a realistic appearance as moonbeams.

The powerful beam projectors with 1500-watt lamps will be necessary for sunlight, to cut through the general light on the stage. These have been mounted in the same manner as the Fresnels and a No. 805 (Light Straw) used with them to give them a bit more warmth than the natural light from these instruments. This light will still appear whiter than the stage-left area lights with their No. 808.

Lighting for the Proscenium Theatre

No.	INSTRUMENT	LOCATION	PURPOSE	LAMP	COLOR	REMARKS
1	6" Ellips'l-Ref'r Spotlight	Beam-L	Area 2L-Warm	750 T12	808	Soft Edge
2	" " " "	" "	" 2L-Cool	"	856	" "
3	" " " "	" "	" 1L-Warm	"	808	Frame off Torm.
4	" " " "	" "	" 1L-Cool	"	856	" "
5	" " " "	" "	" 3L-Warm	"	808	
6	" " " "	" "	" 3L-Cool	"	856	
7	" " " "	Beam-R	" 1R	"	842	
8	" " " "	" "	" 3R	"	842	Frame off Torm.
9	" " " "	" "	" 2R	"	842	Soft Edge
10	6" Fresnel-Lens Spotlight	1st Pipe-L	" 4L Warm	500 T20	808	
11	" " " "	" "	" 4L Cool	"	856	
12	" " " "	" "	" 5L Warm	"	808	
13	" " " "	" "	" 5L Cool	"	856	
14	" " " "	" "	" 6L Warm	"	808	
15	" " " "	" "	" 6L Cool	"	856	
16	" " " "	1st Pipe-R	" 4R	"	842	
17	" " " "	" "	" 5R	"	842	
18	" " " "	" "	" 6R	"	842	
19	" " " "	2nd Pipe-L	" 7L Warm	"	808	
20	" " " "	" "	" 7L Cool	"	856	
21	" " " "	2nd Pipe-R	" 7R	"	842	
22	" " " "	3rd Pipe-R	" 7 Special	"	842	Mat off Drop
23	8" Fresnel-Lens Spotlight	1st Pipe-L	Moonlight	1000 G40	853	Focus on Area 2,3
24	" " " "	" "	"	"	853	" " " 1,2
25	" " " "	2nd Pipe-L	"	"	853	" " " 5
26	" " " "	3rd Pipe-L	"	"	853	" " " 7
27	10" Flood	Scenery-R	Door Backing	250 G30	810	Mount High on Scenery
28	16" Beam Projector	1st Pipe-L	Sun Light	1500 G40	805	Focus on Area 2,3
29	" " "	" "	"	"	805	" " " 1,2
30	" " "	2nd Pipe-L	"	"	805	" " " 5
31	" " "	3rd Pipe-L	"	"	805	" " " 7
32	6"x 6'-0" Striplights					Focus on Painted
33	" "				Amber	Portion
34	" "	On Floor Behind Ground Row	Translucency	300 R40	Blue	Roundels
35	" "		Front Light	Flood	Bl-Green	
36	" "					
37	6"x 4'-6" Striplights	4th Pipe	Translucency	150 PAR 38	861	
38	6"x 6'-0" "	Behind	Backlight	Spot	819	3-Color Circuit
39	" "	Translucency			854	Feed Through
40	" "	Very High				Focus on
41	" "					Translucent
42	6"x 4'-6" Striplights					Portion

172 Stage Lighting

FIGURE 9-7

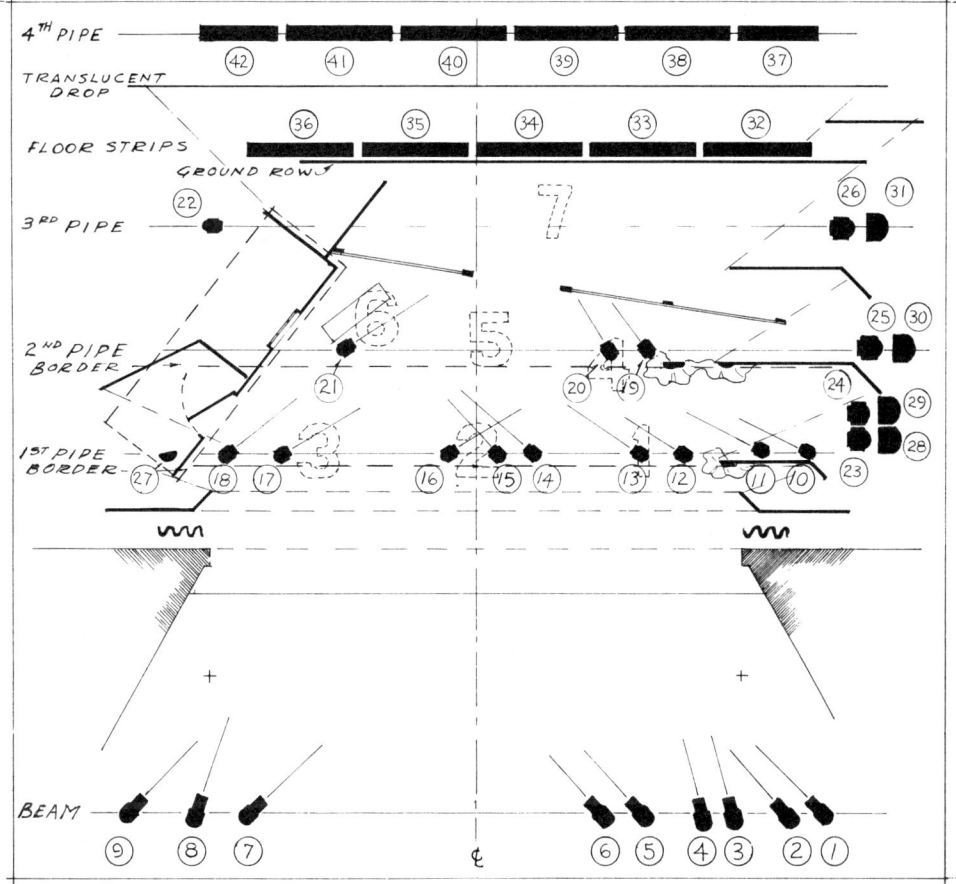

A Realistic Exterior Setting

(Opposite page) Instrument schedule. (This page) Sketch of setting and layout of lighting instruments.

Lighting for the Proscenium Theatre 173

On the stage with limited equipment it is possible to employ the same instrument for suns and moons, changing the color media between scenes, of course.

Translucent Backdrop

And finally we come to the background with a distant view painted opaquely at the bottom. This portion, of course, must be lighted from the front, and therefore five 6-foot lengths of striplights are placed on the floor, not too close, so that their various beams may have room to blend smoothly over the surface. They should be as close to the ground row as necessary to be hidden from the audience (this is especially important if there is a balcony). Because the light to be thrown on this portion is limited to the realistic daylight and nighttime colors, we may use amber, blue-green, and blue roundels over the 300-watt R-floods. Glass is essential here, for plastic would quickly burn out over these powerful lamps.

The upper portion of the backdrop is a true translucency, and therefore its light should come from behind. Four 6-foot lengths and two shorter lengths of strips with 150-watt PAR-spots are flown well above the highest visible part of the translucency and are focused down it to give it a sheet of light. Some form of backdrop might also be hung behind these, to reflect additional light through the translucency. This is a particularly effective device to furnish extra punch. As these strips are focused downwards, standard filters may be used safely. Quite a variation of color is needed for this sky, so the three circuits may well have No. 861 (Surprise Blue), No. 819 (Orange-Amber), and No. 854 (Steel Blue). By mixing the first and last, a daylight sky can be achieved; the 819 and 854 can give a sunset amber, while a touch of 819 added to the strong blue will provide a rich night sky. Many variations of these are possible.

Control

In a setting of this nature it is amazing how rapidly the dimmer requirements mount up. Certainly the twenty-two area spotlights each deserve individual control. The four moons could be ganged but would then require a dimmer of 4000-watt capacity. Similarly the suns could be controlled together, but would need a 6000-watt dimmer or two of 3000 watts each.

The translucency front strips make up as three 20-lamp color circuits of 6000 watts apiece. There are 22 lamps per color circuit in the rear strips, at 3300 watts each.

If the largest dimmers are 2000 watts, then the moons will require two, the suns four, translucency fronts nine, and rear six—a total of twenty-one dimmers!

On many boards this would necessitate ganging area spotlights, with the resulting loss of artistic control. Of course it may be necessary to fall back on awkward replugging between scenes, using the same dimmers for the moons in the second scene as were used for the suns in the first and the left area cools in place of the warms on the same group of controls.

WING-AND-BORDER SETTINGS

The wing-and-border setting presents problems very different from the realistic exterior and interior types. Here realism and plausibility are usually of little concern. Rather, the large expanses of flat scenery demand flat lighting, and against these brilliant backgrounds the actors must be picked out by powerful lighting directed on them. The use of follow spots for this purpose is fairly standard.

Setting for a Musical

Figure 9–8 (pages 176 and 177) shows a wing-and-border set for a typical musical. Because a traveler show curtain with appropriate design is hung immediately behind the house curtain, the house tormentors and teaser have been removed and their functions assumed by a show portal hung just upstage of the show curtain. The zone across the stage just above the portal is usually referred to as "In One." Its upstage boundary is marked by a second traveler, a second portal, and a drop beyond. In turn, some feet upstage of this group is yet another consisting of a second drop, a third portal, and then two more drops. Finally, beyond all is a sky-blue backing.

The several drops will not all be solid cloth; some will be cut out in part so that the audience sees through to other scenic elements beyond. The various drops will work with the curtains and portals in different combinations as the show progresses, while set pieces, furniture, and the like will be moved on and off stage for different scenes. Often special lighting is needed for such pieces.

The sketch shows the three portals, drop No. 2, representing a cut-out of trees, and drop No. 4, a distant view.

Lighting the In-One Zone

In order to provide the punch of light on the actors required by this type of presentation, we have double hung all the area lighting spotlights. This means that in the beams there are twelve 6 × 12 ellipsoidal spotlights, two to a side on each of the three "In One" areas. Care must be taken to focus these spots far enough downstage on the apron to cover the probable movement of the players. In this style of production it is not uncommon for the actors to be brought clear down to the very edge of the stage.

With four instruments on each area, considerable variation in the colors is possible. Rather than simply use the same tints on the op-

Lighting for the Proscenium Theatre

No.	INSTRUMENT	LOCATION	PURPOSE	LAMP	COLOR	REMARKS
1	6" Ellips'l-Ref'r Spotlight	Beam - L	Area 2L Warm	750 T12	826	
2	" " " "	" "	" 2L Cool	"	850	
3	" " " "	" "	" 1L Warm	"	826	Frame to Portal
4	" " " "	" "	" 1L Cool	"	850	" " "
5	" " " "	" "	" 3L Warm	"	826	
6	" " " "	" "	" 3L Cool	"	850	
7	8" Ellips'l-Ref'r Spotlight	Beam - C	Follwspot	1000 T12	Clear	
8	" " " "	" "	"	"	"	
9	6" Ellips'l-Ref'r Spotlight	Beam - R	Area 1R Warm	750 T12	802	
10	" " " "	" "	" 1R Cool	"	842	
11	" " " "	" "	" 3R Warm	"	802	Frame off Portal
12	" " " "	" "	" 3R Cool	"	842	" " "
13	" " " "	" "	" 2R Warm	"	802	
14	" " " "	" "	" 2R Cool	"	842	
15	" " " "	1st Stand-L	Crosslight	750 T12	852	Focus on Area 2,3
16	" " " "	" "	"	500 T12	852	" " " 1,2
17	6" Fresnel-Lens Spotlight	1st Pipe-L	Area 5L Warm	500 T20	826	
18	" " " "	" "	5L Cool	"	850	
19	" " " "	" "	4L Warm	"	826	
20	" " " "	" "	4L Cool	"	850	
21	" " " "	" "	6L Warm	"	826	
22	" " " "	" "	6L Cool	"	850	
23	" " " "	1st Pipe-R	4R Warm	"	802	
24	" " " "	" "	4R Cool	"	842	
25	" " " "	" "	6R Warm	"	802	
26	" " " "	" "	6R Cool	"	842	
27	" " " "	" "	5R Warm	"	802	
28	" " " "	" "	5R Cool	"	842	
29	6" Ellips'l-Ref'r Spotlight	1st Stand-R	Crosslight	750 T12	810	Focus on Area 1,2
30	" " " "	" R	"	500 T12	810	" " " 2,3
31	" " " "	2nd Stand-L	"	750 T12	852	" " " 5,6
32	" " " "	" -L	"	500 T12	852	" " " 4,5
33	" " " "	" -R	"	750 T12	810	" " " 4,5
34	" " " "	" -R	"	500 T12	810	" " " 5,6
35	" " " "	3rd Stand-L	"	750 T12	852	Focus Far
36	" " " "	" -L	"	500 T12	852	" Near
37	" " " "	" -R	"	750 T12	810	" Far
38	" " " "	" -R	"	500 T12	810	" Near
39	16" Beam Projector	2nd Pipe-L	Downlight	1000 G40	802	Focus Downstage
40	" " "	" -L	"	"	802	" "
41	" " "	" -R	"	"	802	" "
42	" " "	" -R	"	"	802	" "
43	6"x6'-0" Striplights				R	
44	" "	Apron	Footlights	150 R40	G	3-Color Circuit
45	" "		Flood		B Roundel	Feed Through
46	" "				828	
47	" "	1st Pipe	1st Border	150 R40	815	
48	" "		Spot		858	
49	" "				828	
50	" "	3rd Pipe	2nd Border	150 R40	815	
51	" "		Spot		858	
52	" "					
53	" "	4th Pipe	Back Drop	300 R40	863	
54	" "		Spot		853	
55	" "				810	

FIGURE 9–8
A Wing-and-Border Setting
(Opposite page) Instrument schedule. (This page) Sketch of setting and layout of lighting instruments.

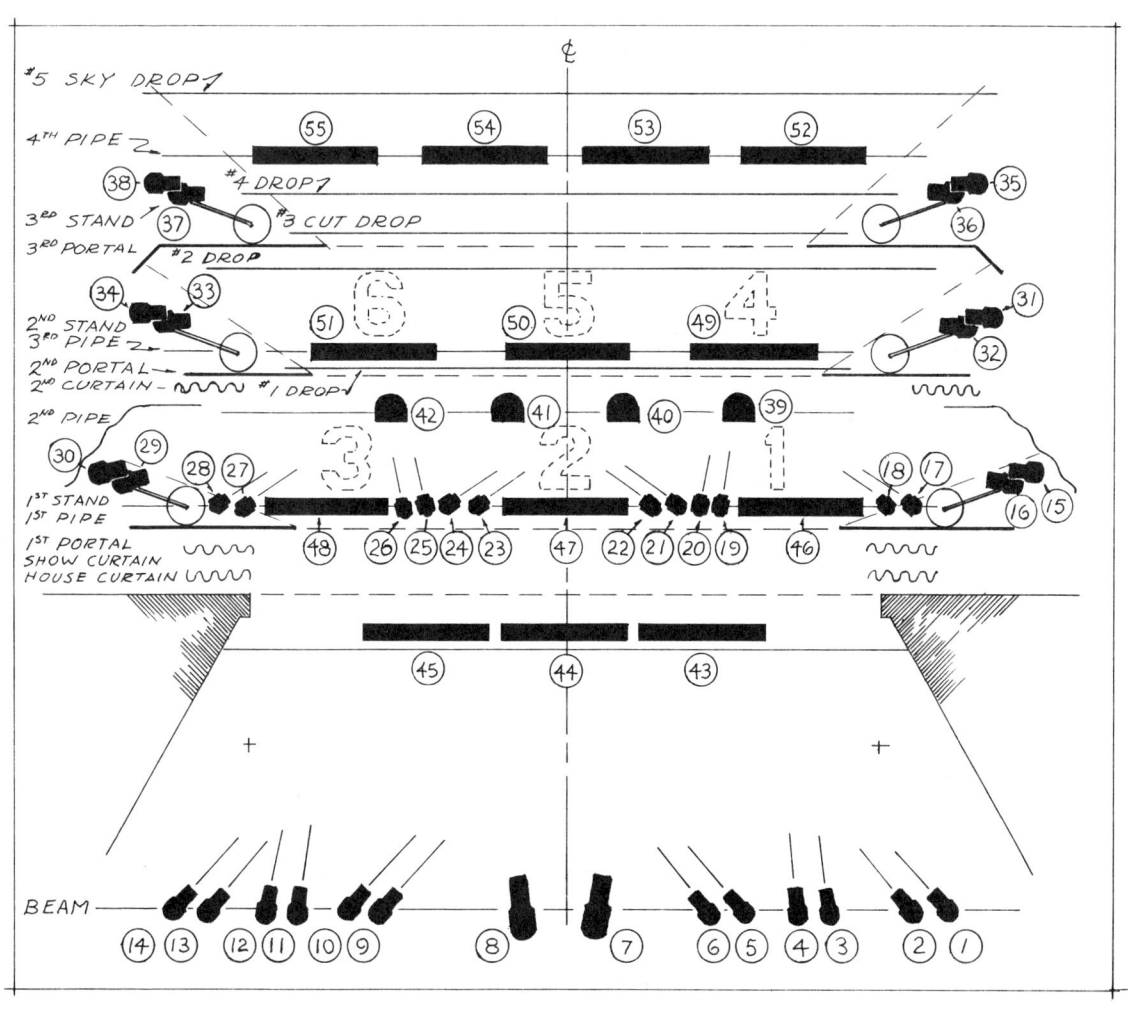

Lighting for the Proscenium Theatre

posite side of the stage, we prefer to put the flattering No. 826 (Flesh Pink) as the warm color on the left and No. 802 on the right. For most productions of this type, a generally romantic feeling is desired, so the cools should not be saturated. No. 850 is a deep enough blue to be used on the left, while the rather neutral No. 842 (Special Lavender) on the right will appear quite cool in comparison to the warm colors used with it.

Follow Spots

Frequently, it is desirable to have special instruments in the beams to illuminate the decorative show curtain. But to keep this layout on the modest side, we have forgone these and will let the footlights do the job. But a pair of 8-inch narrow-beam ellipsoidal spotlights, burning 1000-watt lamps and equipped with irises, are used as follow spots. We assume that operators may be stationed in the theatre's beam. In plants where this is not possible, some other location must be found (for example, balcony, box booms, or rear of balcony projection booth). Musicals without spotlights to accent the leading players on the brightly lighted stage lack a great deal of the theatrical glamor that goes with this sort of presentation. Most of the time these follow spots will be most effective with no color medium at all. If any is used, a No. 825 (No Color Pink) is appropriate. Of course, for occasional and particular purposes other and stronger colors may be used, including a very dense blue filter especially made for ultraviolet effects. With an operator in constant attendance, color changes are easily accomplished.

The In-Two Zone

Moving to the "In-Two" zone, that between the second and third portals, we light the three upstage areas by means of twelve 6-inch Fresnel spots hanging from the first pipe, although 6 × 9 ellipsoidals would also be a good choice. Their colors match the downstage area spotlights, as usual. These instruments must be carefully focused to pass under the second portal without touching the edges with a distracting glare. Many times a third set of spotlights is employed for the "In-Three" zone, but because our stage is not deep, and we are trying to be economical with instruments, we shall hope that the extra light is not needed this far upstage. Of course, viewing rehearsals would tell us for sure.

Side Lighting

Side lighting—lighting from the wings—has become a convention with the wing-and-border setting. It has three important aspects: its low angle from the side adds to the plasticity of the actor's appearance; it can add extra color effects; and it helps to tie together the zones across which it is focused. In each of our six side entrances we have provided two 6-inch ellipsoidal spotlights mounted on boom stands.

The upper instrument is focused across the stage to catch both the center and the far acting areas, and, because of this long throw, it burns a 750-watt lamp and is the narrower beam 6 × 12. The lower one, a 6 × 9 mounted at least 10 feet above stage level, ties in the near and the center areas and uses the 500-watt lamp. Because we are not using strong colors for our regular area spotlights, in these side-lighting instruments we choose No. 852 (Smokey Blue) from the left and No. 810 (No Color Amber) from the right.

Down Lights

Another feature that is becoming almost a must for musicals are the downlights which we have placed over the "In-One" zone. These are hung quite high and just downstage of the traveler curtain and the second portal so that they tend to back-light the actors standing at the front of the zone. A No. 802 filter in these 16-inch beam projectors with their 1000-watt lamps will throw a flattering high light on the head and shoulders of the actors and set them out from the scenery. A second set of down lights over the "In-Two" zone might not be amiss, but our list of instruments is already startlingly long.

Footlights

Striplights have been used extensively to tie in the various portions of the stage, to give tonal washes over scenery and actors, and generally to provide illumination. The footlights consist of the regular three 6-foot lengths, in this case burning 150-watt R-40 lamps behind glass roundels in the primary colors. The unusually high wattage here is to provide a strong wash of light for the show curtain. Musicals and revues can use rather strong footlights to supplement the regular front lighting especially for chorus-line sequences, to throw illumination under large hats, to wash the company with special colors, and the like.

Border Lights

For the first and second borders, three 6-foot lengths each are used. Those on the first pipe must be placed well apart to leave room for area spotlights to be mounted between the lengths; on the third pipe less space is needed. But in both cases somewhat wider extension into the wings is necessary in order properly to wash the scenery hanging upstage of each set of strips. The 150-watt R-40 floods are used with colors approaching the secondaries: No. 828 (Follies Pink), No. 815 (Golden Amber), and No. 858 (Light Green Blue), a combination that should allow almost any tint desired to flood the stage.

The Backdrop

And for the background, the cloth or other surface painted to represent the sky, four lengths of strips have been hung as far downstage from the surface as other flown elements permit so that as smooth a

Lighting for the Proscenium Theatre

wash as possible can be achieved. Here it is necessary to go to the 300-watt R-40 spots because a good punch will be needed. A dark night sky can be achieved by use of a No. 863 (Medium Blue), and if this is a bit too deep it can be lightened a little by mixing in No. 853 (Middle Blue). For a bright daylight sky we add No. 810 (No Color Amber).

Control

There are twenty-four area spotlights, all of which will be working at the same time in several scenes, so no replugging is possible in this production. Although it would be pleasant to have an individual dimmer assigned to each cross-lighting instrument, we can get along by ganging the pair at each location, thereby holding the dimmer requirements to six. The downlights, too, may well be ganged: on a 4000-watt dimmer, if one is available, if not, in pairs on two 2000-watt dimmers.

The footlights and first and second border will each require three 1800-watt circuits—nine all together. But the backdrop calls for three circuits of 4800 watts apiece. On boards with small capacity these loads must be split up in some manner, depending on what is available.

Obviously, individual control over the two follow spots is absolutely essential. The total and minimum demands for this layout, therefore, would be forty-three dimmers that can handle up to 2000 watts each, and three of far greater capacity. And this is a very modest plot for a musical play.

OTHER TYPES OF PROSCENIUM STAGING

Today, the types of presentation that fall within the categories of unit settings, simultaneous settings, or space staging have become increasingly popular. These forms of production generally have very little concern with realistic scenery. Often the scenic elements consist of an abstract arrangement of platforms and possibly a form or two of suggestive (but not very representational) shape. The background frequently will be a surrounding of black velour drapery but may also be an open cyclorama. In either case, lighting which separates the actor from his or her background is imperative.

The scenery may move to help establish various locales, or the lighting designer may be called upon exclusively to set a scene. If this is the case, careful planning as well as extensive communication with both the scene designer and director is of utmost importance. The lighting designer's approach to such a production will have a great deal to do with the number of scenes and their respective complexity. If the script only calls for a few locale changes, the designer may design each scene separately and then combine all into a unified plot. However, if the play has many scenes, the approach will most likely be one of full-stage area lighting with tight control and added special instrumentation when required.

Whether scenic forms are used or not, light plays a major role in the creation and composition of acting space. Movement of light will alter focus and must be considered early in the planning stages. High-angle distribution is often preferred in order to keep the area being lit as tight as possible, but care must be taken to avoid deep facial shadows that could prove disturbing.

The lighting designer must use creative instincts to their fullest potential in supporting the stage action within the limitations of equipment and control. As might be expected, this style of performance presents an exciting challenge to the lighting designer.

10

Lighting for Other Production Forms

So far we have discussed only the types of production presented on a conventional stage, where practically all action is separated from the audience by "the fourth wall." But other forms are rapidly gaining in popularity, forms in which the division between audience area and acting area is less obvious. These vary from a proscenium stage with action coming out into the auditorium on side stages, ramps, and steps to the complete arena form in which the audience surrounds the playing area on all four sides. Techniques useful for lighting in-the-round stages differ from those used for performances done on a proscenium stage.

ARENA PRODUCTION

The designer need not be bothered with lighting the scenery in a truly in-the-round production, for arena staging uses little scenery, and what does exist is adequately lighted by the same beams that strike nearby actors. However, this lack of scenery deprives the designer of valuable mounting positions for instruments, and, more important, eliminates a background. The actors must be lit from all sides, just as they must play to all sides.

Accuracy of Focus

With the spectators crowded closely—often too closely—about the playing areas, instruments that have hard-to-control beams are of little value. Floodlights are impossible. Striplights may be used discreetly and with side maskings to give an overall tonality of rather low intensity. Fresnel spots must be focused with particular accuracy and, in addition, a top hat or barn doors must be added to control the beam spill.

Functions of Arena Lighting

Visibility remains, of course, the primary function in arena-production lighting, and this means that the actors must be effectively lighted for all members of the surrounding audience. Composition takes the form of holding the spectators' attention to the acting areas and thus the lighting must have definition and great precision of form. Tight and specific area control is often required in the arena, adding another compositional requirement to the designer's list. Mood must be accomplished by means of intensity and color toning but both within limited ranges. In addition, the color, texture, and compositional makeup of the stage floor takes on greater visual importance in arena production because of audience viewing angle.

Mounting Positions

Because arena stages and the buildings surrounding them vary so greatly, it is difficult to suggest a typical lighting arrangement. An arena stage in the center of a large gymnasium floor, for example, would probably offer all sorts of lofty and convenient mounting places for overhead lighting instruments, while a formal hall with a plastered ceiling of no great height would present enormous, if not impossible, difficulties. However, let us assume a reasonable amount of overhead flexibility in our discussion of this form of presentation.

Arena Lighting Areas

It is convenient to divide the arena stage into a number of acting areas, each of which can be effectively covered by the beam of a spotlight mounted along a 45-degree angle. Just what type of spotlight this would be would depend on the mounting locations and their distances. If a good, long throw is possible, the 6 × 12 ellipsoidal spotlight with a 750-watt lamp would be fine; for much shorter throws, say of 15 to 20 feet, one of the wider-beam ellipsoidals would work very well.

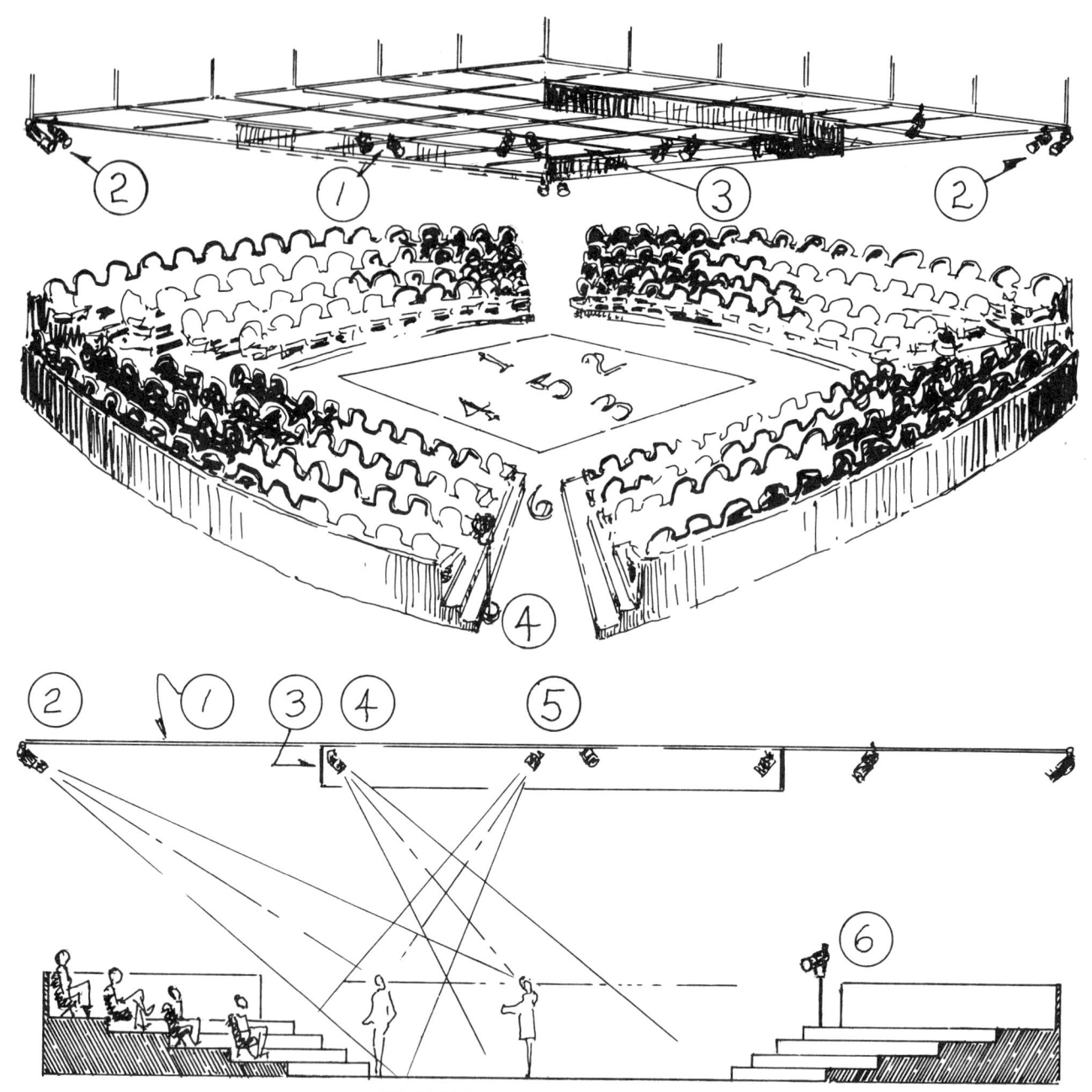

FIGURE 10-1

Arena Stage Lighting Positions

(Top) A perspective view of an arena stage showing a pipe grid over the audience and acting area. (1) The nearest frontal position behind the valance. (2) Extreme position on the outer edge of the grid. (3) Central position over the acting area for down lighting and back lighting. (4) Special position in the aisle for an occasional effect.

The acting areas are numbered from one to five. The number of areas is, of course, optional and would vary with the requirements of the production.

(Above) A cross section through the arena showing the various angles of distribution. (1) Pipe grid. (2) Outside position. (3) Valance. (4) Inner position behind valance. (5) Central position. (6) Special position in aisle.

Stage Lighting

On the proscenium stage each area must be covered by two spotlights, each ideally 45 degrees on the actor. In an arena, however, where the actor is seen from all sides, more instruments are necessary. There are two popular approaches to the solution. One is that three instruments per area be used, evenly spaced about the area and thus at 120 degrees from one another. The second approach is to use four spots on each area, putting them 90 degrees from each other and shooting along the diagonals of the space.

Color in the Arena

With either approach, the system of using one warm and one cool color on each area is no longer applicable. In the three-spotlight plan the third instrument is assigned a neutral color, such as Special Lavender—which, we have seen, appears cool opposite a warm filter and warm opposite a cool one. Light Flesh Pink is also a possibility for scenes that are basically warm and romantic. No color at all also can be quite effective.

The four-instrument system suggests two color variations. In the first, a warm and a cool are used on opposite sides, while the two intermediate instruments have a neutral medium. An alternate approach is to use two warms, each opposite the other, and two cools, also opposite each other. The latter will most often prove more satisfactory.

A word of warning about the choice of colors in arena productions: Because the directionality of the spotlights on each side of each area is so definite, colors show up much stronger on the actors than in a proscenium production, where there is far more mixing of different beams. Or perhaps this seems true to the audience because of its closeness to the action. In any event, the use of more saturated colors is rarely advisable.

Blending

The use of blending strips to give a tonality to the scene, much as first border strips are used on a proscenium stage, may be quite effective if properly handled. Two or three of the 6-foot lengths might be hung down the center line of the arena, or two strips might be placed along opposite sides and focused across the stage. Striplights, so used, must be provided with blinders (side maskings) that will prevent their beams from falling on the audience, particularly that portion of it seated on the opposite side of the stage.

Six-inch Fresnel down lights at flood focus will also provide good blending and color toning. Although Fresnels do not offer as much color flexibility as striplights, they allow for greater control. Finally, don't forget to use top hats.

Lighting for Other Production Forms

Unmasked Instruments

It would be fruitless in a temporary arena setup to attempt to hide the instruments from the audience. They can, of course, be hung and maintained in a neat manner, with wiring carefully tied off and the like. But a frank acceptance of the fact that the instruments are there for all to view is better than a lot of makeshift, dust-catching, and fire-prone draperies.

However, if a stage house has been designed especially for arena production, a false ceiling should be provided with openings through which the beams of light may be focused from instruments hung well above and out of sight. Catwalks must be installed so the electrician can reach all instruments with ease for maintenance, focusing, and color changes.

Blinding the Spectators

The most difficult problem in any form of arena production is to keep the beams of the area spotlights out of the eyes of spectators seated on the opposite side of the stage. As long as light persists in traveling in a straight line, and as long as directors wish to play their actors at the very edge of the arena stage, just so long will a compromise be necessary between a well-lighted actor and a half-blinded spectator.

To solve the problem, the angle of the instrument or instruments spilling into the audience can be raised, but this compromise only helps so much. If the first row of the audience can be raised higher than the stage level, or be set back from it, or both, the problem can be greatly eased. In any event, this is one of the greatest problems confronting the light designer in arena production.

Designing the Lighting for an Arena Production

Should the lighting designer attempt to create the same lighting picture for everyone in the arena audience? Experience has shown that such an approach is quite restrictive and leads to fairly bland lighting. Nonetheless, the designer should always be concerned about the quality of lighting from all viewing angles in an arena theatre.

Figures 10–1 through 10–3 illustrate our sample arena layout with properties in place on the stage floor. There are two boxes in which lighting instruments may be hung overhead. A layout and an instrument schedule for a suitable lighting design are also shown.

The designer has divided the stage into five areas, which have been numbered clockwise from one through four, with area five in the center. Dotted lines on the layout mark the approximate limits of these areas, although it is, of course, understood that actually they will overlap one another and their lights will blend smoothly. The instruments have been numbered systematically, from the top, clockwise around the stage, in the outer box first and then the inner.

No.	INSTRUMENT	PURPOSE	LAMP	COLOR	REMARKS
(1)	6" Ellips'l-Refl Spotlight	Area 1	500T12	803	
2	" " "	" 2	"	803	
3	8" Fresnel Spotlight	Moonlight Special	1000G40	856	Focus Center
4	6" Ellips'l-Refl Spotlight	Area 2	500T12	848	
5	" " "	" 3	"	848	
6	" " "	Divan Special	750T12	826	Frame to Divan
7	" " "	Area 3	500T12	805	
8	" " "	" 4	"	805	
9	" " "	" 4	"	842	
(10)	" " "	" 1	"	842	
11	40° Mini-Ellipse	" 4	500W Q	803	Mat Top
12	6" Fresnel Spotlight	" 5	500T20	803	Top Hat
13	40° Mini-Ellipse	" 3	500W Q	803	Mat Top
(14)	" " "	" 1	"	848	" "
15	6" Fresnel Spotlight	" 5	500T20	848	Top Hat
16	40° Mini-Ellipse	" 4	500W Q	848	Mat Top
17	" " "	" 2	"	805	" "
18	6" Fresnel Spotlight	" 5	500T20	805	Top-Hat
19	4½" Ellips'l-Refl Spotlight	Center Accent	500T12	Clear	Focus Center
(20)	40° Mini-Ellipse	Area 1	500W Q	805	Mat Top
21	" " "	" 3	"	842	" "
22	" " "	Divan Special #2	"	802	Mat to Divan
23	6" Fresnel Spotlight	Area 5	500T20	842	Top Hat
24	40° Mini-Ellipse	" 2	500W Q	842	Mat Top
25	Fixture	Table Lamp #1	40A	–	Gang with #26
26	"	" " #2	40A	–	" " #25

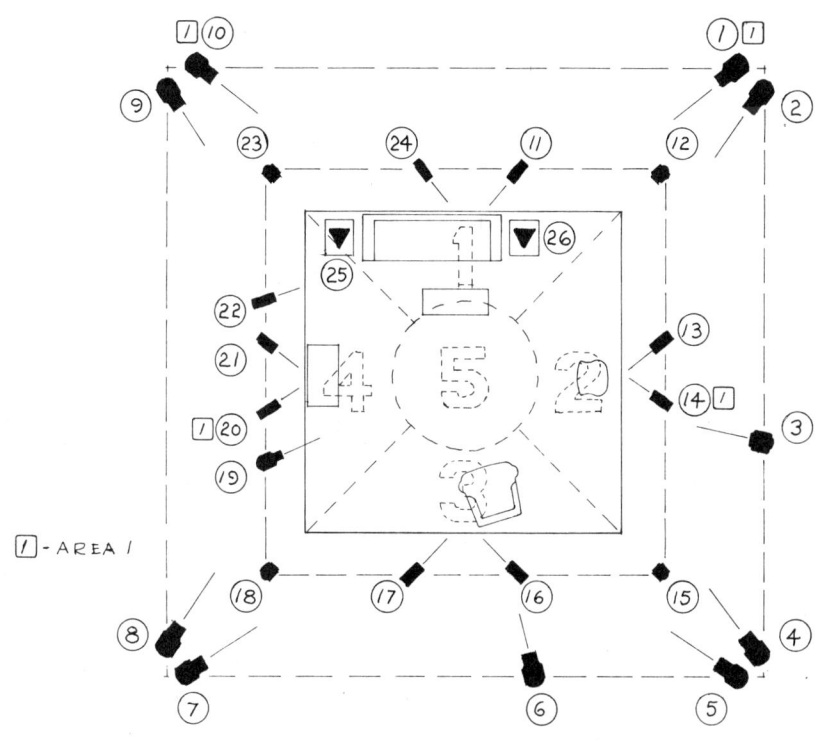

FIGURE 10–2

An Arena-Production Setting
(Left) Layout of lighting instruments.
(Above) Instrument schedule.

Lighting for Other Production Forms

187

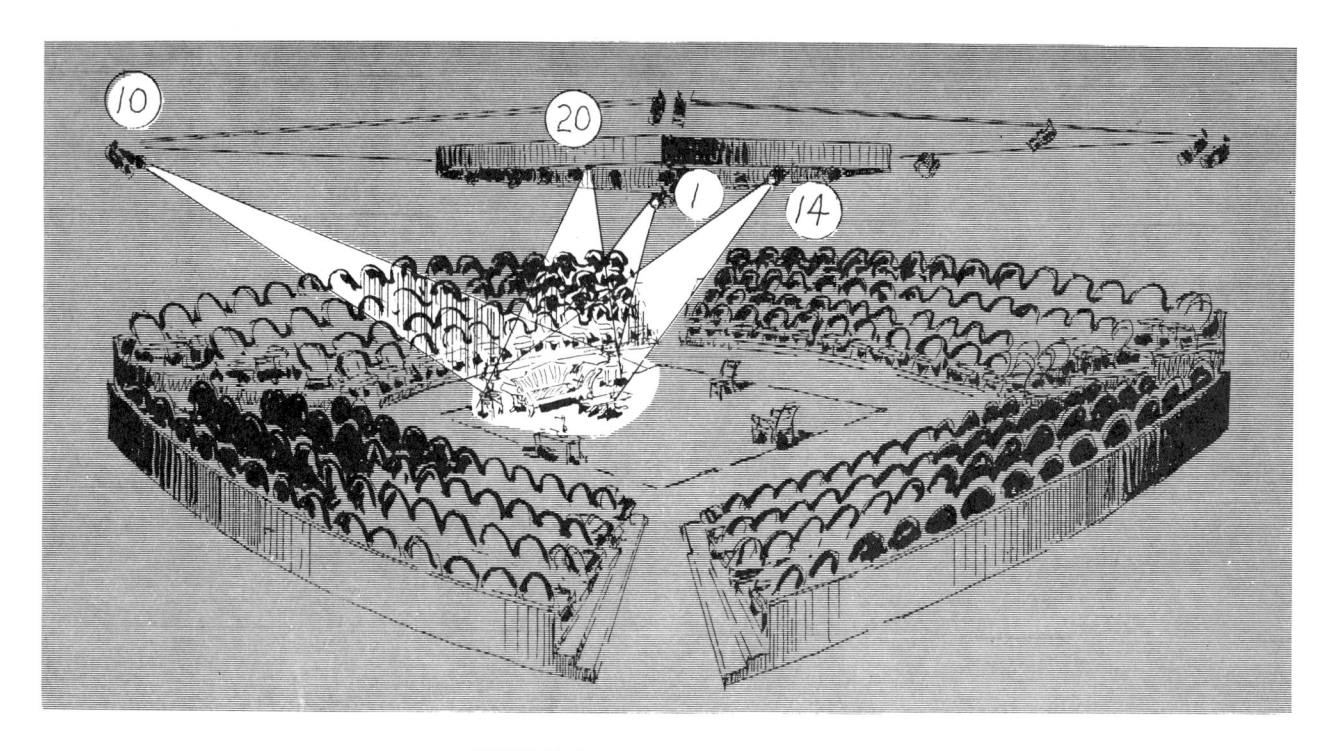

FIGURE 10–3

Arena Stage Lighting Layout

Coverage on one of the five acting areas. Note the four different angles. Note Area 1 in floor plan showing lighting layout, Figure 10–2.

From each corner of the outer box a pair of 6 × 12 ellipsoidal reflector spotlights is focused on the two closest areas, giving each of these two beams of light at approximately right angles to one another. From the inner box two 40° Mini-Ellipse spotlights are focused on each of the same areas. The ERS is used here because the upper portion of its beam can be effectively matted to prevent light from glaring into the eyes of spectators seated on the opposite side of the stage.

Area 5, in the center, is hit from the four corners of the inner box by 6-inch Fresnel spotlights. Here the danger of spill light annoying the audience is less marked than in the outer areas, but top hats are used on the instruments just the same. The typical soft-edged Fresnel-beam pattern is useful to blend this center light with the illumination on the adjacent areas.

The color system in Roscolene plastic is that of opposite warms and cools. The warm light, working diagonally out of the upper-right corner of the layout, is from a Roscolene No. 803 (Pale Gold) Filter. The identical color might have been employed also from the lower left, but the designer preferred to use a slightly different tint, Roscolene No. 805 (Light Straw). In like manner, the cools are not identical: from the lower right is a No. 848 (Water Blue), while opposite it is a No. 842 (Special Lavender). This is not an especially cool color, but it has been chosen here because we are assuming that this is a warm, pleasant type of play. Had it been a cold, stark drama, we might have selected a combination of No. 851 and No. 848 for the cools, while the versatile No. 842 might have been one of the warms, with perhaps no color at all in the opposite instruments.

A few specials have been provided. On the right side there is an 8-inch Fresnel with a No. 856 (Light Blue) gel to give the effect of moonbeams for a brief scene. Instrument 6 is focused carefully on the divan with a romantic No. 826 (Flesh Pink) for a tender moment. Toward the upper-left corner is another divan special with No. 802 (Bastard Amber) for a different scene. Also on the left, a wide-beamed ellipsoidal-reflector spotlight without color serves as an accent on the central area for some special action there. The two table lamps at either end of the divan are practical fixtures, meaning that they will be lit at some point in the production.

Control

Twenty-four dimmers would be necessary for this simple arena layout, assuming that we can repatch one of the specials. Arena and thrust lighting almost always require tighter and more individual control than proscenium production.

THRUST STAGE PRODUCTION

The Extended Apron

There are two forms of theatrical presentation that recently have become extremely popular: the extended apron and the thrust stage. The former is really a variation of regular proscenium production as far as lighting is concerned. Some additional spotlights in the beams, on the balcony front, in side slots in the auditorium walls, and on booms in side boxes can all be used on the extended stage. If the stage is not too deep, it may be back lighted from behind the proscenium, except, of course, when the curtain is closed. The use of striplights and floods is impractical. The only real problem presented is that of keeping the beam patterns from being too prominent on the walls of the auditorium and off the audience itself.

An Approach to Thrust Stage Lighting

Any theatre designed for a thrust stage should include provision for good mounting positions for the lighting instruments. The simplest manner of doing this is a grid of pipes or other mounting structure over the entire stage and extending over the audience as well in all directions as far from the edge of the stage as the height of the grid above the stage floor. There should be a great number of electrical outlets provided on this grid, unless it is the intention to string cables from backstage to the specific instruments. If the grid is not too high,

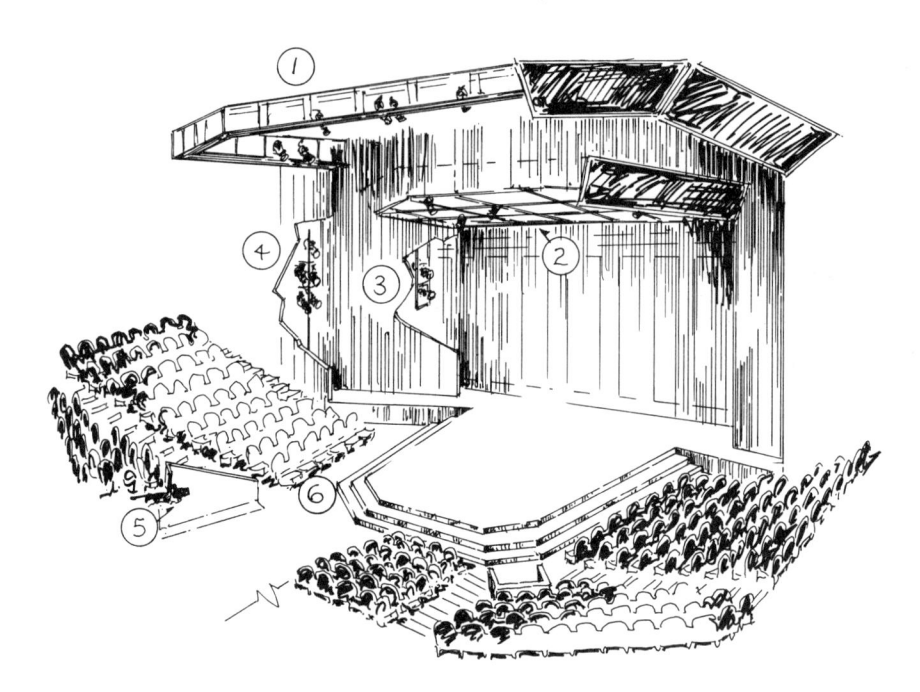

FIGURE 10–4
Thrust Stage Lighting Positions
A perspective view of a thrust stage showing its various lighting positions. The stage division into acting areas would vary with each production. (1) Outer valance position. (2) Second valance and gridiron over stage. (3) Wing ladder, side lighting. (4) Tormentor boom. (5) Vomitory rail. (6) Gutter.

it can be reached by ladders from below. But if it is over 14 feet above the floor, a network of catwalks, so numerous that an electrician can safely reach every inch of the grid from them, should be provided above the pipes.

Boxes or valances to hide the instruments are often provided, but because of the necessity to be able to hang spotlights on any portion of the grid, especially over the stage itself, these devices are not wholly effective. Therefore instruments should be mounted and cabled neatly and securely so as to be neither a distraction nor a danger. Those spectators in the side seats particularly will find that the lenses of instruments focused in their general direction will be in full view. But as long as top hats are used, this should not prove too great a distraction. Care must be taken to mask or frame off the upper part of the beams from such instruments to be sure they do not glare directly into the eyes of those seated facing them. Ellipsoidal reflector spotlights can use their internal framing shutters to good advantage; Fresnels should be provided with barn doors.

Often the arrangement of set pieces and properties will dictate how a thrust stage is best divided into acting areas, and each of these will require several instruments focused on it from several directions. Every actor on a thrust stage is seen from three sides at the same time. Top or back lighting is also essential to set the actor off from the background. Blending and toning are best accomplished by use of soft-beamed spotlights to throw color washes over large portions of the stage.

As with arena staging, strong colors are not desirable on the thrust stage, although we can become somewhat bolder because of the one closed side. Spots to hit the stage at the familiar 45-degree angle from the front might use very pale tints, while other instruments on the same area can take stronger shades of the same basic colors, with those coming in directly from the sides using quite deep tones. The down or back lighting is often not far from white light.

The stage floor becomes a major scenic element in most thrust houses because of the steep audience rake. As in the arena, lighting color, texture, and composition will read quite strongly on the floor.

Designing the Lighting

Figure 10–5 (pages 192-193) shows a sketch of a typical thrust stage with properties and a few scenic pieces set for a play. Also shown are a layout for lighting this production and schedule of the instruments to be used.

The stage divides itself into five natural areas: the upper platform and archway being 1; the central section as outlined by the carpet, 2; and the margin of the platform surrounding the carpet, 3, 4, and 5. The designer has sought to put five to seven instruments on each area, but the difficulty of focusing to cover an area properly without hitting the audience at the same time has limited this in some instances. The further to the side the instruments are mounted, the deeper the colors they use. For this layout Lee filters are employed.

Taking area 1 as an example, we find that it is covered from the front by two 6 × 12 ellipsoidal reflector spotlights, 32 and 36, mounted in the inner box. Two 8-inch ellipsoidals, 1 and 23, strike it from the booms placed in the ramp entrances on either side of the stage. Two more 6-inchers, 27 and 41, are on the ladders hung in the upstage entrances. One 6-inch ellipsoidal works as a back light from above the upstage archway. The colors, working from front to rear on the left side are Lee 117 (Steel Blue), 144 (No Color Blue), and 141 (Bright Blue). On the right side they are 152 (Pale Gold), 151 (Gold Tint), and a double 153 (Pale Salmon). The back light is clear. The other areas use these same colors for instruments working from the same angles.

A pair of 8-inch Fresnel spotlights strikes the entire set from dead ahead to give it a tonal wash that may be varied by dimming the warm and cool instruments to different readings. Two pairs of 6-inch Fresnels, on either side of the inner box, and two pairs of 6-inch ellipsoidals in the ramp entrances work with the others. For the cool wash a 119 (Dark Blue) is used, for the warm wash a 134 (Golden Amber).

A great many specials have been hung. The extreme up-left and up-right corners, which might almost be considered areas in themselves, are each covered by three spots from front and sides, plus a back light. The tunnel entrances through the audience section (called vomitory entrances), the entrances along the ramps left and right, and those at the extreme back, as well as the archway in the center of the backwall, are all lighted. The bench, the window seat, the sofa, and the steps

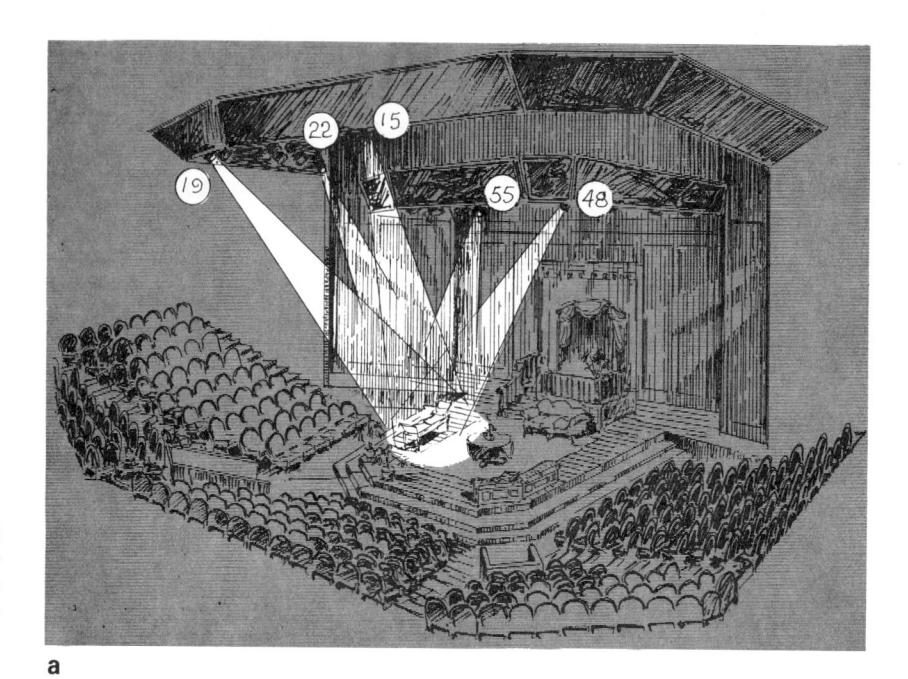

FIGURE 10–5

Thrust Stage Lighting Layout

(a) Isolated coverage of a single acting area, Area 4. Note the five different angles. (b) Floor plan showing lighting layout. Note Area 4. (c) Instrument schedule.

a

b

④ – AREA 4

192   *Stage Lighting*

No.	INSTRUMENT	LOCATION	PURPOSE	LAMP	COLOR	REMARKS
1	8" ELLIPS'L REF'R SPOTLIGHT	LEFT BOOM	AREA 1	1000 T12	144	L. BOOM TOP
2	6" " " "	" "	WASH - WARM	750 T12	134	" MIDDLE SOFT EDGE
3	6" " " "	" "	" - COOL	750 T12	119	" BOTTOM " "
4	6" " " "	2ND. VALANCE-L	AREA 3	1000 T12	141	
5	8" " " "	" " "	" 2	"	141	
6	6" " " "	" " "	" 5	750 T12	141	
7	6" " " "	" " "	" 3	"	144	
8	6" " " "	" " "	WINDOW SEAT	750 T12	144	
9	8" " " "	" " "	AREA 2	1000 T12	117	
10	6" " " "	" " "	LEFT TUNNEL	750 T12	115	FRAME TO TUNNEL
11	6" " " "	" " "	AREA 5	750 T12	117	
12	8" " " "	2ND VALANCE-C	" 3	1000 T12	117	FRAME OFF AUDIENCE
13	8" FRESNEL-LENS SPOTLIGHT	" " "	WASH - COOL	1500 G40	119	BARN DOOR-OFF "
14	8" " " "	" " "	" - WARM	"	134	" " " "
15	8" ELLIPS'L REF'R SPOTLIGHT	" " "	AREA 4	1000 T12	152	FRAME OFF "
16	6" " " "	2ND VALANCE-R	" 5	750 T12	152	
17	6" " " "	" " "	RIGHT TUNNEL	750 T12	115	FRAME TO TUNNEL
18	8" " " "	" " "	AREA 2	1000 T12	152	
19	6" " " "	" " "	" 4	750 T12	151	
20	6" " " "	" " "	" 5	"	153(2)	
21	8" " " "	" " "	" 2	1000 T12	153(2)	
22	6" " " "	" " "	" 4	750 T12	153(2)	
23	8" " " "	RIGHT BOOM	" 1	1000 T12	151	R. BOOM - TOP
24	6" " " "	" "	WASH - WARM	750 T12	134	" MIDDLE-SOFT EDGE
25	6" " " "	" "	" - COOL	"	119	" BOTTOM- " "
26	8" " " "	LEFT LADDER	U.R. CORNER	1000 T12	141	L. LADDER-TOP-FRAMESIDES
27	6" " " "	" "	AREA 1	750 T12	141	" BOTTOM " US
28	6" " " "	" "	U.L. CORNER	500 T12	141	" " " "
29	6" FRESNEL-LENS SPOTLIGHT	1ST VALANCE-L	" "	500 T20	117	
30	6" " " "	" " "	WASH - COOL	"	119	BARN DOOR-OFF AUDIENCE
31	6" " " "	" " "	" - WARM	"	134	" " " "
32	6" ELLIPS'L REF'R SPOTLIGHT	" " "	AREA 1	750 T12	117	
33	6" " " "	" " "	SOFA	"	117	
34	6" " " "	1ST VALANCE R.	"	"	152	
35	6" FRESNEL-LENS SPOTLIGHT	" " "	BENCH	500 T20	152	
36	6" ELLIPS'L REF'R "	" " "	AREA 1	750 T12	152	FRAME BOTTOM
37	6" FRESNEL-LENS "	" " "	WASH - WARM	500 T20	134	BARN DOOR OFF AUDIENCE
38	6" " " "	" " "	" - COOL	"	119	" " " "
39	6" " " "	" " "	U.R. CORNER	"	152	
40	8" ELLIPS'L REF'R SPOTLIGHT	RIGHT LADDER	U.L. "	1000 T12	153(2)	R. LADDER - TOP FRAMESIDE
41	6" " " "	" "	AREA 1	750 T12	153(2)	" BOTTOM " US
42	6" " " "	" "	U.R. CORNER	"	153(2)	" " " US
43	6" " " "	GRID. OVER STAGE	BENCH	750 T12	117	SOFT E. FRAME OFF AUDIENCE
44	6" FRESNEL-LENS "	" " "	AREA 3	500 T20	CLEAR	BARNDOOR " "
45	6" ELLIPS'L REF'R "	" " "	LEFT TUNNEL	750 T12	102	FRAME TO TUNNEL
46	6" FRESNEL-LENS "	" " "	AREA 5	500 T20	CLEAR	BARN DOOR OFF AUDIENCE
47	6" ELLIPS'L REF'R "	" " "	RIGHT TUNNEL	750 T12	102	FRAME TO TUNNEL
48	6" FRESNEL-LENS "	" " "	AREA 4	500 T20	CLEAR	BARN DOOR OFF AUDIENCE
49	6" ELLIPS'L REF'R "	" " "	STEPS	750 T12	152	SOFT E. FRAME TO STEPS
50	6" FRESNEL-LENS "	" " "	AREA 2 DS	500 T20	CLEAR	
51	6" ELLIPS'L REF'R "	" " "	ARCHWAY	750 T12	102	FRAME TO ARCHWAY
52	6" FRESNEL-LENS "	" " "	AREA 2 US	500 T20	CLEAR	
53	6" ELLIPS'L REF'R "	" " "	AREA 3	750 T12	"	FRAME L AND TOP
54	6" FRESNEL LENS "	" " "	SOFA	500 T20	"	
55	6" ELLIPS'L REF'R "	" " "	AREA 4	750 T12	"	FRAME R AND TOP
56	6" " " "	" " "	LEFT RAMP	"	103	" OFF R. WALL
57	6" " " "	" " "	RIGHT "	"	103	" " L. "
58	6" " " "	" " "	UL ENTRANCE	"	103	" " R. "
59	6" " " "	" " "	UR "	"	103	" " L. "
60	6" FRESNEL-LENS "	" " "	UL CORNER	500 T20	CLEAR	
61	6" ELLIPS'L REF'R "	" " "	AREA 1	750 T12	"	SOFT EDGE
62	6" FRESNEL-LENS "	" " "	UR CORNER	500 T20	"	
63	6" " " "	" " "	HALL WAY - L	"	104	
64	6" " " "	" " "	" R	"	104	
65	6" " " "	" " "	WINDOW SEAT	"	CLEAR	BARN DOOR OFF AUDIENCE

Lighting for Other Production Forms

leading up to Area 1 have appropriate coverage. Additional specials might be suggested, particularly as we see the development of the director's staging. Actors might, for example, be placed on the steps leading down from the platform, in which case, of course, suitable lighting would have to be provided.

The ellipsoidal reflector spotlights have been used a great deal in this layout because of the good control we have over their beams. When possible they are soft-edged by shifting the lenses to throw the gate out of focus, so as to cut down on sharp patterns and abrupt changes of intensity on the stage and actors. For the same reason Fresnel spotlights are used when their spill light will not be critical, and even then barn doors are suggested on many instruments.

Variations

Our sample lighting layout is designed for a rather light and charming piece of drama with a simple interior setting. Lighting angles are standard for good visibility and the colors are chosen for their pale tints. The arrangements of color (cool on one side and warm on the other) and angle are derived from proscenium lighting and provide good coverage. However, a two-sided color approach allows for very little variety or color interest and may not be desirable for a production with a number of scenes each demanding specific lighting.

With a minimum of five instruments on each acting area and a color arrangement as shown in Figure 10–6, the designer is provided with several more options.

1. The two warms can act as key light with the cools filling.
2. The two cools can act as key with the warms filling.
3. Any one instrument (except the back light neutral) can be lowered in intensity or dropped out completely, causing a color shift as well as compositional change.

If more than the minimum five instruments per area is possible, even greater variety of color and distribution can be achieved.

For more dramatic productions, the vertical angle of side light can be raised. The following occurs:

1. Higher angle distribution will cause sharper facial and body shadows.
2. Spill into side audience seating is more controllable.
3. Area control can be tighter.

Texture achieved by patterns or gobos can break up the sometimes flat and dull surface of the thrust stage, with high side often being a desirable angle.

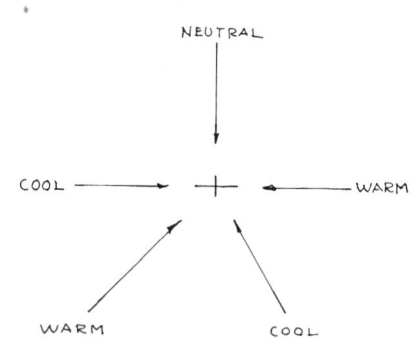

FIGURE 10–6
A Possible Color Key for the Thrust

194　　　　　　　　　　　　　　　　　　　　　*Stage Lighting*

THE FLEXIBLE STAGE

Another form of performance space which should not go without mention is the increasingly popular "black box." This flexible space is primarily intended as an actor's performance space rather than a production facility, but lighting nonetheless is often required. Black box seating can be set up in any number of configurations that will, as a result, define the playing space. Common seating arrangements are:

1. One-sided, or full front—a proscenium-type orientation.
2. Two-sided, or corner staging.
3. Three-sided, or thrust.
4. Four-sided, or arena.
5. Aisle—with seats on two sides of a central aisle.

Lighting the Black Box

Lighting the flexible space is not very different from lighting one of the several theatre forms previously examined except that the lighting positions are generally closer to the stage. But lighting positions must also be flexible. A cross-pipe grid over the entire space is a fair solution to the problem of flexibility. Such a grid will allow lighting instruments to be hung in any position and focused in any direction. Another—and probably better—solution is the tension wire grid (Figure 10–7). One-eighth-inch wire rope is woven in all directions, forming a weight-bearing surface upon which an electrician can walk. Pipes supported from the ceiling are arranged to allow complete hanging flexibility with a minimum of time and effort. The lighting instruments shoot through the thin wire mesh as shown in the photograph. This grid is ideal for the flexible space as well as extremely useful in arena or over-thrust situations.

FIGURE 10–7

The Tension Wire Grid

A woven grid of aircraft cable under tension. Designed as a ceiling grid, it is weight-bearing and gives complete access to overhead lighting positions. (Left) View of a grid installation over the auditorium of a proscenium theatre. (Photo—Eiseman) (Right) Detail of grid and lighting position. Developed by George Izenour; manufactured by J. R. Clancy.

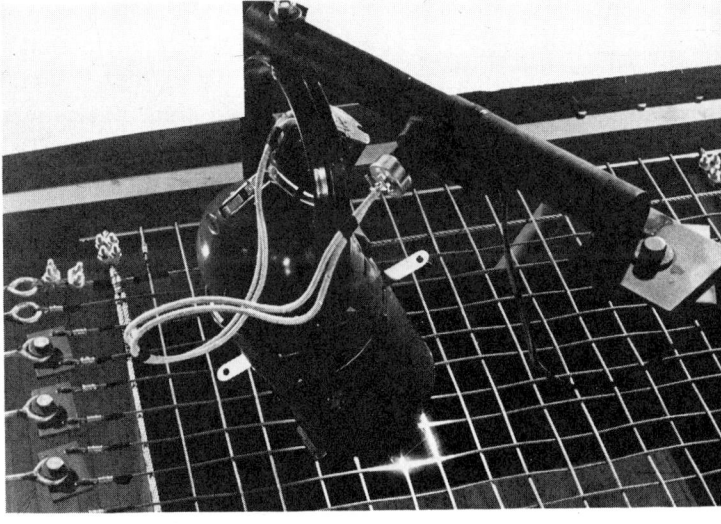

LIGHTING DANCE

The following discussion on lighting for the dance is based in part on the theories and techniques of Thomas Skelton, a leading practitioner in this field.

At first glance, dance, which is almost always performed in a wing-and-border setting on a proscenium stage, would seem to require the same sort of lighting as do other forms of production. But there is one most important difference: when we attend a play we are vitally interested in the face of the actor to tell us character, thoughts, and emotion. This is not true in dance, particularly ballet, in which the position and movement of the dancer's body tell us all. A knowledgeable lover of ballet will scarcely notice a dancer's face and will surely not concentrate on it. The primary concern is movement, which good dance lighting will reveal and emphasize.

To do this, the axis of the principal light should parallel the axis of the movement. Thus a ballerina spinning in a pirouette should have the light hitting straight down on her or straight up from below. The latter, which has been used for trick effects in modern dance routines, would probably not be appropriate for classical ballet. Although light from directly overhead tends to make the human body appear shortened, it is still the best way to accent the rapid turning of the dance.

Assume that a dancer faces the audience and raises her arm gracefully from her side to an angle of 45 degrees above her shoulder. This kind of movement is best accented by a light striking her armpit along the center line of the angle through which her arm was raised. A spotlight about 13 feet away at stage level would fulfill the requirement and would be hidden from the view of the audience if the dancer is close to the wings. If she is farther away, the ideal angle would no longer be possible, but this same location remains the best available position.

Of course it would be quite impractical to attempt to cover every single movement of a dance. A prodigious number of spotlights and an extremely complicated list of cues and light changes would be required. But provision can be made for some of the most significant moments and for more general lighting that will best suit the major movements of the work. The light designer must attend as many rehearsals as possible and take careful notes before sitting down at the drawing board. Fortunately, dances do fall into certain basic patterns of movement which can usually be covered successfully by one or more of the areas suggested in Figure 10–8.

Location of Instruments

The following are the more usual mounting positions for instruments (almost invariably spotlights).

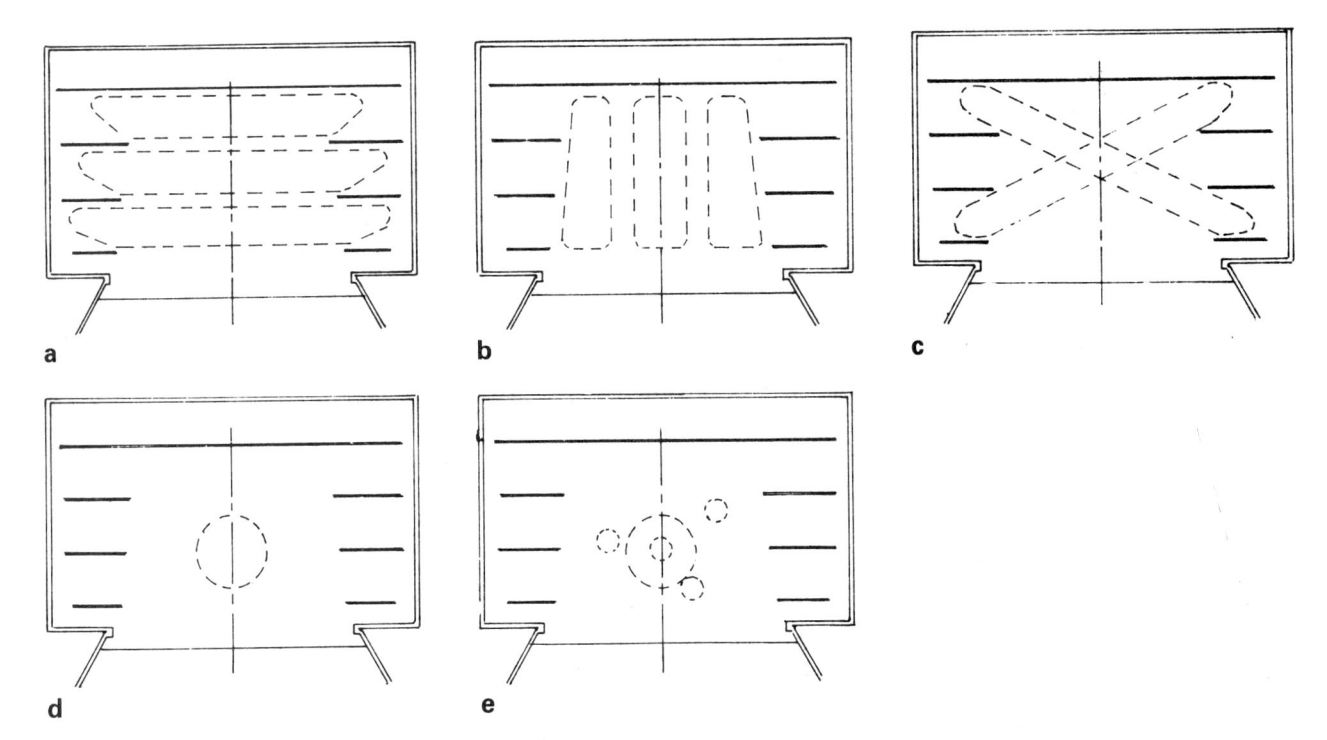

FIGURE 10–8

Lighting Areas for Dance

These coincide with the principal movements of the dancers on the stage. (a) *Cross-stage.* Dancers emerge from and disappear into the wings, dance across the stage, and work in lines that parallel the footlights. (b) *Up-and-down stage.* Dancers move toward the footlights and away again. In ballet the chorus frequently poses along the sides while the principals take center stage. (c) *Diagonal movement.* A most important aspect of modern dance. Dancers emerge from upstage wings and exit downstage on the opposite side, or vice versa. (d) *Center stage.* An obvious location for important dancing. The principal, or principals, or a small group, frequently work here in a circular pattern. (e) *Special Spots.* These may be any place on the stage (a few possibilities are indicated) in which a tight movement by the leading dancer is performed.

Low Front. For the low-front position, the lights might be mounted on a low balcony rail. Although light from this angle tends to wash out body form, a little is desirable for the sake of visibility and/or color washing.

Medium Front. These lights would be mounted on a second balcony or a beam position. Again, this does little for the body and accentuates the shadows of the dancers' costumes on their legs. This angle corresponds with the 45-degree visibility light common to theatrical presentation and can be used as such if necessary.

High-Front. Roughly at a 60-degree angle, high-front is much more useful for dramatic presentation than for dance. This angle casts serious costume shadows on the legs of an otherwise beautiful ballerina.

Low-Side. For the low-side position, light would come from the floor of the wings. Although an unnatural angle, it is flattering to dancers, for it tends to lift the body. Low-side lighting instruments are called

Lighting for Other Production Forms

"shin kickers" or "shin busters" for obvious reasons. They are normally clear or colored with very light tints, and their light can fairly effectively be cut off the floor surface in order to eliminate scallops from the beams.

Medium-Side. For the medium-side position, lights are mounted about 8 or 10 feet above the floor in the wings. This may be regarded as *the* basic dance-lighting angle. It throws a wash across the stage with little important shadowing. It may be desirable to mount one or two additional spotlights a few feet higher to carry across to the far side of the stage. In this case both long- and short-throw spots are focused so that the centers of their beams are parallel. Medium-side should not be confused with high-side, which is described below.

High-Side. Light in the high-side position comes from 15 to 20 feet high in the wings or from the ends of electric battens (such units are called "pipe ends"). If too high an angle is chosen, the light will tend to push the dancers down and make them seem squat. However, a 60-degree high-side can be very effective for a dramatic moment and is particularly useful in modern dance.

Straight-Back. In the straight-back position, light comes from above but also from behind the dancer. This is a very fine position, for it highlights the body in space, separating it from the background, and it does not cause one dancer to throw a shadow on the next one.

Diagonal-Back. Like the straight-back position, light comes from above and behind the dancer but from an angle to the side as well. Frequently this is more desirable than straight-back because more of the dancer's body is lighted.

Down-Light. In the down-light position, lights are mounted directly overhead, an effect that tends to push the body down. They are useful only for specialized moments.

Follow Spots. The follow spot may come from the house or from some on-stage location. This must be unobtrusive and should be used with a superior operator who can keep it so. Of course, in musical comedy dancing and the like, the blatant follow spots are all part of the show.

Booms

Low and medium side lighting require floor stands or booms as hanging positions. A dance concert or ballet will almost always call for a boom in each wing on both sides of the stage. This can total twelve booms for a large production. It is traditional to hang lighting instruments to the side of booms in the theatre, but for dance they should be mounted straight out from the boom pipes. In this way, the boom will take up as little wing space as possible, allowing more freedom for dancer entrances and exits (often leaps into the wings).

Booms must be clean and safe, with safety ties from the top of the pipe to the grid. Cable to booms will be neatest if run up the boom and onto an electric pipe for circuiting. However, many times floor pockets will have to be used. If this is the case, run the cable straight off-stage from the boom and then turn up- or down-stage to floor pocket locations. Cover the cable with carpeting and tape it securely.

Caution. Inexperienced dancers may try to use light booms as balance bars to warm up. Discourage this practice without being rude.

Color

For most ballet, strong colors are not desirable, but a basic tint certainly is. Pale lavender is frequently used, but for some ballets tradition may prescribe some other tint. Whatever color is selected becomes the neutral for the particular ballet. The other shades work in relation to it, and when blended together on the stage, approximate the neutral. Thus if lavender is the neutral, a violet next to it will appear quite warm and a light blue will appear cool, while the violet and blue together will mix to lavender.

An excellent effect is obtained by use of advancing and receding colors, which add apparent depth to the stage. The use of slightly cooler tints on the upstage dancers will make them appear farther away than they would seem otherwise. Likewise, warmer shades on the downstage dancers will bring them even farther forward. Care must be taken in using this technique, however. The tints must not be so far apart that the dancers visibly change color as they move through the zones.

The use of stronger colors for modern dance, especially in the side lights, is a common technique for expressing mood. Double hanging from the sides with a light tint or no color mixing into a more saturated color can offer the designer much variety.

Cueing and Other Considerations

Cue placement for a dramatic piece is often dictated by the rhythm of the work. This is even more true of dance. Movement nearly always corresponds to the music, and cueing should do the same. The cues for a ballet should be called by the stage manager from the score. The lighting designer should become extremely familiar with the music before beginning the design.

Dancers maintain balance by finding their "center." The lighting designer can help them by placing a "spotting light" or "centering light" in the auditorium. This should be a small 7½- or 15-watt red light located dead center at head height from the stage.

Lighting for Other Production Forms

FIGURE 10–9

Sketch for *Giselle*, Act II

The scale and style of both modern and classical ballet provide unique lighting opportunities. Realistic illumination is of less importance than atmosphere and color. Even classical ballet is a theatrical extension of life into a highly stylized performance technique.

The Dance Plot

Figure 10–10 is a lighting layout designed by Pat Simmons for the second act of the classical ballet *Giselle*. The scene is a wooded bower sheltering Giselle's grave (Figure 10–9) and the color is basic moonlight blue that warms a little as dawn approaches at the end of the ballet.

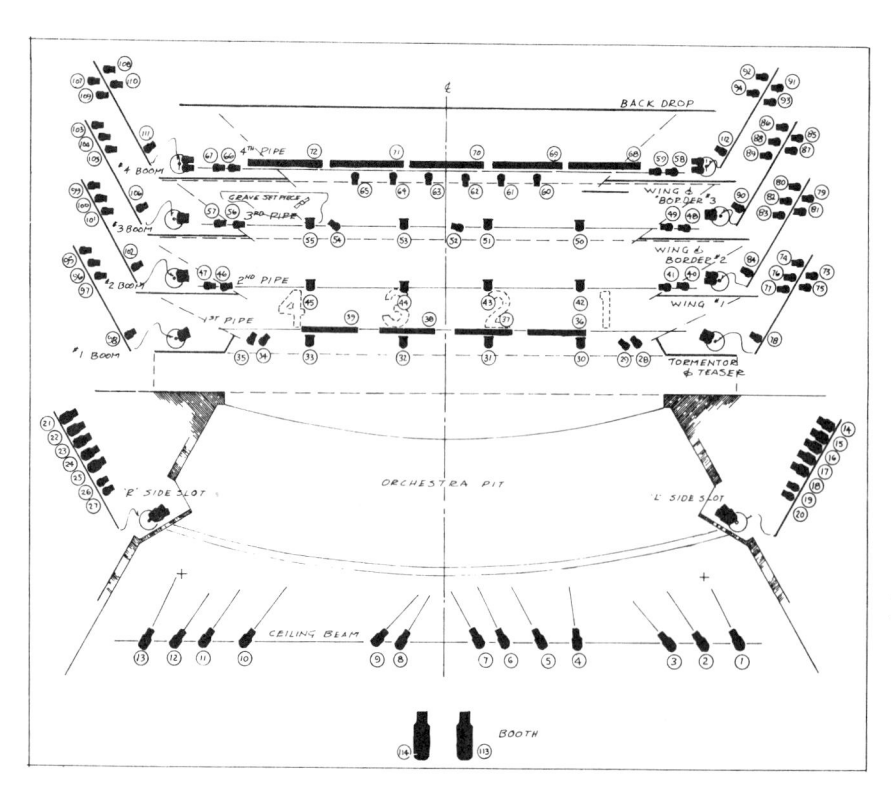

FIGURE 10–10

Lighting Layout for Ballet

(Left) Layout for *Giselle*, Act II. Note that only the down-one zone has been divided into conventional lighting areas. The balance of the plot is more dependent on side, down, and back lighting for effect. (Page 201) *The Instrument Schedule.* All color is Roscolux. (Layout courtesy of Pat Simmons, lighting designer, Pittsburgh Ballet Theatre).

Stage Lighting

The thirteen front-of-house sources are 8 × 10 ellipsoidals located in the ceiling beam and all colored in Roscolux No. R65 (Daylight Blue). Cross lights from auditorium side slots both left and right are a deeper shade of blue (No. R68—Sky Blue). Pipe-end instruments create a fairly high side light in the same blue used front-of-house, while Fresnel down lights covering the entire dance space are colored in No. R79 (Bright Blue). Six-by-twelve ERS back lights on the fourth pipe are colored in R64 (Light Steel Blue) and R51 (Surprise Pink). These colors, which are slightly less saturated than those examined so far, were chosen to punch through the other color and rim the dancers with light.

The design thus far uses a great deal of blue. But we have yet to look at the all-important side light. Both sides are again colored in R68 with the shin kickers in R64 for increased intensity. Additional side light is added stage left for the slow fade to dawn. These instruments are in R37 (Pale Rose Pink) and R18 (Flame). Two follow spots shoot from the rear-of-house booth. The follow spots will stay with the principals while the corps of dancers and scenery are bathed in blue moonlight.

Lighting for Other Production Forms

11

Scenic Projection, Practicals, and Special Effects

LIGHT AS SCENERY

Much has been said and written about the use of light in a supportive role to reveal the actor and illuminate the scene. Light, however, can become the basic element of a production. In recent years the use of light as scenery has reached an extreme height in popularity. Many reasons can be pointed out: (1) the increased use of theatre forms other than the proscenium stage, such as the thrust and arena stages where light is more obviously a major part of the total visual effect; (2) the impact of modern film and video techniques on live theatre as a stimulus for the use of film and multimedia experiments; (3) the tremendous advances in stage lighting technology assisted by the computer revolution; and (4) the more specific and complete training of designers in the use of lighting as a design element.

The consolidation of all these influences has led to a new attitude toward the use of light as a design element in all but the most conventional stage setting.

This new concept of lighting does not mean conventional illumination will disappear. Nor does it mean that scenery and the scene designer will cease to exist. It should also be apparent that flashy lighting does not fit every play or production and that the role of the lighting designer is routinely supportive more often than it is freely innovative.

Light begins to be a scenic element the moment an open source is present on the stage. Such motivating lights as realistic chandeliers and sconces generally bring elegance and high style to the scene. On the other hand, gaudy carousel lights or burlesque runway lights are frankly decorative and theatrical in their impact. Although motivating lights can make a strong visual contribution to the total design, they are a supporting element and normally not the basic scheme of production.

PROJECTED SCENERY

The most familiar and accepted application of light as scenery is through the use of projections. Projections and projected scenery (usually backgrounds) are not new to the theatre. They are as old as the "magic lantern," which entered the theatre in the 1860s, before the incandescent lamp. The early experiments with the projection of moving images, first as crude animations and then later as motion pictures, are well-known events in theatre history. The resurgence of projections in modern theatre is the result not only of improved equipment design but also of a change in attitude toward their use.

Paint versus Light. It is most important to realize that a projection is *light* and not *paint* and that there is a world of difference between the two media. Because color in light is more brilliant than in paint, and has a limited value scale by comparison, its use in a projection is more dramatic and eye-catching. For these reasons, when projections are used as background to substitute for painted scenery, the actor may have to fight for attention. This is not to say that projections do not work as background, for they can, either at controlled levels of intensity or in a highly dramatic situation. The director and designers soon learn that the most successful use of a projection is not as a substitute realistic background, but as a medium of its own, where it expresses itself best in abstract or thematic terms and almost becomes an additional actor.

The inexperienced designer may be tempted to consider projection as a means of saving either time or money. This reasoning is totally fallacious. Good projections require a great deal of effort and often more lead-time than standard theatrical scenery; they must never be considered a last-minute production detail. In addition, projection equipment is very expensive to buy and often difficult to rent.

Both paint and light, as individual mediums of expression, have their advantages and disadvantages. Thus, it is important to realize that one is *not* the substitute for the other. This is one of the places where everyone concerned, the director and the scene and lighting designers, must be in full agreement and completely knowledgeable, or misconceptions will develop that will adversely affect the end result.

FIGURE 11-1

Light as Scenery

(a) The exposed light sources are a part of the visual composition. *Stop the World, I Want to Get Off,* by Leslie Bricusse and Anthony Newley. Set Designer—James Hooks; Lighting Designer—Steve Ross. (b) A curtain of light. The shape of visible light rays turns light into substance and becomes the design form. An early use of high-intensity low-voltage light sources by Josef Svoboda, the Czechoslovak scenographer. Light rays are caught in a special aerosol spray of minute electrostatically charged oil-emulsion droplets capable of staying suspended in the air for a prolonged time. The hyperdense air catches the light and takes on a form of eerie solidity. A light column is the central portion of the design by Svoboda for Wagner's *Tristan und Isolde*. (c) Curtain or walls of light for Verdi's *I Vespri Siciliani* (*Sicilian Vespers*). (Photos reprinted from *The Scenography of Josef Svoboda* by permission of Wesleyan University Press. Copyright © 1971 by Jarka Burian.) [Continued on page 206]

a

204 *Stage Lighting*

b ↑   c ↓

d

Lighting as Scenery
(d) Projected scenery. A simple, direct use of projected images as a design form in a show curtain for *Anastasia* by Guy Bolton, a dye-painted translucent muslin curtain with projected photographs from the balcony front. Designer—John Ezell.

Projection Techniques

Reduced to its simplest elements, the projection process consists of a light source, the object or slide, the projected object or image, and the projection surface most commonly known as the screen, although it is possible to project the image onto almost any type of surface.

The image is projected by two different methods: lens projection or shadow projection. Though both images are shadows in essence, the term shadow projection is used to define all projections obtained without a lens.

The projection apparatus may be placed in front (downstage) of an opaque screen for a front projection, or at the rear (upstage) of a translucent screen for a rear projection. For a front projection the source is normally hidden from view of the audience. It must also be placed so that it has a clear throw onto the screen. In a rear-projection arrangement the problem of hiding the source is solved, although backstage space still has to be kept clear of the throw to the screen (Figure 11–2).

The Shadow Projector

Of the two methods of projection, shadow projection is the easiest to achieve. Because the process depends upon direct emanation from the light source, without lens, the image is not as sharp or intense as a comparable lens projection.

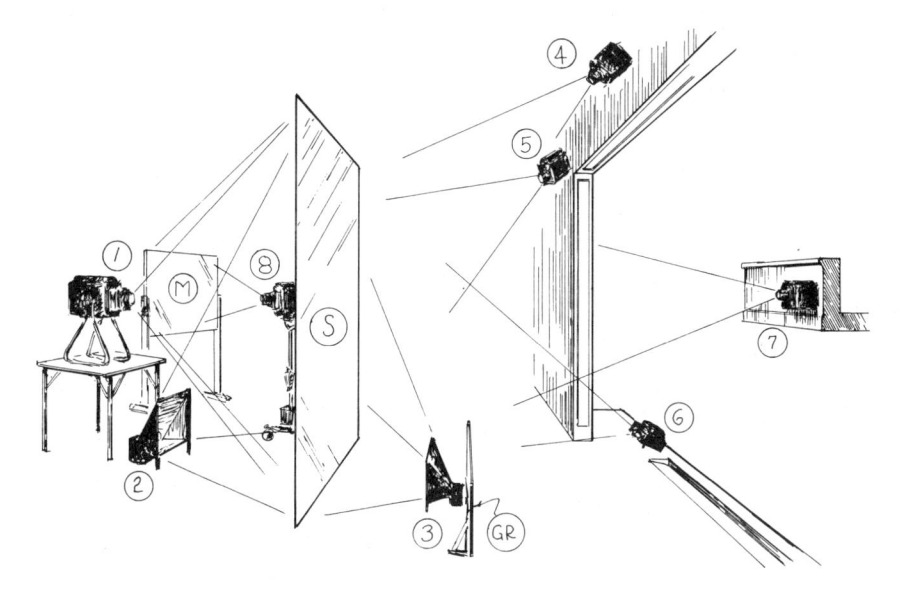

FIGURE 11–2

Screen and Projector Positions

The screen (S) is in the center of the stage. *Rear projections.* (1) Lens projector on platform to align with the center of the screen. (2) Linnebach projector on floor. *Front projections.* (3) Linnebach on floor masked by a groundrow. (4) Center teaser position. (5) High tormentor position. (6) Side apron position. (7) Balcony front. *Rear projection under limited space conditions.* (8) Lens projector angled upstage into a first surface mirror (M), which redirects the image onto the screen.

The Linnebach Projector. The basic instrument for straightline, shadow projection is the familiar device known as the Linnebach Projector (Figure 11–3a). It is a large, plain hood with a source of light—sometimes an arc but more often a high-wattage incandescent lamp—at the center of a system of diverging sides. The outer edge of the hood has a slot for holding the slide.

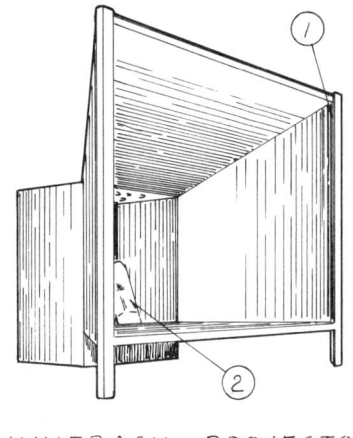

LINNEBACH PROJECTOR
a 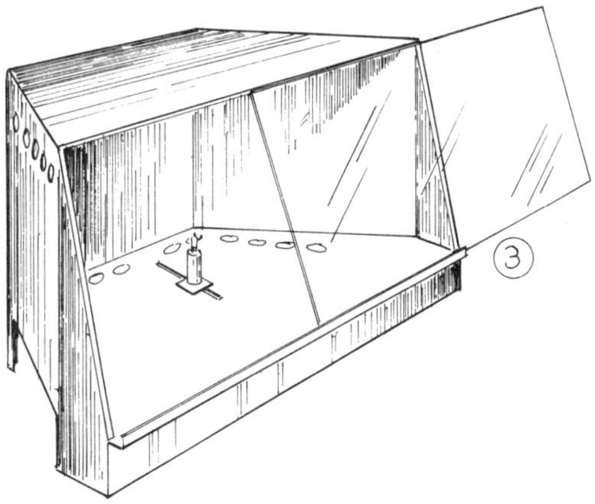   b

FIGURE 11–3

(a) The Linnebach Projector. (1) Slide holder. (2) Concentrated-filament T-shaped lamp. (b) Low-voltage, high-intensity Linnebach. A small, specially built shadow projector using a small source for a sharp projection. (1) Section view showing the position and adjustment of light socket. (2) General Electric Quartzline lamp, FCS 24 volts. The lamp, though miniature, is about 250 watts. It was designed for use in photographic studios. Adapted for use on the stage, it requires a variable transformer to reduce voltage. (3) Slide.

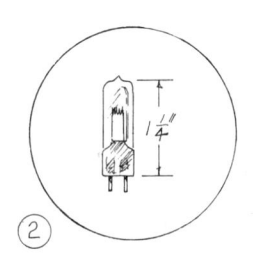

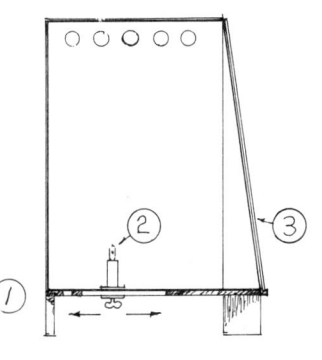

Scenic Projection, Practicals, and Special Effects

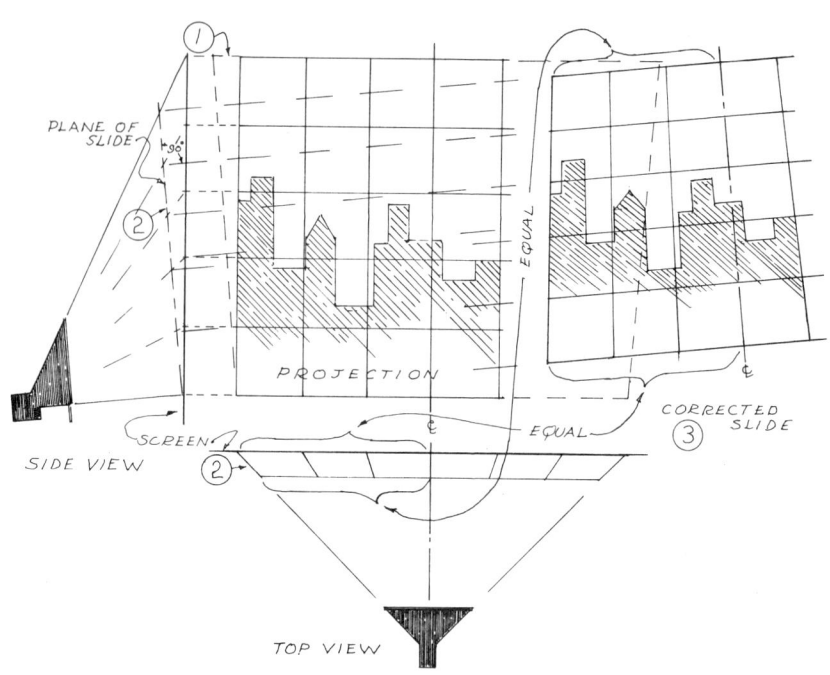

FIGURE 11–4

Correction of Distortion

The Linnebach projector is tilted backward to project the image high on the screen. The plane of the slide is no longer parallel to the screen, resulting in a distortion of all vertical lines in the image. The diagram shows the method of countering the distortion with a corrected slide. (1) Keystoning or distortion of the rectangle. (2) Reference line established in side view parallel to the plane of the slide. It is then located in the top view and vertical line plotted. (3) Corrected grid is constructed perpendicular to the plane of the slide and the verticals are plotted with information from the top view. The corrected slide is drawn into the new grid.

The slide of the Linnebach projector or any variation of shadow projector can be a simple cardboard cutout or painted glass. If the slide is kept parallel to the screen there is no distortion of the image on the screen. It is not always possible to place the instrument and the slide in this ideal relationship, hence the designer must be able to cope with distortion. Once the position of the instrument has been determined image distortion can be corrected by building in a counter distortion in the slide. Distortion on one plane is, of course, easier to correct than on two planes. Figure 11–4 diagrams the methods of correcting simple and complex distortions.

Figure 11–3b illustrates a Linnebach projector using a high-intensity low-voltage lamp (ANSI Code = FCS). Low-voltage lamps are desirable for shadow projectors because of their reduced filament size. The smaller the lamp filament, the clearer and sharper the image.

The Cinebach Projector. Another variation of the Linnebach is the Cinebach projector, a homemade device that has proved extremely satisfactory for lighting the curved plaster cyclorama of a small stage. In its simplest form it is two D-shaped plywood panels, each about 20 inches wide, fastened about 24 inches apart to a plywood back piece. A sheet of acetate or of plastic color medium, clear or tinted, is tacked around the edges. On the bottom panel is a socket with a large-wattage lamp. Ventilation holes are drilled through both bottom and top panels, and frequently light baffles are built to shield these (see Figure 11–5).

Any sort of design may be painted on the plastic, just as on a conventional Linnebach slide. Because of the curved surface, this device is especially effective for lighting a curved surface and can be valuable even if no more than a plain blue wash is required for a sky. If the Cinebach (which gets its name from the use of Cinemoid as a slide material) is to be placed at the bottom of the curved cyclorama, the top panel may be built smaller than the bottom one to permit the light to spread upward more smoothly.

The Lens Projector

The second and more complex type of instrument for projecting an image is the lens projector. The light source in a lens projector is concentrated on the slide surface by a condensing lens system. The illuminated slide is then transmitted into an image as it passes through the objective-lens system. The size of the image on the screen is determined by the beam-spread capacity of the objective-lens system (focal length). There are adjustments within the system of lenses (lens train) to bring the image of the slide into sharp focus.

Lens projectors used for theatrical performance vary a great deal, and selection depends on the specific application desired. However, there are several guidelines to follow:

1. The longer the throw or the larger the image, the brighter the light source should be.
2. A large slide size will produce a clearer image than a small slide.
3. The larger the slide format, the more expensive and bulky the equipment.

Slide sizes vary from the convenient 35mm (1.346 × 0.902 inches) to the large continental size of 9 × 9 inches.

The Plano-Convex Effect Head. Figure 11–6 (page 210) is an illustration of what once was the lens projector workhorse of the theatre, the effect head. It is an assemblage on the front of a plano-convex spotlight and consists of a condensing lens, slide holder, and objective-lens system. The effect head is so named because it turns an ordinary working spotlight into a lighting instrument that produces effects beyond the spotlight's normal powers of illumination.

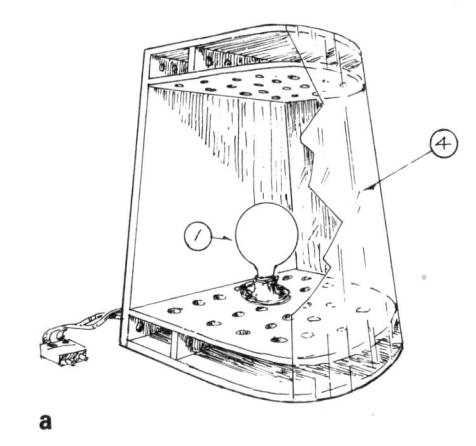

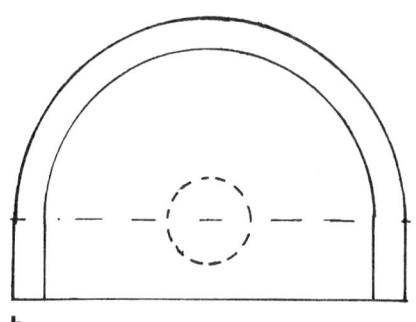

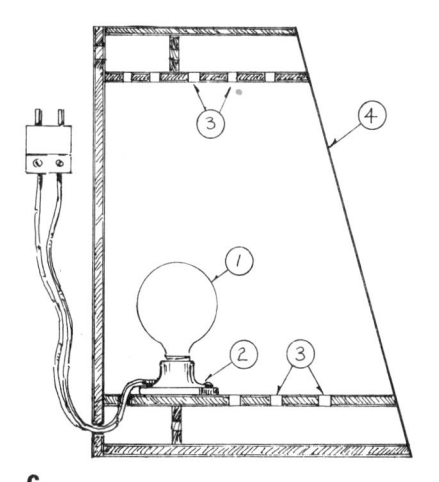

FIGURE 11–5
The Cinebach
(a) A pictorial representation. (b) Section. (c) Plan. (1) High wattage lamp. (2) Socket for lamp. (3) Ventilation holes. (4) Curved sheet of clear or colored plastic.

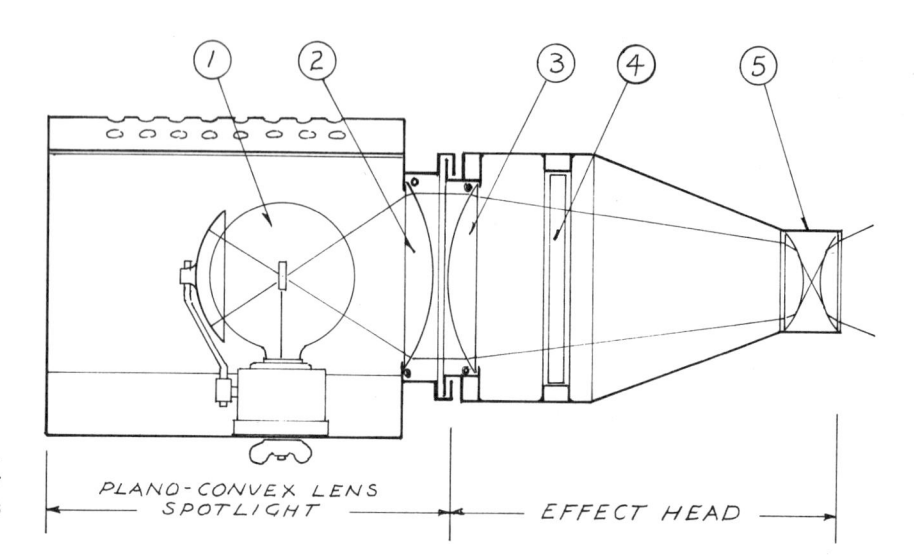

FIGURE 11–6

The Lens Projector

(1) G-shaped lamp. (2) Plano-convex lens. (3) Additional concentrating lens (or "Dutchman"). (4) Slide. (5) Objective-lens system.

There is an additional piece of apparatus that can be applied to the effect head assembly. A drumlike device with a motor drive known as an effect machine can be mounted on the spotlight at the slide position. It provides moving effects such as water ripples, flames, snowflakes, and the like. These are expensive and the results are rather too obvious for the tastes of today's audience.

The "Scene Machine." The "Scene Machine" is a modern imitation of the plano-convex lighting instrument with an effect head (Figure 11–7). This scenic projector, distributed in the United States by The Great American Market, takes a 4 × 5-inch slide and is available with a high intensity 1200-watt or 2000-watt quartz lamp. The projector head (equivalent to the plano-convex spotlight) is sold separately from the slide carrier and objective-lens systems. Lenses are available in focal lengths of 4, 6, 8, 10, 12, and 16 inches. Optional equipment includes a spiral machine, disc machine (which acts as a remote-control slide changer), film machine, and other types of effect heads. Although fairly expensive, this is one of the few useful large-format scenic projectors available in the United States.

The Kodak Carousel Projector. Very few people in this country are unfamiliar with the Carousel projector. While the theatre has used this projector for years, it has only recently become the best choice of 35mm projectors because of its improved lamp. Keep in mind the following valuable bits of information about this lamp and the projector in general:

1 The standard lamp recommended by Kodak is the ELH (300 watt, 30-hour life). An acceptable substitute is the ENG (300 watt, 4-hour life). While the life of the ENG is only a fraction of that of the ELH, its light output is greatly increased. It is the ENG that enables the Carousel to be a viable scenic projection unit.

FIGURE 11-7
The "Scene Machine"
Shows film loop rollers. Manufactured by Ryudensha Co., Japan.

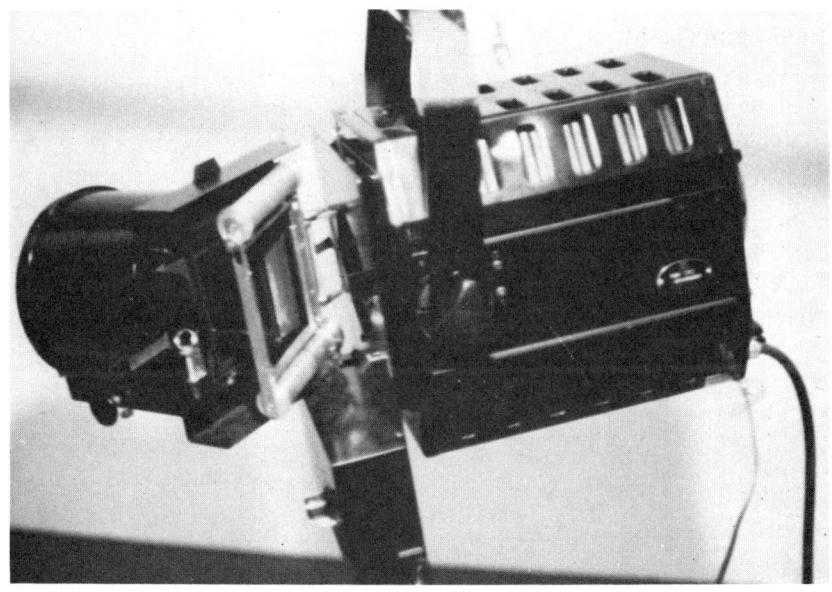

2   The Carousel as wired cannot be dimmed because of its fan and slide-changer motor, although Kodak manufactures a dissolve unit which will cross-fade two projectors. However, it is possible to add an external dimmer in-line with the projector's lamp without any sort of rewiring. A two-pin male plug (Radio Shack Cat. No. 274–342) fits into a pair of holes in the rear of the projector and interrupts power to the lamp. Power need only be directed through any remote dimmer of 300-watt or greater capacity. *Caution*: Power is supplied from the projector, through the dimmer, to the lamp—one may not connect the projector to a conventional stage circuit and dimmer without causing a short circuit.

Scenic Projection, Practicals, and Special Effects

3. While Kodak sells a large range of its own lenses, Buhl Optical Co. manufactures an even larger range of superior lenses. Focal lengths of Buhl lenses made to fit the Carousel projector begin at a very wide 1 inch and go to a narrow 9.5 inches. These lenses are available in varying speeds, with the faster lenses being best for scenic projection.

Kodak sells 25-foot extension cables for the projector's remote controller, allowing control over projectors hung over-stage or placed in the auditorium. One final thing to remember is that the Carousel operates on a gravity-feed principle for changing slides. This means that the projector cannot be tilted too much in any direction without danger of slides jamming.

Arc Projection. High-intensity arc lamps mounted in a scenic projector provide a great deal of intensity for long-throw applications. Several arc projectors for both film and slides are available to the theatrical designer, but all have the disadvantage of being impossible to dim (Figure 11–8).

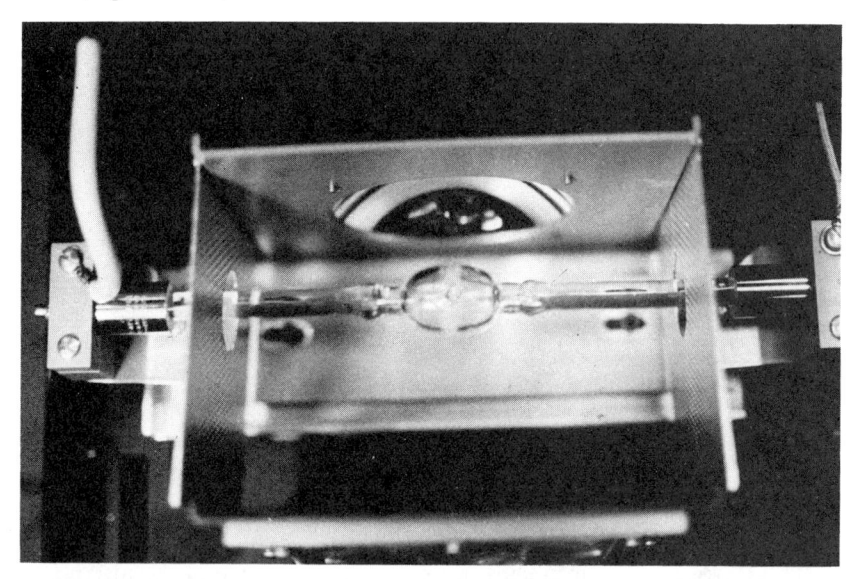

FIGURE 11–8
Short-Arc Lamp Slide Projector
The Metro-lite ME 100 produces a sharp, high-intensity image. (Top) HMI 2500-watt lamp. (Bottom) Projector with top removed showing position of lamp, color filter, slide holder, condensing lens and objective system (George Snell Associates).

The Overhead Projector. The most unusual instrument in the lens-projector category is the overhead projector. Its large slide deck (about 12 × 12 inches) is a translucent, horizontal surface with the light source underneath. The slide image, after passing through a vertically mounted objective-lens systems, is redirected by a mirror onto the screen (Figure 11–9).

The advantages of the overhead projector, which was originally designed to animate or illustrate the classroom lecture, are twofold: (1) The large area of the slide permits handpainted slides, allowing the photographic process to be omitted, thereby saving time and money, and (2) the horizontal position of the slide deck provides the opportunity to bring movement to the image. On-the-spot animation is possible by such actions as moving transparent film across the slide deck, agitating with an air jet a shallow transparent dish of colored dyes in oil or water, or blowing smoke across the deck. The movement of smoke across the deck can appear on the screen as a descending fog, rising smoke from a fire, or the engulfing black cloud of an approaching storm.

The overhead projector is not as efficient as a regular lens-projector, but because of its wide-angle objective system it can work close to the screen. It functions best with short-throw, small-image projections.

The overhead projector obviously requires an operator and therefore cannot be used in a remote position. It is best for rear projections, although it has been used for front projections from an extreme off-stage side position.

The Opaque Projector. There is another lens projector that has not been mentioned: the opaque projector. The slide, which is opaque, is reflected by mirrors into the objective-lens system and projected onto the screen. Because the slide is not transparent the image is not as bright; thus, the inefficiency of the instrument renders it impractical for stage use. Its chief use in the theatre is to facilitate the cartooning and painting of scenery. If a drawing bearing a grid of scaled squares is projected to match over a corresponding full-scale grid of a scenic element or drop, it can serve as a quick guide for drawing an enlargement of the original painting.

The Television Projector. The television or video projector is a complex and highly specialized piece of equipment that is capable of projecting a live televised image. It has been used as a dramatic extension of action on stage or of a scene occurring just offstage. Intimate business or emotions expressed by live actors can be supported by simultaneously enlarged television projection elsewhere on the stage.

Gobos. One form of lens projection that does not require any special apparatus other than a common ellipsoidal reflector spotlight is the gobo, also known as a cookie. The gobo is a sheet of highly heat-

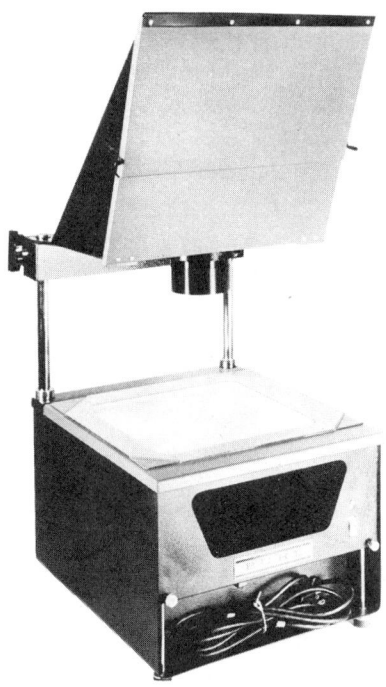

FIGURE 11–9
Overhead Projector
Wide-angle overhead projector with a 10 x 10-inch transparent slide deck. The objective-lens system can be operated vertically, as shown, or swung into a horizontal position. The hinged shutters at the top protect the mirror, which is at a 45-degree angle to the slide surface (Buhl Optical).

Scenic Projection, Practicals, and Special Effects

resistant material from which some shape, pattern, or design has been cut. When placed at the gate of an ellipsoidal spot, this pattern is projected by the lens (or lenses) onto any appropriate surface.

Commercial equipment houses sell gobos in a variety of designs; some are fairly realistic, but most are simply pleasant patterns. These are frequently used in television, where the background is rarely in sharp focus, to give interest to an otherwise plain drop or wall.

Patterns may be home-designed and cut from heavy aluminum foil or the bottom of a cheap tin pie plate. Two especially useful effects are clouds, cut from foil, which may be wrinkled slightly to give out-of-focus soft edges, and stars, made by pricking tiny holes through a piece of tin kept carefully flat to make all edges sharp. Both are projected in a white light against a blue drop or cyclorama.

Regrettably, neither color nor fine detail can be used at the present because the only transparent material that will withstand the terrific heat at the gate of an ellipsoidal spot is a very expensive clear ceramic requiring special paints and a carefully controlled fixing process not available to the public.

FIGURE 11-10

Slide Projection Equipment

A few of the many slide and film projectors available for projected scenery. Separated into slide sizes and automatic slide-changing capabilities, they are: (a) Hi-Lite (Buhl Optical) 35mm carousel changer, 1200 watts (incandescent or quartz). A dependable changer, small, good in remote positions. The same projector, a modified Kodak Carousel, can be adapted to a Zenon package for a more brilliant source but less flexible dimming capabilities. (b) Pani 5000-watt scenic projector. Uses 180mm square slides; optional automatic slide magazine available—Strand Century. (c) 5000-watt 7 x 7-inch slide projector. Its one-for-one optics (1-foot coverage at a 1-foot distance) makes it good for wide-coverage rear projections. The 7 x 7-inch slide size is large enough to be hand-painted if desired as well as adaptable to a conventional 5 x 7-inch film size in Ektachrome color transparencies. (d) A 16mm 500-watt Baur film projector with an ECU-RP (Extreme Close Up Rear Projection) lens and a built-in mirror system; lens—Buhl Optical. (e) Film loop projector (moving projection) with speed control; Kliegl Bros. Film Machine (moving projection).

Stage Lighting

The Mathematics of Projection

To eliminate trial-and-error methods of selecting lenses and placing projectors, the use of the following simple formulas should be understood:

> F = Focal length of lens.
> D = Projection throw distance.
> S = Slide size.
> I = Image size.

$$F = \frac{D \times S}{I}$$

$$D = \frac{F \times I}{S}$$

$$I = \frac{D \times S}{F}$$

Remember that all these distances must be expressed in the same units, usually inches. If the horizontal dimension of the slide is used, the horizontal dimension of the image will be obtained; if the vertical measurement of the image is needed, one must use the vertical measurement of the slide.

The Screen

Aside from the increased efficiency of projection equipment, the innovative exploitation of the screen or projection surface is perhaps the greatest contribution to the imaginative use of light as scenery. Projected scenery has graduated in a very short time from the large single-screen background to multiscreen compositions and to an infinite variety of sizes, shapes, and three-dimensional forms.

Under conditions where time and money are no obstacle the possibilities of the highly dramatic and imaginative use of projection is unlimited. The leader and prime innovator in the development of light as scenery is without a doubt the Czechoslovakian scenographer, Josef Svoboda. His inventive and artistic genius has unlocked traditional scenery and lighting practices and opened the doors to a less restricted attitude toward scene design and lighting.

Figure 11–11 (page 216) illustrates a few of the many screen arrangements and projector positions. They range from a single rear-projection screen, a mixture of both rear- and front-projection screens, multishapes and sizes to three-dimensional front-projection surfaces.

FIGURE 11–11

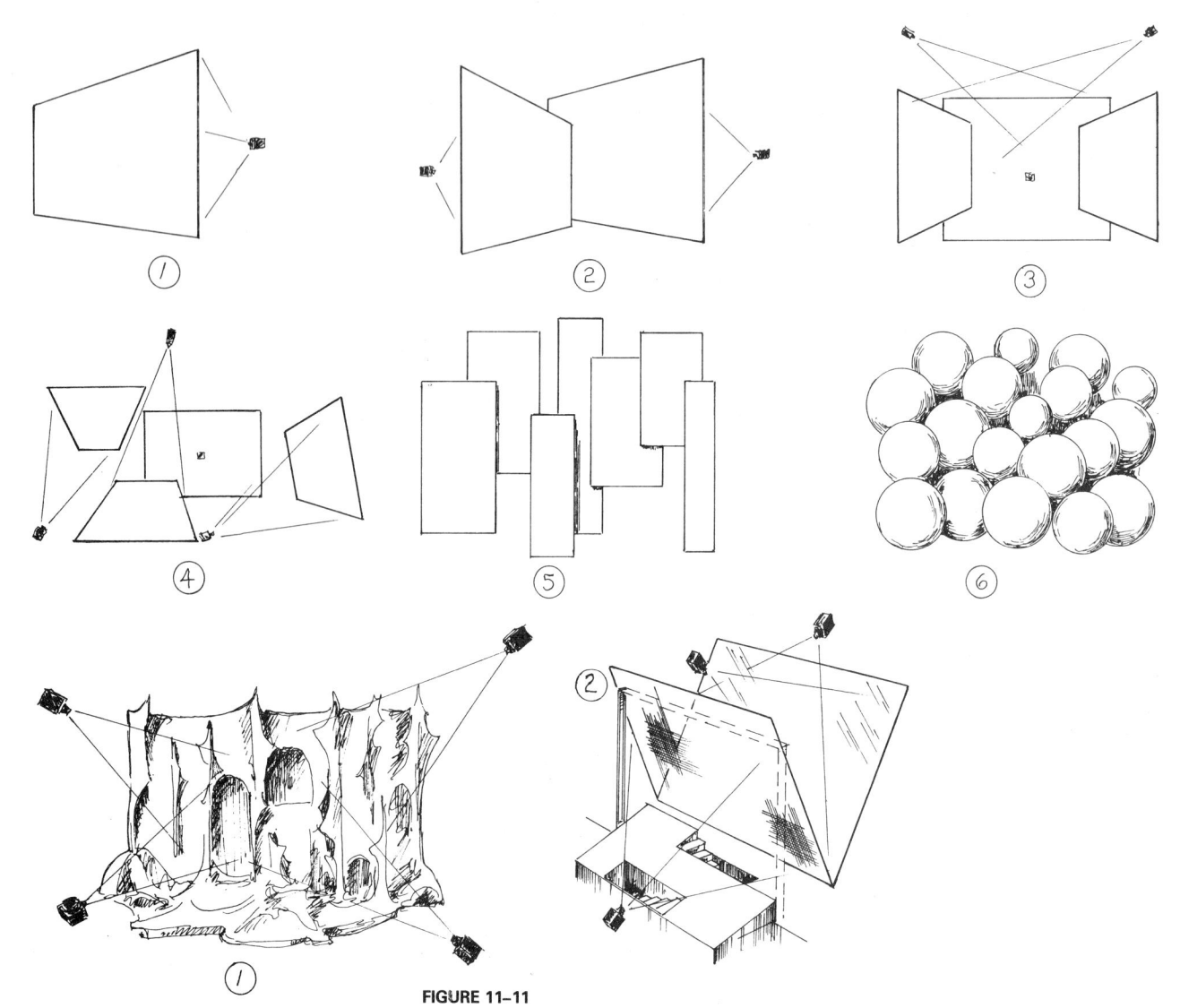

Projection Screen Arrangements

Rear projections. (1) Single screen. (2) Double rear-projection screen arrangement. (3) Two front-projection screens right and left, with rear-projection screen in center. (4) Multiscreen arrangement. (5) Three-dimensional surface made up of flat planes designed for a single projection. (6) A projection surface of balloons or Styrofoam spheres. (Bottom sketches) (1) Sculptural surface planned for many angles of projection. (2) Slanted surfaces. The downstage screen is scrim, providing the possibility of front, rear, and see-through projections.

Front Projection versus Rear Projection

The single screen, rear-projection technique has been used as background for dramatic productions for some time. The original location of the projector and screen was governed by the need of having an operator, as well as the reluctance to stop thinking of the screen as a painted drop. A rear-projection screen is translucent enough to diffuse the bright spot of the projector's source, yet transparent enough to

FIGURE 11-12
Multiscreen Technique

The use of many screens is best illustrated by the work of the originator, Josef Svoboda. Although the production of *The Journey* repeats the square screen, the technique can involve a variety of screen shapes and sizes, each with its individual slide projector. The screens are deliberately treated as projection surfaces and not as scenic background. The organic harmony or contrasting interplay of the several screens can fluctuate in scenic style from a documentary to a kind of surrealistic reality. (Photos reprinted from *The Scenography of Josef Svoboda* by permission of Wesleyan University Press. Copyright © 1971 by Jarka Burian.)

transmit the image. A professionally made rear-projection screen is constructed with the greatest density in the center to offset the hotspot of the projector source and is polarized to allow for equal distribution of the light. Because of the general high density of a rear-projection screen a lot of light is stopped; consequently a rear projection requires a higher intensity to equal a similar projection from the front.

Scenic Projection, Practicals, and Special Effects

Front projections have become more popular and practical for two reasons: the first, which has been mentioned frequently, is the change in attitude from thinking of projections as a substitute for painted scenery, and second, the great improvement in the efficiency and reliability of remote-control projection equipment.

Front projection does have the disadvantage of having to throw from a more extreme angle or a greater distance than does a rear projection because of the necessity of hiding the instrument from the view of the audience.

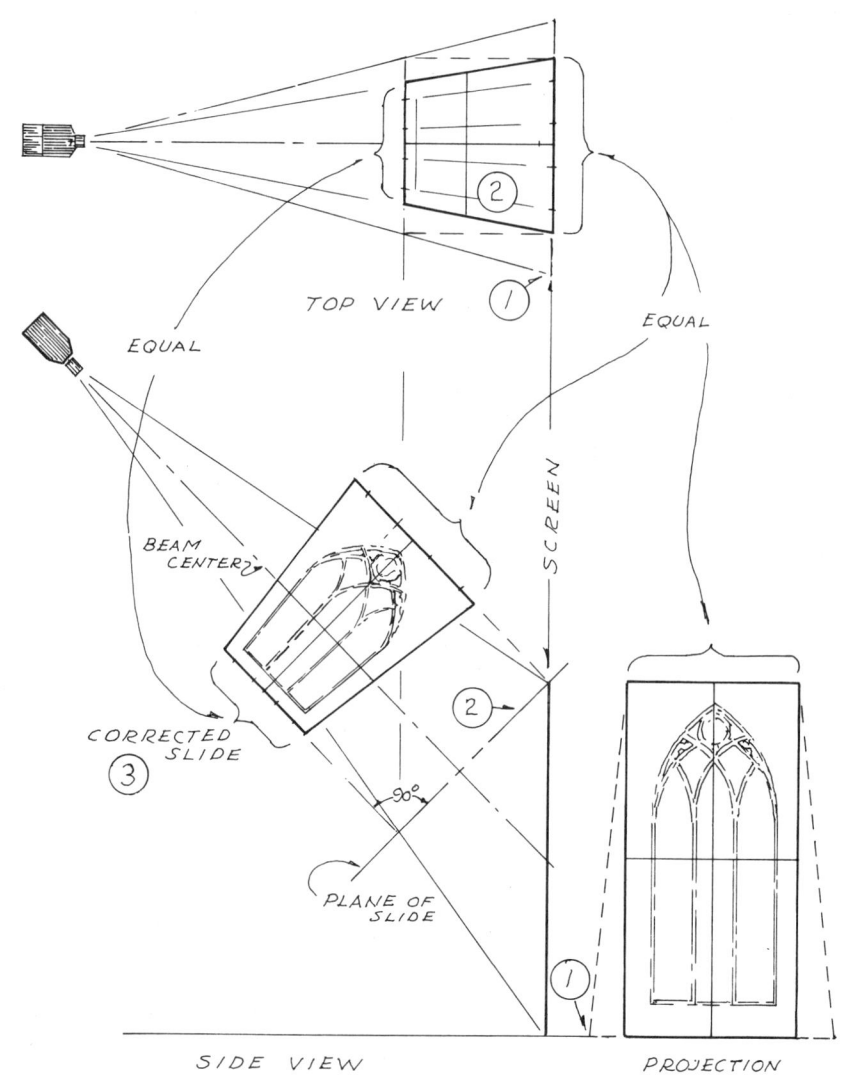

FIGURE 11–13

Distortion Correction for a Lens Projection

The projection position is perpendicular to the screen in top view but angled in the side view, resulting in a keystone distortion (1) of the image. Reference line (2) is constructed parallel to the plane of the slide. The counter distortion is plotted in the top view of the slide plane (2). The corrected slide (3) is drawn perpendicular to the reference plane with information from the top view.

Stage Lighting

Distortion. The extreme angle of a front projection also causes distortion problems. They are not insurmountable but do necessitate extra drawing for the scene designer. If the slide is to be a photographed transparency, the designer has to make two designs. The first is the projection as it is to appear free of distortion, and the second shows the built-in counter distortion that is to be photographed and processed into a color transparency for the slide. If the slide is not too small or too detailed it can be painted directly on the slide glass using the same counter-distortion control. The correction process for one-plane distortion is diagramed in Figure 11–13. The corrected grid on the slide should, however, always be checked under actual conditions before painting or photographing any quantity of slides.

To demonstrate distortion-correction solutions for projections involving two-plane distortion, a small, mixed-media production of Elmer Rice's *The Adding Machine* is shown in Figure 11–14 (page 221). The steps taken to make the slides for a pair of sharply angled front-projection machines are depicted. The expressionistic style of the play allowed for the strong visual statement of projections as an extension of the actor. Larger productions, more screens, or different angles of projections would follow the same approach for distortion solutions.

Not all distortions need to be corrected. There are times when the distortions of an angled projection are accepted as part of the design, especially if the slide is abstract or nonobjective in style.

Projections and the Actor

The lighting of the actor in relation to a projected background is very tricky and varies with the direction of the projection, front or rear. Any projection suffers from reflected light on the front of the screen, which tends to wash out the intensity of colors and design in the image. Care must be taken to choose angles to light the actor that will not reflect off the floor onto the screen (Figure 11–15, page 222).

In addition to the control of distribution, bounce light can be minimized in other ways: (1) The reflective quality of the floor can be deadened with a cover of black or dark gray felt or carpeting; or (2) reflected light can be kept off the screen by hanging a seamless black scrim about a foot in front. It serves to absorb the reflected light but does not affect the quality of the image.

The reflected light problem can also be helped by the design and position of the screen or the image on the screen. If, for example, the screen or the image on the screen begins about 4 feet or more above the floor, it is less likely to suffer from bounce light. This elevation coupled with the directing technique of keeping actors away from the screen by maintaining a so-called neutral zone of about 4 feet makes it easier to light the actor and not lose the intensity of the projection.

Back lighting and side lighting are especially helpful in separating the actor from a projected background. Otherwise, it is difficult com-

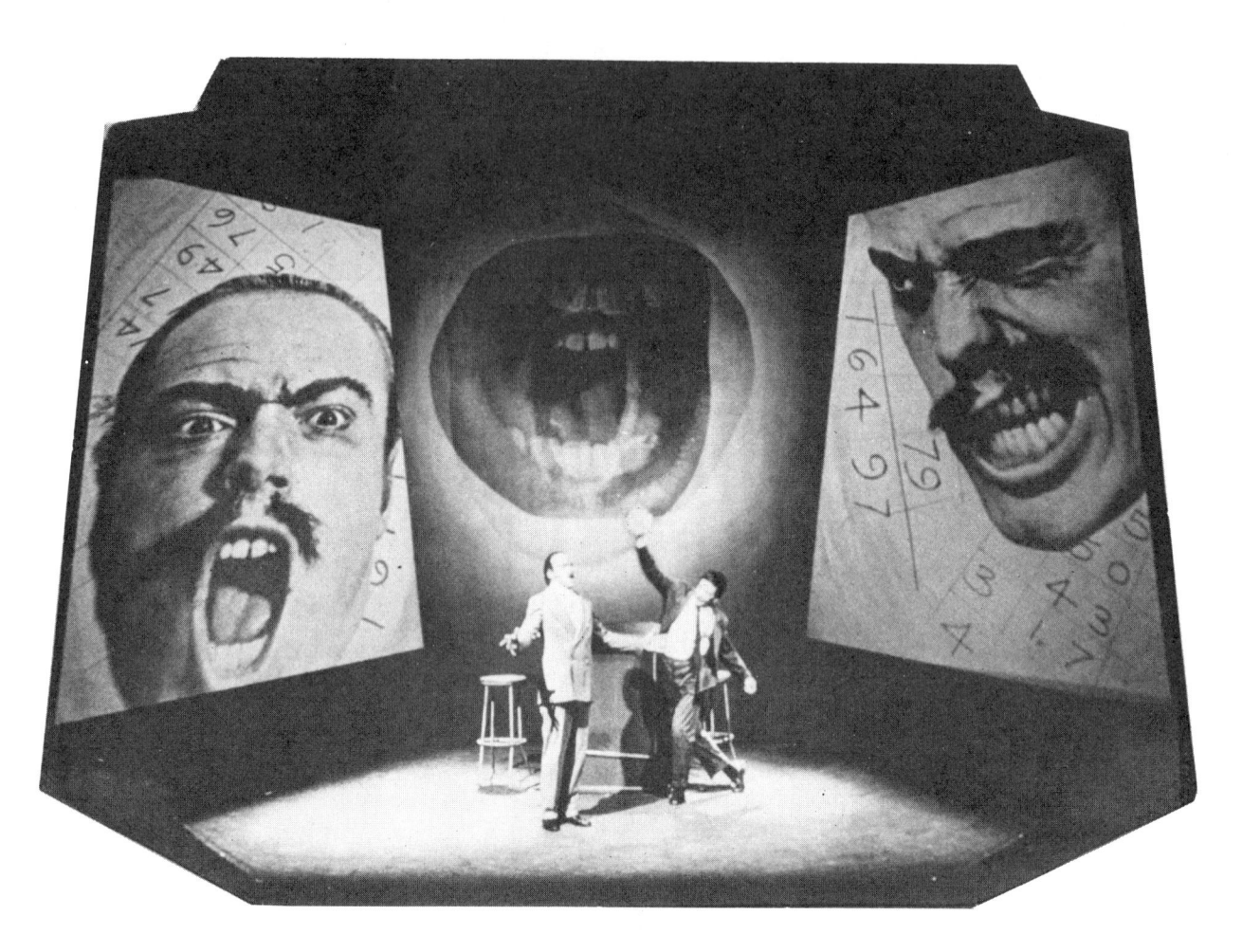

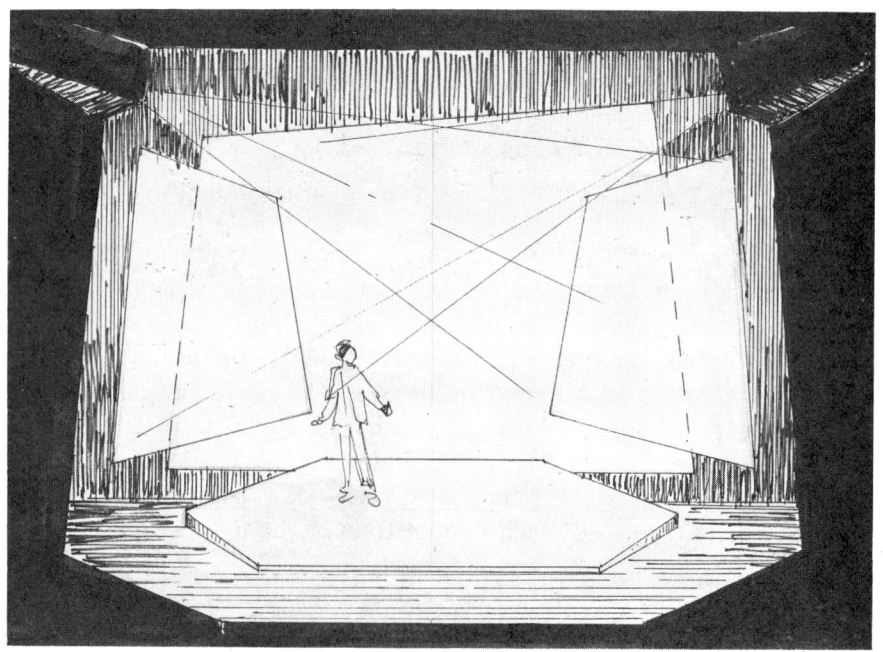

Stage Lighting

FIGURE 11-14

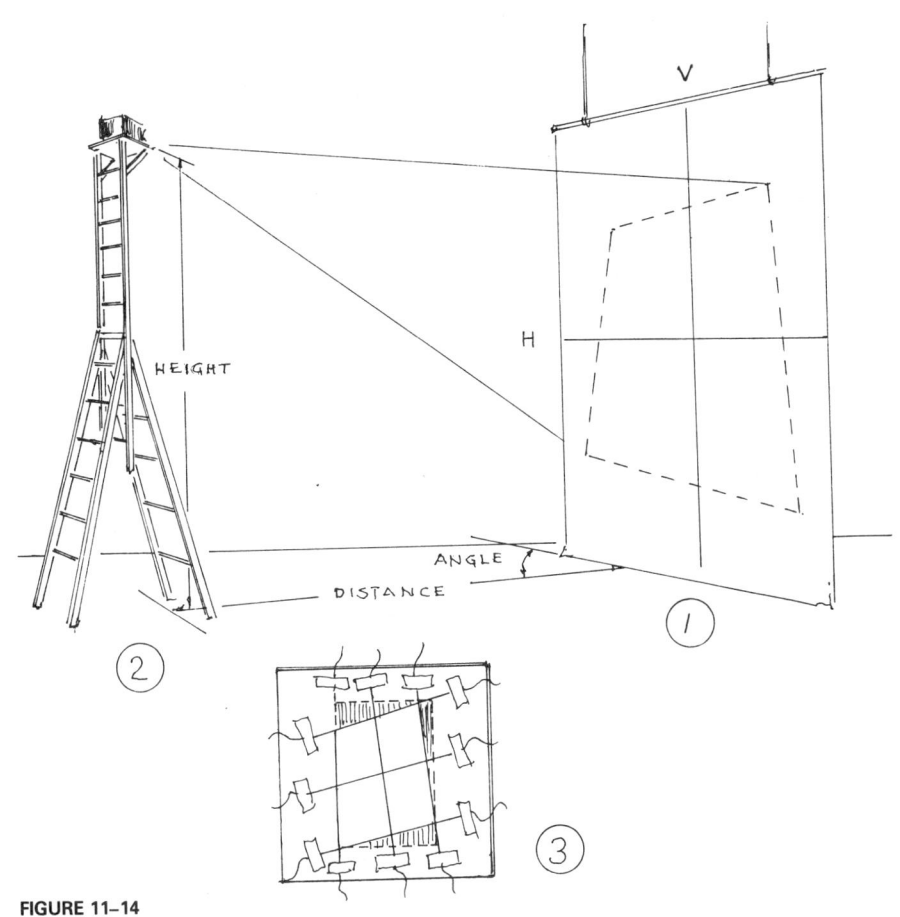

Projected Scenery

To illustrate the planning and execution of projected scenery, an all-projection production of Elmer Rice's expressionistic play *The Adding Machine* is illustrated. (Left, top) The pulsating images on the screen heighten the action in the scene. (Bottom) Sketch of the screen arrangement. Three screens were used, two small downstage front-projection screens backed by a large rear-projection screen. (Above) Sketch showing the method used to figure the counterdistortion of the front-projection slides caused by the steep angle of projection. (1) A temporary screen was hung at the site of the finished screen. The shape of the planned screen was drawn on the temporary surface with established horizontal (H) and vertical (V) center lines. (2) The right projector position at the top of the ladder duplicated the distance, height, and angle of the final mounting position in the upper stage right of the portal. (3) Taped threads on a clear 35mm slide were moved by trial and error until the projection of the threads matched the outline and cross lines on the screen. The projector was tilted slightly to bring one projected edge of the slide into alignment with the upstage edge of the screen.

positionally to balance the intensity of the background and the area lights without one or the other becoming dull.

The use of front projections allows greater creativity in the design of the screen. It may be three-dimensional or it may be pierced, to permit action behind or through the screen. In a more practical vein, the screen position can be farther upstage, thereby giving more space to the actor and providing for an occasional scenic element.

Scenic Projection, Practicals, and Special Effects

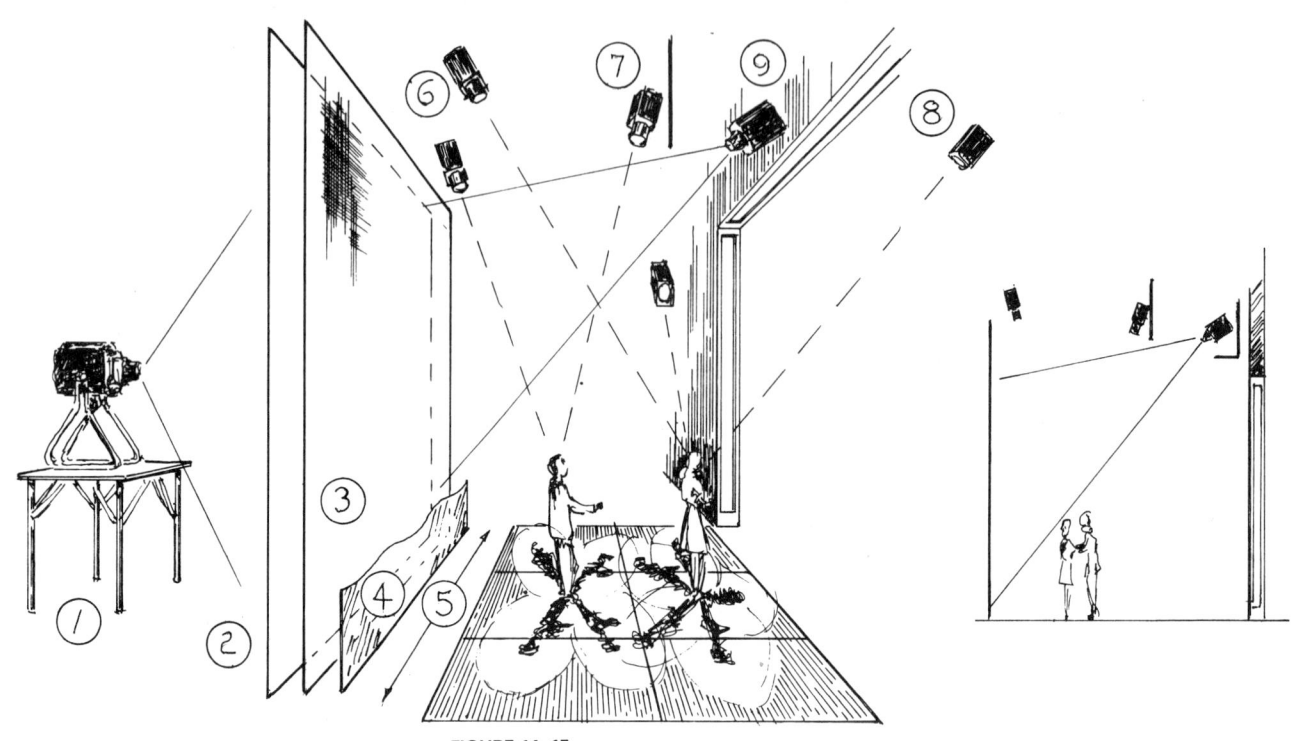

FIGURE 11-15
Projections and the Actor
The effective use of large-scale projections as a background requires special lighting techniques. To avoid undue spill of reflected light onto the screen, the acting-area lights are kept at a steep angle along with the obvious use of back and cross lighting to throw the actors' shadows away from the screen. (Left) Diagram of a rear-projection setup. (1) Rear-projection machine. (2) Rear-projection screen. (3) Black scrim drop hung in front of screen to absorb reflected light from the front. (4) Groundrow or screen frame to kill light reflected from the floor. (5) Unit area, called neutral zone, about 3 or 4 feet in front of screen. (6) Back light on actor to help define him against a projected background. Note top hat or funnel on the front of the spotlight to prevent a flare of light onto the screen. (7) Sharply angled upstage-area spotlights to keep light and shadows off screen. (8) Front-area ceiling spotlight. The normal angle is usually good. (9) Center teaser position for front projection. (Right) Front-projection setup. The lighting of the actor remains the same. The black scrim is removed to allow projections from the teaser position. Note the angle of front projection. It is planned to miss actors at the edge of the neutral zone.

Front projections can also frankly involve the actor as a projection surface or use the shadow that he or she casts as a part of the image. The imaginative mixture of light, projections, and performers is so successfully executed by Alwin T. Nikolais and his dancers that their performances are both a stimulating experience in the theatrical form of sight and sound and epitomize light as scenery (Figure 11–16).

Light as a Scheme of Production

In his productions of Wagner's *Tristan und Isolde* and Verdi's *I Vespri Siciliani (Sicilian Vespers)*, Josef Svoboda uses light as a scheme of production (Figure 11–1). Another quite different but equally effective use of light and projection is shown in Figure 11–17 (pages 224-225). These illustrations and photographs are from the English National Opera's 1979 production of Britten's *The Turn of the Screw*.

Stage Lighting

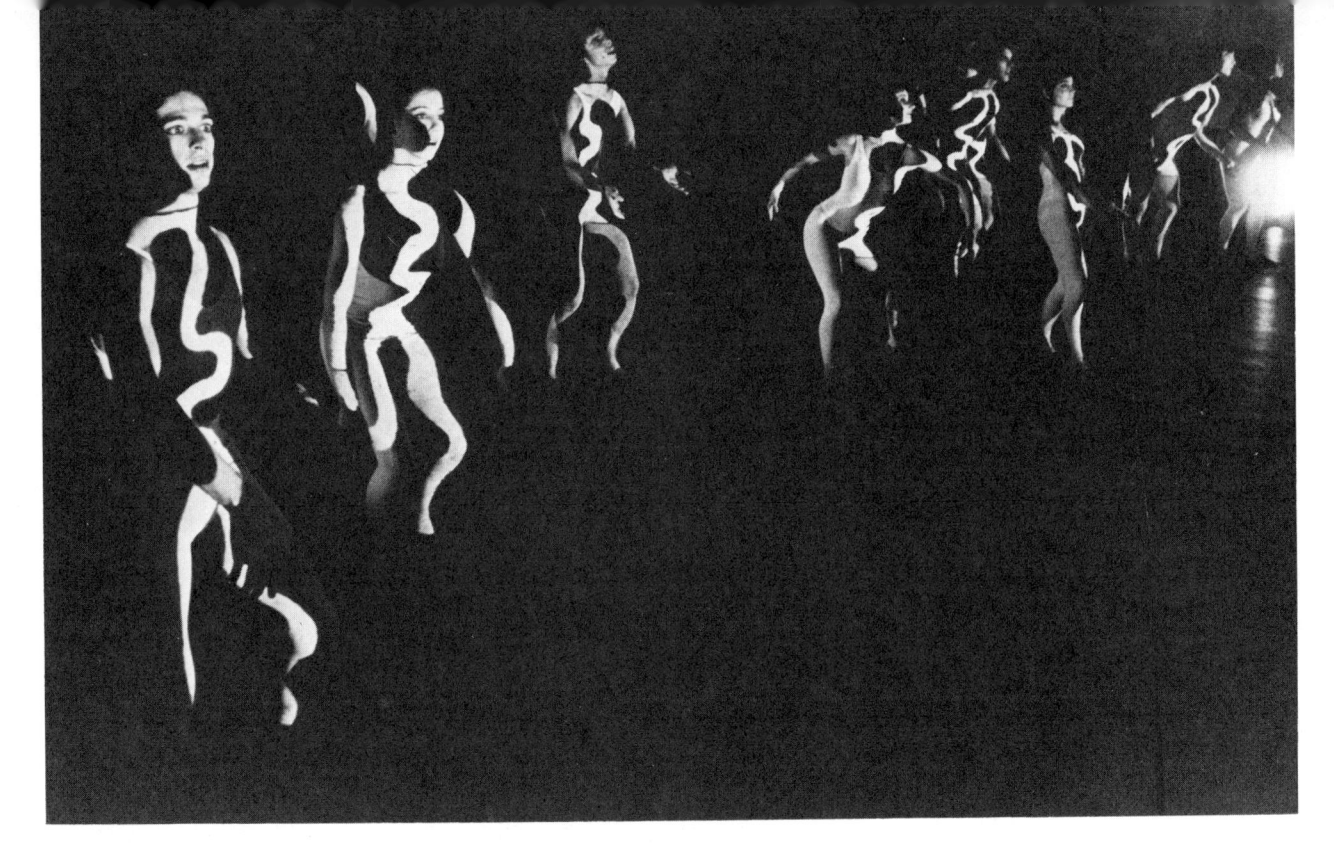

FIGURE 11–16
Projections on the Actor
The abstract form of the dance adapts easily to the unconventional use of projections on the actor or performer, thereby heightening theatricality and visual impact. *Scenario,* a production of the Nikolais Dance Theater (Photo—Oleaga).

The expanded metal screens shown in Figure 11–17a were reception surfaces for both front and rear projection. Kodak Carousel projectors and Pani 5000 watt projectors as well as Strand's Patt 752 projectors were all employed from front-of-house, stage-left and stage-right wings, and backstage. Note the extremely effective use of texture on the stage floor in Figure 11–17.

PRACTICALS

Practicals refer to on-stage working light sources such as lanterns, lamps, fireplaces, or candles. The wiring and maintenance of such units are the responsibility of the electrical department, and their use is sure to be a concern of the lighting designer. Playwrights or directors will call for practicals for any of several reasons:

1. The particular light given off by a practical will enhance the desired mood of a scene.
2. The use of a practical will indicate time of day, season, or even period.
3. Practicals help reinforce the reality of a scene or location.

Scenic Projection, Practicals, and Special Effects

a

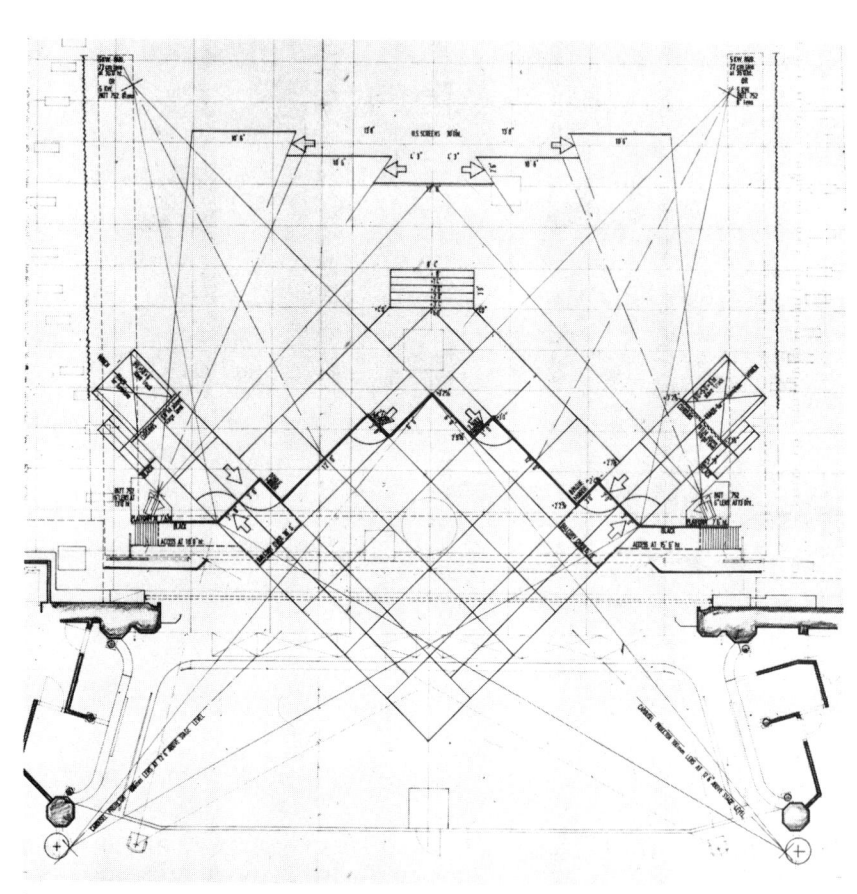

b

FIGURE 11–17

Light as a Scheme of Production

Bly, a gloomy Victorian country house, is the locale for the English National Opera's production of *The Turn of the Screw* by Benjamin Britten. The eerie mood of the opera lends itself to the extremely effective use of projected scenery as the action moves rapidly through fifteen variations. (a) Line drawing shows the arrangement of screens that form the basic setting. A third screen, upstage, occasionally adds

224 *Stage Lighting*

c

greater depth to the composition. The surface of the basic set is an expanded metal screen allowing projections from the front and rear as well as a clear view of the upstage screen when necessary. Walls perpendicular to the two major planes were covered with mylar mirror to reflect the image of the projection. (b) Floor plan shows relationship of screens and location of projectors. (c) Photographs of two of the many variations. Scene Designer—Patrick Robertson, Lighting Designer—David Hersey. Projections were by Mr. Robertson. (Photos—courtesy Noel Staunton, Technical Director, English National Opera, London Coliseum)

Scenic Projection, Practicals, and Special Effects **225**

One rule to remember in dealing with practicals is that whenever possible they should be controlled by dimmers. Never allow an actor to switch on a major motivating practical and then expect your light board operator to support it on cue—it simply doesn't work.

Fire Effects

Open fires are rarely convincing on the stage. Yet play after play calls for them. If it is possible to design the setting so that the hearth is located in a side wall, reasonably good results can be attained by simply letting a flickering light move over the far corner of the fireplace. Even this must be kept at low intensity so as not to take attention from the actors.

All too often the demands of the script force the designer to put a fire in full view of the audience. If no flames are required, then a mere glow, through crumpled gelatin (orange and red), broken glass splashed with translucent orange paint, or the like, will suffice. If flames must be shown, then a glow on some form of rising smoke, or on thin streamers of chiffon or China silk, blown upward by a small fan, can be used. Another method of simulating fire from a fireplace is to use a slowly rotating drum covered with crumpled foil and painted in various fire colors. Lights mounted above the drum in the hearth and out of audience sight are then trained upon the turning cylinder. The designer can also go to the extremes of using a color organ or one of the several available flicker generators hooked up to various colored low-wattage lamps.

In every case, however, the designer is placed on the horns of this dilemma: whether to make the fire effects so realistic as to grab the attention of the audience or so phony as to arouse their ridicule. It must be stated emphatically that, on the whole, the less fire effect you can get away with, the more fortunate you and your production will be.

Flames. Torches are particularly difficult to simulate. Perhaps a flashlight hidden in the handle and focused on streamers of very light silk is as good a solution as any, but it is not very convincing, even when the torch is stationary and the silk can be blown upward by a hidden fan. Perhaps a smoke device can be incorporated and the flashlight trained on its fumes. If real flame is necessary, a can of Sterno is securely mounted in the top of the torch, but liquid fuel must never be used.

Oil-burning lanterns should never be used on the stage. To begin with, their use is strictly against all fire rules and insurance regulations. A real hazard is presented by their use, for in case of accident the stage will become flooded with blazing oil. Fortunately, oil lanterns conventionally have glass chimneys which can be realistically smoke-stained to hide a small lamp bulb placed inside.

If the lantern is never moved during the action, it can be connected to the regular stage wiring and dimmed up and down from the control board. Of course, actors, when pretending to adjust the wick, or touch a match to it, or whatever, must always be careful to mask this fakery by placing their bodies between the lantern and the audience until the process of dimming has been completed. If a lantern is to be carried about the stage a battery must be hidden within it and a silent switch provided for the actor to control.

Candles. Unlike oil lanterns, candles, which usually extinguish themselves when dropped, are permissible on most stages if properly handled. In some locations they must be encased in transparent mica shields. If you have any doubts about the legality of using candles on stage, consult the local authorities. In no case should candles be placed near draperies or other easily flammable materials, including human hair and frilly costumes.

Even if candles are allowed, however, they probably should be avoided, for their bright light and particularly their flickering at the smallest breath of air can be most distracting for the audience. Very effective faking of candles can be done by means of a small battery or pencil flashlight hidden in a white paper tube. A tiny lamp on the top, with a twist of colored gelatin about it gives a steady and quite convincing glow.

Lighting Fixtures

Chandeliers, wall sconces, table lamps, and similar household lighting fixtures generally offer no vast problems except for the wattage of the lamps actually used in them. Such fixtures should never be counted on to produce all the light that seems to emanate from them. Frequently they are in quite the wrong locations to light the faces of the actors playing near them, so additional illumination must be provided by spotlights especially mounted for the purpose, or the acting area lights may be varied to give the effects desired.

This is particularly true when the fixtures have bulbs visible to the audience, for these, if at all bright, will throw a most annoying (even blinding) glare. Such bare bulbs must always be of extremely low wattage, and even then may have to be dimmed still further. Obviously little light will emanate from such fixtures, so the extra instruments become doubly important.

But if the bulbs are shielded by shades, then the glare is hidden and extra large-wattage lamps may be used to give a more realistic effect on an already bright stage. Such shades must be quite opaque, of course, or brown paper linings can be put inside them. Often an additional baffle must be placed over the bulb to prevent an unsightly hot spot on the walls and ceiling of the setting.

Scenic Projection, Practicals, and Special Effects

SPECIAL EFFECTS

All uses of light that are not directly involved in lighting the actor or illuminating the scene may be grouped in the category of special effects. Examples include explosions, fires, ghosts, or psychedelic lighting. Working out special effects is almost always enjoyable but can take a great deal of time. They should not be left to the end as an afterthought.

Moon and Stars

Some day a playwright undoubtedly will call for a realistic sun on the stage! Until then we have quite enough trouble with the moon and stars that are so often required. If the background is in the form of a cloth drop or cyclorama, quite a realistic moon can be devised by cutting the desired shape—fully round or crescent—into a large sheet of thin material such as cardboard or plywood, which is pressed firmly against the back of the drop. A small spotlight is then focused on the cutout from the rear. If the background is not a cloth, then a projection from an effects machine or an ellipsoidal reflector spotlight with an iris or a gobo may be used from the front.

Stars can be quite effective, but are tricky to handle. The tiniest bulbs obtainable look like great blobs of light against a darkened sky. It is advisable to tape these over; a mere pin-prick will pass enough light. If a dark-blue gauze or scrim is hung a few feet in front of the sky drop, it will help cut down excessive brightness and also will hide the wiring to the star bulbs. When the cyclorama is a permanent one of plaster or wood, tiny holes are often drilled through it and clips provided on the back to hold the little lamps in place. Usually for such effects, strings of low-voltage lamps can be bought at any hobby shop together with an appropriate transformer. Even Christmas tree strings can be used.

Stars can be projected from the front but, unless they are done by the gobo technique, they are rarely convincing, for even the best slide equipment reproduces them as large and somewhat indistinct smudges of light. For unrealistic, stylized effects, both stars and moon can be projected by a Linnebach with good results.

Lightning

Lightning is a device in many plays. Fortunately, it is usually not necessary to show forks of light springing from the sky, but only the sudden, rapid, and irregular bursts of high illumination as seen through windows or coming from the wings. By striking and breaking the contacts rapidly, a carbon arc can be used to give excellent results for this purpose. In fact a so-called arc striker that makes this even easier to handle is available commercially.

Another method is to switch rapidly on and off a number of small sources. It is better to use a striplight with many white and daylight-blue lamps of low wattage than a single large source which would respond more slowly to the irregular, staccato timing of typical lightning. A special switch may be devised to make the closing and the opening of the circuit easier to control.

Large photoflash bulbs, although fairly expensive, create a wonderfully bright burst of light. They can be mounted in an old plano-convex housing (with or without lens) or a simple tin can to avoid unwanted spill. Some photoflood lamps have a quick response time and also deliver a good deal of intensity.

If the lightning flash has to be seen against the sky, a projection must be used. Because of the slow response of the high-wattage lamp, it is well to have the instrument already turned on and an operator stationed at it to reveal and conceal the beam of light by means of a cap or other masking device. And several different slides should be provided, rather than show the same shaped flash again and again. Scratches on black-painted slides can be drawn quite realistically for these.

Explosions and Flashes

To produce these offstage, in the wings, the same general techniques can be applied as were suggested for lightning flashes, with the addition of mechanically produced noises when required. But for the same effects on the stage, in view of the audience, a flash pot is necessary.

A good flash pot consists of a metal pan with a tight-fitting wire screen over it. The bottom is covered by a piece of asbestos board, to which two electric terminals are fastened (small brass screws will do very nicely) but they must be carefully insulated from the box itself or a short circuit will develop. The two terminals may be about 1 inch apart. They are connected respectively to the two wires of a circuit that also contains a switch. Between the two terminals a single, very thin strand of copper wire is strung, wound firmly around each screw and lying flat on the asbestos board. A small quantity of flash powder is poured over this wire, covering all portions of it. When the switch is closed, the thin wire will burn out, igniting the powder. After each use the wire and powder must be replaced.

A variation of the flash box uses a fuse of very low amperage set in an appropriate fuse clip or socket. The fuse is cut open—in the case of a plug fuse by prying out the isinglass window—with a cartridge fuse by cutting away part of the paper cover. Care is taken not to damage the fuse link. The resulting cavity is then filled with the flash powder. As with the flash box, the opened fuse and the powder must be renewed after each use.

Flash powder, when set off in this way, gives a good burst of light, but little smoke. If smoke is desired, some sal ammoniac powder may be mixed with the flash powder. In any case, the flash device must be well protected with a screen and should never be fired close to flammable materials or to people.

Caution. Flash pots are extremely dangerous. Serious injury can happen if they are misused. It is a good precaution to include a low-wattage warning lamp in-line with the flash pot cable and close to the box itself. The lamp burning will indicate that the box is "live" and dangerous.

And a most important warning: *very little powder should be used at one time—and it should never be tamped down,* but poured loosely into place.

A commercial flash pot system called "Pyro-Pack" is available and tends to be safer than the older flash boxes. A number of dramatic effects can be achieved by using this system.

Fog and Smoke Effects

Many devices are used to produce smoke on the stage, but none is completely satisfactory. Perhaps the best known is sal ammoniac powder, which after a few moments in a hot plate or in a heating cone will give off a good volume of white smoke. In ordinary quantities this is neither too odorous nor dangerous to breathe, but if allowed to become too dense, it can be very unpleasant. Cinnamon powder may be added to sweeten the smell for the actors. Sal ammoniac powder has disadvantages. It cannot be started suddenly, nor can it be stopped on cue. It is also extremely corrosive on the producing elements.

Titanium tetrachloride combines with the moisture present in the air to give off a thin smoke that rises well. By adding a little water to it, or dropping a pinch of the powder into water, an instant response is produced that can be very effective, though the fumes are dangerous if breathed in quantity.

Dry ice can be dropped into water for a small quantity of smoke, but this tends to fall instead of rise. Dry ice may be quite effective in a fog machine (a metal drum with a heating element to keep the water from freezing when the solid carbon dioxide is lowered into it). If the drum is provided with a cover, quite a flow of fog can be produced suddenly and directed around the stage by means of a hose (Figure 11–18).

Smoke bombs are very smelly, impossible to control, and leave a greasy coating on the scenery and costumes. Steam is clean, but requires special piping and produces a loud hissing that makes it impractical for quiet scenes.

One device for generating smoke seems to be superior to any of the others mentioned. It consists of a container which is filled with a special liquid in which a heating coil is submerged. A handle for easy carrying is provided, and a plunger to pump the smoke about the stage at the desired rate and intensity. This mist tends to rise, but a

FIGURE 11-18

Fog Machine

Solid carbon dioxide or dry ice changes state from a solid to a vapor without becoming a liquid. The rapidity of the change is increased when dry ice is submerged in hot water. The result is an almost instantaneous cloud of dense fog. (Center left) Assembled fog machine. (Left) Top removed showing dry ice basket on end of the plunger. (Center right) View into the tank revealing electric heating element to heat water. (Bottom left) Loading basket with crushed dry ice. (Bottom right) The plunging of the dry ice in hot water produces a blanket of fog. (Pictures courtesy Richard Thompson)

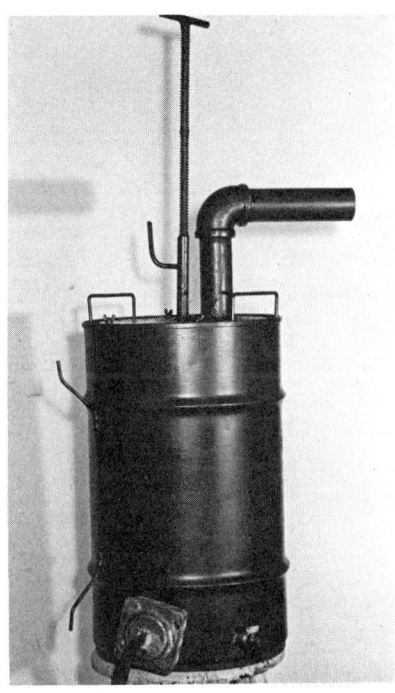

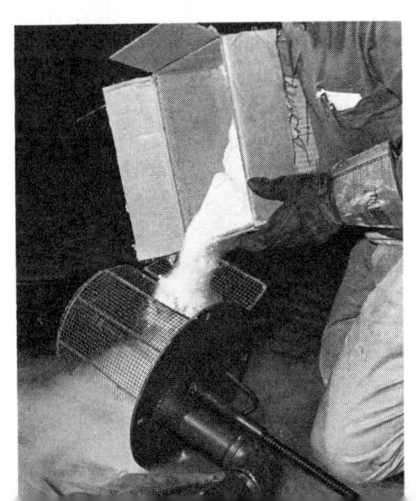

FIGURE 11–19

Portable Fog Machine

Small, lightweight tank vaporizes "fog juice" with electric heat. Fog is dense, white, and dissipates quickly. Basket can be attached to front of machine with dry ice to slow dissipation. Machine develops enough pressure to fill the stage very quickly. It can also be forced through PVC tube to remote parts of the stage. (Distributor—Mutual Hardware)

cage is provided that may be filled with dry ice and fastened over the nozzle of the container. When this is done, the fumes hug the floor. Plastic hose hidden about the stage has proved an easy way to make this mist appear wherever wanted. A second fluid may be used to help disperse the smoke, and several essences are available to scent it pleasantly. Their value is strictly a matter of individual taste. Actually, the fumes are not dreadfully unpleasant (Figure 11–19).

Controlling Smoke. Anyone using smoke of any nature on the stage is frequently faced with the problem of preventing it from flowing or blowing to where it is not wanted. Heavy fog that tends to hug the stage floor may easily spill over the footlights into the auditorium—a touch that is seldom appreciated by the audience.

The lighter-than-air smoke that rises is subject to the slightest breeze or draft. A ventilator at the top of the stage house may draw it swiftly upward, a cross-draft may set up eddies and swirls, while an exhaust fan that evacuates stale air from the auditorium can bring the smoke billowing into the house.

Ultraviolet Effects

One field in which it is impossible to surpass the carbon arc follow spot is in the use of ultraviolet effects. Because the output from this instrument is rich in these very short waves, a black-light filter that removes practically all the visible waves will still permit the ultraviolet ones to pass through in good quantity. Objects painted with a medium susceptible to such waves will glow under this stimulus and, if all other light is removed from the stage, weird and unworldly effects can be achieved.

Stage Lighting

EFFECT PROPERTIES

There was a time in theatre history when visual and sound effects were the major concern of the property department. Before the advent of high-fidelity recording many sound effects were created mechanically by the property person. Most of these old machines are now gathering dust in the property room. An adequate sound system can bring any effect to the audience with a truer quality and a more sensitive control than any mechanical sound effect. There is one possible exception: the effect of offstage gunfire. The recordings of distant battle scenes are fairly convincing, but close rifle or revolver shots are better when a gun with blank cartridges is fired backstage.

More as historical record than as modern practice, Figure 11–20 (page 234) shows some of the mechanical sound effects that are a part of the property department. Directors, on occasion, have requested old mechanical sound effects for their theatrical quality rather than having the movielike realism of electronic sound.

Although some visual effects have become electrified, most are still produced mechanically. Smoke, fire, and flash explosions are usually electrically controlled; however, smoke also can be made nonelectrically (Figure 11–21, page 235).

Some familiar visual effects that are mechanical are the snow cradle and rain pipes, which are shown in Figure 11–22 (page 235) along with other special effects that call upon the ingenuity of the stage technician and property person to rig and trigger on cue.

Breakaways

Many times pieces of furniture, dishes, or other objects have to break on stage. The chairs that collapse and the flagpole that falls down in *Cockadoodle Dandy*, the bullet fired through the windowpane in *The Front Page*, or a railing that breaks during a fight scene are a few examples of properties or scenery breaking on cue and in a predetermined manner.

In Figure 11–23, a railing breakaway is prebroken and lightly glued together. Thin strips of orange crate are tacked to the back of the repair to give a convincing splintering sound as the railing breaks again. The pattern of the break is carefully planned in order to control the fall of the pieces in the same manner for each performance.

Breakaway Windowpanes and Mirrors. Breaking real glass on stage is somewhat dangerous. Flying glass and broken glass left on the floor can be a hazard. If an actor must be close to breaking glass it is sometimes desirable to use other materials. One familiar substitute used often in the motion picture industry is candy glass. Candy glass, or hardened sugar and water, is prepared like old-fashioned rock candy. After a supersaturated solution of sugar and water is brought to about 260 degrees Fahrenheit it is poured on a smooth surface into a thin

FIGURE 11–20

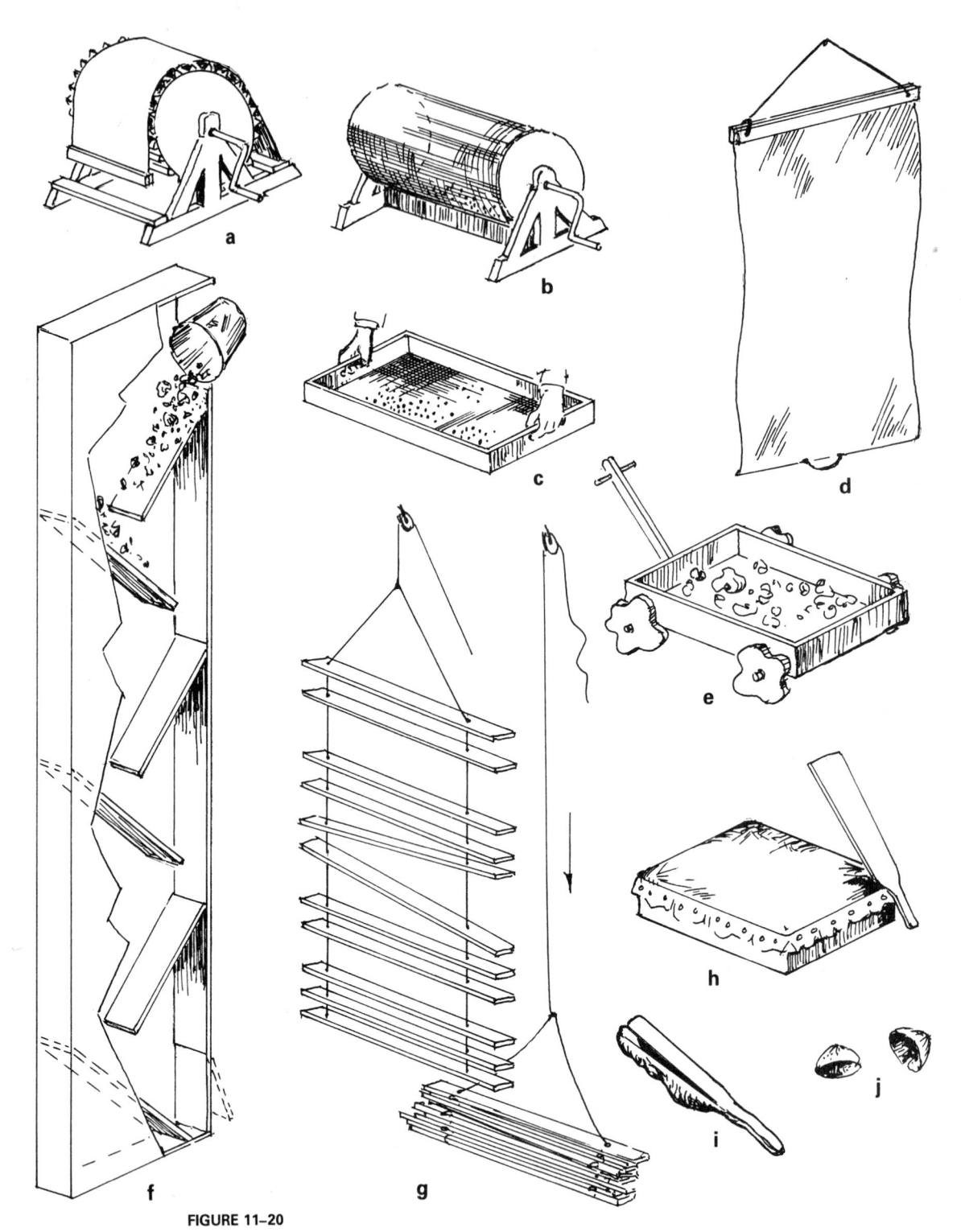

Mechanical Sound Effects

(a) Wind machine. (b) Rain, shot in rotating drum. (c) Rain, shot in tray with wire-screen bottom. (d) Thunder sheet. (e) Rumble cart. (f) Falling rubble after an explosion. (g) Wood crash. (h) Gun shots. (i) Slap stick. (j) Horses' hoofs.

Stage Lighting

FIGURE 11–21

Smoke Effects

(a) Smoke bomb. (b) Dry ice and water. (c) Heated sal ammoniac. (d) Heated mineral oil. (e) Squib, means of electrically firing a flash or firecracker. (f) Flash box containing flash powder over low-amperage fuse wire for electrically firing flash and smoke.

FIGURE 11–22
Visual Effects

(a) Snow cradle. (b) Rain pipe. (c) Water reflection.

Scenic Projection, Practicals, and Special Effects 235

sheet. The sheet hardens into a clear, transparent solid. Candy glass, however, has a low melting point and may soften under stage lights or excessive handling.

Pottery Breakaways. Opaque shapes, such as teacups, dishes, or small objects of art are much easier to make into breakaways. Because they are not transparent, inexpensive pottery or china pieces may be prebroken and lightly glued together again to insure their breaking on stage. As the second breaking usually shatters the piece beyond reclaiming, a breakaway should be prepared for each preformance.

Special opaque breakaway shapes can be prepared by casting a mixture of plaster and Styrofoam into a mold of the shape. To keep the casting hollow for easy breaking requires a core mold, which makes the whole casting process very complicated and time-consuming.

If the authenticity, both in sound and looks, of the breakaway object is extremely important to the play a replica can be made in clay bisque. A clay slip or solution of powdered water clay and water is poured into a mold of the object and after setting a few minutes is poured out. A thin shell of clay adheres to the mold, making a hollow casting of the object. After drying thoroughly (48 hours) the raw-clay casting is fired in a ceramic kiln to bisque hardness. A great number can be prepared this way.

Electrically Triggered Breakaways. To cue a breakaway in a remote position it is frequently easier to use an electrial trigger rather than a manual operation. A chandelier shattered by gunfire, a picture falling off the wall, or the decapitation of the weathervane cock in *Annie Get Your Gun* are a few examples of remote breakaways.

FIGURE 11-23
Breakaway Railing
(a) Railing prepared for breaking: (1) Prebroken spots, lightly glued. (2) Loose spindles, lightly glued. (b) Railing after breaking: (1) prepared hinge points.

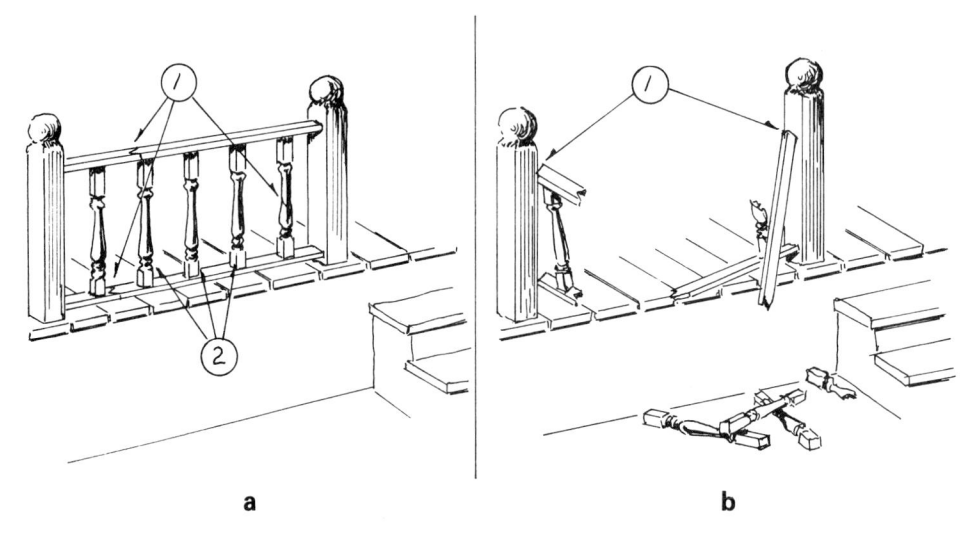

A mousetrap spring can be released by shorting out the low-amperage fuse wire that is rigged to hold the spring under tension. Melted fuse wire can also be used to break a support chain of a chandelier (Figure 11–24).

The magnetic power of the solenoid coil can be used to withdraw the support of a picture on the wall or as a trigger for any other breakaway. When a current is passed through the coil of the solenoid it becomes an electromagnet which draws the spring-loaded center pin into the coil. Upon breaking the circuit the pin is released with considerable force. Either action can be used to trigger a breakaway.

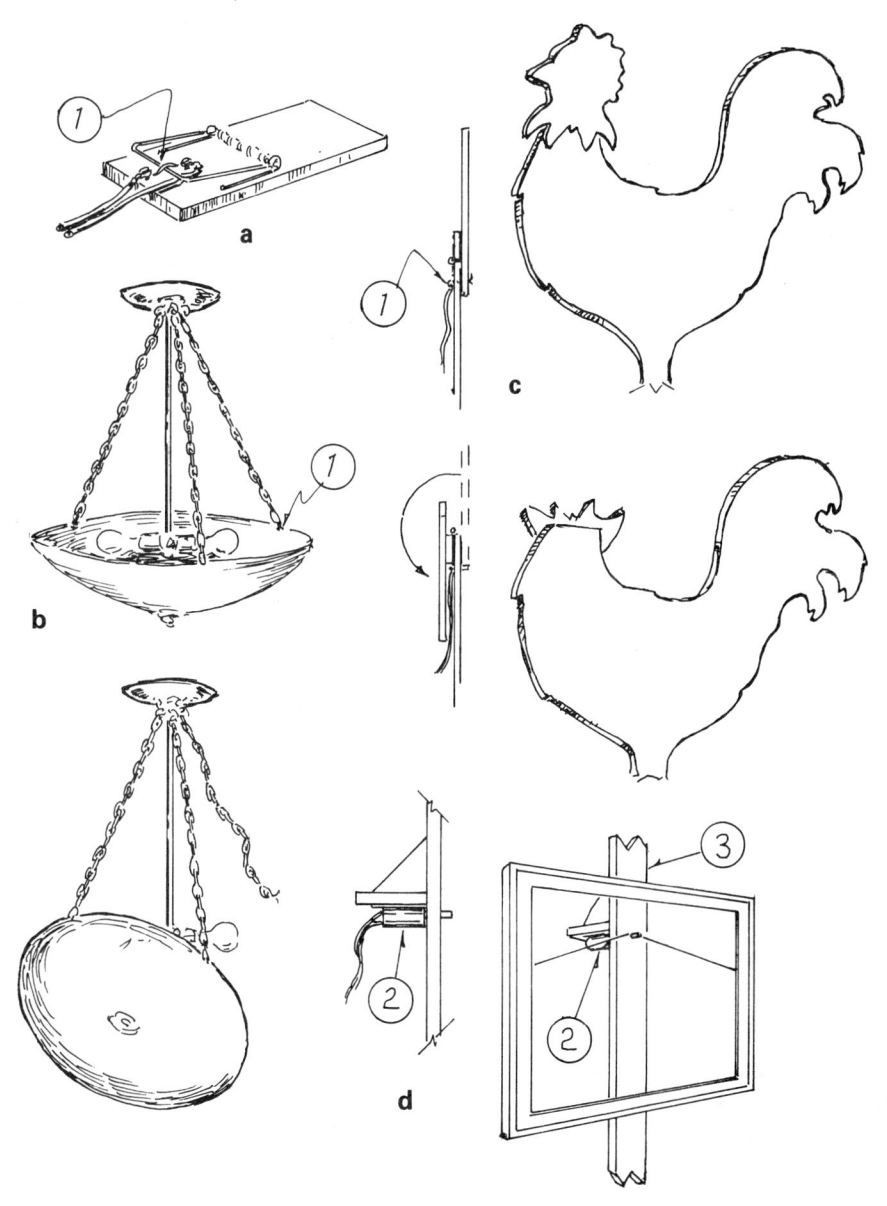

FIGURE 11–24

Electrically Triggered Breakaways

(a) The mousetrap is a simple mechanism that can be used to trigger a breakaway: (1) Fuse wire holding trap in "set" position. An electrical short melts fuse wire and the trap is sprung. This action can be used to break glass or spring load a hinge as in c. (b) Breakaway chandelier: (1) Fuse wire link which can be located anywhere on chain. The effect is helped if there is a little sand or dust in bowl to spill after the break. (c) Decapitating a weathervane cock: (1) Fuse wire holds spring-loaded hinge in upright position. Head folds behind body when fuse wire melts. 3- to 5-ampere fuse wire usually works best. If spring is too strong fuse wire can be doubled for strength. (d) Falling picture. (2) Solenoid coil mounted on rear of (3) picture batten. In off position the spring-loaded pin is extended through the batten to hold picture frame in place. When current is sent into the coil the pin withdraws and picture falls.

Scenic Projection, Practicals, and Special Effects

Glossary

Arc Light A spotlight that has for its source an electric current arcing between two electrodes.

Amperage The rate of flow of an electric current through a conductor. The capacity of an electrical conductor.

ANSI American National Standards Institute. The ANSI Code is a three-letter code used to identify lamps.

Anti-Pro or **A.P.** *(In front of the proscenium)* A front-of-house lighting position often located in the ceiling of the theatre.

Asbestos Fire-retardant curtain located at the proscenium opening.

Automated Fixture A lighting instrument whose focus and color is remotely controlled.

Avista Change of scene or movement of scenery in full view of the audience.

Backstage Much the same as *offstage* but used generally in reference to stage workers and stage machinery rather than to actors.

Barn Doors A device consisting of two or four hinged metal flaps which is placed in front of a fresnel spotlight to reduce the beam spread in one or more directions.

Beam Port A front-of-house lighting position located in the ceiling of the theatre.

Blackout The instantaneous killing of all stage lights.

Bloom Specular reflection from mirror or highly polished surface.

Boards Slang for stage.

Boom or **Boomerang** A vertical pipe for mounting spotlights.

Border Lights *see* Striplight.

Bounce Reflected diffuse light off the floor or walls.

Box Booms Lighting booms located in front-of-house box-seat positions.

Bumper Metal hoop fastened to a batten carrying lighting instruments to protect them from flying scenery and the scenery from hot instruments.

Bump-up Sudden movement of lights to a higher intensity.

Channel A lighting control path. *Channel* replaces the term *dimmer* in modern usage.

Circuit Established paths of electricity.

Company Switch A distribution panel with hook-up terminals to supply the power for a traveling company's switchboard. Usually three-wire 220 volts, 600 amps on a side.

Control Short for a theatre's control

or dimming system. Also the location of said system.

Cross Fade To fade from one lighting set-up to another without going through a dimout.

Cue A visual or audible signal from the stage manager to execute a predetermined movement of lights or scenery.

Cyc Short for cyclorama.

Deck Stage floor.

Diffusion A plastic medium placed in the color holder of a spotlight to break up the light in a variety of ways.

Dim Change the intensity of a light, either brighter or less bright.

Dimmer Apparatus for altering the flow of electric current to cause a light to be more or less bright.

Dimmer-per-Circuit A system in which an individual dimmer is permanently assigned to each stage circuit.

Disconnect *see* Company switch.

Douser Mechanical means of putting out a light.

Downstage The area nearest the footlights and curtain.

Dutchman Condensing lens in a lens projector.

EMF Electromotive force or voltage.

ERF Stage jargon for ellipsoidal reflector floodlights.

ERS Stage jargon for ellipsoidal reflector spotlights.

Fill Light Wash or soft light that fills in the light on the face from the direction opposite the key light.

Flood Widespread focus on a spotlight. Also, short for floodlight.

Floodlight A lighting instrument that produces a broad spread of light. Often misapplied to other lighting apparatus.

Focus (1) The direction in which a lighting instrument is aimed. (2) Adjustment of the size or shape of a light beam.

FOH Front-of-house. Anything located on the audience side of the proscenium arch.

Follow Cue A cue timed to follow an original cue so quickly it does not warrant a separate cue number.

Follow Spot A high-intensity, long throw spotlight requiring an operator in order to follow action on stage.

Footcandle The measurement of illumination; the amount of light from one candle that will fall on a surface one foot from the candle.

Fresnel (correctly pronounced Fre' nel) A lens recognized by its concentric rings. The spotlight designed to use this lens.

Front Lighting Illumination on the stage from instruments placed in the auditorium.

Frost *see* Diffusion.

Funnel Also known as a top hat. A short metal cylinder placed in front of a spotlight to reduce the beam spread.

Gobo A metal cutout used with a spotlight to obtain a patterned beam.

Halation Undesirable spreading of light from a spotlight. A halo of light around the beam.

Head Spot Very narrow beam from a spotlight focused on an actor's head. Also called *pin spot*.

Hook-up A lighting schedule which lists instruments by dimmer number.

House Curtain Main curtain of a proscenium theatre designed to tie in with the house decoration. Also called act curtain.

IA Short for IATSE—International Alliance of Theatrical Stage Employees. The stagehands' union.

In-one Foremost downstage acting position, traditionally in front of oleo.

Interconnect A flexible system allowing the electrical connection of any stage circuit with any dimmer. Also called patch panel.

Iris Mechanical means of closing the aperture of a spotlight.

Juice Commercial slang for electricity.

Jumper Cable connecting two or more lighting instruments.

Key Light Accent or highlight on actor's face, usually from the direction of the motivating light for the scene.

Keystoning Distortion of a projected image when the projector is oblique to the screen.

Klieglight A type of spotlight sold by Klieg Bros. *Klieg* is often used as a synonym for any bright light.

Ladder Hanging ladderlike frame for mounting spotlights.

Lamp (1) Correctly, the name of what is often called a light bulb. (2) In the commercial theatre the term for any lighting instrument, particularly a spotlight.

Lead Cable from power supply.

Left Stage To the actor's left as he or she faces the audience.

Lekolite A type of spotlight sold by Century-Strand. *Leko* is often used as a generic term for any ellipsoidal reflector spotlight.

Light Leak Unwanted spill from an instrument or through scenery.

Load Lamp or instrument.

Lumen Intensity measurement of a source of light.

Mask Conceal from the audience, usually by scenic pieces or neutral hangings, any portion of the backstage area or lighting equipment.

Mat Shutter or matting material over the face of a spotlight to change the shape of the beam.

M.E. Slang for master or head electrician.

Nanometer Wavelength unit in electromagnetic spectrum.

Offstage Out of sight of the audience. Away from the center of the stage.

Ohm An electrical measurement of resistance in a circuit.

Ohm's Law A statement of the relationship of current, electric potential, and resistance in a circuit. It may be expressed by the equation: $I = \dfrac{E}{R}$.

Oleo Traditionally the in-one back-

Glossary

drop. A decoratively painted ad-drop from vaudeville days.
Olivette Old stand floodlight.
On and Off Referring to scenery sitting parallel to the footlights.
Onstage In sight of the audience. Toward the center of the stage.
P and **OP** Promp and Opposite Promp. An English and old American method indicating the left and right side of the stage. *Promp* was the side of the prompter or stage manager.
PAR Short for parabolic aluminized reflector lamp.
PAR Head Slang for PAR 64 lighting instrument.
Patch Panel *see* Interconnect.
P-C Plano convex lens or lighting instrument.
Pigtail Short length of lead cable.
Pile On Adding one preset to another with channels operating on a highest-takes-precedence basis.
Pin Spot *see* Head spot.
Plot Short for lighting plot.
Practical Descriptive of something that can be used by the actor, like a window sash that can actually be raised or a light that can be switched on and off.
Preset A pre-arranged lighting set-up held in readiness for later use.
Quartz-iodine Early name for what is now known as the tungsten-halogen lamp.
Return Element of scenery that returns the downstage edge of the setting offstage to the right of left.
Right Stage To the actor's right as he or she faces the audience.
Roundel A glass color filter for lighting instruments.
Scenography (In European theatre, scenographie) Literally, the graphics of scenery, drawing, and painting. In modern usage, combining the design of scenery, lighting, and costumes into a single visual concept.
Scoop Slang for ellipsoidal reflector floodlight.
Section A Sectional view of the stage used by the lighting designer to determine masking, lighting angles, and throw distances.
Sharp Focus Narrow-beam focus of a spotlight.
Shop Order A lighting rental equipment list for the purpose of bids.
Short Slang for short circuit, the term for the escape of electricity from its prescribed path.
Shutter A beam-framing device located at the aperture of an ellipsoidal reflector spotlight.
Slash A diagonal beam of side lighting on a stage drapery or window curtain creating an arbitrary pattern of light.
Spot Focus Narrow beam focus.
Spotlight A lighting instrument with a lens that throws an intense light on a defined area. The term is often misapplied to other lighting instruments.
Stage Left and **Stage Right** *see* Left stage and Right stage.
Strike Take down a setting. Remove properties or lights.
Strips or **Striplight** A number of light sources closely adjacent to one another creating a "line of light." Most often used for cyc lighting.
Switchboard Fixed or movable panel with switches, dimmers, and so forth to control the stage lights.
Teaser Top or horizontal member of the adjustable frame downstage of the setting.
Template *see* Gobo.
Top Hat *see* Funnel.
Tormentor Side or vertical members of the adjustable frame downstage of the setting.
Track A control board term meaning a channel's intensity reading will automatically appear in all presets until otherwise instructed.
Trim Mark designating the height of a line set. **High Trim** Height of a flown piece when in *out* position. **Low Trim** Height of flown piece when in an *in* (or working) position.
Tungsten-Halogen An improved form of the incandescent filament lamp which contains a small quantity of a halogen gas in the bulb.
Up and Down Reference to scenery sitting perpendicular to the footlights.
Upstage On the stage but away from the audience.
USA United Scenic Artists. Theatrical union for scenic artists; scenery, costume, and lighting designers; and allied crafts.
Voltage The pressure behind electrical flow.
Wattage An electrical term for the rate of doing work.
Wash Low angle front-of-house lighting sources which illuminate in a general manner.
Wings Area offstage right and left, stemming from the era of wings and backdrops.
X-Rays Old expression designating the first row of border lights.
Zone A single stage-left to stage-right lighting area; most often used in dance lighting.

Additional Reading

The following books are recommended as supplementary reading, either to broaden the reader's view of the field or to assist him in understanding knotty problems. They would form an invaluable nucleus for the private library of anyone genuinely interested in the field.

The general list contains books of broad approach to the whole stage-lighting picture, and offers material of value in several facets of theatre lighting. The Supplementary titles contain matter related to specific aspects, and also include a few periodicals that frequently carry articles of interest to the lighting designer for the stage.

GENERAL

Bellman, Willard F. *Lighting the Stage: Art and Practice,* 2nd ed. New York: Chandler, 1974.

Bentham, Frederick. *The Art of Stage Lighting,* 2nd ed. New York: Theatre Arts Books, 1976.
 Covers the field well, but for the American reader the British terminology is sometimes confusing.

Fuchs, Theodore. *Stage Lighting.* Boston: Little, Brown, 1929.
 Many portions are outdated today, but there is much pure gold still to be found in it.

Gassner, John. *Producing the Play,* rev. ed. New York: Holt, Rinehart and Winston, 1953.
 Contains a capsule survey of the field by some of Broadway's most successful lighting practioners.

Gillette, J. Michael. *Designing with Light.* Palo Alto; Mayfield, 1978.

Kook, Edward F. *Images in Light for the Living Theatre.* New York: privately printed, 1963.

McCandless, Stanley. *A Method of Lighting the Stage.* 4th ed. New York: Theatre Arts Books, 1958.
 Though it does not go into the more technical aspects, this is probably the most influential book ever published on the subject.

McCandless, Stanley. *A Syllabus of Stage Lighting,* 11th ed. New York: Drama Book Publishers, n.d.
 A reference book and dictionary of all stage-lighting terms.

Pilbrow, Richard, *Stage Lighting,* rev. ed. New York: Drama Book Publishers, 1979.
 An extremely find design book, but does not cover lighting mechanics.

Rosenthal, Jean, and Wertenbaker, Lael. *The Magic of Light.* Boston: Little, Brown, 1972.

Rubin, Joel E., and Watson, Leland H. *Theatrical Lighting Practice.* New York: Theatre Arts Books, 1954.
 A survey of the usual lighting practices of all types and levels of dramatic production.

Sellman, H. D. *Essentials of Stage Lighting.* New York: Appleton-Century-Crofts, 1972.

Warfel, William. *Handbook of Stage Lighting Graphics.* New York: Drama Book Publishers, 1974.

Williams, Rollo G. *The Technique of Stage Lighting.* London: Pitman, 1952.
 Especially good on color. British terminology may confuse.

SUPPLEMENTARY

Bureau of Naval Personnel. *Basic Electricity.* New York: Dover Publications, Inc., 1962.
 Clear and simple presentation of the fundamentals of electricity. The best available text.

Colortran, Burbank, Calif. Equipment catalogues.

General Electric Company. Cleveland. *Fundamentals of Light and Lighting,* 1956.
 Excellent material on color, sources, and behavior of light.

General Electric Company. Cleveland. *Large Lamp Bulletin.*
 Almost a textbook on sources. Excellent illustrations.

GTE Sylvania Lighting Handbook, 7th ed. Danvers, Mass.: GTE Sylvania Lighting Center, 1985.
 Very good information on lamps and basic lighting considerations.

Illuminating Engineering Society, New York, *IES Lighting Handbook.*
 Pertinent information on color, instruments, equipment, and use.

Kliegl Bros., New York. Equipment catalogues.

Strand Century Company, New York. Equipment catalogues.

Tabs.
 This little magazine is brought out four times a year by Strand Electric and Engineering Co., Ltd., London and is available by writing to Rank Strand, P.O. Box 51, Great West Road, Brentford, Middlesex TW8 9HR, England.

Theatre Crafts.
 Published nine times a year by Theatre Craft Associates, P.O. Box 630, Holmes, PA 19043.

Lighting Dimensions.
 Published seven times a year by Lighting Dimensions Publishing, Inc., P.O. Box 471, South Laguna, CA 92677.

Index

Absorption, color, 107
Accessories, spotlight, 64–65
Acetate, 117
Acting area, lighting the, 126–127, 129
Action
  placing, in stage lighting, 15
Actor
  colored light and, 117–118
  lighting the, 120–121
  projections and the, 219, 222–223
Additive mixing, 105–106
Alternating current, 27–28
Ampere, 25
Arc light, 38, 49, 51
Arc projection, 212
Archway, 166
Area control, 131–132
Area specials, 131
Area spots, 170
Arena theatre
  design for, 186, 188–189
  lighting for, 182–189
Atomic theory, 19, 21
Autotransformer dimmers, 85, 87

Back lighting, 121
Backdrop
  translucent, 174
  wing-and-border, 179–180
Backing strips, 167
Batten tapes, 143–144
Batteries, 23
Beams, 63, 67, 73
Black box (flexible stage), 195
Blending in arena production, 185
Blinding, spectator, 188
Boards: *see* Control(s)
Booms, 165
Border lights, 179
Breakaways, 236–237
Broadway lighting practices, 150, 151

Candles, 227
Carbon arc light, 50–51
Ceiling, losing the, 169–170
Cheat sheet, 145
Chroma, 104–105
Cinebach projector, 209
Circuit breakers, 35
Circuits
  projection of, 35–36
  series and parallel, 30–31
  see also Dimmers
Color, 103
  arena, 185
  for dance, 199
  design and choice of, 136–137

Color (*cont.*)
  designing with, 111, 117
  electromagnetic spectrum, 104–105
  filtering of, 107
  lamp, 41
  mixing of, 105, 113
  paint, 108, "plate 4"
  primary, 106
  in stage lighting, 8, 9, 13
Color key
  as communication device, 145
  and instrument, 141
Color manipulation, 103
Color media, 117–118, 119
Color modification, 115
Color temperature, 48
Color vision, 108
Color wheel, 107–108
Colored glass, 118
Cool colors, 112
Combination reflectors, 58
Complementary hues, 106–107
Composition, "in stage lighting" 10
Computerized memory systems, 98, 101
Conductors, electrical, 21–22
Connectors, electrical, 31, 33
Control(s)
  area, 131
  arena production, 189
  beam, 63
  electronic: *see* Electronic control
  intensity, 83, 102
  instruments for light distribution, 63
  lighting distribution and, 62, 78
  realistic exterior, 174–175
  realistic interior, 169
  wing-and-border, 174
Cues, 146, 156–157, 199
Currents, electric, 23–28

Dance, lighting, 196–201
Dance plot, 200–201
Dichroic reflectors, 58
Diffusion material, 119
Dimension(s)
  stage lighting, 12–13
Dimmer-per-circuit system, 93
Dimmer readings, 137
Dimmers
  archaic forms of dimming, 84–85
  autotransformer, 85, 87
  electronic, 88–89
Direct current, 27–28
Distance of throw, 215
Distortion, 218
Distribution, light, 8
  flexibility in, 130

Double-hung spotlights, 130
Down lights, 179, 198
Downstage areas, 163–164
Dress rehearsals, 146

Electrically triggered breakaways, 237
Electricians, 152
Electricity,
  atomic theory of, 19, 21
Electromagnetic spectrum, 104–105
Electromagnetism, 23
Electronic control, 88, 101
  types of, 93, 101
Electronic dimmers, 88–89
Ellipsoidal reflector spotlight (ERS), 67, 72
Ellipsoidal reflectors, 55, 57
Equipment,
  in Broadway theatre, 50
  hiring, 151
  safety and care of lighting, 82
  testing electrical, 36–37
Explosions, 229
Extended apron (stage), 189

Feder, Abe, 3
Field angle, 69–70
Filtering, color, 107
Fire effects, 226–227
Flames, 226–227
Flashes, 229–230
Flexibility, 130
Flexible stage (black box), 7, 195
Floodlights, 74, 166
Focal length, 59
Focal point, 59
Focusing, 146–147, 156–157, 183
Fog effect, 230–232
Follow spots, 76–77, 178
  position, 116–198
Footlights, 179
Fresnel lenses, 59–60
Fresnel spotlights, 65, 67
Front projection, 216–219

Gaseous discharge lamps, 38, 51
Gelatin, 117
Generators, 23, 25
Glass, colored, 118
Glossary, 238–240
Gobos, 213
Goncharova, Natalya, 110

Hanging cardboards, 144
High-front position, 197
High-side position, 198
Hook-up, instrument schedule, 141

Hues(s), 104
　twelve principal, 108

Incandescent lamp, 38, 42
In-one zone, lighting the, 67, 70
Instrument annotation, 139–140
Instrument(s)
　choice of, in design, 134–136
　and color key, 141
Instrument(s) (cont.)
　for lighting distribution control, 63
　location of, dance, 196–198
　for realistic exteriors, 170, 173
　for realistic interiors, 161, 169
　unmasked, 186
Instrument schedule, hook-up and, 141
Insulators (electricity), 21–22
Intensity, 8
　and color, 109
　and color overload, 110
　in stage lighting, 8
Intensity control, 83, 101
Interaction of color, 110
Interconnect system, 90, 93
In-two zone, lighting the, 178
Inverse Square Law, 109

Kodak Carousel projector, 210–212

Lamp bases, 42
Lamp bulbs, 40, 41
Lamp filaments, 39, 40
Lamp life, 45–46
Lamps, identifying and purchasing, 47–48
Lens projectors, 209–214
Lenses, 58, 61
Light
　and color: see Color, 103
　distribution control and quality of, 62, 78
　reflection of, 53, 58
　refraction of, 53, 58, 60
　as scenery, 202–203
　sources of, 38
Lighting, 1, 18
　actor, 120
　arena production, 182–189
　background, 131, 134
　Broadway practices with, 150–151
　for the commercial theatre, 150–151
　dance, 196–201
　design decisions on, 134, 136
　designer of, 3
　distribution control of, 62–78
　and electricity: see Electricity
　fixtures, 227
　flexible stage, 195
　functions of, 14, 18
　and fundamentals of design, 10, 14
　intensity control, 83, 102
　laboratory, 148–149
　and light plot, 137, 147
　planning the, 152, 158
　proscenium theatre, 5, 7, 160, 180
　qualities of, 8, 10

regional theatre, 158, 159
section in lighting plot, 141–142
sketch for, 1–2
and theatrical form, 4, 7
for thrust stage, 7, 189–194
Line,
　in stage lighting, 10, 12
Linnebach projector, 207
Losing the ceiling, 168
Low-front position, 197
Low-side position, 198
Low-voltage connection, 92, 93
Lumen output, 47

McCandless, Stanley, 3, 112
Magic sheet, 144
Magnetic amplifier, 89
Manual systems, electronic control, 94, 97
Manufacturers, color, 119
Mastering
　electrical dimmer, 87
　group, for electronic control, 97
　mechanical dimmer, 86
Mathematics of projection, 215
Measurement, units of, for electricity, 25, 27
Medium-front position, 197
Medium-side position, 198
Memory systems
　computerized, for electronic control, 98, 101
　designing with, 101
Mirrors
　breakaway, 233
Mixing
　color, 105, 113
Mood, scene design for, 16
Moon, 228
Moonlight, 171
Mounting positions (arena lighting) 183
Move-in, 156
Movement
　in stage lighting, 10, 13
Musicals, setting for, 175
Musser, Tharon, 101
Mylar, 117

Ohm, 26
Ohm's law, 27
opaque projector, 213
Opening, after, 157
Overhead projection, 213

Package boards, autotransformer, 87
Paint
　light versus, 103
PAR (parabolic aluminized reflector lamps), 42, 44
PAR can, 74
Parabolic reflectors, 42, 44, 55
Parallel circuits, 30–31
Perception color, 109
Photoelectricity, 28
Piezoelectricity, 23
Plano-convex effect, 209–210

Plano-convex lens, 58–59
Plano-convex spot sizes, 65
Plano-convex spotlight, 63, 65
Plastic media for color, 117
Plot
　dance, 200–201
　light, 137, 147
Pottery breakaways, 236
Powder formula (electricity), 26
Practicals, 223–227
Pre-move-in, 153
Preset systems for electronic, 96
　control, 94–97
Primary colors, 106, 107
Production,
　and lighting style, 5
　see also specific types of stages
Projection
　scenery, 203–223
　techniques of, 206
Projectors, 206–214
Properties,
　effect, 233–235
Proscenium theatre,
　lighting for, 5, 7, 160, 180
Put-in, 146

R (reflector type) lamps, 42, 44
Realistic exteriors, 170, 175
Realistic interiors, 161, 170
Rear projection, 216–219
Reflection, light, 53, 58
Reflectors, 55, 58
Refraction, 53, 58, 61
Regional production, 158
Rehearsals, technical and dress, 147
Remote control, operator and, 101, 102
Repertory theatre, 159
Resistance dimmers, 84, 85
Road shows, 157
Rosenthal, Jean, 3

Safety
　with electricity, 37
　light equipment, 81, 82
Saturable-core reactors, 88
"Scene Machine," 211
Scenery
　colored light and, 114, 115
　light as, 202–203
　projected, 203–223
Scheme of production, light as, 222
Screen, 215
Series circuits, 30–31
Service power, electric 28–29
Setting(s),
　exterior, 170
　stage, 139
　wing-and-border, 175–177
Set-up, 156, 157
Shadow projector, 206–209
Short-arc lamps, 50–51
Side lighting, 122–125, 178–179
Silicon controlled rectifiers, 90
Sketch(es), 1–2
　lighting, 1–2

Index　　**243**

Sky, color on the, 115–116
Smoke effects, 230–232
Special effects, 228–237
Specials, realistic interior, 167
Spherical reflectors, 56
Spotlights, 63, 72
Stages: *see specific types*
Stairway, 164–165
Stars, 228
Step lenses, 59–60
Stock productions, 158–159
Story, staging the, 17
Straight-back position, 198
Striplight, 75–76
Subtractive mixing, 107
Sunbeams, 166
Sunlight, 171
Svoboda, Josef, 6, 205, 217
Switches, electric, 34

Technical rehearsals, 147
Television projector, 213
Testing, electrical equipment, 36–37
Texture
    in stage lighting, 13
Theatre,
    lighting and forms of, 4, 6
    see also specific types of theatre
Theatre plan, 139
Theme, 16
Thermoelectricity, 23
Thrust stage, lighting for, 7, 189, 194
Thyratron tubes, 89
Time
    design for place and, 15
    movement and, 10
Total theatre (total environment), 7
Training, lighting designer, 4
Triple hanging, 130

Tungsten-halogen lamps, 44–45

Ultraviolet effects, 232
Unmasked instruments, 186
Upstage areas, 164

Value, 105
Visibility, 14–15, 131
Volt, 25

Warm colors, 112–113
Watt, 26
Wattage output, 47
White light, 111
Wing-and-border settings, 175, 177

X-rays, 166